EXPERT SYSTEMS
FOR BUSINESS

EXPERT SYSTEMS FOR BUSINESS

Edited by
Barry G. Silverman

Addison-Wesley Publishing Company

Reading, Massachusetts · Menlo Park, California · Don Mills, Ontario
Wokingham, England · Amsterdam · Sydney · Singapore
Tokyo · Madrid · Bogotá · Santiago · San Juan

Library of Congress Cataloging-in-Publication Data

Expert systems for business.

Includes bibliographies and index.
1. Business — Data processing. 2. Expert systems
(Computer science) I. Silverman, Barry G.
HF 5548.2.E96 1987   006.3 ' 3   86-20672
ISBN 0-201-07179-7

ABCDEFGHIJ-HA-8987

To Rachel and Joel
and all other three and five year olds (in fact or in heart)
whose joyful use of software to extend their abilities, interest,
and creativity is an inspiration and a design goal.

PREFACE

Computerized support systems are not new to business and despite all the recent hype, expert systems (ESs) and artificial intelligence (AI) must come to grips with the same time-tested business and management issues confronting other support systems if they are to penetrate this marketplace successfully. How AI/ES is coping with the important business-related issues is the principal concern of this book.

The goal is to assist the business-oriented lay person in learning about the realities of what AI/ES can reliably deliver by explaining actual applications and developments in a clear, familiar-language fashion. At the same time, each chapter is intended to help AI/ES practitioners and students better appreciate the issues that business applications must resolve by sharing a number of lessons learned from individuals currently attempting real business applications. Each author, an experienced AI/ES practitioner, takes a hard look at selected business-related issues, explaining ways that are currently being pursued to aid with AI/ES techniques.

The business-related topics covered in the chapters of this book are eclectic and wide ranging, a partial list includes management, accounting, procurement, operations management, factory supervision, resource allocation, executive and financial decision making, inventory management, and project management. While there is a little bit of something for everyone, the real story captured by this book is the struggle to insert a new technology successfully.

In particular, this book explores three distinct but related types of AI/ES efforts: (1) expert system (ES) and expert support system (ESS) applications to business problems with lessons learned, (2) the state-of-the-art in embedding ES technology in familiar office and business automation products, and (3) the longer term more research-oriented efforts that hope to open the way to next-generation technology.

The expert system revolution has occurred quite rapidly and most of the relevant work that answers business peoples' and managers' questions exists in diverse and scattered places. The books that do exist tend to focus either on rather technical, how-to-do-it topics or on the original research work that led to the expert system "craze." The small amount of literature that exists on business applications leaves one unsatisfied. Only a small peek at the "other player's cards" is generally documented.

Among the questions that are repeatedly heard and that this book attempts, in part, to address are

1. What are the principal elements of the AI landscape from a business usage viewpoint, and which of these promise genuinely useful tools? What truly is an expert system? Isn't it only clever programming?

2. Many expert systems have been developed for medical and scientific applications. But are there successful systems for business applications? Are they truly successful by managerial criteria as well as by the technical criteria of the developers?

3. Do natural language interfaces really work for database and other systems? Can this technology be adapted to facilitate end-user interaction?

4. How should a layperson go about exploring the possibilities for developing an expert system, natural language interface, or other AI technology for a specific application? What special personnel, software, hardware, and other resources are needed? What has already been done in my application area?

5. What are the relationships among expert systems, artificial intelligence, decision support systems, management information systems, and modeling and simulation? To what extent do these disciplines interact and contribute to one another? For example, can "expert systems" be used to make a decision support system more intelligent?

This book attempts to answer many of these and similar questions in terms of the following:

- *Practical issues* relating to the introduction and usage of expert systems and artificial intelligence in business environments based on actual efforts to do so
- *Realistic constraints* that define the tasks that expert systems and artificial intelligence can and cannot solve — what is achievable today versus what is a research subject
- *Actual experiences* with existing tools and systems: descriptions, evaluations, and lessons learned relating to specific applications
- *Related topics*

Probably the most important issue that many business-oriented AI/ES applications must face is that the managers and personnel in the business world often must cope with ill-structured problems in relatively short time frames, all in the presence of political and organizational realities. Ill-structured problems are not routine or well-defined with standard conditions, nor are they easily solved by immediate application of well-known procedures or decision rules. Examples of ill-structured problems include innovation, executive decision making, and diagnostic evaluations by project managers. One could use any other situation in which neither the goal nor the procedure for accomplishing the goal are well understood at the outset.

Many practicing managers, accountants, planners, and supervisors demonstrate a keen appreciation (should I say intuitive understanding) for the fact that concrete, right-brained thought is an essential component of effective business practice. For example, a 20-year-old Harvard student (Land) produced the first practical light-polarizing material, and Apple Computer Corporation was launched by a couple of "kids" in their garage.

Fletcher L. Byrom, former president and chief executive officer of Koppers Company, a "Fortune 200" firm, makes the same point for executive decision making:

> Among all people I have worked for and admired, I have observed one Universal trait, and that is a well-developed intuition....I'm not arguing against the use of sound reasoning based on facts. All I'm saying is that when it comes to the point of decision, you have to...be able to depend on what your intuition tells you. (*Dunn's Review*, September 1969)

Numerous evidence suggests that managers spend much of their time in communication, interfacing, and casual conversation. Mintzberg, in the *Harvard Business Review*, observed that the executive prefers concrete current information, even gossip, to the written (summary) information of the routine documents. Dreyfus, in turn, suggests that managers "seek and use such information to facilitate a nonanalytical situation-recognition ability.... Situational understanding not only facilitates recognition but, at the same time, resolution."

This brief discussion has attempted to highlight several realities with which AI/ES, like any other business technology, must come to grips. In short, combining the nature of ill-structured problems, on the one hand, with the nature of intuitive thought, on the other hand, leads to a relatively clear picture of the reason(s) for the nonuse of so many of the "rational computerized aids." Or as Ouchi, the author of *Theory Z* points out: "Managers are often heard to complain that they feel powerless to exercise their judgment in the face of quantitative analysis, computer models, and numbers, numbers, numbers." People are used to dealing with ambiguous poorly defined situations and with "growing" a decision. The use of prescriptive decision analysis methods can have the potential of "freezing" the situation and eliminating flexibility. Creativity may be stifled, options not in the "recipe" may be overlooked, and the value of seeking information in terms of reflective time may be eliminated. Many "formal" (mathematical *or* computerized) procedures can be correlated positively with such deleterious effects beyond some minimal threshold.

Realities such as these present an array of intimidating challenges and opportunities for AI/ES to conquer. In particular, this text organizes the chapters into major parts that cover five potential AI/ES approaches to the realities of business applications. These parts reflect a taxonomy of types of business-related approaches including: (1) expert support systems (ESSs) for applications that are highly unstructured, (2) expert systems (ESs) for more well-defined applications, (3) embedding AI/ES technology in existing business automation products, and (4) cognitive modeling to better understand business personnel so that next-generation technology can be evolved. Such classifications are reflected in the five parts of this book.

Part I Building an Expert System Capability

Part I sets the stage for the sections that follow. Chapter 1 defines ESs and how they work; Chapter 2 examines the broad set of potential applications of ES for management and business settings; and Chapter 3 provides insight into how to manage and control an ES project.

Part II Expert Support Systems

Part II clearly shows the humility and care with which experienced AI/ES practitioners are approaching the ill-structured problems of the business world. The authors of these four chapters uniformly feel that *AI/ES cannot replace the human*, it can only support the human. All four chapters explore expert support systems (ESS) that utilize AI/ES to extend the human's capability. The ESS is an important phenomenon, and it is a logical extension to information and decision support systems.

Part III Expert Systems

The authors of the two chapters in Part III are bolder than those in Part II as they uniformly imply that their expert systems can ultimately replace human managers and supervisors at a number of important tasks. Several reasons for these conclusions are probed in the introductory commentary; however, at least part of their approach includes cognitive modeling of supervisory behavior. The advanced topic of cognitive modeling is presented more directly in Part V.

Part IV Integrating Expert Systems into the Business Environment

In addition to ESS and ES applications in areas such as, but not limited to, accounting, procurement, and operations management, AI/ES practitioners are vigorously adding generic expert system capabilities and extensions to existing business support environments. A number of generic capabilities are addressed in these five chapters including: (1) building AI parsers that can read business reports and routine documents, (2) embedding expert system techniques in spreadsheets, data base systems, and other common business automation products, and (3) constructing management workstations that utilize AI/ES to support business project personnel working in team environments.

Part V Next-Generation Technology

While the chapters in the other parts of this book for the most part probe the insertion of relatively off-the-shelf technology (i.e., ESs, ESS, or embedded AI/ES), this part explores the road to the next generation of AI capability. Only by attempting to understand how the manager's or executive's mind truly works can major breakthroughs be made. While cognitive modeling research and development is a lengthy and expensive process, without it business can only hope to have the marginal improvements offered by ESSs, well-defined ESs, and ES extensions to existing automation. These three chapters explore the research frontier and illustrate the state of development of one of the next generation of AI tools for business application.

The bottom line appears to be that AI/ES can make the transition out of the lab and into business applications, but the profitability of the applications often arise from better support of, not replacement of, existing personnel. It is important to complete these applications and to reap the profits, cost savings, and quality improvements they offer. However, it is equally important to continue the advancement of what is known about how business people think so that even more profit-bearing next-generation AI/ES tools can be evolved.

ACKNOWLEDGMENTS

There are a number of people who helped with this project and to whom thanks are due. My thanks first to the reviewers, and especially to Jerrold May of the University of Pittsburgh, whose careful and insightful comments contributed enormously to improvements in both the quality and integration of 17 separate chapters into a single book. Thanks are also due to Peter Gordon of Addison-Wesley, to several individuals at TIMS-CAIMS who tried to give this project a boost, and special thanks to Carl Heimowitz. Last but not least, Marie Barnes's meticulous handling of much of the correspondence and typing greatly helped this book come out as soon as it did. Unfortunately, none of the above can be blamed for any errors, shortcomings, or insufficiencies of integration. Whatever weaknesses remain are the responsibilities of the editor alone.

Washington, D.C.   B.G.S.

CONTRIBUTORS

Robert Blanning
Owen Graduate School of Management
Vanderbilt University
Nashville, TN 37203

B. Chandrasekaran
Department of Computer and Information
    Science
The Ohio State University
Columbus, OH 43210-1277

Chen-Hua Chung
Department of Management
College of Business and Economics
University of Kentucky
333C Commerce Building
Lexington, KY 40506-0034

Daniel A. De Salvo
Federal Systems
American Management Systems, Inc.
Arlington, VA 22209

Jesse F. Dillard
College of Business
The Ohio State University
Columbus, OH 43212

Peter Duchessi
Department of Management Science and
    Information Systems
State University of New York at Albany
Albany, NY 12222

Lance B. Eliot
Expert Systems Laboratory
University of Southern California
Los Angeles, CA 90089-0021

Kenneth J. Fordyce
International Business Machines Corp.
Data Systems Assurance
Internal Zip 53SE/446
Kingston, NY 12401

Fred J. Ganoe
School of Business
West Georgia College
Carrollton, GA 30118

Amy E. Glamm
Federal Systems
American Management Systems, Inc.
Arlington, VA 22209

Eric Gold
Department of Social and Decision Sciences
Carnegie-Mellon University
Pittsburgh, PA 15213

Nancy Green Hall
School of Business and Economics
Mercer University
Atlanta, GA 30341

Henry Hamburger
Navy Center for Applied Research
    in Artificial Intelligence,
Naval Research Laboratory
Code 7510
4555 Overlook Avenue S.W.
Washington, D.C. 20375-5000

Franz Hatfield
The Analytic Sciences Corporation
1700 North Moore Street, Suite 1220
Arlington, VA 22209

Clyde W. Holsapple
Management Information Research Center
Krannert Graduate School of Management
Purdue University
West Lafayette, IN 47907

Dr. Adolfo Lagomasino
AT&T Bell Laboratories, Room 1A-605
Holmdel, NJ 07733

Jay Liebowitz
Department of Management Science
School of Government and Business
    Administration
The George Washington University
Washington, D.C. 20052

Dana A. Madalon
The Analytic Sciences Corporation
1700 North Moore Street, Suite 1220
Arlington, VA 22209

Vassilis S. Moustakis
Department of Management and Production
    Engineering
School of Engineering
Technical University of Crete
Aghiou Markou Str.
Chania, Crete 73100 Greece

Daniel E. O'Leary
School of Accounting
University of Southern California
Los Angeles, CA 90089-1421

Brian Phillips
Tektronix Laboratories
Tektronix, Inc.
P.O. Box 500, M/S 50-662
Beaverton, OR 97077

Kamesh Ramakrishna
Digital Equipment Company
77 Reed Road
Hudson, MA 01749

Richard L. Roth
Desktop A.I.
1720 Post Road East
Westport, CT 06880

Dr. Andrew P. Sage
Dean, School of Information Technology
    and Engineering
George Mason University
Falls Church, VA 22030

Brian Schott
Decision Sciences Department
Georgia State University
Atlanta, GA 30303

James R. Slagle
Computer Science Department
University of Minnesota
Minneapolis, MN 55455

Jeffrey L. Staley
Tektronix Laboratories
Computer Research Lab
Tektronix, Inc.
P.O. Box 500, M/S 50-662
Beaverton, OR 97077

Kar Yan Tam
Krannert Graduate School of Management
Purdue University
West Lafayette, IN 47907

Thomas C. Varley
Management Consulting and Research, Inc.
5113 Leesburg Pike, Suite 509
Falls Church, VA 22041

Thomas Whalen
Decision Sciences Department
Georgia State University
Atlanta, GA 30303

Andrew B. Whinston
Department of Computer Science and
    Management Information Research
    Center
Krannert Graduate School of Management
Purdue University
West Lafayette, IN 47907

CONTENTS

xv

1

BUILDING AN EXPERT SYSTEM CAPABILITY

The ultimate objective of this book is to help business people in their quest to achieve organizational objectives (e.g., increase net revenues, improve customer satisfaction, achieve product shifts, etc.). The motivation is not to push a new technique, but to help the reader assess *if* and *where* that new technique might be fruitfully applied. AI/ES technology should be implemented only where it can be cost justified.

Completing a knowledge-based system, however, is not the same as conducting a knowledge-engineering investigation. The latter provides general insight into how experts and practiners perform their jobs and as such must be treated in part as a technique for the assessment of organizational productivity improvement needs. Understanding how to set up a knowledge-engineering project is a worthy goal in its own right, whether or not it culminates in a knowledge-based system.

Obviously no single text can give the reader the depth of background necessary to complete the entire knowledge-engineering job. This book instead attempts to survey the "waterfront"—to point the reader toward the important concepts and to steer the reader away from the pitfalls. While much more is hoped for, if by the end of this text the reader is able to set up a knowledge-engineering project and to detect when it is proceeding down a nonproductive path, then the authors will have achieved some of their objectives.

The expert system revolution has occurred quite rapidly, and most of the significant work that answers managers' questions exists in diverse and scattered places. The books that do exist on expert systems tend to focus either on rather technical, how-to-do-it topics or on the original research work that led to the expert system craze. The small amount of literature that does exist on business applications leaves one unsatisfied. Only a small peek at the "other player's cards" is generally documented.

Among the questions that are repeatedly heard and that this book attempts in part to address are:

1. What are the principal elements of the AI landscape from a business usage viewpoint, and which of these promise genuinely useful tools? What truly is an expert system? Isn't it only clever programming?

2. Many expert systems have been developed for medical and scientific applications. Are there successful systems for business applications? Are they truly successful by managerial criteria as well as by the technical criteria of the developers?

3. Do natural language interfaces really work for data base and other systems? Can this technology be adapted to facilitate end-user interaction?

4. How should a layperson go about exploring the possibilities for developing an expert system, natural language interface, or other AI technology for a specific application? What special personnel, software, hardware, and other resources are needed? What has already been done in my application area?

5. What are the relationships among expert systems, artificial intelligence, decision support systems, management information systems, and modeling and simulation? To what extent do these disciplines interact and contribute to one another? For example, can "expert systems" be used to make a decision support system more intelligent?

This book attempts answers to many of these and similar questions in terms of the following:

1. *Practical issues* relating to the introduction and usage of expert systems and artificial intelligence in business environments based on actual efforts to do so.

2. *Realistic constraints* that define the tasks that expert systems and artificial intelligence can and cannot solve. What is achievable today versus what is a research subject.

3. *Actual experiences* with existing tools and systems – descriptions, evaluations, and lessons learned relating to specific applications.

4. *Related topics.*

Part I is an introduction to the AI/ES field. It addresses many of the issues, terminology, definitions, and fundamentals built upon in later chapters. In particular,

1. Chapter 1 introduces and defines expert systems, knowledge representation, chaining and inference engines, knowledge engineering, expert support system issues, and benefits and limits of ESs. This chapter was distributed to all other authors to avoid repetition of definitions throughout this book, and it is occasionally referred to by the other authors.

2. Chapter 2 picks up where Chapter 1 left off in terms of the types of business applications to which AI/ES can be fruitfully applied. In particular, the author surveys the fields of finance, marketing, operations, accounting, R&D management, and human resource management. The six chapters of Parts II and III of this book can be viewed as examples of two of the items on this list – operations and accounting.

3. Chapter 3 describes an expert data base system; however, its role in Part I is primarily to elucidate the knowledge-engineering process. The authors review a variety of knowledge-engineering techniques and focus the reader's attention primarily on the importance of structuring a knowledge-engineering effort.

Armed with these three sets of fundamentals – definitions/concepts, types of business applications, and structuring of knowledge-engineering efforts – it is hoped that the reader can more fully appreciate the material offered in the remaining chapters. It is also expected that these three chapters will help the reader begin to formulate answers to many of the questions listed earlier in this commentary.

1

Should a Manager "Hire" an Expert System?

Barry G. Silverman

This chapter introduces the manager to a new type of corporate helper called an expert system (ES) by attempting to answer two questions. The first is: Should a manager hire an ES? The answer is explored in terms of the relevancy, appropriateness, feasibility, optimality, and likelihood of success of an ES for a managerial application. After determining an ES is indeed appropriate, a second question remains: What is this new helper like? This question, perhaps the one most often asked by managers, concerns what an ES is, whether it can be trusted, how it will fit into the organization, and if it truly differs from other computer programs. The remainder of this chapter attempts an answer to the second question.

1.1   INTRODUCTION

This chapter attempts to answer two questions: (1) What are expert systems (ESs)? and, (2) Will expert systems (ESs) be valuable for the reader's application?

Since the answer to the second question requires the elaboration of a "rule base" concerning when and how best to use ESs, it is convenient to use that rule base as a set of examples in the dialogue addressing question 1. That is, the reader will learn about ESs by seeing how to build an ES that can offer advice on what problems it thinks it can successfully solve.

Specifically this paper overviews the promise of ESs (Section 1.1.1), airs concerns about the applicability of the ES approach to management (Section 1.1.2), answers question 1 on what is an ES (Section 1.2), and provides a fuller treatment of the answers to question 2 (Section 1.3).

1.1.1   The Promise of Expert Systems

Expert systems have emerged in the past five years as computer programs that draw on the organized expertise of one or more human experts. The computer takes the expert advice of humans, coded as a series of rules, and applies it to a specially structured knowledge base containing information about a real or hypothetical situation. By taking actions specified by the rules, the computer simulates the behavior of human experts in confronting the same situation.

During the encounter between a human nonexpert seeking advice and a (computerized) "expert" providing consultation, there are three key types of information transfer (Shortliffe and Fagan, 1982):

1. The expert requests relevant information about the case under consideration.

2. The expert offers a recommendation based upon the data that are available.

3. If the nonexpert requests it, the expert explains the basis for decisions made.

This latter feature distinguishes an expert system from an expert aid or intelligent support system. That is, intelligent support systems (e.g., decision support systems, natural language processors, and traditional computer programs) often address only the first two features. Expert systems encompass all three features; however, they generally cannot offer as many and as diverse capabilities as expert aids. These differences are important and will be further clarified in later sections. Expert systems and intelligent support systems (expert aids) are important to management, and both are addressed here. A single term, *knowledge-based systems*, will be used henceforth when referring to both of them.

Dozens, perhaps hundreds, of expert systems have been developed for a number of different problem domains ranging from medicine, en-

TABLE 1.1
PROBLEMS THAT KBSs CAN TACKLE*

Problems	Knowledge-Based Systems Solutions

Shortage of Human Expertise
Scarce, expensive, hard to duplicate and
  upgrade
Fallible and capacity limited
Mobile, vulnerable, and mortal
	KBSs Reduce Skill Shortages
	Widely distributable, cheap and easy to
	  run, duplicate, and upgrade
	Can exceed human capacity, especially in
	  complex problems
	Cannot resign, lose interest, or die

Management Concerns for the Future Growing business turbulence Acquisition of competent management Too little time for problems Information overload/irrelevance Lack of trained personnel Material resource availability	**KBSs Assist with Some Concerns** Assist policy analysis and strategy Augment management skills Help formulate and solve known problems Are decision oriented Provide educational applications Assist exploration, cut risks and costs

Computing—a Broken Promise
Systems inscrutable to users
  difficult to converse
  difficult to comprehend
  expensive to modify
  hard to encourage use of information
    technology
Software development costly
Uncomputable problems
Negative trade balance
	KBSs Return Early Hopes
	Bridge man-machine gap
	  talk users' language
	  can explain reasoning
	  trivial to modify
	  best route to encourage use of informa-
	    tion technology
	Progress in automatic programming
	Heuristic approaches most workable
	Opportunity to improve trade balance

Complex Systems Becoming Dangerous
False missle alerts
Three-Mile Island
Air traffic control
	KBSs Return Human Control
	"Human window" can be engineered to
	  return human comprehension and
	  enable faults to be spotted and disasters
	  to be averted

*Adapted from Ellis (1983).

gineering, finance, and science and covering tasks such as diagnosis, design, problem solving, planning, repair, search, interpretation, training, monitoring, and control, to mention a few. A common feature of these applications is that their structure includes (1) a natural language system for conducting the dialogues with the user, (2) an "inference engine" for controlling the processing both of the dialog with the user and of the internal store of knowledge, and (3) an internal store of problem domain and task knowledge called here a *knowledge base*. A discussion of these three structural elements will follow.

Numerous articles and reports have been generated either as documentation of these original applications or as surveys and reviews (Shortliffe and Fagan, 1982; Feigenbaum, 1977, 1982; Hayes-Roth, Waterman, and Lenat, 1983; Duda and Gaschnig, 1981). While there have been critics, most material is extremely favorable and indicates results such as those summarized in Table 1.1. Knowledge-based systems (KBSs), in general, and expert systems, in particular, appear to help when human expertise is in short supply, when jobs become problematical, when computer-person interfaces are vital, and when it is necessary to extract from humans judgments that are crucial to emergency settings.

At first glance it might seem that an expert system could never excel over its human "creator" or "mentor." In one sense this is true. An expert system cannot be programmed to perform a task that no human knows how to do. But unlike a human expert, the computer is always "calm," and does not develop "tunnel vision" in an emergency the way humans do. Also, a human can apply only his or her own expertise to a situation, but it is hoped that an expert system can apply the expertise of several human advisors simultaneously. Human experts can become fatigued, ill, or tempermental. An expert system is always alert and never has a bad day. Finally, an expert system is the property of the company. It cannot accept a better offer somewhere else and leave the company the way humans do.

1.1.2   Concerns about Expert Systems

This section returns to question 2 ("Will ESs be valuable for you?") and offers some tentative answers based on who will build the expert system and on whether it is appropriate.

Who Should Build It?   The construction of knowledge-based systems is often referred to as "knowledge engineering." Such efforts typically require close collaboration between human experts in the application of interest and "knowledge engineers" familiar with the construction process.

The fundamental point of who builds the system is that knowledge engineering work is too important to be left in the hands of a few computer programmers who call themselves "knowledge engineers." One reason why this is true is that there is a greater demand for knowledge engineers than there are graduates of the field. Another reason is that experience has shown that narrowly focused technicians (even when available) are incapable by themselves of designing man-machine systems that are of long-standing utility. For example, the modeling and simulation literature is filled with computerized techniques paid for by organizational sponsors and developed by operations researchers working on their own that could be used no more than once (see Majone and Quade, 1982; Dreyfus, 1982; Silverman, 1985a). The management information systems literature contains a similar number of citations of data banks brought on-line in isolation by the electronic data processing staff; these banks fell to equally alarming levels of disuse (see Ackoff, 1962; Lucas, 1975; Zmud, 1979).

There is no reason to expect knowledge-based systems to be any different. There is a narrow technical role for computer scientists to fill in the knowledge-engineering job (i.e., writing the actual computer code). However, if the management profession does not assume the bulk of the knowledge-engineering job, it may not be done at all. Or worse, it will be done badly.

The most important reason for managers to get directly involved, however, is that knowledge engineering, when done properly, examines the entire work flow, habits, and procedures of the organization.

The knowledge-engineering issues confronting the manager who is cognizant of the nature of expert knowledge encompasses many far-reaching questions such as organization and job design, worker productivity, employee training, and expert performance assistance. Knowledge engineering is a potentially powerful approach to the identification of productivity problems and corrective opportunities ranging across the full set of managerial functions. In short, knowledge engineering is largely a management-related endeavor.

Is an Expert System Appropriate? In terms of why an expert system is appropriate, it is possible via the knowledge-engineering technique to elicit from well-respected, expert knowledge engineers a knowledge base concerning the facts and heuristics associated with where, when, and how, an ES approach should be applied. That is, we will now begin the construction of an ES that can answer such a question.

The knowledge base of an expert system consists of facts and heuristics. The *facts* constitute a body of information that is widely shared, publicly available, and generally agreed upon by experts in a field. The *heuristics* are mostly private, seldom-discussed rules of good judgment (rules of plausible reasoning, rules of good guessing) that characterize expert-level decision making in the field. For example, part of the knowledge base that will be used here to answer the appropriateness question has been culled from the open literature (see references already cited; Kinnucan, 1985; and Hayes-Roth, 1984), while other portions of it have been learned from this author's and his colleagues' experiences (Silverman, 1985a–d, 1983; Silverman, Moustakis, and Robless, 1984) as briefly summarized in Table 1.2. The content of the rules of Table 1.2 will be addressed in this section, while discussion of syntax and format will be briefly postponed.

The question to be answered is indicated in Table 1.2 as the "goal," while the pathway to an answer is expressed as the "top-level rule." This top-level rule* indicates that: "IF" four conditions are satisfied "THEN"

---

*The reader should note that numerous other methods of representing such heuristics exist and are in common use in expert systems. For example, the same knowledge could be expressed as a semantic net, as an object-attribute-value triplet, or as a frame-slot formalism to mention just three alternatives. For the sake of this chapter's consistency, however, only IF-THEN rule formalisms will be utilized.

TABLE 1.2
A RULE SET DESCRIBING WHEN TO "HIRE" AN EXPERT SYSTEM

Goal
Determine if an ES approach is appropriate

Top-Level Rule
IF: The ES approach is
   1.   Relevant
   2.   Feasible
   3.   Optimal
   4.   Success-Oriented
THEN: An ES approach will be appropriate (cf 100).

Second-Level Rules
Relevancy Rule
IF: 1.   There is a recurring shortage of skilled employees, or
   2.   Problems regularly arise requiring innumerable solutions to be considered, or
   3.   Job excellence requires unreasonably high levels of human training, or
   4.   No single person can know the requisite problem-solving expertise, or
   5.   Difficulties in applying existing knowledge routinely cause management to work around basic problems,
THEN: Expert systems are a relevant solution technique (cf 85).

Feasibility Rule
IF: 1.   The problem typically takes a few minutes to a few hours to solve, and
   2.   No controversy over problem domain rules exist, and
   3.   Problem domain experts exist, and
   4.   Problem domain knowledge can be cast into existing representational techniques,
THEN: An expert systems approach appears feasible (cf 85).

Optimality Rule
IF: 1.   It is necessary to reason with erroneous data, uncertainty, and make hundreds or thousands of judgments (heuristics), and
   2.   Inference engine planning, scheduling, and control procedures are more appropriate than conventional software program layouts, and
   3.   Interaction with human users via natural language is required, and
   4.   The computer program must be able to explain why it is asking a question, and
   5.   The computer program must be able to justify its conclusions,
THEN: An expert system is the optimal approach (cf 100).

Success Rule
IF: 1.   Solutions in the problem domain are of high value, and
   2.   Top management supports an expert system approach, and
   3.   An existing expert system kit can be used as the core of the application, and
   4.   An iterative prototyping approach can be pursued in which initial problems can be solved with a limited subset of the experts total knowledge, and
   5.   Training cases and test cases are available for gradually augmenting and evaluating the expert system, and
   6.   An "apprenticeship" approach can be adopted in which experts will review and critique each incremental version's solutions, and
   7.   The knowledge-engineering team has a successful track record,
THEN: The expert system approach is likely to be a success (cf 75).

the goal can be satisfied. Each of these four conditions, in turn, is determined by its own "second-level rule." If all four second-level rules are satisfied for a given application then all four conditions of the top-level rule are satisfied, and one would be relatively confident that an ES approach is appropriate: certainty factor (cf) is 100. Thus, the four second-level rules—relevancy, feasibility, optimality, and success—contain the keys to the answer being sought.

The "relevancy rule" indicates the five situations that most commonly lead businesses to explore the ES approach. The more of these situations that look familiar the more the ES approach is likely to be relevant to a given application. As an example, the illustrative ES satisfies the relevancy rule for most organizations since they do not have the in-house expertise to pinpoint the innumerable applications that could help solve basic problems.

Simply being relevant does not guarantee feasibility. Four additional conditions are needed as shown in the "feasibility rule." Use of the illustrative ES of this chapter satisfies the feasibility rule since determining whether an ES is appropriate typically takes an expert a few hours (for a first impression) using problem domain rules. Of course a knowledge engineer's time and availability are tight, but doing this once leads to an ES that can alleviate him or her from having to repeatedly answer the same appropriateness questions in the future.

Although relevant and feasible, an ES is not optimal relative to other approaches unless it can solve yet five more conditions as embodied in the "optimality rule." The illustrative ES satisfies the optimality rule not only because of conditions 3, 4, and 5 and not only because the inference engine approach is the most productive one to facilitate the processing of the dialogue and the rules, but also because numerous heuristical and uncertain inferences will invariably have to be made in addressing the goal. That is, it is not so much the clean-cut, yes-or-no answers to each condition of each rule that make the job tough. Rather the expertise is involved with interpreting and combining the varying degrees of belief commonly associated with each answer.

Finally, relevance, feasibility, and optimality are of little use if seven conditions likely to lead to a successful ES cannot be fulfilled as delineated in the "success rule." The author has personally witnessed two ES projects fail: one in the prototype stage for lack only of condition 2; and a second ES, after substantial development effort, due to obstacles associated with conditions 5 and 6. For the illustrative ES of this chapter, the top-level and second-level rules of Table 1.2 are sufficient to build a simplified version that meets the success rule conditions, although a few of the third-level, fourth-level, and fifth-level rules are elaborated in the remainder of this chapter. For the illustrative ES all seven conditions of the success rule can be satisfied for the author's own organization and application areas.

1.2 WHAT IS THIS NEW TYPE OF "EMPLOYEE" LIKE?

As "employees" expert systems may be thought of as drones without general intelligence. They are brilliant workaholics at their jobs but incredible dullards with no opinion on any other subject. Further, they require extensive "training" and apprenticeship periods before they become qualified for the position they are to fill.

Expert systems come in numerous forms based on type of knowledge representation, inference, and/or control strategy adopted. Since one of the more well-known types of expert systems is the rule-based, backward-chaining form,* this will be used as an illustrative case. One illustrative case is sufficient to elaborate the *general* nature of expert systems (particularly so for the uninitiated), however, deviations of other types of expert systems from the illustrative case are common and occasionally will be pointed out.

1.2.1 Why Bother Defining Expert Systems?

Numerous managers have asked: "Isn't any computer program that does a job formerly done by a human an expert system?" Given the technique differences and subtleties alluded to in the preceding two paragraphs it is no surprise that this is a point of confusion.

There is, in truth, no definitive answer to this question. On the one hand, any computer program that satisfies the consultative definition and has an architecture/methodology similar to the illustrative ES of this chapter is clearly an ES. However, how much relaxation of these tenets is permitted before a program is no longer an ES? Further, why bother trying to establish such a position? If a program reliably replaces a former employee, isn't that all a manager really needs to care about?

To a manager who sees only the end result, making a subtle distinction between ES and "other" programs may appear unimportant. After all "medicine is medicine," and the patient frequently cares only that a physician administers a medicine that works with minimal side effects. Blind trust is undesirable, however, for two reasons. First, the "physician," in this case, the knowledge engineer, requires guidance concerning the location and nature of the ailment or bottleneck for which an expert system programming solution (medicine) is a possibility—this is an interactive problem identification. The better informed the manager (patient), the quicker (and cheaper) the knowledge engineer's job. Put another way, the more a manager can clarify his or her requirement, the

---

* Backward chaining, the testing of hypotheses stored in the knowledge base, is useful for selection problems and related situations in which an exhaustive consideration of hypotheses and evidence is desired. Forward chaining, on the other hand, starts with problem symptoms, evidence, or conditions and quickly zeros in on the relevant hypothesis or conclusion that explains the symptoms. Forward chaining is more appropriate to such applications as process control, simulation, and planning.

less likely the product design will be wrong and the more likely the end product will do what he or she desires. Second, the knowledge engineer is prone to human error as discussed earlier and should not be allowed to create an expert system in isolation. This would also violate most of the conditions of the success rule.

How then does a manager recognize an application with ES potential? Aside from the consultative, architectural, and methodological conditions about to be elaborated upon, several other factors are clear indicators. If automation of time-consuming clerical functions by amassing and processing large volumes of data is required, then it is probably a traditional data processing application. If a well-known algorithmic approach with only a few judgmental heuristics will solve the problem, then a traditional computer programming approach is most likely warranted: the "horsepower," effort, and software overhead of an expert system will be wasted at best and generally unusable. Find an application that requires hundreds or thousands of judgmental heuristics (a few minutes or hours of a professional's time for interpreting, diagnosing, planning, scheduling, etc.) and you have found a potential ES application. Next, the five rules explained in Table 1.2 must be applied to the potential expert system.

1.2.2 What Is an ES Architecture and How Does It Behave?

Expert systems are created by knowledge engineers who build a knowledge base containing facts and rules about some particular application or problem domain and who attach this knowledge base to an inference engine (hopefully one already exists). The expert system can then engage a user in a natural language (also a preexisting capability) question-and-answer consultation about the application chosen using the knowledge base to reason about the problem and make a recommendation or conclusion. During or after a consultation, the user can request explanations of the system's reasoning process or ask the system to justify its conclusions. Figure 1.1 illustrates an ES architecture.

The inference engine is activated when the user begins consultation at which time it looks for a goal specification(s) within the knowledge base. A *goal* is an expression whose value is to be sought by the inference engine during the consultation. For example the goal of an expert system using the rules of Table 1.2 as its rule base would be: "Determine whether an expert systems approach is appropriate."

The inference engine adopts this goal expression as a task and seeks a value for this expression through the following steps:

1. It first tries to directly compute the value of the expression (e.g., in the case of an arithmetic expression), the result of the computation is returned as the value of the expression.

FIGURE 1.1
ILLUSTRATIVE EXPERT SYSTEM ARCHITECTURE

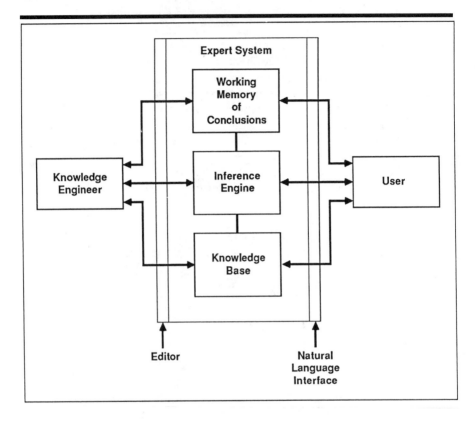

2. Failing in step 1, it reasons the value of the expression may be noted in the working memory. If so, the inference engine simply returns that value.

3. Failing in step 2, it searches its knowledge base entries sequentially until it comes across an entry that can be used to find a value for the expression. It then uses that knowledge base entry to do so.

4. If no pertinent knowledge base entry is found, the inference engine asks the user to supply a value for the expression currently being sought. The response is appropriately noted in working memory.

As an example, consider the goal mentioned above. Steps 1 and 2 would fail, but step 3 would lead the inference engine to the top-level rule of Table 1.2. Since this rule actually returns a set of four valueless expressions (i.e., relevant, feasible, optimal, successful), the inference engine treats each clause one at a time as a new goal expression for which it must find a value. That is, it repeats the four steps for the first subgoal. Once again step 3 will prevail, and once again in this example the result is still further valueless expressions. That is, the relevancy rule is located in the knowledge base, and its five IF conditions pose five new expressions for which the inference engine must locate the value. If no further rules exist in the knowledge base concerning the five relevancy conditions, when the inference engine repeats its four value-seeking steps (for each of the five IF conditions of the relevancy rule of the example knowledge base) it will arrive five separate times at step 4: ask the user.

The natural language capability of the expert system will now formulate these clauses as questions to be posed to the user, such as "Is there a recurring shortage of skilled employees?" The user in turn may respond "yes," "no," or "why?" In response to a "why" the inference engine simply prints out "I am trying to determine the values of the expressions in the relevancy rule that states: IF (1)...THEN...." In response to a "yes" or a "no," the inference engine records the value in working memory and proceeds to the processing of the next expression.

This process is repeated tirelessly by the engine until all the values of all the subgoal expressions are determined. At this point the goal itself may be evaluated and a recommendation can be formulated.

This discussion has intentionally simplified the nature of step 3 (knowledge base search), the syntax of rule entries, the process of testing a rule, and the treatment of certainty factors. Each of these will now be addressed more fully.

1.2.3   What Exactly Is a Rule?

A *rule* is a knowledge base entry of the form

```
if       CONDITION
then     ACTION
```

Where CONDITION is a proposition often of the form:

EXPRESSION = VALUE

Propositions may be joined by various combinations of the Boolean connectors "AND," "OR," and "NOT" as shown in Table 1.3. (Table 1.3 shows a third-level rule that could be added to the rule set of Table 1.2 to elaborate upon condition 3 of the success rule.)

ACTION is also generally made up of propositions of the form:

EXPRESSION = VALUE cf N

ACTIONS may contain "AND," but *not* "OR" or "NOT." They may not conclude values for several different expressions. The two conclusions of

TABLE 1.3
EXAMPLE ES-KIT RULE FROM THE THIRD LEVEL OF THE RULE SET

IF:	1.	A suitable ES kit exists in-house (AND)
	2.	Its availability is assured (AND NOT)
	3.	It runs on a computer which is fully utilized (OR)
	4.	A suitable ES kit can be purchased with available funds (AND)
	5.	The licenses (hardware and software) & postimplementation concerns are affordable (AND)
	6.	A computer is available for using the kit (OR)
	7.	A suitable hardware environment can be purchased within budget constraints (AND)
	8.	The ES kit supports integration into a KBS environment,
THEN:	1.	An existing ES kit can be used as the core of the application (cf 90) (AND)
	2.	An existing ES kit will not be useful (cf 30).

Table 1.3 are valid. One could not legally add a third conclusion such as:

"(3) Employees should be taught how to use this kit."

This is ill-formed, because the conclusion of the rule would now provide values for two different expressions (using a kit and teaching the kit.)

A rule is considered pertinent when its conclusion can provide a value for the expression currently being sought. If a pertinent rule is encountered while an expression is being sought, each of the clauses within the conditions of the rule is tested. If all of the propositions in the conditions of the rule are found to be true, the rule succeeds, and the values within the conclusion are noted in working memory with the appropriate certainty factors. If any of the clauses within the conditions of the rule are found not to be true, the rule is said to fail (unless an "OR" within the premise offers another clause to try) and the inference engine continues looking for another knowledge base entry that can help find a value for the expression being sought.

1.2.4   Suppose an Expert Is Not Sure of a Rule?

An important feature of an expert system is its ability to cope with intuitive and uncertain knowledge as expressed by degree of belief in the value of an expression. The degree of belief of a value is given by its certainty factor, an integer between 0 and 100, where:

- 100 represents complete certainty, that is the value is believed to be true
- A minimum threshhold of belief is represented by 20, for example
- 0 represents no belief at all, that is the value is felt to be false

Certainty factors less than 100 may arise because (1) a user may be unsure of his or her answer to a question, (2) a fact in the knowledge base has an attached certainty factor, or (3) the conclusion of a rule contains a certainty factor. If no certainty factor is given, 100 is assumed.

As mentioned earlier, the clauses that comprise the condition of a rule are generally propositions of the form EXPRESSION = VALUE. To test the truth of a clause of this form, the inference engine seeks EXPRESSION and compares the resultant value with VALUE. If the resultant value is believed with a certainty of at least some threshhold, for example 20 (a cf of 20 or greater), and matches the value specified in the proposition, that clause is considered true and the next clause is examined. If the resultant value is believed with less than a certainty of 20, or does not match the value specified in the proposition, the clause is considered untrue. This causes the rule to fail, unless the proposition is part of an OR clause within the premise that has not yet been proven false.

Another feature of cfs is captured in the conclusion of the "ES-kit rule" (Table 1.3). Here an apparent contradiction exists in that a kit is concluded to be useful with a cf of 90 and *not* useful with a cf of 30. The expert who put forth this conclusion is not simply irrational. Rather, the cf numbers should not be construed as probabilities that should sum to 100, but as judgmental measures reflecting degree of belief in a conclusion expression when confronted by the evidence offered in the values of the conditions. In other words, the evidence provided by the conditions is sufficient to give the expert a high degree of belief (cf 90) that an ES kit can be used, while the same evidence is insufficient to entirely rule out the possibility of a failure with that kit. The two expressions of the conclusion are apparently measured by the expert against somewhat different factors.

As a result cfs are "phenomenological" rather than theoretically rigorous. That is, they are used because they tend to work. Further, cfs represent an important mode of inexact reasoning in expert systems, and most kits expect the user to specify cf levels. Due to their phenomenological nature, however, theoreticians have postulated numerous alternatives: Zadeh's Fuzzy Sets, Bayes' Theorem, and the Shaefer-Dempster approach are several of the alternatives argued forcefully by their proponents (G.E. Corporate Research, 1983).

1.2.5   What about Different Pieces of Evidence?

Independent knowledge base entries may conclude the same value for an expression with various degrees of certainty. The inference engine combines these certainty factors (see Figure 1.2) via a formula such as:

$$((100 * CF1) + (100 * CF2) - (CF1 * CF2))/100$$

FIGURE 1.2
COMBINING CERTAINTY FACTORS

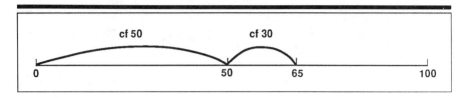

For example, suppose a knowledge base contains:

(Rule 1)	IF:	Preferred Kit = In-House
	THEN:	Best Kit = In-House Kit

(Rule 2)	IF:	In-House ES Kit = Is Available
	THEN:	Best Kit = In-House Kit

(Rule 3)   Preferred Kit = In-House Kit (cf 50)

(Rule 4)   In-House ES Kit = Is Available (cf 30)

Then, the inference engine will determine that

Best Kit = In-House Kit (cf 65)

provided no user dialogue concerning availability or preferred kit cfs transpired.

Conversely, the certainty of a conclusion of a rule is reduced if the belief of a condition is uncertain. The formula used here is:

CF-noted = (CF-of-conclusion * CF-of-condition)/100

For example, given the rule:

(Rule 1)	IF:	In-House ES Kit = Available
	THEN:	In-House Kit = Best Kit (cf 50)

Suppose this stimulated the inference engine to prompt the user for the value concerning "Available" to which the user responded

In-House ES Kit = Available (cf 40)

The inference engine would then determine

Best Kit = In-House Kit (cf 20)

because of the multiplication operation.

Other formulas exist in the inference engine to govern other possibilities by which evidence can be combined. For example, when multiple expressions exist in the conditions or conclusions of a rule, a set of formulas governs the combination of these expressions' individual cfs depending on the type of Boolean connector (AND, OR, NOT), user-specifications, and so forth. These are elaborated at length in other, more technical publications, and their repetition here is unimportant to furthering a generic understanding of the nature of inexact reasoning as already established in this short explanation.

1.3   CAN THIS NEW "HELPER" BECOME A TEAM PLAYER?

Up to this point we have explored answers about ES questions posed by managers. It is equally important to explore the elements of a manager's job. By elucidating the nature of managerial work, answers can be offered to the knowledge engineer's question "What is a management expert system?" Minimally, these answers should provide guidance pertaining to the five rules of Table 1.2. More generally, these answers might form the beginnings of an ES design specification that a manager can give to his or her knowledge engineer.

In a manager's world, evidence and problem symptoms frequently arise from numerous sources and in a variety of forms often on a moment's notice and in a crisis mode. Sources include conversations (hallway, telephone, ad hoc meetings), staff memos and notes, stray articles and news items, routine and periodic performance reports, and contracted and/or algorithmic (model- or spreadsheet-based) studies. A manager's response(s) to the problem stimuli will inevitably flow through similar channels but in a reverse direction via queries, directives, or status reports (see Figure 1.3).

In between the stimulus and response, the manager passes inputs through a series of internal filters, weighs the evidence, asks for clarifications, considers alternative courses of action, obtains more clarificational inputs, and weeds out dominated or politically unwise alternatives until hitting upon a satisfactory direction. In day-to-day problem solving this direction is often chosen on the basis of a "feel," that is, a warm sensation in the gut developed only after buying and wearing out 30 three-piece suits. The response is chosen because it parallels a stable, untroubled organizational state the manager has encountered in the past. The manager probably cannot entirely explain why this is a stable state, only that in his or her judgment it is.

In this intuitive approach the manager will not expect an ES to replace him or her. Rather, an ES is needed to interact with him or her, to act as an intelligent assistant, to extend his or her capabilities of considering alternatives or additional information, to point out factors embedded or missing in the stimuli that might have a bearing on the decision to be made, to inform him or her of conclusions it has reached, and to be able to explain its questions and/or conclusions.

The reader probably has already suspected that ESs are not panaceas. When compared with a manager or an expert staff member, they appear

FIGURE 1.3
TYPING AN EXPERT SYSTEM INTO THE MANAGER'S WORLD

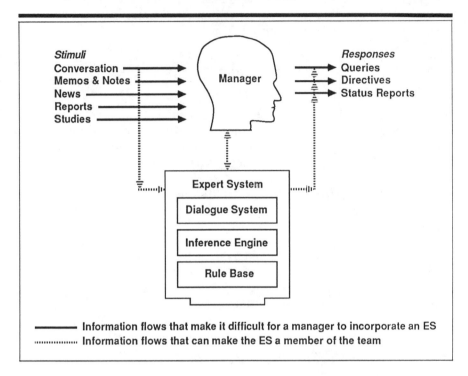

narrow, brittle, and shallow. Unlike such humans, ESs do not resort to reasoning from principles, analogies, or common sense. But ESs do have to elicit input evidence (data from memos, news, reports, or results of computational procedures) to make their educated guesses. They must be able to trace their questions and answers back to many of these elicited inputs in the same way that managers would if they were forced to verbalize their thought process.

In other words the ES must receive and process much of the same stimuli the manager accumulates in order to assist the manager to form a response. This input and output can either flow entirely through the manager (or a typing designee) or it can be *somewhat* automated as indicated in Figure 1.3 by the solid and dashed lines, respectively. If the manager has to pause and delay his deliberations to interact with an ES, the benefits of that interaction will be doubtful. In fact, after one or two trials the manager's ES would fall to disuse.

Bringing an ES into the team thus suggests three rather intimidating requirements: (1) enhancing the language system to facilitate flexible, rapid, adaptive input and possibly verbal intercourse as well; (2) readily converting written inputs (memos, notes, news, periodic reports, etc.) to electronic form directly "digestible" by the ES; and (3) interfacing the ES with existing electronic (computerized) aids so that it can automatically, without a need for the manager or a programmer's involvement, retrieve and send information from/to the relevant electronic mail bulletin boards; data bases, management information systems and document files; electronic spreadsheets and other decision aids; report-writing text editors; and graphics generators.

These three requirements suggest a variety of fourth-level rules needed to clarify several of the terms and conditions mentioned in Table 1.3. For example, it is now possible to more clearly define a "suitable ES kit" that "supports integration into a KBS environment" as called for by conditions 1, 4, and 8 of the ES kit rule (Table 1.3). The reader should be able to apply this new found understanding of rule syntax to write out such rules based on the text in the preceding paragraph: these will not be formally elaborated here.

More important is whether any ES kits yet exist that satisfy the three requirements. The answer to this question is directly addressed in the five chapters contained in Part IV of this book.

In terms of the first requirement, ES kits are being sold with enhanced language and editing systems (Kinnucan, 1985; and Silverman, 1985d) including (1) multiple windows for viewing different aspects of the dialogue simultaneously, such as working memory, questions, allowable answers, and rule-based reasoning explanations, (2) visual and graphical displays that change in real time and as appropriate during the course of the dialogue to draw the user's attention to relevant portions of a diagram or to values of critical parameters or chains of reasoning, and (3) well-documented, easy to use, natural language or touch (mouse, touch-screen, etc.) techniques for utilizing the features in (1) and (2) and for inputting and editing answers, questions, rules, and so forth.

In terms of the second requirement, optical character reader and video technology is available, and given the proper document formats it may prove appropriate in limited circumstances. This is currently proving quite popular in certain circles for making documents, maps, and diagrams, available to managers via their desktop CRT displays. Rare is the application using optical technology to feed inputs to an expert system; however, more and more organizations are computerizing periodic reports and forms—a point that brings up the next requirement.

In terms of the third and last requirement, a few ES kits have overcome the "closed box" syndrome and permit direct interface between their (proprietary) software and other software packages such as, but not limited to, data base management systems (DBMS), report-writing text editors, spreadsheet systems, and electronic mail/communications modules. Those interfaces require considerable programming skill and effort to utilize.

A couple of ES kits, largely considered to be exploratory in nature, go beyond simple interfaces of other packages and offer a complete environment containing tools to build many of the features one might desire (Kunz, Kehler, and Williams, 1984; Stefik, et al., 1983). That is, instead of shooting for the stars and offering an ES capable of replicating a manager's behavior, these kits aspire to the more realistic goal of enabling the knowledge engineer to craft a manager's assistant in the fullest sense. These tools include many of those features mentioned in the three preceding paragraphs and a number of tools not discussed here, all "bundled" together in an artificial intelligence (LISP) computer—these are forerunners of fifth generation technology.

The added costs of this approach are: (1) learning to master such a computer and environment takes time, (2) the manager's applications must be created on this machine or interfaced to it, and (3) hardware is expensive—each user must buy a LISP machine. The advantages of this approach, aside from those already mentioned, are yet to be proven. No one knows whether the resulting productivity increase will be sufficient to overcome the added costs and risks.

1.4   CONCLUSION

This chapter has served to introduce and define expert systems by attempting answers to two major questions commonly asked by managers.

First, what are Expert Systems? The answer to this question has been investigated by offering answers to a set of related questions. What is an ES like? Why bother defining ESs? What is an ES architecture? How does it behave? What exactly is a rule? How does an ES handle uncertainty? How does an ES combine different pieces of evidence?

Second, will ESs be valuable for the manager's application? The answer to this question has been investigated by offering answers to a second set of related questions. What is the promise of ESs? What are the concerns? Who should build an ES? Is an ES appropriate? Is a given ES project relevant? Feasible? Optimal? Success-oriented? Can an ES become a "team player?" Can it be integrated into the manager's environment?

A set of rules indicating when ESs will be appropriate to a managerial application were elaborated as part of the answer to the latter set of questions. An illustrative ES capable of manipulating these rules and diagnosing whether an ES is appropriate to a given application was then described as part of the answer to the first set of questions.

In describing the illustrative rule set and ES, a number of issues were purposely simplified. Nevertheless, it is felt that a basic understanding of ESs has been established to which a manager can add technical details gracefully and without serious conceptual reorientation. While simplified in technical detail, the descriptions presented here are accurate and faithful.

REFERENCES

Ackoff, R. (1962), "Management Misinformation Systems," *Management Science*, 14(4):B–147–156.

Dreyfus, S.E. (1982), "Formal Models vs. Situational Understanding: Inherent Limitations on the Modeling of Business Expertise," *Office: Technology and People*, 1(1):133–165.

Duda, R.O., and Gaschnig, J.G. (1981), "Knowledge-Based Expert Systems Come of Age," *Byte*, September, pp. 238–276.

Ellis, P. (1983), "Expert Systems – A Key Innovation in Professional and Managerial Problem Solving," *Information Age*, January, pp. 2–6.

Feigenbaum, E.A. (1977), "The Art of Artificial Intelligence: Themes and Case Studies of Knowledge Engineering," *Proceedings of the Fifth International Joint Conference on Artificial Intelligence*, AAAI, pp. 1014–1029.

Feigenbaum, E.A. (1982), "Knowledge Engineering for the 1980s," Computer Science Dept., Stanford University, Palo Alto, Calif.

Hayes-Roth, F. (1984), "Knowledge Based Expert Systems," *Computer*, October, 263–273.

Hayes-Roth, F., Waterman, D.A., and Lenat, D.B., eds., (1983), *Building Expert Systems*, New York: Addison-Wesley.

Kinnucan, P. (1985), "Software Tools Speed Expert System Development," *High Technology*, March, pp. 6–21.

Kunz, J.C., Kehler, T.P., and Williams, M.D. (1984), "Applications Development Using a Hybrid AI Development System," *AI Magazine* 5(3):41–54.

Lucas, H.C. (1975), *Why Information Systems Fail*, New York: Columbia University Press.

Majone, Q. (1982), *Pitfalls of Analysis*, New York: John Wiley & Sons.

Shortliffe, E.H., and Fagan, L.M., (1982), "Expert Systems Research: Modeling the Medical Decision Making Process," Stanford, Calif.: Stanford University (Tech. Memo HPP-82-3).

Shortliffe, E.H., and Fagan, L.M. (1983), "Analogy in Systems Management: A Theoretical Inquiry," *IEEE Transactions On Systems, Man, and Cybernetics*, (SMC-13), pp. 1049–75.

Silverman, B.G. (1985a), "A Behavioral Approach to Multigoal Decision Making," in B. Dean, ed., *Project Management*, New York: North Holland.

Silverman, B.G. (1985b), "Expert Intuition and Ill-Structured Problem Solving," *IEEE Transactions on Engineering Management*, February, pp. 29–32.

Silverman, B.G. (1985c), "INNOVATOR: An Expert System for Management of Modeling and Simulation," *Proceedings of the International Test and Evaluation Conference*, November.

Silverman, B.G. (1985d), "Development Tools Update," *The Institute for Management Science, College on AI Newsletter*, Spring, pp. 3–4.

Silverman, B.G., Moustakis, V.S., and Robless, R. (1984), "Expert Systems and Robotics in the Space Station Era: Design Considerations," *Institute for Artificial Intelligence Report*, Fall.

Stefik, M., Bobrow, D.G., Mittal, S., and Conway, L. (1983), "Knowledge Programming in LOOPS," *AI Magazine*, 4(3):3–14.

"Survey of Uncertainty Representation in Expert Systems," *Proceedings of the Second Workshop of the North American Fuzzy Information Processing Society*, available from G.E. Corporate Research and Development, Schenectady, N.Y.

Zmud, R.W. (1979), "Individual Differences and MIS Success: A Review of the Empirical Literature," *Management Science*, 25(10): 969–979.

2

A Survey of Issues in Expert Systems for Management

Robert W. Blanning

The purpose of an expert system for management (ESM) is to capture the specialized knowledge and experience of line managers and the staff analysts who support them and to apply this knowledge and experience to individual management decision problems. Three issues relevant to the design and implementation of ESMs are examined: (1) the types of problems for which ESMs might be suited, (2) certain technological issues in ESM development, and (3) potential business application of ESMs.

2.11 INTRODUCTION

The growing number of successful applications of expert systems in such areas as medical diagnosis and geological prospecting (Barr and Feigenbaum 1982; Hayes-Roth, Waterman, and Lenat 1983; Weiss and Kulikowski 1984; Miller 1984; Harmon and King 1985; and Waterman 1986) has led to suggestions that expert system technology may also be used to help managers to make decisions and implement them (Reitman 1982; Fox 1983; Gorry and Krumland 1983; and Reitman 1984). The purpose of an expert system is to capture the specialized knowledge and experience of practicing professionals and apply them to individual problems. We are concerned here with expert systems for management (ESMs), which capture the specialized knowledge and experience of line managers and the staff analysts who support them (e.g., financial analysts, market research analysts, etc.) and apply them to problems in management decision making. ESMs have been developed in such areas as portfolio management, the auditing of accounts receivable, the analysis of financial statements, and personnel assignment (Michaelson and Michie 1983; and Blanning 1984c), and many more applications are anticipated (Blanning 1987). For example, ESMs might be developed for financial planning, market research, budget variance analysis, and so forth.

As ESMs become more widely developed and implemented, certain technological and managerial issues will arise. For example, managers now have available to them a variety of computer-based information sources, such as management science models, management information systems (MISs), and decision support systems (DSSs). It appears likely that many ESMs will not be stand-alone systems but will have to be integrated, possibly in an informal way, with other types of computer-based information systems. In addition, it appears unlikely that ESMs will be equally productive or desirable in all of the functional areas of an enterprise — such as finance, marketing, operations, and so forth. Rather, different components of an organization will be affected by ESMs in different ways, and it will be useful to anticipate the organizational components in which ESMs are most likely to be found and the problems to which they will be applied. In this chapter, three tasks are undertaken. First, we identify three types of problems to which ESMs have been applied. The ESM applications described here are developmental efforts initiated at universities and industrial research laboratories, but they may well lead to commercially available systems. Second, we examine the technological (i.e., knowledge engineering) issues relevant to ESM development. Finally, we explore the possible business applications of ESMs.

2.2 ESM PROBLEM TYPES

There are several ways in which ESMs might be classified. One is by the technology employed (e.g., the structure of the knowledge base, the functions performed by the inference engine, etc.). Another is the level of the organization (strategic, tactical, operational) at which the ESM is implemented. Yet another possible breakdown is by the functional area of an organization in which the ESM is found (e.g., finance, marketing, etc.). This approach will be taken in Section 2.4. Finally, one can classify ESMs by the type of decision problem for which the ESM provides support. This is the approach that will be used in this section.

There are three areas in which ESMs have been developed in the past, and it is likely that these areas will continue to provide a useful description of the ESMs that will be developed in the future. Each of these areas will be examined in a separate subsection. It should be noted that the ESMs described here are experimental at present. That is, they have been developed at universities and industrial research laboratories and are not yet commercially available. However, as more research is done and field testing is performed, ESMs of this type may be shown to be quite useful in practice. Presently, it is not clear why these three problem areas, rather than other possible ones, have initially been explored. However, it appears that the areas described here contain fundamental management problems for which ESM technology is appropriate or at least promising. We now examine the three problem types, and the fledgling attempts to confront them, in detail.

2.2.1   Resource Allocation

An important function of management is to allocate scarce resources, such as budgets, equipment, personnel, floor space, and so forth. It is understandable that some ESMs have been developed for this purpose—that is, to evaluate resource allocation proposals or to recommend an allocation that satisfies the objectives of the manager responsible for the allocation.

The first ESM was a portfolio management system that modeled a bank trust officer preparing portfolios for his clients (Clarkson 1963). The user enters the size of the account, certain client preferences (e.g., for growth stocks), and other relevant information about the client and the trust (e.g., the client's place of legal residence and income tax bracket). The output is a recommended portfolio.

The system consists of a data base, a knowledge base, an inference engine, and a user interface. The data base consists of two files. The first is a list of industries available for investment and, within each industry, a list of acceptable companies. The second file contains information about the economic and financial performance of the U.S. economy, each of the industries, and each of the companies. The knowledge base consists of a set of rules that are applied to the data base to select a portfolio that meets client requirements. The rules are based on certain characteristics of the companies (e.g., sales, earnings, cash flow per share, profit margin, etc.)

and on industry and general economic data. The inference engine implements the rules by beginning with a list of all available stocks and successively eliminating those that are not appropriate to the needs of the client until a satisfactory portfolio is developed. Finally, the user interface receives the input describing client preferences and status and prints the portfolio.

Two important tasks in the construction of this and any other ESM are knowledge acquisition (i.e., the construction of the knowledge base — in this case the development of the rules for client analysis and stock selection) and system validation. Knowledge acquisition was accomplished by eliciting protocols from a bank trust officer. A *protocol* is a transcript of the verbal statements and responses (to questions) of an expert as he performs a task. Two tasks were presented to the trust officer. The first was the preparation of portfolios for real clients, and the second was the reading and interpretation of financial articles and reports on trust fund management. The trust officer made comments to the knowledge engineer (i.e., the person who constructed the ESM) about how he was preparing the portfolio and what he thought of the articles. The knowledge engineer used these protocols to construct the rules in the knowledge base. System validation was accomplished by having the trust officer and the ESM each prepare portfolios for four of the bank's new clients. The results were quite similar.

This ESM was a pioneering effort. It was the first ESM and was one of the first expert systems of any type. However, most of the ESMs now being developed differ from this pioneering effort in three respects.

First, few ESMs are now validated by comparing the output of the ESM with the judgment of the person or persons used to construct it. Rather, the output is compared with the judgments of other experts. Second, most current inference engines not only apply the knowledge base to the problem at hand to produce a recommended solution, but they also provide additional information. For example, they often contain explanation facilities. When an ESM requests information from a user, the user can enter "WHY" and be given an explanation of the intended use of the requested information by the ESM. Thus the user can compare the effort needed to generate the input (when this is difficult) with the likely benefits. Similarly, when an ESM presents a result to a user, the user can enter "WHY" and be given an explanation of the reasoning that led to the result. Finally, many ESMs make use of certainty factors so that their users may judge the confidence that they may have in the recommendation of the ESM.

The effort described above, published in 1963, did not lead to other ESMs for almost 20 years. Expert systems in general and ESMs in particular have only recently flourished as practical and commercial possibilities, even though the idea of modeling expertise in an explicit computational form was first implemented, at least on an experimental basis, more than

20 years ago. The reason is that during the 1960s most researchers in artificial intelligence believed that they could reproduce intelligent behavior by discovering and invoking a few fundamental laws of reasoning that would be repeatedly (often, recursively) implemented on powerful computer systems. Examples include software systems for playing games, proving theorems, and so forth. The failure of this approach to achieve more than mediocre reasoning performance led researchers during the 1970s to believe that any effective reasoning system must contain a large amount of domain-specific knowledge, which in turn has led to a growing number of attempts to develop expert systems, including ESMs.

Another type of ESM useful in resource allocation is one that evaluates investment proposals. Bohanek, Bratko, and Rajkovic (1983) have developed a system, called DECMAK, for the evaluation of capital budgeting proposals. The system is a domain-independent "shell"— that is, it is not modeled after a particular user solving a particular type of problem. Rather, the user enters a set of rules to be used in the analysis of a particular class of projects (e.g., the way in which economic characteristics are to be combined with other characteristics to lead to an evaluation). These rules, along with a set of certainty factors, form the knowledge base of DECMAK, which was then applied to a particular capital budgeting proposal. The result is a recommendation concerning the desirability of the proposed investment and an explanation, when requested, of DECMAK's reasoning procedures.

ESMs are not the only type of computer-based systems that provide decision support to managers allocating resources. Other systems, based on such operations research techniques as linear programming, have been in use for more than 20 years (Palmer et al. 1984). These systems differ from ESMs in that most of the information they contain is causal information (e.g., unit costs, facility capacities, etc.) rather than expert knowledge. Although building causal models requires expertise, in ESMs this expertise is made explicit and is separated from causal information and from the reasoning procedures (in the inference engine) that applies it to a specific problem. We may expect that the increasing availability of ESMs will make it possible to solve a broader range of resource allocation problems than have been addressed in the past with operations research techniques.

2.2.2   Problem Diagnosis

Managers are expected to anticipate inchoate problems in their organizations and to take action to correct them before they become seriously damaging. Examples are cost overruns, schedule delays, and sudden declines in sales. To this end, managers receive periodic control reports, such as budget variance reports, that often contain indicators of possible problems, and they must diagnose any problems and take steps to correct them. In this respect, managers are similar to certain other professionals, such as doctors and geologists, for whom expert systems have been developed. Therefore it is not surprising that ESMs have been developed for problem diagnosis and especially for the diagnosis of impending financial problems.

An example of such a system is AUDITOR, an ESM that audits trade accounts receivable—that is, it recommends whether delinquent customer credit accounts should be reported in a company's financial statements as collectable (Dungan and Chandler 1985). The user is asked a sequence of questions (e.g., whether the customer is still an active customer, whether more recent items have been fully paid, etc.), and he or she enters a number between -5.0 and +5.0 to indicate the degree to which the statement is true. The output is a judgment as to whether the account is collectable, along with a probability estimate.

The knowledge base is a set of 39 rules, containing certainty factors, that relate such antecedents as whether the customer is still active to the collectability of the account. The rules were obtained by eliciting protocols from auditors in a public accounting firm. The auditors were first asked to supply a list of "cues"—that is, factors, such as whether the customer is still active, that they felt were important in assessing collectability—and these were used to construct an initial set of rules. The knowledge engineer then showed the rules to the auditors and asked them to judge the "relative strength" of each rule in order to arrive at two certainty factors (called positive weights and negative weights) for each rule. The inference engine was Advice Language X (AL/X), a commercially available domain-independent inference engine that received the user input for a delinquent account and applied the rules to produce a judgment concerning collectability. After a trial run of the system, the knowledge engineer made several adjustments to the initial set of rules (i.e., some were discarded and others added) and to the certainty factors so that AUDITOR produced judgments consistent with those of the professional auditors.

System validation was accomplished in two ways—by means of an "open-book" validation and a "blind" validation. In the open-book validation, the validator (i.e., the expert or experts with which the ESM is compared) was an audit manager practicing in the same public accounting firm that employed the auditors used to develop AUDITOR. He was shown the work papers for ten delinquent accounts (five accounts for each of two clients), and his judgments were compared with those of AUDITOR. They agreed in nine of the ten cases. In the blind validation, the validator was an audit manager in a different public accounting firm. AUDITOR was applied to eleven delinquent accounts for one of the firm's clients. The validator was shown the judgments of AUDITOR and of human auditors in the firm (without being told which was which) and a set of "fact sheets" describing the account. (This is called a Turing test.)

In all but one case the human and AUDITOR judgments were the same, and the validator agreed with the human judgment in the remaining case.

Another example of a diagnostic ESM is one developed to analyze the financial health of a company based on published financial data about the firm and its industry (Bouwman 1983). The system is based on protocols elicited from professional financial analysts and students in a graduate course on financial analysis. Its output is a narrative description of the financial status of a company and an explanation of how the published financial figures suggest the conclusions concerning financial status. For example, the system might explain a low profit margin by noting that the company had invested in an expansion of production capacity far in excess of that needed to meet demand.

An important discovery made during the knowledge acquisition process is that financial analysts presented with a plethora of data about a company (e.g., annual reports and other public domain reports that must be filed with the Securities Exchange Commission) do not attempt to use all of the data in arriving at a judgment concerning financial status. Rather, they look for a few qualitative indicators that summarize these data. The knowledge engineer uncovered five such indicators: a simple trend (e.g., an increase or decrease over time of net income), a complex trend (e.g., recovery to a previously held level), a comparison with an industry norm, comparison of two or more financial measures, and an application of a simple heuristic (e.g., that earnings should be positive). These were used to construct the rules in the knowledge base.

2.2.3 Scheduling and Assignment

The scheduling of logistical activites and the assignment of discrete resources (people, machines, etc.) to tasks or responsibilities are well-studied problems in operations research, and algorithms have been developed to determine optimal or near-optimal schedules and assignments—ones that maximize or minimize a performance measure (e.g., completion time, cost, etc.) without violating a set of specified given constraints (Coffman 1976; and Graves 1981). The principal differences between these algorithms and the ESMs that have been developed in this area are that (1) the ESMs are not based on a single performance measure to be optimized, but rather they attempt to satisfy several objectives, (2) the problem as presented to the ESM may be infeasible (i.e., the constraints as given may collectively define a null set), and (3) the purpose of the ESM is to suggest an acceptable relaxation of the constraints that will result in a feasible schedule or assignment.

An example of such a system is NUDGE, an ESM for scheduling business meetings. The user enters a set of requirements for the meeting (e.g., the type or purpose of the meeting, who is to attend, a range of times within which the meeting should be held, etc.), and NUDGE interacts with its user to find a suitable time, place, and attendance list. For example, if there is no time at which all of the designated attendees are available, then NUDGE will infer from the type or purpose of the meeting and the capabilities of the people who were not on the list of attendees which substitutions might be acceptable, and it will request permission to make a substitution.

NUDGE's knowledge base contains a great deal of common sense information about different types of meetings, the characteristics of potential attendees, and certain preferences of its user (e.g., preferences for a particular time of day or for a particular location for the meeting). The knowledge base differs from those described previously in that it is not based on rules, but on frames. A *frame* is a directed graph consisting of a node representing an entity in the real world (e.g., a type of meeting, a person, etc.) and one or more arcs designating certain properties of the entity, along with other nodes (called *slots*) containing the values of the properties. Frame-based ESMs such as NUDGE derive their power from the types of property values that an entity can have. For example, a property value might be a numeric or other symbolic value or set of values, a default value that can be overriden by the user, an algorithm for calculating a value, or the name of another frame. Thus a frame can "inherit" property values from other frames. NUDGES's knowledge base is a library of interrelated frames that combines information about meetings, purposes, people, times, and places, and it uses the library to assist its user in arriving at a satisfactory schedule.

Other ESMs for scheduling and assignment have been developed in the problem domains of factory scheduling, office automation, and human resource management. An example is ISIS, a frame-based system for factory scheduling (Fox and Smith 1984). ISIS performs a constraint-directed search for an acceptable production schedule when the constraints involve due dates, inventories, costs, schedule stability, resource availability, machine capacities, precedence of operations, and certain preferences of factory management (e.g., a preference for using one machine over another whenever possible). ISIS considers the relevance and importance of the various constraints and attempts to resolve conflicts among them. Another such system is ODYSSEY, a frame-based ESM for scheduling business trips (Fikes 1981). ODYSSEY contains procedures for resolving inconsistencies and ambiguities in a user's stated trip requirements. Yet another system is OMEGA, a rule-based ESM for personnel assignment (Barber 1983). OMEGA helps a user to assign available personnel to job openings when inconsistencies in job requirements, personnel qualifications, and the availability of travel funds for reassignment must be resolved.

2.3 TECHNOLOGICAL ISSUES
IN ESM DEVELOPMENT

There are two sets of technological issues relevant to ESMs. The first include issues that arise in the development of any expert system (e.g., knowledge acquisition, the design of the inference engine, etc.). These topics are collectively called *knowledge engineering*. In examining knowledge-engineering issues, we will focus on those that differ, at least in emphasis, from those that arise in the development of other types of expert systems. The second set of issues are those that concern the relationship between ESMs and other computer-based decision aids that are increasingly being made available to managers (Blanning 1984b).

2.3.1 Knowledge Engineering

Five issues that generally arise in the development of expert systems will also arise in the development of ESMs. The first is *the structure of the knowledge base*. Most ESM knowledge bases consist of a set of if-then rules. For example, AUDITOR (Section 2.2.2) contains rules that relate such variables as whether the delinquent account is still active to the likelihood that it will be settled. As with other types of expert systems, these rules are obtained by eliciting protocols from managers experienced in performing the task in question.

Rules such as these are only one of the types of relationships between important variables that make up the information available to a manager. There are three other types of relationships found in most organizations, and it may be necessary to integrate these with expert rules. The first type derives from economic theory or other theories relevant to the management of an enterprise. Examples are the net discounted present value criterion and the payback criterion often used in investment analysis. The second type of relationship includes rules mandated by legal or other authority. The accounting rules set forth by the Financial Accounting Standards Board, the Internal Revenue Service, and the Securities Exchange Commission are an example. The third type consists of causal relationships, such as those describing plant capacities, substitutability between raw materials, and so forth. Although nonjudgmental relationships such as these are found in many expert systems, the sheer number of such rules that will appear in many ESMs suggests that some ESMs will have a two-level knowledge base, one for the judgmental rules and one for the nonjudgmental ones.

The second issue is *knowledge acquisition*. As in the case with other types of expert systems, knowledge acquisition for ESMs will be accomplished primarily by means of protocol analysis. However, there is another source of information concerning managerial behavior. Managers, unlike most other professionals, have been studied in some detail

(Carlson 1951; Mahoney, Jerdee, and Carroll 1965; Stewart 1967; Mintzberg 1973; and Kotter 1982), and attempts have been made to explicate their judgmental and decision-making processes (Mintzberg, Raisinghani, and Theoret 1976). Knowledge engineers may be able to make productive use of this body of literature during the knowledge acquisition process, both in determing an appropriate structure for the knowledge base and in interpreting protocols to determine specific rules and the values of any parameters associated with them.

The third issue is *the design of the inference engine*. The purpose of an inference engine is to: (1) request and receive information from a user concerning the problem to be solved, (2) access the knowledge base to arrive at a judgment and/or recommendation concerning the problem and report them to the user, and (3) explain or demand why it has requested its input data and how its results were obtained (i.e., to explain the chain of reasoning that led to its judgment and/or recommendation).

There are two additional functions that might be performed by ESM inference engines. Surveys (Naylor and Schauland 1976) and case studies (Boulden 1975) concerning the way managers use planning models (i.e., causal models used in long-range planning) suggest that an important feature of these models is that they facilitate sensitivity analyses (or "what if" studies). Furthermore many of the planning languages that have been developed to assist in the construction and use of planning models contain special features for sensitivity analysis (Naylor and Mann 1982). They also contain report writers that help their users to format pro-forma financial and operating reports. Inference engines for ESMs will probably contain sensitivity analysis commands and report writers as well.

The fourth issue is *system validation*, which will be accomplished by comparing the output of an ESM with that of human experts for the same problem input. One important question is whether laboratory experiments or field studies are more revealing (Blanning 1984a); the answer depends on the relative merits of contextual realism and experimental control. Another question concerns the specificity of results. Although some management judgments and decisions (e.g., production schedules) can be made explicit, others cannot. Examples are the cause of a significant budget variance or the best way to introduce a new product. The problem is not that these are difficult to determine, but that it is often difficult to compare two solutions to determine how similar they are. Case studies written for business school pedagogy address problems of this type, and they usually lead to substantial disagreement, some of which is caused by difficulties in comparing solutions.

The fifth issue concerns *the user interface*. Most ESMs, like most expert systems, have structured user interfaces. However, the development of natural language data base query processors (Tennant 1981) and the suggestion that similar processors be developed for decision models (Blanning 1984d) suggest that less structured interfaces be developed for

ESMs. One intermediate possibility is menu-based natural language query processing, in which a user assembles words or symbols taken from menus on a CRT to construct a natural language query (Tennant 1984). This may provide sufficient structure to avoid ambiguities without constraining the user unnecessarily.

2.3.2   The Integration of Information Sources

The ESMs described in Section 2.2, like most expert systems, are stand-alone systems—that is, they are not integrated with other computer-based information systems. This will probably change in the future. There are two other types of computer-based information widely available to managers. The first is stored data and the output of data analysis software (e.g., statistical packages), and the second is the output of (causal) decision models (e.g., linear programming models of transportation networks, Monte Carlo simulations of production facilities, deterministic models of the financial structure of a firm, etc.). Expert knowledge may well supplement (but not replace) these two established information sources to become a third type of available information.

Each of these three types of information—stored data, decision models, and expert knowledge—must be stored, processed, and integrated (see Table 2.1). Data are stored in a data base and processed by a data management system; models are stored in a model bank and processed by a model management system; and knowledge is stored in a knowledge base and processed by an inference engine.* In each case the purpose of the software is to insulate the user from the physical aspects of information organization and processing—that is, from the retrieval of data, the execution of models, and the application of knowledge.

An important issue in ESM development is what type of interaction, if any, should take place between these three types of information systems. One possibility is that an ESM may be used to integrate systems;

---

*Of these three topics, model management is the newest and least developed. See Bonczek, Holsapple, and Whinston (1982), Konsynski (1983), and Blanning (1983).

TABLE 2.1
SOURCES OF MANAGEMENT INFORMATION

Type of Information	Information Base	Software for Information Processing
Stored Data	Data Base	Data Management System
Decision Models	Model Bank	Model Management System
Expert Knowledge	Knowledge Base	Inference Engine

thus information from all three sources might be combined in response to a single user query (Blanning 1985). In addition, the ongoing investigation of the relationships between expert systems and data management systems (Kerschberg 1984; and Wiederhold 1984) and of the similarities between data management and model management (Blanning 1983) suggests that intermediate information structures possessing some of the properties of data, models, and knowledge may be developed.

2.4 POTENTIAL BUSINESS APPLICATIONS OF ESMs

In Section 2.2 we described several developmental ESMs, classified by the type of management problems for which they provide decision support. In this section we examine briefly the major functional areas of an organization in which ESMs might be useful and the management decisions within these functional areas that they might support.*

2.4.1 Finance

There are three areas in which ESMs might be useful. The first is the preparation and analysis of investment proposals. Although investment analysis is founded on economic logic, and ESM may be useful in obtaining the parameters to be used in economic rules (e.g., projected cash flows) and in comparing economic and noneconomic considerations. The second area is financial market analysis. The efficiency (or near efficiency) of financial markets suggests that ESMs are unlikely to be useful in stock selection (except possibly for new issues), but they might be useful in eliciting the risk preferences of portfolio owners and other relevant information (e.g., tax information). The third area is banking (e.g., cash management and credit evaluation for industrial lending).

2.4.2 Marketing

Many marketing decisions (e.g., product pricing, advertising and promotion, new product introduction, brand management, and the design of sales territories) require substantial amounts of subjective judgment. Subjectively based "decision calculus" models are sometimes used in making these decisions, but they require considerable brand-related expertise on the part of their users. If this type of expertise were incorporated into

---

*This material is taken from a research effort being completed at the Owen Graduate School of Management at Vanderbilt University to identify potential ESM applications in business. It will soon be described in detail (Blanning 1987). Additional members of the project team are Brian E. Barkocy, Joseph D. Blackburn, Germain B. Boer, Paul K. Chaney, John R. Deckop, Timothy M. Devinney, Thomas A. Mahoney, Paul K. Makens, Ann C. Seror, David W. Stewart, Robert A. Ullrich, and Anthony J. Zahorik.

these models and if other features (e.g., explanation facilities) were added, they would become ESMs.

2.4.3   Operations

This is an area in which much causal modeling has been done, including modeling based on heuristic search techniques. ESMs of the type discussed in Section 2.2.3 may be very useful in operations management. Possible decision areas include capacity planning, facilities scheduling and design, activity scheduling, materials management, inventory planning and control, work force management, and quality planning and analysis.

2.4.4   Accounting

Accounting is a rule-based profession, the rules being mandated by such rule-making bodies as the Financial Accounting Standards Board, the Internal Revenue Service, and the Securities Exchange Commission. However, expertise is needed to select the most appropriate rules and to supply data needed to implement the rules. For example, in structuring a lease, it is necessary to estimate the fair market value of the asset being leased, which requires the expertise of experienced accountants. ESMs may be useful in both financial accounting (e.g., auditing) and management accounting (e.g., cost accounting and budgeting).

2.4.5   Research and Development (R&D) Management

Most of the issues that arise in R&D management are similar to those that arise in other areas of management, but the nebulous nature of R&D projects often makes it difficult to obtain hard data for decision making. Three areas in which ESMs might be useful are budget allocation and project selection (e.g., an ESM might elicit information about project risk from researchers), project scheduling and control (e.g., an ESM might elicit information about partial project success), and determining appropriate modes of communication among related projects.

2.4.6   Human Resource Management

Human resource management is similar to accounting in that there are externally mandated rules that must be followed, and it is similar to R&D management in that expertise is not as well recorded and understood as it is in some of the other areas. Even so, there are five areas for which ESMs might be appropriate: staffing (e.g., matching job requirements with applicant capabilities), compensation (e.g., job evaluation), training and development (e.g., assessing skill levels and the need for training), employee assistance (e.g., counseling), and employee relations (e.g., grievances).

2.5 CONCLUSION

During the past decade information systems researchers and practitioners have become increasingly interested in the application of information processing technology to the solution of unstructured or semistructured management problems. The systems produced by these researchers and practitioners, often called *decision support systems* (DSSs), provide convenient and flexible user interfaces to stored data and decision models (Keen and Morton 1978; Alter 1980; and House 1983). More recently the emphasis in this area has been on dialogue management (as a supplement to data management and model management) and the application of artificial intelligence techniques (such as heuristic programming and knowledge representation) to decision support (Bonczek, Holsapple, and Whinston 1981; and Sprague and Carlson 1982). It appears that ESMs may most productively be viewed not as a radical departure in the application of information processing technology to decision making, but as an evolutionary outgrowth of DSS technology. We may expect that many of the troublesome issues that will arise during the development and implementation of ESMs, such as formulating messy problems, overcoming the skepticism of potential users, and coping with the inevitable failures that accompany the introduction of any new technology, will be similar to those that have arisen during previous attempts to develop and implement DSSs. Although these issues are not easily resolved, their solution is far more promising in an environment that views ESMs as an additional tool for meeting the objectives of DSSs, rather than in one that views ESMs as a totally new and different type of system. It seems reasonable to suggest that ESM developers will be more productive if they attempt to work closely with those experienced in the development and implementation of DSSs, rather than if they stress the differences between ESMs and the more traditional types of DSS.

ACKNOWLEDGMENT

This work was supported by the Dean's Fund for Faculty Research of the Owen Graduate School of Management at Vanderbilt University.

REFERENCES

Alter, S.L. (1980), *Decision Support Systems: Current Practice and Continuing Challenges.* Reading, Mass.: Addison-Wesley.

Barber, G. (1983), "Supporting Organizational Problem Solving with a Work Station," *ACM Transactions on Office Information Systems*, 1(January): 45–67.

Barr, A., and Feigenbaum, E.A. (1982), *The Handbook of Artificial Intelligence*. vol. II, Los Altos, Calif.: William Kaufman.

Blanning, R.W. (1983), "Issues in the Design of Relational Model Management Systems," *Proceedings of the National Computer Conference*, June, pp. 395–401.

Blanning, R.W. (1984a), "Knowledge Acquisition and System Validation in Expert Systems for Management," *Human Systems Management*, 4(Fall): 280–285.

Blanning, R.W. (1984b), "Issues in the Design of Expert Systems for Management," *Proceedings of the National Computer Conference*, July, pp. 489–495.

Blanning, R.W. (1984c), "Expert Systems for Management: Possible Application Areas," *DSS-84 Transactions*, April, pp. 69–77.

Blanning, R.W. (1984d), "Communicating with Management Information Systems in Natural Language," *Communications of the ACM*, 27(March): 201–207.

Blanning, R.W. (1985), "Expert Systems for Management: Research and Applications," *Journal of Information Science*, 9(March): 153–162.

Blanning, R.W., ed. (1987), *Foundations of Expert Systems for Management*, Köln: Verlag Rheinland (to appear).

Bohanek, M., Bratko, I., and Rajkovic, V. (1983), "An Expert System for Decision Making," in H.G. Sol, ed., *Processes and Tools for Decision Support*, Amsterdam: North-Holland, pp. 235–248.

Bonczek, R.H., Holsapple, C.W., and Whinston, A.B. (1982), "The Evolution from MIS to DSS: Extension of Data Management to Model Management," in M.J. Ginzberg, W. Reitman, and E.A. Stohr, eds., *Decision Support Systems*, Amsterdam: North-Holland, pp. 61–78.

Bonczek, R.H., Holsapple, C.W., and Whinston, A.B. (1981), *Foundations of Decision Support Systems*, New York: Academic Press.

Boulden, J.B. (1975), *Computer-Assisted Planning Systems*, New York: McGraw-Hill.

Bouwman, M. (1983), "Human diagnostic Reasoning by Computer: An Illustration from Financial Analysis," *Management Science*, 29 (June): 653–672.

Carlson, S. (1951), *Executive Behavior*, Stockholm: Strombergs.

Clarkson, G.P.E. (1963), "A Model of the Trust Investment Process," in E.A. Feigenbaum and J. Feldman, eds., *Computers and Thought*, New York: McGraw-Hill, pp. 347–371.

Coffman, E.G., Jr. (1976), *Computer and Job Shop Scheduling Theory*, New York: Wiley.

Dungan, C.W., and Chandler, J.S. (1985), "AUDITOR: A Micro-computer Based Expert System to Support Auditors in the Field," *Expert Systems*, 2(October): 210–221.

Fikes, R.E. (1981), "Odyssey: A Knowledge-Based Assistant," *Artificial Intelligence*, 16(July): 331–361.

Fox, M.S. (1983), "The Intelligent Management System: An Overview," in H.G. Sol, ed.,*Processes and Tools for Decision Support*, Amsterdam: North-Holland, pp. 105–130.

Fox, M.S., and Smith, S.F. (1984), "ISIS – A Knowledge-Based System for Factory Scheduling," *Expert Systems*, 1(July): 25–49.

Goldstein, I.P., and Roberts, B. (1982), "Using Frames in Scheduling," in P.H. Winston and R.H. Brown, eds., *Artificial Intelligence: An MIT Perspective*, vol. 1, Reading, Mass.: Addison-Wesley, pp. 257–284.

Gorry, G.A., and Krumland, R.B. (1983), "Artificial Intelligence Research and Decision Support Systems," in J.L. Bennett, ed., *Building Decision Support Systems*, Reading Mass.: Addison-Wesley, pp. 205–219.

Graves, S.C. (1981), "A Review of Production Scheduling," *Operations Research*, 29(July–Aug.): 646–675.

Harmon, P., and King, D. (1985), *Expert Systems: Artificial Intelligence in Business*,. New York: Wiley.

Hayes-Roth, F., Waterman, D.A., and Lenat, D.B., eds. (1983), *Building Expert Systems*, Reading, Mass.: Addison-Wesley.

House, W.C., ed. (1983), *Decision Support Systems: A Data-Based, Model-Oriented, User-Developed Discipline*. New York: Petrocelli.

Keen, P.G.W., and Morton, M.S.S. (1978), *Decision Support Systems: An Organizational Perspective*, Reading, Mass.: Addison-Wesley.

Kerschberg, L., ed. (1984), *Proceedings of the First International Workshop on Expert Database Systems*, I and II, October.

Konsynski, B.R. (1983), "Model Management in Decision Support Systems," in C.W. Holsapple and A.B. Whinston, eds., *Data Base Management: Theory and Applications*, Dordrecht: D. Reidel, pp. 131–154.

Kotter, J.P. (1982), "What Effective General Managers Really Do," *Harvard Business Review*, 60 (Nov.–Dec.): 156–167.

Mahoney, T.A., Jerdee, T.H., and Carroll, S.J. (1965), "The Job(s) of Management," *Industrial Relations*, 4 (Feubary): 97–110.

Michaelson, R., and Michie, D. (1983), "Expert Systems in Business," *Datamation*, 29 (November): 240–246.

Miller, R.K., ed. (1984), *The 1984 Inventory of Expert Systems*, Madison, Ga.: SEAI Institute.

Mintzberg, H. (1973), *The Nature of Managerial Work*, New York: Harper & Row.

Mintzberg, H., Raisinghani, D., and Theoret, A. (1976), "The Structure of 'Unstructured' Decision Processes," *Administrative Science Quarterly*, 21 (June): 246–275.

Naylor, T.H., and Mann, M.H. (1982), *Computer Based Planning Systems*, Oxford, Ohio: Planning Executives Institute.

Naylor, T.H., and Schauland, H. (1976), "A Survey of Users of Corporate Planning Models," *Management Science*, 22 (May): 927–937.

Palmer, K.H., Boudwin, N.K., Patton, H.A., Rowland, A.J., Sammes, J.D., and Smith, D.M. (1984), *A Model Management Framework for Mathematical Programming*, New York: Wiley.

Reitman, W., ed. (1984), *Artificial Intelligence Applications for Business*, Norwood, N.J.: Ablex.

Reitman, W. (1982), "Applying Artificial Intelligence to Decision Support: Where Do Good Alternative Come From?" in M.J. Ginzberg, W. Reitman, and E.A. Stohr, eds., *Decision Support Systems*, Amsterdam: North-Holland, pp. 155–174.

Sprague, R.H., Jr., and Carlson, E.D. (1982), *Building Effective Decision Support Systems*, Englewood Cliffs, N.J.: Prentice-Hall.

Stewart, R. (1967), *Managers and Their Jobs*, London: Pan Books.

Tennant, H. (1984), "Menu-Based Natural Language Understanding," *Proceedings of the National Computer Conference*, July, pp. 629–635.

Tennant, H. (1981), *Natural Language Processing*, New York: Petrocelli.

Waterman, D.A. (1986), *A Guide to Expert Systems*, Reading, Mass.: Addison-Wesley.

Weiss, S.M., and Kulikowski, C.A. (1984), *A Practical Guide to Designing Expert Systems*, Totowa, N.J.: Rowan and Allenheld.

Wiederhold, G. (1984), "Knowledge and Database Management," *IEEE Software*, 1 (January): 63–73.

3

Structured Design of an Expert System Prototype at the National Archives

Daniel A. De Salvo
Amy E. Glamm
Jay Liebowitz

This chapter presents a case study of a software development project, during which American Management Systems, Inc. (AMS) built a prototype expert system for the National Archives and Records Administration (NARA). Some of the highlights of this project include the following:

- The final product was a medium scale (about 300 rules) expert system. The software acts as a "front end" which helps users retrieve information from a data base on an IBM-PC/AT microcomputer. It does this by implementing as "rules of thumb" the methods that archivists use to search for information.
- The project team either adapted or developed new structured software design techniques for this project. They used model building as their major design paradigm.
- The project team applied project planning and management techniques to deliver this system on time and within strict budget constraints.

3.1 INTRODUCTION

This project started in the last half of 1985, when AMS had just begun to design a large-scale information storage and retrieval (ISAR) system for the Archives. The Archives had already started several other projects to see how digital imaging, high-accuracy optical character recognition, and other new information technologies might contribute to the ISAR.

The Archives' goal was to apply the findings from these various projects to the ISAR's design. The overriding concern was to find out if these new technologies were practical, reliable, and appropriate.

There were, therefore, two major constraints on this project. First, the project team had to produce definitive answers to some key questions. In particular, the Archives had to know if expert systems were practical at all, before committing scarce resources to investigating them further. Second, the information gathered from this project had to be available in time to influence the early stages of the ISAR system design. Because the first stages of the ISAR design were already underway, the project had to produce a system within about four and one-half months, complete an evaluation of it by the end of approximately five months, and document the project by the end of about six months total elapsed time.

This project therefore was a practical example that supports the following premise:

> Knowledge systems will never be commercially acceptable until we can develop them on time and within a budget, just as we do with the more conventional systems.

Structured systems development methods are the keys to doing this, just as they are in more traditional systems implementations. Many of the structured design tools we need are available from two closely related disciplines: *systems analysis*, the study and design of "traditional" algorithmic computer systems, and *knowledge engineering*, the study and design of knowledge-based or inferential computer systems.

Structured methodologies have already been put to good use in the development of both algorithmic and knowledge-based systems. However, project planning, knowledge acquisition, and system verification/validation are areas that still present significant challenges to the developer of commercial or government expert systems.

The National Archives encouraged a carefully structured systems development approach. The main elements of the system development strategy and some of the tools that have proven useful include the following:

- Requirements analysis — This was the first step in the system's development, during which the system's environment was fully described using narratives and data flow diagrams (De Marco 1979). This step was actually performed during the larger system design effort from which this project arose.

- Knowledge acquisition—During this phase, information was collected about the information handling process as performed by the domain experts—highly skilled archivists. This phase was highly dependent on the use of logical models of the system's behavior and knowledge-level analysis of the heuristics employed by the archivists (Clancey 1984).
- System development—During this phase, the system software was developed using structured programming techniques (Ziegler 1983; Page-Jones 1980; and Powers, Adams, and Mills 1984) adapted from algorithmic systems design methods.
- System assessment—This is the phase during which the system's behavior was evaluated for (1) its ability to emulate the domain experts and (2) what the project experience suggests about the usefulness of employing expert systems at the Archives.

In this chapter, we discuss three specific techniques that were applied to the development of the system. They are (1) the use of a "traditional" requirements analysis, (2) the use of system models as a key element in the knowledge acquisition process, and (3) the application and results of a quantitative system evaluation process.

Other techniques included in the discussion, but not addressed here in detail, are the use of structured programming, multiple experts, and techniques for managing the multiple tasks associated with the project.

This chapter has eight sections. In addition to the Introduction, Section 3.1, and the Conclusion, Section 3.8, they are

- Section 3.2—*Environment and working hypothesis for the prototype,* which outlines the working methods and environment of the archivist and the rationale for building this system
- Section 3.3—*The need to apply systems analysis techniques to the structured development of expert systems,* which discusses why we believe conventional analytical techniques are applicable to expert systems and which gives a brief overview of how we tied the various phases of the project together
- Section 3.4—*The use of a functional requirements analysis in building the expert system,* which defines the role of a preliminary requirements analysis in the system design process
- Section 3.5—*The use of models as an integral, analytical tool,* which discusses various system models and how they were used during the knowledge acquisition process
- Section 3.6—*Application of a scheme for system assessment,* which discusses the purpose, scope, and application of the assessment methods
- Section 3.7—*Brief review of the system,* which discusses the system, its major components, and their construction

3.2   ENVIRONMENT AND WORKING HYPOTHESIS FOR THE PROTOTYPE

The Archives comprise a large and complex, mostly manual, information system, which the archivists manage and maintain. We believed an expert system should be able to capture and use at least some of the expertise of the archivists. Therefore, we determined to test that hypothesis by building a prototype that would emulate at least some key parts of the archivist's expert behavior. Since the need to retrieve records is the key factor in determining how they will be arranged and handled, we determined to try to emulate the retrieval process.

The Archives is charged with preserving historically significant records of the federal government and with making those records available to the public for research. The types of records include: photographs, microfilm, machine-readable records, cartographics, bound volumes, and standard documents.

These holdings are arranged *hierarchically* to reflect the work done by the agencies. Therefore, the Archives' records are currently organized into an artificial set of groupings that reflect the Archives' view of how the government functions. For example, the *record groups*, or artificial collections, of the Bureau of Land Management (BLM) reflect such things as geography or accounting functions, whereas the original records were organized to reflect the internal organization of the various parts of BLM. The archivist or researcher must therefore go to the *series*, or basic level of the Archives' record structure, to see how the records were actually arranged by the agency.

This method was originally developed in order to make a large and complex records system manageable in several ways, including: (1) to establish a certain *intellectual control* over the records by defining a common view that could be shared among archivists, (2) to establish some kind of stable records structure that did not have to be changed every time an agency was reorganized, and (3) to reflect the activities of the government in such a way that the archivists could effectively relate the records organization to the sometimes broad or unfocused inquiries posed by researchers.

While this kind of arrangement ensures that the records are preserved in historical context, it narrows somewhat the means for accessing those records. For example, the primary *finding aid*, or directory, to the records is the *records description*, the main component of which traces the origin, or *provenance*, of the records. The content of the records is outlined in the records description, but again, the descriptions are organized to reflect the work done by the author agencies, rather than by topic or subject.

Various finding aids have been prepared for research purposes, including some very good topical finding aids. However, there is no comprehensive set of finding aids that provides researchers with subject or topical access to all of the Archives' holdings. This is largely due to the fact that archival holdings comprise mostly source documents (e.g., original working papers, memoranda, etc.). Establishing subject indexes to these kinds of records is more difficult (unless the subject of the query is the creator of the records) than for published works, which are inherently topical. Even after the advent of the Archives' large-scale information system, comprehensive and effective subject access will probably take years to develop, if only because there is such a massive amount of information to be drawn out of the billions of pages of Archives' documents.

Yet, archivists have developed a series of methods for (1) abstracting from researchers' inquiries the subjects that may be contained in federal government records and (2) efficiently searching those records in order to retrieve information.

It is clear that the archivist must understand the function of the agency that created the records, in order to know what kind of information would be contained in its records. For this kind of information, the archivist must rely on the *administrative histories* of the federal agencies that created the records. For example, to know that information about water rights is available in the BLM records, it is necessary to know that the BLM was charged with conducting several major programs concerning water rights.

The archivist's knowledge of the administrative histories thus comprises a view of the records, organized according to the activities of the federal agencies and mapped to the hierarchical records structure. This view is dynamic, changing as the archivist learns more about the records, about the administrative histories, or about how different parts of the view relate to specific kinds of inquiries.

We had two reasons for believing that an expert system could successfully imitate the archivist's record search techniques:

1. Interviews with archivists showed that they can describe their work and the knowledge they use to do it as a set of discrete judgments with known inputs and outputs. This made it much simpler to describe the work of archivists within a logical structure and thus to turn that logical structure into a straightforward computer program.

2. The average time an archivist takes to answer an inquiry, based on a quick sample of cases, appeared to vary from less than one minute to no more than one-half hour (discounting the time it may take to physically handle records). This is a good indication that the archivist is pulling information directly out of memory, rather than performing logical calculations of great depth. The ability to pull information directly from memory ("if you want to answer this question, look here") indicates that the archivist has reduced the complex retrieval process to a set of highly organized and crystallized rules of thumb or heuristics, which may be applicable for use in an expert system.

FIGURE 3.1
Archivist's Use of Shared Knowledge and Reference Data*

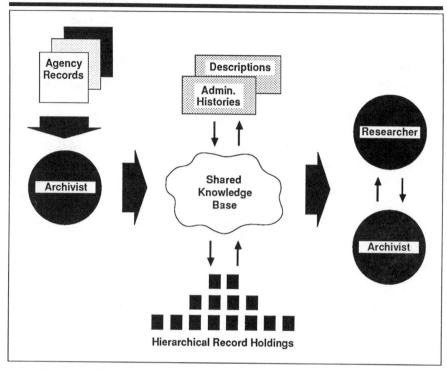

*The Archives' records management environment is conceptually straightforward. Agencies re-lease their records to the Archives, where an archivist generates records descriptions. Rolled into those descriptions, and available from other sources such as the *Government Handbook*, are the administrative histories of the agencies. Administrative histories describe what the agency responsibilities were—for example, the programs they adminstered, what larger agencies they were a part of, and so on.

The records descriptions contain a little of that same information and a lot of data on the *prove-nance* of the records: who created them, when they were created, what kind of records they were (e.g. correspondence) and so on. The records themselves are arranged hierarchically to reflect the organiza-tional structure of the government entity that created them.

Archivists also help researchers use the records, since the archivists share a body of knowledge between them about what kinds of information are located in what kinds of records, and so on. A lot of the shared knowledge that archivists develop over time goes toward knowing how to interpret a re-searcher's questions in terms of the administrative histories. For example, because an archivist knows the program areas administered by a certain agency, that archivist can interpret what kinds of information should be contained in the agency files.

As Figure 3.1 shows, the archivists rely heavily on their shared knowledge about (1) the Archives' organization, (2) the existing finding aids such as administrative histories and records descriptions, and (3) rules of thumb about how best to search the records to find specific kinds of information. This knowledge comprises an invaluable *institutional memory*.

The knowledge acquisition process revealed that archivists use heuristics to (1) control the search strategy, and (2) manipulate and communicate specific facts about the records. For example, specific topics that are abstracted from the researcher's broad inquiry may be heuristically matched to what the archivist knows about the content of specific records. Inherent in this is the archivist's empirical and tactical selection and management of specific search techniques (e.g., best-first).

Knowledge acquisition further indicated that the archivist uses internal lists (e.g., facts about records) and a knowledge indexing scheme that accommodates several views of the Archives' data in order to formulate search paths. These views include: a network of predetermined, generalized search paths related to specific classes of topics; hierarchical views of the records, which correspond to their arrangement and description; and views of the functional topics contained in the records. The last views correspond to the activities engaged in by the agency (e.g., water conservation) and are derived from both the administrative histories and the archivists' knowledge of the record contents.

3.3   THE NEED TO APPLY SYSTEMS ANALYSIS TECHNIQUES TO THE STRUCTURED DEVELOPMENT OF EXPERT SYSTEMS

The regular use of expert systems in practical business environments will not happen until potential commercial or government buyers are confident that expert systems fit in with other systems, other projects, limited budgets, and their organizations' schedules. Systems analysis already comprises a well-developed discipline of techniques for structuring, planning, and implementing "traditional," or deterministic, software. At least some of those techniques can be combined with knowledge-engineering techniques to improve our ability to plan, manage, and execute knowledge systems and buyer confidence in the process.

This project, in a small scale, successfully applied conventional systems analysis to the development of an expert system. We found the same general approach to be applicable to both kinds of project: (1) define the concept and role of the system, usually through a requirements analysis; (2) use available analytical tools such as models to express and refine that concept through the various stages of the project; and (3) define each step of the project as a collection of smaller, logically discrete operations.

3.3.1   Some Potentially Applicable Systems Development Approaches

Several systems development approaches have been designed and used over the years. Some of these, pertaining to software life cycles, were written by Davis (1974), Quade and Boucher (1978), Mandell (1979), Freeman and Wasserman (1977), Peters (1981), Metzger (1973), Boehm (1976), Silverman (1985), and Liebowitz (1984). These methodologies are outlined in Figures 3.2 and 3.3.

FIGURE 3.2
STEPWISE SYSTEMS ANALYSIS METHODOLOGIES*

Davis	Quade and Boucher	Mandell	Freeman**

1. Definition
  a. Feasibility assessment
  b. Information analysis
2. Physical design
  a. System design
  b. Program development
  c. Procedure development
3. Implementation
  a. Conversion
  b. Operation and maintenance
  c. Postaudit
	1. Problem
	2. Formulation
	3. Search
	4. Evaluation
	5. Interpretation
	6. Verification
	7. Suggested action
		1. Design situation
		  a. Problem recognition
		  b. Determination of objectives
		  c. Study present system
		  d. Design new system
		  e. Propose solution
		2. Implement
		  a. Detailed system design
		  b. File design
		  c. Develop programs
		  d. Develop documentation
		  e. Develop test data
		  f. System test
		  g. Conversion
		3. Evaluate
		  a. Efficiency analysis
		  b. System modification
		  c. Postaudit
			1. Needs analysis
			2. Specification
			3. Architectural design
			4. Detail design
			5. Implementation
			6. Maintenance

*See reference list for complete source of these methodologies.
**In addition to the reference see Peters, L.J. (1981), *Software Design: Methods and Techniques*, New York: Yourdon Press.

FIGURE 3.2 (Cont.)
STEPWISE SYSTEMS ANALYSIS METHODOLOGIES*

Metzger**	Boehm	Silverman (1985)	Liebowitz
1. (System) definition	1. System requirements	1. Requirements identification	1. Problematic state of affairs
2. Design	2. Software requirements	2. Design, development, test and integration	2. User
3. Programming	3. Preliminary design	a. Analogous programs	a. Value hierarchies
4. System test	4. Detailed design	3. Operation and maintenance	b. World views
5. Acceptance	5. Code and debug	4. Collection	3. Problem identification
6. Installation and operation	6. Test and preoperations	5. Disposal	4. Motivation
	7. Operation and maintenance		a. Novel, innovative methodologies
			5. Analogical reasoning
			a. Existing methodologies
			6. Chosen methodology
			7. Design
			8. Validation
			9. Testing and evaluation
			10. Forecasted results
			11. Implementation
			12. Critique/ Postaudit

*See reference list for complete source of these methodologies.
**In addition to the reference see Peters, L.J. (1981), Software Design: Methods and Techniques, New York: Yourdon Press.

FIGURE 3.3
SILVERMAN'S SUGGESTED APPROACH

1. Initiate knowledge-engineering project.

2. Explore the domain for a knowledge-engineering view.
   a. Construct idealized view.
   b. Describe actual activity.
   c. Pinpoint needs/bottlenecks in the project.

3. Recommendations
   a. Formulate knowledge-based system related recommendations.
   b. Make other recommendations.
   c. Act on other recommendations (i.e., accommodate suggestions).

4. Obtain approval and guidance to proceed.

5. Design and integrate knowledge-based system into the domain.

6. Verify knowledge-based system.

7. Validate knowledge-based system.

8. Evaluate knowledge-based system.

9. Resulting knowledge-based systems (spin-offs)

While each of these methodologies is different, each does allow for some form of stepwise progression from concept to finished product. Yet many expert systems are still being developed in a fashion consistent with academic or research projects, in which the exercise is often more important than the final product.

For example, Figure 3.3 shows Silverman's (1984) suggested stepwise, structured approach to expert systems development. This approach clearly recognizes the need to identify key steps in the project management process that can be tied to specific stages in the expert systems development cycle. For example, step 2 of his approach, shows that an idealized view of a knowledge system can be developed and then brought into line with practical constraints.

As noted above, the National Archives' project had four main activities: (1) a preliminary requirements analysis, (2) knowledge acquisition, (3) system development, and (4) system assessment. The approach we took to the Archives' project does not contradict Silverman's. For example, the requirements analysis led, at a lower level, to the activities described in step 2 of his approach; our use of logical system models was a key tool in a two-way communication between the project team and the archivists, which corresponded to step 3 of his approach; and steps 6, 7, and 8 of his approach correspond to the system assessment scheme used in the Archives' project.

However, there are some differences between the approach we took on the Archives' project and Silverman's approach. For example, as shown in Figure 3.3, his outline highlights the need to gain approval from the client at each step of the development cycle. At each step of the development process in the Archives' project, the team was required to document what they intended to do with a work plan and to demonstrate that they had completed the work, either by producing written documentation or working software. This is common operating procedure for most governmental or commercial clients outside of the research arena.

The process of getting the client's approval for each completed project task was dictated by long experience and governmental requirements. Therefore, the project team could concentrate on evaluating the interactions between those tasks, one with the other. This is illustrated in Figure 3.4.

We have not included the functional requirements process in Figure 3.4. There are two reasons for this: (1) the functional requirements analysis was done as part of a different, large-system design, and (2) it is a preliminary step to the other three processes and would have been represented as a logically separate function. However, Figure 3.4 does show the development cycle beginning at the completion of the requirements analysis. This is represented by the oval at the top left of the figure labeled "GFR" for "general functional requirements," which is the document that describes the requirements analysis.

Figure 3.4 is a modified program evaluation and review technique (PERT) chart. For this illustration, we have removed some of the lower-level detail regarding documents that had to be delivered, approval steps, and the numerous code-test-debug-test cycles.

Section 3.5 will address the use of models as an analytical tool. However, as Figure 3.4 shows, the use of models helped tie the entire project together. For example, the GFR provided the basic information from which the project team developed two models: (1) an *empirical model* of the archivist's activities and (2) a simple *modular software model*, which noted that the final software could be completed with three major modules. The project team then worked with those two models and interviewed archivists in order to develop a series of progressively more complex, *logical software models*, which defined the basic logical and functional relationships between each of the software modules. Work on the software itself did not begin until the logical model had been fairly well developed—enough so that we named it the "phase II" version.

As with the models, software development was a top-down process. Most of the software was written in M.1, a prologue-based expert system shell. Like most AI development environments, it facilitates top-down implementation as well as the top-down design employed by most systems developers. In that respect, the use of an AI language enhanced the traditional, top-down conceptualization techniques that are usually recommended for all programming projects.

3.3.2 Current Approaches to Structured Programming of Expert Systems

Rapid prototyping has recently gained wide acceptance as a systems development technique for both traditional and expert systems. The underlying approach is to quickly build working models or emulations of important system components, let users work with and comment on the result, and refine the final system concept to accommodate those comments. Usually, work starts on one or more of the following key systems components:

- The user interface, which is often the part of a system that gets the most immediate and critical attention
- Primary logic, such as accounting calculations, which have to be built into the system in order to demonstrate that it works at all
- Preliminary data structures, so that the project team can start to load initial test data into the system

Rapid prototyping is a structured technique, in the sense that (1) there are definable, repeatable steps in the process and (2) a higher-level design such as the primary system logic and user interface, drives the lower-level programming process, such as data file or knowledge base manipulation. However, rapid prototyping has often been the only system development technique used to build expert systems, without the extensive preliminary planning and design so familiar to traditional systems developers. This is acceptable or even desirable in a laboratory environment but not in the business world.

We suggest that rigorous examples exist in conventional systems analysis for systems planning and that these proven approaches can be adapted to developing expert systems without constraining either the creativity of the development process or the usefulness of its products. For example, *data flow diagrams* — a "traditional" systems analysis tool (De Marco 1979) — were used to describe the problem domain and perform a functional requirements analysis of the proposed system during the Archives' project; as discussed below, this preliminary analysis provided a number of benefits to the planning and development processes.

Tools that have proven useful in other projects include characteristic charts and attribute hierarchies and/or graphs, all derived from the knowledge-engineering arena. Decision tables, "borrowed" from systems analysis, have aided knowledge engineers in understanding and showing

FIGURE 3.4
DEVELOPMENT OF THE EXPERT SYSTEM PROTOTYPE

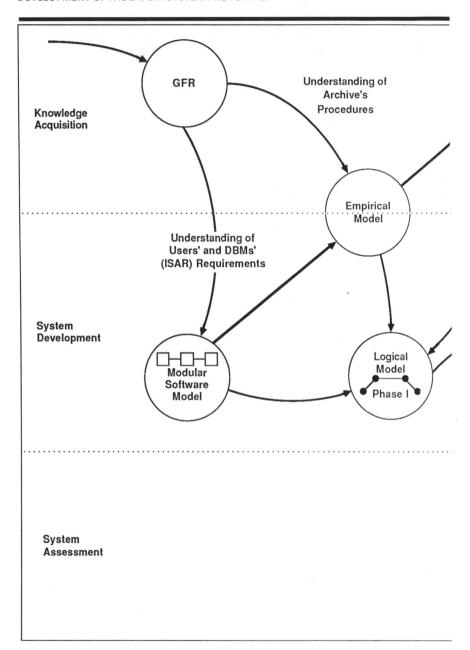

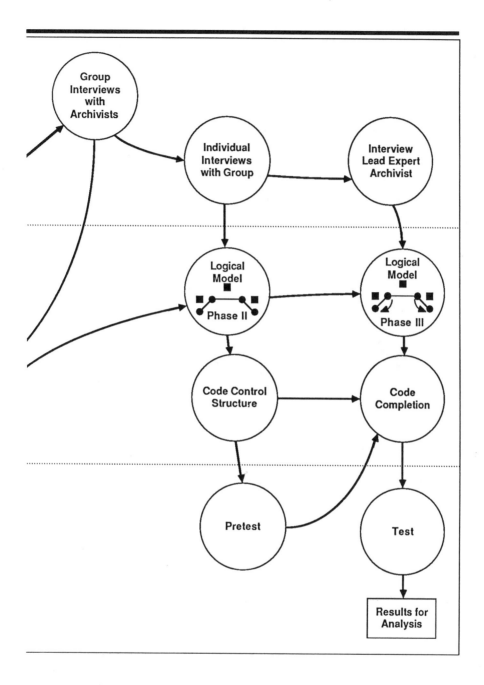

which rules are being fired, and the expert system's line of questioning in response to a given user input. Other tools, derived from "traditional" systems analysis, which are useful in the programming process include the following (see Davis 1974; Page-Jones 1980; Powers, Adams, and Mills 1984; and Glass 1982):

- Visual table of contents (VTOC)
- Warnier-Orr diagrams
- System flowcharts
- Synchronized flowcharts
- PERT charts
- Petri nets
- Hierarchy-input-processing-output (HIPO) charts
- Decision trees
- Threads
- Builds
- Data flow diagrams
- Top-down design
- Structured design
- Data dictionary
- Structured English/pseudocode

The Archives' project benefited from a structured approach that (1) "borrowed" tools from conventional systems analysis, such as the use of data flow diagrams, and (2) applied some knowledge-engineering tools, such as Clancey's (1984) knowledge level analysis techniques, in a fashion that would be familiar to "traditional" systems builders.

We therefore believe the knowledge-engineering process can be improved through formalization and standardization of expert system building methods. This may allow developers of expert systems to repeat the experience of "traditional" systems builders and increase the amount of reuseable software they write, thereby reducing the level of effort and resources required to implement their systems.

3.4   THE USE OF A FUNCTIONAL REQUIREMENTS ANALYSIS IN BUILDING THE EXPERT SYSTEM

A great deal of a knowledge engineer's time in building a system goes toward understanding both the environment and the client's expectations for the system. A "traditional" functional requirements analysis can shorten this process significantly and provide a sound basis for defining the major components of the system design.

The functional requirements analysis was, in this case, performed during a previous project. The major data flows and archival processes were evaluated during interviews with archivists and other Archives staff. The resultant documents provided an empirical view of the archival information handling process, graphically depicted in data flow diagrams (De Marco 1979).

One of the major advantages of this approach is that it produces a set of specifications — narrative and graphic — for the empirical performance of the system. Knowledge engineering is, after all, a creative science, wherein we try to build systems that imitate the behavior of a human expert, even though the underlying computer system is vastly different from the human mind in its form, functions, and capabilities.

As DeMarco (1979) says:

> In classical [systems] analysis, we first try to see the operations from the user's viewpoint; i.e., we interview him and try to learn from him how things work. Then we spend the rest of our time trying to document the working of modified operations *from the system's viewpoint.* (Notice that this approach is pervasive in unstructured technology; a flowchart, for instance, is design documentation from the system's point of view.)
>
> The inversion of viewpoints occasioned by Structured Analysis [data flow diagramming] is that we now present the workings of a system as seen by the data, not as seen by the data processors. The advantage of this approach is that the data sees the big picture, while the various people and machines and organizations that work on the data see only a portion of what happens.

In this project, our understanding of how data moved and changed within the host environment helped greatly in the following ways:

- The initial requirements analysis provided a high-level understanding of the system's major processes, thereby allowing the project team to establish the major software modules early in the project.
- Once the software modules and functions were defined, structured programming was possible, because (1) major system functions could then be consistently identified with specific parts of the software, (2) logically discrete functions could be identified for each part of the software, (3) those logically discrete functions could be broken down into pseudocode, and (4) programming could begin. All of this required that some initial order be placed on the structure of the system, which is often very difficult for expert systems.
- Understanding the flow and forms of data allowed the team to clearly define the format for encoding facts into the system. For example, archivists work with multiple series of lists that follow specific formats; by accommodating the same forms, the system inherited (1) an ability to work congenially with an underlying, list-based information storage and retrieval system and (2) a form of knowledge representation that is both understandable to and maintainable by the archivists.

The formal benefits of doing an initial functional requirements analysis are difficult to estimate. However, our experience indicates that at least two or more complete overhauls of the knowledge base were avoided as a result. One of the reasons for this was the amount of information the project team gained about the information that is exchanged between archivists. Once the project team had identified what knowledge was used and exchanged during the inquiry and search processes, it was possible to classify and organize that knowledge. Therefore we suggest that:

> A preliminary functional requirements analysis is appropriate in the design of both conventional and knowledge-based systems.

3.5 THE USE OF MODELS AS AN INTEGRAL, ANALYTICAL TOOL

An important strategy in this system development effort was the use of models to: (1) codify, and thereby help maintain a coherent view of the system throughout the project and (2) save time and resources by using the models as a vehicle for iteratively constructing, changing, and refining the system design.

Several kinds of systems representations were used over the course of the project:

- During the requirements analysis — the initial stage — of the project, data flow diagrams, narratives, an empirical model, and a modular software model were developed. Figures 3.5, 3.6, and 3.7 show or describe data flow diagram models. Figures 3.8 and 3.9 show at a high level the empirical and modular software models, respectively. The data flow diagrams and narrative representations provided significant insights into the system's inputs, its outputs, its representation of facts, and its working environment.
- During the knowledge acquisition phase, the empirical model and modular software models contributed to the development of a logical model of the system. The logical model is derived from (1) Clancey's (1984) method for knowledge level analysis and (2) the notational method employed by Teknowledge, Inc. in their Knowledge Engineering Methodology program. The logical model provided the foundation for a coherent view of both the project and the emerging system.

3.5.1 How Data Flow Diagrams Were Used in Building the Expert System

Data flow diagrams are a tool of conventional systems analysis. The systems analyst can use them to improve his or her understanding of (1) how an organization or system handles information, and (2) how the final system will have to behave. Just as with all good design tools, data flow diagrams should also help the analyst develop a reasonably objective and comprehensive view of some situation, which is necessary in knowledge engineering as in any analytical discipline.

During the initial stages of the Archives' project, the design team used a set of data flow diagrams that had been prepared as part of the Archives' long-term information systems development effort. These provided a capsule summary of the Archives' environment that was very useful to the knowledge-engineering process.

For example, Figure 3.5 shows a high level view of what happens when a researcher — a member of the public — asks for information from the Scientific and Natural Resources Branch of the National Archives. Figure 3.6 gives a brief explanation of data flow diagram technique. Please note that, in order to follow De Marco most closely, the diagram in Figure 3.5 should be broken into a series of simpler diagrams. However, we have included this one because (1) it is the one actually used on the project, and (2) it is reasonably comprehensive.

The Scientific and Natural Resources Branch (which the Archives identifies with the NNFN mail code seen in Figure 3.5), was the primary site of the prototype. The project's primary domain expert works with records of the Bureau of Land Management (BLM), which are under the control of the Branch.

As Figure 3.5 shows, there are several major points at which the researcher's inquiry stimulates the movement of information. At each of those points, one or more archivists or members of the staff have to evaluate that information and may confer with other archivists or members of the staff.

For example, when a researcher makes an inquiry (see oval 1.0 of Figure 3.5), it is screened and routed to a particular archivist with knowledge of some particular set of records. In order to perform just this one function, at least the following knowledge must change hands:

- The subject of the original inquiry
- Potential topics addressed in federal records that may pertain to the inquiry
- The archivist(s) or other members of the staff who may know more about the topics and where they may be found
- At least the basic protocol for handling an inquiry

Figure 3.7 is drawn one level of detail deeper into the interaction between researcher and archivist. It shows the exchange of information and knowledge that occurs when the researcher presents an inquiry to an archivist, who then "translates" the often-ambiguous question into a set of discrete topics that might be addressed in federal government records.

An examination of Figure 3.7 will show that at least the following types of knowledge, in addition to those noted previously, must change hands among one or more individuals:

FIGURE 3.5
HIGH-LEVEL DATA FLOW DIAGRAM OF THE RESEARCH PROCESS IN THE ARCHIVES'
SCIENTIFIC AND NATURAL RESOURCES BRANCH*

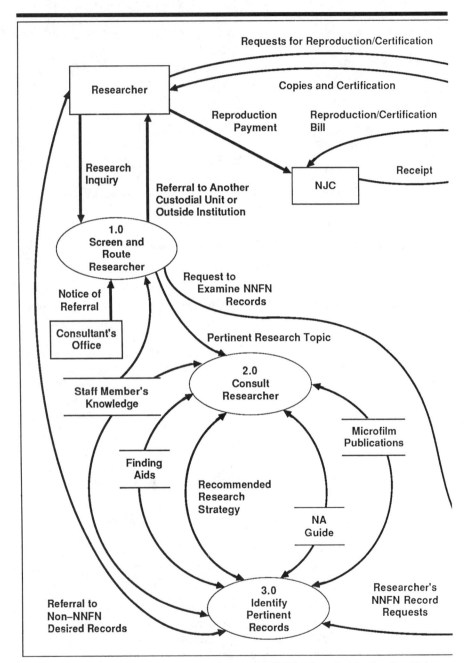

*Adapted from American Management Systems, Inc. (1985), volume II of the *Functional Information Requirements for the Office of the National Archives.*

58

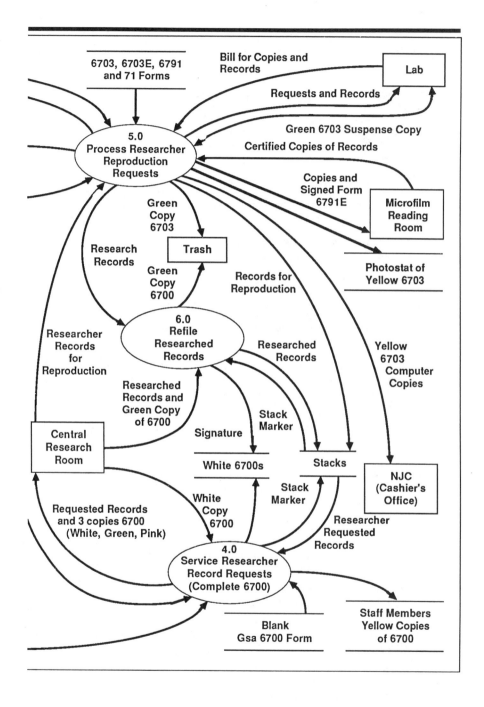

6703, 6703E, 6791 and 71 Forms

Bill for Copies and Records

Lab

Requests and Records

5.0 Process Researcher Reproduction Requests

Green 6703 Suspense Copy

Certified Copies of Records

Copies and Signed Form 6791E

Microfilm Reading Room

Green Copy 6703

Trash

Research Records

Green Copy 6700

Records for Reproduction

Photostat of Yellow 6703

6.0 Refile Researched Records

Researched Records

Yellow 6703 Computer Copies

Researcher Records for Reproduction

Researched Records and Green Copy of 6700

Signature

Stack Marker

Central Research Room

White 6700s

Stacks

Requested Records and 3 copies 6700 (White, Green, Pink)

White Copy 6700

Stack Marker

NJC (Cashier's Office)

Researcher Requested Records

4.0 Service Researcher Record Requests (Complete 6700)

Blank Gsa 6700 Form

Staff Members Yellow Copies of 6700

FIGURE 3.6
DATA FLOW DIAGRAM CONVENTIONS AS USED HERE*

- *Processes* are represented by an oval. A process is any activity that acts on information to produce an output. Each process is given a name describing the operation that it performs. In cases in which an operation is extremely complex, a discussion of the precise steps or subprocesses that combine to make up that process will be included.

- *Data flows* are packets of information in motion, represented by arrows. Each arrow is labeled with a descriptive name explaining the data that it represents. Each process has inputs (information that it requires) and outputs (information that it produces). From the viewpoint of the data flow diagram there is no distinction between inputs and outputs. An output from one process is often an input to another process. Collectively, inputs and outputs are called data flows.

- *Files* represent data at rest. A file is any temporary or permanent repository of information. Any location where data is temporarily stored between processes or any set of information that is part of the system and provides different data to more than one process is a file. For example, a collection of manuscripts qualifies as a file under this definition.

- *Sources* or *destinations* for data are represented by a box. A box represents any person or organization, lying outside the context of the system being examined, that is a net originator of information input to the system or a receiver of information output from the system. Any person, agency, or external system that is not part of the system being examined but contributes inputs to or receives outputs from the system being examined is represented by a box.

*Adapted from American Management Systems, Inc. (1985), volume II of the *Functional Information Requirements for the Office of the National Archives.*

- The researcher's specific areas of interest, such as the time period (oval 2.3) of the event or activity in which the researcher is interested
- A knowledge of how to go about translating the researcher's inquiry into appropriate topics
- The applicability of the inquiry to other sets of records than those to be found in the Scientific and Natural Resources Branch (NNFN)
- The specific parts of government agencies that may have been involved in activities pertaining to the inquiry at the time of their occurence
- A knowledge of the contents and use of various search tools, such as published guides, microfilm, or archivists' notebooks

FIGURE 3.7
THE RESEARCH TOPIC TRANSLATION PROCESS*

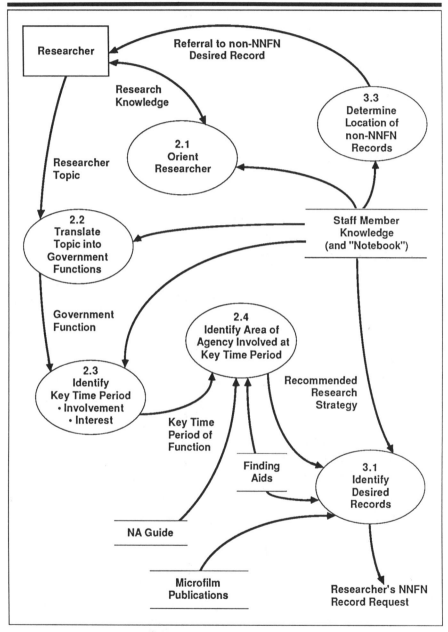

*Adapted from American Management Systems, Inc. (1985), volume II of the *Functional Information Requirements for the Office of the National Archives.*

Therefore we suggest that:

The data flow diagrams provided two important kinds of information to the design team: (1) a conceptual view of the data that the underlying information system would have to process and (2) an initial inventory of the different kinds of knowledge that might be embodied in the system. Subsets of the data and the knowledge were then more easily selected for inclusion into the actual system. A conventional systems analysis technique helped bound the domain of the expert system and, in so doing, helped solve one of the more difficult problems of expert system design.

3.5.2   The Empirical Modular and Logical Software Models

The differences between the empirical, modular, and logical software models are as follows:

- The *empirical software model* (see Figure 3.8) represents the way the archivist's job appears to the outside observer (in this case, a previous project team). It was developed as a convenient, generalized, high-level representation of the archivist's use of lists. As the figure shows, it is a somewhat richer model, even at this high level, than the modular software model, but it still embodies the same three major components.
- The *modular software model* (see Figure 3.9) was used during the initial knowledge acquisition phase as a convenient framework for describing the system's inputs and outputs. As Figure 3.9 shows, it is a simple "black box" model, with modules that correspond to the main parts of the empirical model.
- The *logical software model* (see Figure 3.10), and its succeeding refinements, show the major functional modules of the system. Again, as Figure 3.10 shows, its major modules correspond to the empirical model's.

During the knowledge acquisition phase, the logical model was used in two ways:

1. The model served as a visual representation of what the archivists were saying during the interviews. Initially, the project team conducted group and individual interviews with five archivists, and the model provided a common view of the way they made inferences. With the model as a backdrop, the project team was able to obtain concrete lists of facts and heuristic rules and associate them with specific, logical parts of the retrieval process.

2. The model served as the conceptual design of the physical system. The inferences represented by the model were made progressively more detailed during the project — well after the project team had actually started to write software. At one point, a large schematic of the logical

FIGURE 3.8
EMPIRICAL SOFTWARE MODEL*

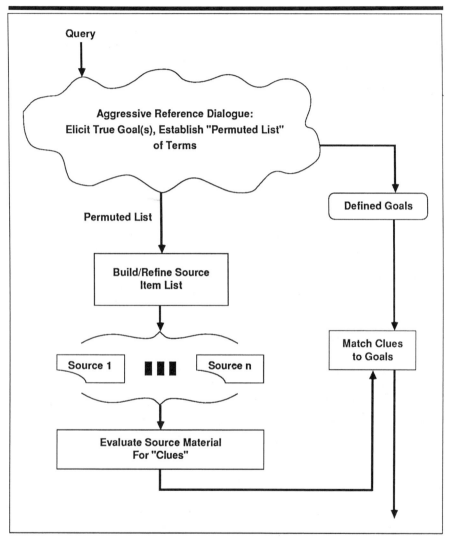

*On a high level, the retrieval process consists of (1) an interview, whereby the archivist engages the researcher in a dialogue to extract from the researcher's broad subject those topics that can be answered by information found in federal government records; (2) the archivist — by relating those to-pics to goverment program areas or his or her own knowledge of record content — sets up a list of rec-ords that might satisfy the topics, which in expert systems parlance can be referred to as *query goals*: and (3) the archivist helps the researcher work through the process of finding and using the appropriate rec-ords.

model was drawn on a blackboard, and 4-by-5-inch index cards with pseudocode rules written on them were stuck to it in order to help evaluate the interdependencies of the rules.

FIGURE 3.9
MODULAR SOFTWARE MODEL

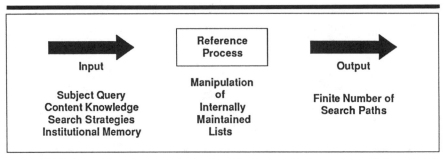

*This is the modular software model developed for the expert system prototype. It shows the reference process used by the archivist as a "black box" that accepts input to create an output. The input is the query, and the output is a list of records that will provide an answer to the query.

Both group and individual interviews were used during knowledge acquisition, with the models serving as the focus of discussion. Initially, five archivists, each of whom are responsible for a different area of records within the Archives, were interviewed in a group setting, where a consensus could be reached on the proper form for the model. Each of the five were then interviewed separately, in order to ascertain which group of records was the best target site for the prototype. Finally, in-depth knowledge acquisition was carried out with one archivist—Renee Jaussaud—when it was determined that the records for which she is responsible were the best subject for the prototype.

The group interviews provided an opportunity to do two things: (1) carefully examine, with the help of an expert, each of the five records areas in order to select the most appropriate one and (2) obtain a consensus of opinions and advice on the logical system model from a group of experts.

By obtaining a consensual agreement from all of the archivists on the form of the logical model, the project team (1) was assured that the basic form of the model was correct and (2) was provided with important insights into how and to what extent the practices of the five archivists differed.

The individual interviews served to further refine the logical model. The process of examining and revising the logical model provided both the archivists and the project team with valuable insight into the design and operations of the future system.

With the model as a framework, key decisions made by the archivist during the search process were located conceptually in the program's structure. For example, the model helped clarify where query abstrac-

FIGURE 3.10
LOGICAL SOFTWARE MODEL*

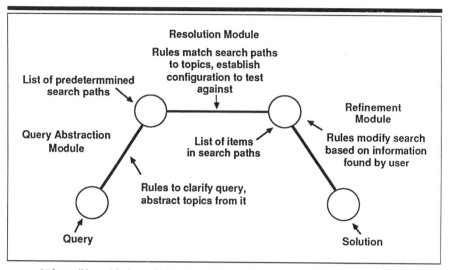

*After talking with the archivists about this model of the retrieval process we worked it into a model developed by Dr. William Clancey for what are called *classification-type expert systems*. Classification systems, which include diagnostic and catalog selection systems, are designed to recursively refine the definition of a subject area or question until it becomes small and limited enough to match to some real object.

In this model, the notational graphics—courtesy of Teknowledge, Inc.—serve much as a HIPO chart would in giving a conceptual view of a process as it goes from general to specific. The three parts of the model are named here to correspond to the specific applications. Abstraction produces a list of potential topics out of a general query.

Resolution maps those to program areas and then to specific sets of records. In the process, it works from the highest, or *record group* level of the records organization, to the lowest practical level, the record *series*. The refinement part of the model logically represents the place where the archivist and the researcher progressively review and discard the records they retrieve.

The model was used during interviews with the archivists to help determine (1) where each module's functions should begin and end and (2) the parameters that have to be passed between modules, in this case in the form of lists.

It is worth noting that the models helped us in working with multiple experts. Although the bulk of the work was done with one expert archivist, Renee Jaussaud of the Office of the National Archives, we did a substantial amount of work with as many five experts at one time. The ability to pull together a large design team is, we feel, essential to successfully developing commercial software.

tion—the process of analyzing the inquiry for its content—ends and where resolution—the process of mapping query content to the record structure—begins.

The facts and heuristics associated with each logical process could then be much more clearly defined and placed within the proper software module prior to any code being written. For example, the query abstraction process contains a wealth of heuristics to match, to the researcher's query, topics that may be addressed by federal government records. The resolution process, however, uses a much more generalized set of heuristics to manipulate detailed facts (e.g., about the records, the administrative histories, etc.) as it maps the topics to specific sets of records.

Therefore we suggest that:

> The expert tends to view what he or she does as a cohesive process (also, see Chapter 1). However, the use of models: (1) allowed rules to be grouped efficiently, thereby improving software efficiency and (2) allowed much more compact software routines to be written to manipulate a small data base in which the majority of facts and lists are maintained.

3.6   APPLICATION OF A SCHEME FOR SYSTEM ASSESSMENT

3.6.1   Overview of the System Assessment

The purpose of the system assessment was to test three aspects of the system's performance:

1. The system's *recall*. This test was based on the answers to sample research questions. The expert archivist, Renee Jaussaud, drew up a list of the record series that she would recommend as places to look for answers to the sample questions. The system's answers were then compared to hers, to see what percentage of the series recommended by the archivist were also recommended by the system. That percentage reflects the system's ability to recall, from its data base, the names of all *record series* that might contain information pertinent to a particular query. A *record series* is normally the smallest set of records that the Archives handles. A series might contain a group of individual documents, file folders, and so forth. The Archives has catalogued the individual files in some series, but by and large the series is the basic element of archival control.

2. The system's *precision*. This test was based on the same sample questions as the test for system recall. Here the system's answers were compared to the archivist's to see if the system suggested any records that the archivist would not have recommended. That is, the more of these "wrong" answers given by the system, the higher the degree of imprecision in its responses.

3. The system's *behavior*. This test was based on a hands-on review of the system by the expert archivist, members of an Archives' project review committee, and the project team. It is a partially subjective review of what the system is like to use. For example, the archivist must ask the researcher questions in the right order, in order for the researcher to understand the reasoning behind the questions. The system's ability to mimic this kind of behavior was evaluated during this test. Other factors, such as how quickly it performed certain tasks, were also evaluated.

The assessment process was conducted as follows:

1. An *assessment team* was established to conduct the test. Members included the software design team, the primary domain expert, and several members of a project review committee, which the Archives had established to monitor the progress of the project.

2. A set of *sample inquiries* was developed by the project team and the primary domain expert. The domain expert then answered the inquiries by suggesting records series that might be appropriate to each of the queries.

3. The same inquiries were run through the system.

4. The *responses* of both the archivist and the system were researched to determine how many correct, wrong, or missed answers had been made. The research identified 100 record series that were pertinent to the test questions. The archivist failed to identify some on the first pass but recalled them easily while researching the answers. The system failed to identify some of the series, primarily because some keyword indexing data had not been entered into the data base, although one case was wrongly identified because of a software problem. Interestingly enough, the system identified some of the cases the archivist had missed and, when the proper data was entered into the data base, the system successfully recalled the cases it had missed before.

5. The expert archivist and the review committee worked with the system for several days and determined that its behavior was appropriate. As a good example of the value of letting an organization actually work with a prototype of a system, the review committee suggested a number of features that a production version of the system should have.

3.6.2 The Quantitative Tests for Recall and Precision

As Figure 3.11 shows, the archivist and the system together identified 100 series as possible places to look for answers to the sample inquiries. The sample cases are all unique, although the same series may appear more than once if it is applicable to more than one research inquiry.

The key factors in the system's recall and precision scores were: (1) the system logic, which performed well, although 1 series out of the 100 was misidentified because we did not write software to specifically compare the geographic areas of the inquiry and the records; (2) the system's data base, in which not all of the series were completely described, therefore causing the system to pass over 21 and misidentify 1 more of the 100 cases (this was later corrected); and (3) the limited thesaurus built into the system (it did not have a match for 1 search term), which resulted in 3 series being wrongly identified.

FIGURE 3.11
100 SERIES RETRIEVED BY THE ARCHIVIST AND THE SYSTEM*

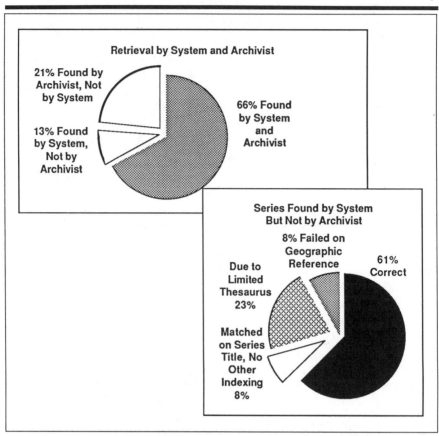

*This figure shows the relative performance of the system and the archivist in identifying records that might apply to the sample inquires. The system missed some retrievals altogether, as did the archivist, when both of the identified series were examined after the test. Significantly, the system was able to retrieve some series that the archivist missed on the first pass. The right-hand chart defines the series that the system found but the archivist did not. A significant portion (61%) turned out to be correct. The others were wrong for one of three reasons: (1) the series was retrieved based on subject but was in the wrong geographic area, because no specific geographic data were included in the index; (2) the temporary thesaurus created in the system made a weak match between terms (in this case, "hydro-electric power" was matched to the term "water-power" which, because of the limited text search capabilities in the prototype, matched on the subject index term "water"—out of four series retrieved that way, only one had information on hydro-electirc power) and (3) a plain lack of indexing (in this case, predecessor records to the Bureau of Fisheries, were retrieved on the title line reference to "fish").

The system's recall and precision were calculated as follows:

$$\text{Recall} = [(R2\text{-}RS)/R2] * 100$$

where *R2* is the number of series identified by the archivist, and *RS* is the number identified by the archivist that is not in the system's data base.

This is a *limited technical definition of recall but sufficient to compare the system to the archivist as benchmark.* Therefore

$$\text{System Recall} = [(81\text{-}21)/81 \, ^* \, 100 \ = 74\%$$

This is a fairly low level of recall. To increase this, the expert system would have to be married to a powerful conventional information retrieval system. Conventional systems often recall several times more records than a highly experienced human would have. The expert system would thus act to counterbalance this effect.

$$\text{Precision} = (S1/S) \, ^* \, 100$$

where S is the set of records series identified by the system, and $S1$ is the set of records that both the system and the archivist identified.

Therefore

$$\text{Initial System Precision} = (66/100) \, ^* \, 100 = 66\%$$

This is a *limited definition of precision* but, as with the recall calculation above, it is sufficient to compare to the archivist as a bench mark. It is also a much lower score than we had anticipated. After examining the data, however, we adjusted the score for inaccuracies in the raw data. The calculation then becomes

$$\text{Precision(Adjusted)} = [S1/(S\text{–}Sc)] \, ^* \, 100$$

where Sc is the number of series that we felt were retrieved because of the data errors.

Therefore

$$\text{Precision(Adjusted)} = [66/(100\text{–}31)] = 96\%$$

This would be a very good score. In practice, after updating the data base, the score hovered around 91 to 92% during several postassessment trials. That is still a good score, but it indicates that the quality of data in any system directly affects its value—no less so with an expert system.

3.7   A BRIEF REVIEW OF THE SYSTEM

As Figure 3.12 shows, the system's construction is very straightforward. Most of the software was built using the M.1 expert system "shell" or development environment, as a series of knowledge bases, each of which is a collection of heuristics that the system uses to direct the information retrieval process.

The system is implemented on an IBM-PC/AT, with 640KB of main memory and currently occupies something less than 400KB of disk space.

FIGURE 3.12
THE SYSTEM COMPONENTS*

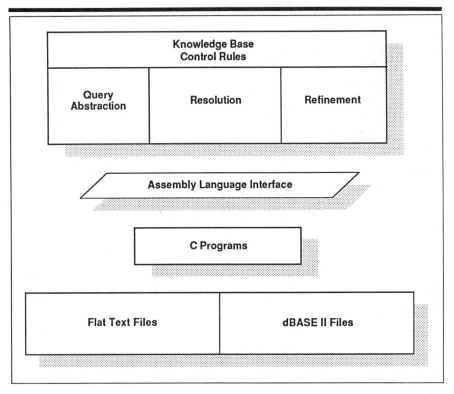

*The system's construction is straightforward. Most of the programming effort went into build-ing the knowledge base as a series of IF-THEN rules in the M.1 system shell. M.1 is an expert system shell from Teknowledge for the IBM-PC built in Prologue and assembly language. It has good support for re-cursive functions—something we needed with all the list manipulations we were doing.

The system manipulates some dBASE II files, via external M.1 calls to C. We used the Computer In-novations' C86 compiler, because it provides almost all of the DBMS functions we needed. The bulk of the files the system uses comprise flat data files that contain facts about the records, cues the system picks up during the search process, and so on.

The software is menu-driven, as a natural language processor would have reduced the memory available for the knowledge bases and would have increased the cost of the prototype. It currently comprises about 300 rules and 1200 lines of C and assembly language source code.

3.7.1   The System Components

The system has five main components. They are:

1. The *knowledge bases*. These are subdivided into four functional modules, each of which operates part of the retrieval process. The knowledge bases are written in the M.1 expert system shell and contain four modules of backward-chaining rules: (1) *control rules*, which control the flow of the program; (2) *query abstraction*, which uses rules and certainty factors to determine the most important topics contained in a set of general subjects that the user identifies; (3) *resolution*, which first matches topics to the general types of documents (e.g., personnel records) that may have answers to an inquiry and then identifies specific sets of records in the underlying data base; and (4) *refinement*, which allows the user to cycle back through the process if desired.

    2. An *assembly language interface.* This allows the M.1 software to call and execute other programs. For example, an M.1 rule can contain the following command to open a data file:

    IF external (150, [open, series, series]) = ["ok"]

    THEN data base is open.

The assembly language interface picks up the command and passes it to a program — "150" — written in C. This opens the particular file — "series" — which is indexed on a field named "series." The C program then sends "ok" back through the interface to M.1 to indicate that the file is open.

    3. *C language programs.* This prototype uses C language programs to do most file handling chores. For example, dBASE II files contain information on the record series, which are the common units of records in the Archives' files. The knowledge base software, using C programs through external calls, searches the dBASE II files to find topic indices series titles, or other information. In some cases, the C program, as in the preceding example, sends information from the dBASE II file directly back to M.1. In other cases, the data are temporarily stored in simple text files, which the M.1 software can then read directly from disk. Passing data directly through the assembly language interface is much faster than creating and reading a disk file. However, the software is implemented in version 1.2 of M.1, which unlike the current version can only pass 80 characters at a time to a C program. Therefore, whenever large quantities of information have to be picked up by the knowledge bases, text files are used.

    4. *Flat text files.* The M.1 shell can read and interpret certain kinds of flat text files. In this prototype, text files are used primarily to store the various lists that the system makes use of during processing, including facts and information about the records or the search process. For example, Figure 3.13 shows a sample of a file called "subjects.txt." This file contains a list of the research subjects the system can address. As the figure shows, these files are in a very straightforward form; they can be used in much the same way that data tables would be in a conventional system. Therefore the system can be expanded and maintained by changing or enlarging the lists with which it works, since the knowledge base contains generalized rules for interpreting the lists.

FIGURE 3.13
EXAMPLE OF A FLAT TEXT FILE*

```
          subs = subject-water_resources.
          subs = subject-land_resources.
          subs = subject-territories.
          subs = subject-economic_development.
          subs = subject-transportation.
          subs = subject-environment_conservation.
          subs = subject-alaska.
          subs = subject-indians.
          subs = subject-national_resources.
          subs = persons.
          subs = documents.

          subj_infos = water-resources.
          subj_infos = and-resources.
          subj_infos = economic-development.
          subj_infos = territories.
          subj_infos = transportation.
           bj_infos = environme   onservation.
            hi inf  = alas
```

*This figure shows a sample of a flat text file, "subjects.txt." The file represents two kinds of information. The top section shows research subjects ("subs") that the system will present to the user in a menu. The bottom section defines which of those subjects ("subj_infos") the system can provide an explanation, or "help" menu, for. This scheme is somewhat redundant, but it is quicker for the system to read these facts directly than to have the M.1 shell manipulate them internally. This kind of data redundancy would be eliminated in a production system.

5. *dBASE II files.* dBASE II files are used in much the same way as the flat text files. However, data are extracted from them using C language routines, which are under the control of the knowledge base and search and sort files much more efficiently than the M.1 software could. The titles of record series, for example, are contained and indexed into dBASE II files.

As noted previously, control rules guide the general flow of processing within the system. For example, to paraphrase the top-level control rule:

IF the introduction has been presented to the user

AND query_abstraction is done

AND resolution is done

AND refinement is done

THEN consultation is over.

The software attempts to evaluate each of the arguments to the IF-THEN statement in order. For example, there is a rule that ends with the statement "THEN query_abstraction done." The system must evaluate each argument of the second rule before it can determine whether query_abstraction is indeed done. Some of the rules analyze data, some drive a process such as menu generation, and so on. By chaining backward through the rules in this fashion, the system imitates a simple, mechanistic form of deductive logic with which it narrows down the possible set of records that pertain to the researcher's inquiry.

3.7.2 Building the System

The actual software took about 11 weeks to build, as Figure 3.14 shows. A good part of the effort, however, was devoted to analyzing and documenting what the team had learned about the Archives, about applying expert systems in the archival environment, and about designing and building expert systems on microcomputers.

Therefore, although Figure 3.15 shows the knowledge engineer's time tapering off toward the end of the project, it is because the graph reflects only that time spent by the expert archivist, Renee Jaussaud, and the lead knowledge engineer (systems analyst), Amy Glamm, on either (1) actually writing the software or (2) performing the system assessment tests. In fact the level of effort stayed quite steady over the entire five months of the project.

Ultimately, the test of analytical techniques comes in our ability to use them to deliver what we promised. The project was completed within its schedule and budget constraints. That was not a surprise. However, we were interested to note that the pattern of software growth and the number of hours spent writing the software did not follow some previous patterns found in many expert systems projects.

For example, our previous experience indicates that program size may grow and shrink several times during an expert system development. This occurs as the knowledge bases are (1) tossed together during knowledge acquisition and (2) refined and optimized afterward. This cycle can repeat itself several times.

By taking a structured approach, we were able to avoid this. As Figure 3.14 shows, we reduced our knowledge base by approximately four questions during the seventh week of the project, when we decided not to install a function to trap the results of inquiry pattern matching to a disk file.

We also found that the use of models made a tremendous difference in our ability to work independently of the domain expert. Ms. Jaussaud, the primary domain expert, would work for several half-day sessions on a new part of the rules. Then, she could use the model as a guideline for making comments on the behavior of the system.

For example, during the first six weeks of the project, as Figure 3.15 shows, the domain expert spent an increasing amount of time working directly with the knowledge engineer. Then, for about the next four weeks,

FIGURE 3.14
GROWTH OF SOFTWARE DURING PROJECT*

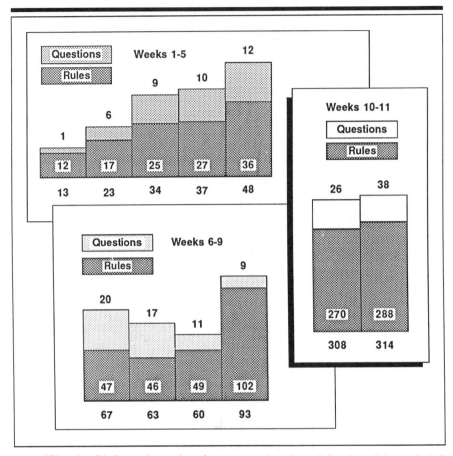

*"Questions" indicates the number of program routines devoted directly to dialogue; "rules" shows the number of rules used either for inferring search strategies or handling data. The first five weeks were spent building "core" software. During the last six weeks, the user interface was refined (the number of dialogue rountines actually decreased) and the number of rules more than tripled.

they worked apart except for one or two meetings per week of a half day each. As the system neared its completion during the fourth month of the project, they worked more closely together again, primarily refining the system's dialog and the order in which it asks questions. As Figure 3.14 shows, the number of questions the system could ask increased dramatically between the ninth and eleventh weeks of the project.

Finally, Ms. Jaussaud participated in the hands-on evaluation of the system, as well as several follow-on meetings that were devoted to discussing and analyzing the results of the project.

FIGURE 3.15
HOURS SPENT BY THE EXPERT ARCHIVIST AND SYSTEM ANALYST/KNOWLEDGE ENGINEER*

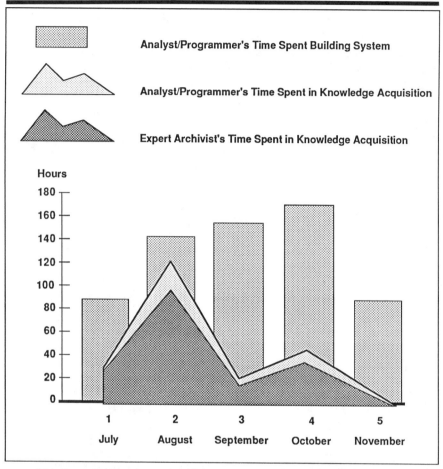

*This figure compares the amount of time spent by the expert archivist and the AMS systems analyst programmer. Not shown are the lesser amounts of time spent by oversight committee members from the Archives, lead systems and management personnel from AMS, etc. As the figure shows, the archivist's involvement (black plot) was heaviest at the beginning of the project, while the systems analyst/ programmers's time involvement was fairly steady, when both the amount of time spent working on the system (background bars) and time spent in knowledge acquisition sessions with the expert (gray plot) are taken into account.

Based on this experience, we suggest that:

The use of structured design and analysis techniques can permit expert systems development to proceed with essentially the same regularity of effort and predictability that exemplify conventional systems developments.

3.8   CONCLUSIONS

Structured systems development methods from both "conventional" systems analysis and knowledge engineering have been successfully applied to this prototype expert system. This and other evidence (Boehm 1976; Silverman 1984, 1985; Liebowitz 1984; and Clancey 1984) suggests (1) that other, more rigorous, structured techniques from classical systems analysis may be merged to develop expert systems and (2) that there should be cost savings and other benefits associated with doing so.

Certainly, a prime goal in managing any software development effort is to avoid wasted effort. Two key elements required to ensure that are (1) good communications among the project team members and (2) a cohesive view of the role, purpose, and functions of the emerging system that is shared by both users and developers of the system (Davis 1974; Quade and Boucher 1978; Powers, Adams, and Mills 1984; and American Management Systems, Inc.).

We believe that management goal was met during this project through the application of three key techniques:

1. The use of an initial requirements analysis, which established the system's role, its purpose within a defined environment, and the functions required of it

2. The use of various system models that (1) provided a means for the users and developers of the system to agree on the design of the emerging system and (2) eliminated at least some of the initial false steps associated with a rapid prototyping effort

3. Quantitative measurement of the system's behavior — in this case a measure of how completely and accurately it retrieved information — that (1) helped the system users put their own hands-on evaluation of the system into perspective and (2) helped clarify the differences between this system and one built for a similar purpose with conventional technology.

This was a limited project to build a small computer system. Therefore our experiences and the results of our efforts cannot be construed to be too far reaching. We hope, however, that this provides useful information for those who wish to develop expert systems while taking advantage of the body of knowledge developed during conventional systems developments.

ACKNOWLEDGMENT

We wish to acknowledge the kind advice and assistance of Frank Burke, Archivist of the United States, William Yoder, American Management Systems, Inc., and Ted Weir of the National Archives. We would also like to thank the five archivists who participated in the initial knowledge acquisition, Robin Cookson, Sara Jackson, James Rush, Richard Myers, and the archivist who spent much time on the project, Renee Jaussaud.

REFERENCES

American Management Systems, Inc. (1985), *Functional Information Requirements for the Office of the National Archives, Volumes I–III.*

Boehm, B.W. (1976), "Software Engineering," IEEE Computer Society, December.

Clancey, W.J. (1984), "Knowledge Acquisition for Classification Expert Systems," Stanford University Heuristic Programming Project working paper (HPP 84-18), July.

Davis, G.B. (1984), *Management Information Systems: Conceptual Foundations, Structure, and Development*, New York: McGraw-Hill.

De Marco, Tom (1979), *Structured Analysis and System Specifications*, New York: Yourdon Press.

Freeman, P., and Wasserman, A.I. (1977), *Tutorial on Software Design Techniques*, IEEE Computer Society, April.

Glass, R.L. (1982), *Modern Programming Practices: A Report from Industry*, Englewood Cliffs, N.J.: Prentice-Hall, Inc.

Liebowitz, J. (1984), "Determining Functional Requirements for NASA Goddard's Command Management System Software Design Using Expert Systems," Washington, D.C.: George Washington University, Ph.D. dissertation, December.

Mandell, S.L. (1979), *Computers and Data Processing: Concepts and Applications*, St. Paul, Minn.: West Publishing.

Metzger, P.W. (1973), *Managing a Programming Project*, Englewood Cliffs, N.J.: Prentice-Hall.

Page-Jones, M. (1980), *The Practical Guide to Structured Systems Design*, New York: Yourdon Press.

Peters, L.J. (1981), *Software Design: Methods and Techniques*, New York: Yourdon Press.

Powers, M.J., Adams, D.R., and Mills, H.R. (1984), *Computer Information Systems Development: Analysis and Design*, Cincinnati, Ohio: South-Western Publishing.

Quade, E.S., and Boucher, W.I. (1978), *Systems Analysis and Policy Planning: Applications in Defense*, New York: Elsevier.

Silverman, B.G. (1984), "Chapter One: Nature of an Expert's Knowledge," Institute for Artificial Intelligence Technical Report, Washington, D.C.: George Washington University.

Silverman, B.G. (1985), "Software Cost and Productivity Improvements: An Analogical View," IEEE Computer Society, May.

Ziegler, C.A. (1983), *Programming System Methodologies*, Englewood Cliffs, N.J.: Prentice-Hall, Inc.

II

EXPERT SUPPORT SYSTEMS

What is a good decision? Attempts to answer this question have generated not one but hundreds of answers, which at the risk of some imprecision can be characterized as varying between two extremes. At the one extreme, there is reliance upon "rational man" approaches or frameworks. The decisions are assumed to be based on perfect knowledge, that is, the decision maker knows exactly all the probabilities of each of the potential outcomes as well as their values. This process is highly quantitative and supposedly comprehensive in relation to problem solving and maximization of goals. However, it often disregards irrationalities of individual decision makers. It generally fails to recognize the subjective nexus between decisions and world views of decision makers and decision executors. Consequently, solutions are often unacceptable to the policy makers and, if accepted, are sometimes difficult to implement for sociopolitical reasons.

At the other extreme is incrementalism, the bureaucratic approach, or "muddlin' through." Advances are made in small steps (disjointed marginal adjustments), and there is rarely any drastic change. It assumes that there is not one right decision but a continuous stream of minor decisions. However, it is politically pluralistic, practical in real settings, permits tradeoff/revisions of views, tolerates ambiguity, and is sensitive to power struggles and the concerns of interest groups. This approach is sometimes called "the art of the possible." However, it implicitly assumes that the shorter the projected effect term and the smaller the effect scope, the easier it is to nullify or compensate for iatrogenic effect. Incrementalism may be a good approach when the original decisions were good. If the original decisions were bad to begin with (or if conditions have substantially changed), then they will still be bad after muddling.

The pursuit of the second approach does not mean that a decision maker is innately irrational. The inherent complexities and interconnectedness of our society dictate that rationality, in most circumstances, is neither clear-cut nor automatically determinable, particularly when multidimensionality is considered. Robert T. McNamara, a former secretary of defense and a pioneer of systems thinking, explains this intermingling of approaches. First it is wrong to look upon intuition and analysis or minds and machines as rivals or alternatives. Properly used they complement each other. We have seen that every systems analysis is shot through with intuition and judgment. Every decision that seems to be based on intuition is probably shot through with species of analysis.

In the AI/ES field, computerized systems that attempt to assist in the middle ground are known as expert support systems (ESSs). ESSs are logical extensions of management information systems (MISs) and decision support systems (DSSs) that include certain degrees of AI/ES capability. Some of the more popular capabilities an ESS might add to the worker's environment include, but are not limited to:

1. *Procedural cuing*—Reminds the user of all the steps; suggest steps overlooked; provides step advice when requested; cues the user in on the latest and most recent techniques and organizational changes.

2. *Issue identification/resolution support*—Several ESS functions would be useful to support the handling of issues, particularly ones that recur from case to case and stage to stage. For issues that it knows how to resolve, the ESS should provide a batch operation mode useful for sensitivity analyses.

3. *Corporate memory*—Reminds the user of what was previously learned about the problem under study; and holds the user's past sessions in a secure yet intelligent directory. (Also connects to predecessor's directories who held the user's position previously and on a need-to-know basis).

4. *Similar results* — Automatically recalls results and lessons learned on similar problems, systems, and components by other users; and feeds these results to the user as needed and in limited, progressive, deepening dosages.

5. *Cross-stage advisor* — Connects the user to relevant results available from earlier stages on that problem including what was tested, why, what was learned, and what still needs to be studied.

6. *Interoperability* — Puts the user in touch with interoperability considerations and with points of contact at other departments.

7. *Training* — For newcomer users, provides numerous help and explain features via the natural language facility. Also provides lessons, learned files and instructional documentation.

The chapters of this part of the book illustrate a number of the ESS features. They also demonstrate an interesting variety of techniques for knowledge collection and representation and for reasoning/inferencing.

Chapter 4 gives a thorough survey of the notable auditing applications and of their purpose, design, structure, and development status. The discussion also cites a large number of limitations that ESSs in general and accounting applications in particular must cope with.

Chapter 5 makes the simple and eminently reasonable claim that approximate reasoning is needed in ESSs and that fuzzy linguistic variables are useful knowledge representation forms. The authors then describe four classroom-oriented examples and conclude by discussing the concept of a manager's "apprentice."

Chapter 6 provides insight into the behavior of expert decision makers since it focuses on a real task performed by actual procurement personnel. This is a useful case study in the problems of trying to understand an ill-structured problem domain. The authors explain how they utilized in-depth interviews, protocol analyses, and deep knowledge collection to evolve an ESS for pricing decisions.

Chapter 7 explores the applicability of frames, rules, and forward chaining to support acquisition strategy makers and concludes that one of the key benefits of the process is in gaining a better understanding of how acquisition planning occurs. (This lesson sounds all too familiar to any and all who have attempted operations research models). This chapter also briefly introduces the concept of a Blackboard expert system, a topic more thoroughly discussed in Chapter 17.

4

The Use of Artificial Intelligence in Accounting

Daniel E. O'Leary

The purpose of this chapter is to review the work that has been done to date in the area of artificial intelligence and expert systems in accounting. Currently, there are few applications that have been implemented commercially and only a few prototype expert systems that have been developed. This chapter summarizes those systems, reviews the knowledge base and inference engine of those applications, and compares those systems to each other and to expert systems in medicine and mineral exploration. Finally, this chapter summarizes some limitations and provides some extensions of expert systems in accounting.

4.1 INTRODUCTION

The purpose of this chapter is to review and extend the use of artificial intelligence (AI) and expert systems (ES) in accounting. The primary focus of this chapter is on expert systems, although other uses of artificial intelligence also are discussed.

4.1.1 Previous Reviews of AI/ES in Accounting

There have been earlier reviews of some business expert systems (Michaelsen and Michie 1983) and auditing-based decision support systems (DSS) and expert systems (Messier and Hansen 1983; Bedard, Gray, and Mock 1984; and Dillard and Mutchler 1984). However, there has been substantial work in *accounting* expert systems since these reviews were written.

A theoretical framework for developing ESs in auditing is expected from Lewis and Dhar (1985). Finally, an analysis of the potential implications of expert systems on the accounting industry from the perspective of a public accounting firm is given in Elliot and Kielich (1985).

4.1.2 The Plan of This Chapter

Section 4.2 briefly reviews some characteristics of accounting and then relates accounting and ESs. In Section 4.3 characteristics of one of the best known and most discussed accounting ESs are examined. Section 4.4 summarizes various AI/ES accounting applications, and Section 4.5 analyzes those applications in terms of their knowledge bases and inference engines. Section 4.6 relates the accounting ESs to each other, and Section 4.7 compares the ESs in accounting to those in mineral exploration and medicine. A discussion of the limitations of ESs in accounting appears in Section 4.8. Section 4.9 reviews some related ESs from other disciplines and briefly discusses some extensions of ESs in accounting. A brief summary appears in Section 4.10.

4.2 WHY AI/ES IN ACCOUNTING?

Researchers have generated some ESs for analysis of accounting-based decision processes. This section addresses why management needs to know about AI/ES in accounting and analyzes the feasibility and desirability of AI/ES in accounting.

4.2.1 Why Does Management Need to Know about AI/ES in Accounting?

Management will be concerned about AI/ES in accounting for two primary reasons. First, the development of AI/ES affects management's allocation of resources. Second, AI/ES in accounting contains knowledge and reasoning about accounting-based decisions. Accordingly, the extent those decisions affect or are affected by management reflects the importance to management.

In the first situation, management's allocation of resources will be affected by the resources expended on AI/ES. The systems may reduce payroll costs or enhance decision making. However, the systems also will require an investment of time and dollar resources. As a result, management will be concerned that AI/ES in accounting is cost beneficial in the long run.

In the second situation, management's information and decisions are impacted by accounting information. The type of impact on management's decisions depends on the functional area.

Functional Areas of Accounting   There are five functional areas of accounting: auditing, management accounting (planning and control systems), tax, accounting information systems, and financial accounting.

As noted by Arens and Loebbecke (1984),

> Auditing is the process by which a competent, independent person accumulates and evaluates evidence about quantifiable information related to a specific economic entity for the purpose of determining and reporting on the degree of correspondence between the quantifiable information and established criteria. (p. 1)

In the *auditing* process there are three branches of auditors: external auditors, internal auditors, and EDP auditors. External auditors are from outside the firm (certified public accountants), and internal auditors are from within the firm. *External auditors* issue an accounting opinion about the financial statements. The opinion directly impacts the credit of the firm and the ability of the firm to generate capital. Thus management is concerned with the decision process by which the external auditor generates the opinion. *Internal auditors* review the operations of the firm. As a result, management is concerned that the internal auditors have the appropriate tools to ensure an adequate review. *EDP auditors* are either external or internal auditors concerned with the audit of computer-based systems. Accordingly, management is concerned that EDP auditors have the appropriate tools and expertise to assess and develop the controls required for the computerized accounting system to minimize the loss of resources through improper controls.

Management accounting (planning and control systems) develops information to meet the needs of decision makers. As a result, management is concerned with the expertise used in the development and maintenance of the planning and control systems.

Tax accounting relates the tax law to the needs of individuals and corporations. This branch of accounting is characterized by its relationship to the Internal Revenue Service (IRS). Tax accounting decisions have a direct impact on the cash flow of the firm. Accordingly, management is concerned with the expertise of the tax advice it receives.

Accounting information systems (AIS) refers to the computerized accounting information systems that are developed to meet management's and external users' requirements. Accordingly, management and external sources are concerned with the expert systems used to develop and implement the AIS.

Financial accounting deals with the general purpose accounting reports and financial statements (Kieso and Weygandt 1983). This branch of accounting is characterized by its link to requirements of accounting disclosure by the Security and Exchange Commission (SEC) and the Financial Accounting Standards Board (FASB). Accordingly, management will be concerned that the firm meets the legal requirements of disclosure.

4.2.2 ESs and Generic Tasks

Accountants are concerned with a number of ES generic tasks that have been the source of ESs from other disciplines: interpretation, diagnosis, monitoring, scheduling, planning, and design (Hayes-Roth, Waterman, and Lenat 1983).

These generic tasks generally differ across the functional areas in accounting. For example, an auditor's primary activity is the diagnosis and treatment domain. Internal auditors perform a number of monitoring activities. Accounting firms must schedule audits and audit personnel. Tax accountants face a configuration of tax laws and client activity for diagnosing the best plan. Management accountants (planning and control) design planning and control systems. This suggests that there is no one typical AI/ES application in accounting.

4.2.3 ES Characteristics and Accounting

Chapter 1 listed some characteristics of expert systems. Those characteristics included: (a) tasks can be decomposed into segments, (b) knowledge can be expressed in the form of rules and heuristic judgments, and (c) expertise is scarce and expensive.

The task characteristics vary across accounting functions; however, accounting tasks often are characterized by decomposability.

Accounting is characterized by knowledge in the form of rules and heuristic judgments. Large sets of accounting rules are provided by the IRS, SEC, FASB, and individual companies. Heuristic judgments are made in all functional areas of accounting (e.g., tax planning).

Accounting expertise often is in short supply and almost always expensive. The existence of certifications such as a certified public accountant (CPA) indicates the existence of a distinction between a neophyte and an expert.

The relationship of these characteristics to accounting suggests that accounting is a *feasible* domain for ESs.

4.2.4   Complex Accounting Problems

The accountant faces a broad base of complex problems. Hansen and Messier (1982) show that some audit problems are NP-complete (nondeterministic polynomial), which are effectively intractable for traditional optimization methods. The tax accountant and the auditor face compliance with a broad base of rules established by the IRS, SEC, and FASB. Management accountants (planning and control) face ill-structured systems design problems.

Accordingly, accountants have developed heuristic methods to analyze these problems. However, as the problems and the computer technology changes, accountants are faced with developing new tools to meet these changes. The complexity of accounting problems and the available set of responses to the problems indicate that accounting is also a *desirable* domain for the development of ESs.

4.3   A SAMPLE ACCOUNTING EXPERT SYSTEM

This section examines an accounting ES that probably has received more attention than any other accounting ES. TAXADVISOR (Michaelsen 1982a, 1982b, and 1984; and Michaelsen and Michie 1983) is a prototype tax ES. This system has at least four characteristics in common with other accounting ESs: designation of a highly specific problem, study of a human expert(s), translation of that process into a computer program, and performance of the activity at a human level. These characteristics also are used in the next section to discuss other accounting ESs.

First, TAXADVISOR was developed to resolve a specific problem in tax accounting—in particular, to make recommendations concerning estate planning. Second, TAXADVISOR models the decision processes of a tax expert. In particular, it (a) performs a screening process to determine if it can help the client, (b) gathers information for making recommendations, and (c) finds a solution that reflects the objectives and situation of the client. Third, the system translates the process using a series of IF-THEN rules as modeled using an ES shell. Fourth, the system produces results similar to those of human experts.

4.4   PREVIOUS RESEARCH*

The systems that have been developed in accounting using AI/ES fall into three categories: systems in use, prototype systems, and conceptual design/systems in process. *Systems in use* refers to those systems that are or will be in use. *Prototype systems* refer to those systems that have been

*This paper examines previous research from a number of different sources: the *Peat Marwick (1985) Interim Report* of research grants for auditing, Miller's *1984 Inventory of Expert Systems*, the new *Expert Systems* journal, the *Accountant's Index*, accounting Ph.D. dissertations, major accounting journals (few artificial intelligence publications to date), and unpublished working papers and presentations at major conferences known to the author.

designed to understand the particular processes and are not necessarily for use in the commercial world. *Conceptual design/systems in process* refers to those applications for which the system has been planned but not implemented.

4.4.1   Systems in Use

There apparently is only one artificial intelligence–based system that will be in use in accounting (Willingham and Wright 1985). Peat, Marwick, Mitchell and Company have developed an ES that is a loan evaluation system for use in the audit of banks. The system examines the collectability of term and collateral loans. The system was built using an expert system shell/kit (Insight 2) and has over 1000 rules.

Peat, Marwick, Mitchell and Company apparently has future plans for the use of other systems (Elliot and Kielich 1985). Some expert system shell vendors have indicated that other accounting firms have purchased their product for developing expert systems. In addition, an expert system for capital budgeting (Reitman 1985) is scheduled to be in commercial use in the near future.

4.4.2   Prototype Systems

The largest category of work completed to date using artificial intelligence in accounting is the prototype. These systems are summarized in Table 4.1.

AUDITOR   AUDITOR (Dungan 1983 and 1985; and Dungan and Chandler 1983) was developed to make diagnostic judgments concerning the adequacy of a firm's allowance for bad debts. The system modeled the judgment of an auditor using an ES shell (AL/X). The system performed on a level similar to an expert.

EDP AUDITOR   EDP AUDITOR (Hansen and Messier 1982, 1985a, and 1985b) was developed to assist in the audit of computerized accounting systems. The system modeled the diagnostic judgments of an auditor using an ES shell (AL/X).

AGGREGATE   AGGREGATE (Munakata and O'Leary 1985) was developed to aid in the design of accounting information systems by developing aggregated financial statements from a set of accounts in order to improve management decision making. The system modeled the aggregation judgments of a management consultant using Prolog.

ICE   ICE (Kelly 1984) is a prototype expert system designed to aid in internal control evaluation. Unlike other accounting-based ESs, ICE in-

TABLE 4.1
A SUMMARY OF AI/ES PROTOTYPE SYSTEMS IN ACCOUNTING

System Name	Function	Subject	Language/Shell	Type
AUDITOR— Dungan (1983)	Audit	Auditing allowance for bad debts	AL/X	ES
EDP AUDITOR— Hansen and Messier (1985a, 1985b)	EDP audit	Auditing advanced EDP systems	AL/X	ES
AGGREGATE— Munakata and O'Leary (1985)	Accounting information systems	System design of aggregated financial statements	Prolog	ES
ICE— Kelly (1984)	Audit	Audit planning process	INTERLISP	ES
TICOM— Bailey et al. (1985)	Audit	Internal control evaluation	PASCAL	AI*
TAXMAN— McCarty (1977)	Tax planning	Corporate reorganizations	MicroPLANNER /LISP	AI**
TAX ADVISOR— Michaelsen (1982a, 1982b)	Tax planning	Estate tax planning	EMYCIN	ES

*They suggest an interface with an ES.
**TAXMAN II is being developed (Miller 1984).

cludes knowledge about the clients of an audit firm, including information about their management, the industry, and the economy. The system modeled diagnostic judgments of auditors using LISP.

TICOM   TICOM (Bailey et al. 1985) is an analytic query tool that incorporates AI concepts such as knowledge representation and graph simplification in the design, analysis, and evaluation of internal controls.

TAXMAN   TAXMAN (McCarty 1977; and Miller 1984) was a model of the facts of certain corporate cases and some concepts from the IRS that produced the tax consequences of corporate reorganizations. The system used AI concepts in knowledge representation. The model was built using the judgment of a tax attorney using LISP.

4.4.3   Conceptual Design/Systems in Process

A number of systems have been developed to the conceptual design stage or are in the process of being built. These systems are summarized in Table 4.2. Because these systems have not been completed at the time this chapter was written they are not discussed in further detail.

TABLE 4.2
A SUMMARY OF REPORTED AI/ES CONCEPTUAL DESIGNS IN ACCOUNTING

Application	Description
Analytic Review — Braun (1983)	A problem of concern to the external auditor/CPA. Emulates auditor decision used in determining the relative importance of analytic review information compared to other audit evidence.
Price Analysis — Ramakrishna et al. (1983) and Dillard, Ramakrishna, and Chandrasekaran (1983)	Primarily a concern of the internal auditor. The system would analyze prices for fairness and reasonableness. Developed for the U.S. government. A design only.
Accountant's Opinion Formulation — Dillard and Mutchler (1984)	A problem of concern to the external auditor/CPA. Reviews the question of how auditors form an opinion of the financial statements. Addresses the issue of going concern. A design only.
Internal Controls — Meservy (1984)	Designed to help auditors evaluate the quality of the internal control systems.
Going Concern — Biggs (1985)	Addresses the issue of going concern judgment.
Capital Budgeting — Reitman (1985)	Designed for use by corporate management in the analysis of capital budgeting problems. Currently developing a prototype system in LISP.

4.5   ES COMPONENTS AND ACCOUNTING-BASED ESs

The knowledge base and the inference engine generally differ across functional applications of accounting-based ESs. If an expert system shell is used, then the shell defines the available set of knowledge representation schemes and inference engines.

4.5.1   Knowledge Base

ES applications in accounting have made use of two different knowledge base structures: rules and frames.

Rules   Rules are structured as "if . . . then . . . ." The majority of the applications of ESs in accounting have used a rule-based approach. Typical of the rule-based approach is the rule in Hansen and Messier (1985a):

If: 1) Message control software is complete and sufficient, and
         2) Recovery measures are adequate, and
         3) Adequate documentation is generated to form a complete audit trail
Then: There is strong suggestive evidence (.8) that controls over data loss are adequate.

Another example of the rule-based approach is given in Michaelsen (1984). An example rule (in abbreviated form) is as follows.

| If: | 1) The client and/or spouse does wish to shift property income to another (not for support), etc. for at least ten years or until the death of the beneficiary, . . ., |
| Then: | It is definite (1.) that client should transfer assets to a short-term trust. |

Frames   The use of a frames representation of knowledge has received only limited attention in accounting systems. A frames representation uses a networking approach to summarize a number of attributes associated with accounting concepts. Typically the knowledge is networked together using multiple frames to summarize the knowledge of the expert.

In Munakata and O'Leary (1985) a frame-based knowledge representation was used by attributing a set of characteristics to accounting titles. One frame was used to determine the "importance" of various words in an accounting title. For example, the system analyzes "net electric plant in service" to find that "plant" is the most "important" word, in that the characteristics in the next frame are a function of this word. The next frame assigns attributes to accounting titles according to the time dimension and the liquidity dimension of the most important word. For example, cash is a short-run asset and the most liquid asset.

In Kelly (1984) three levels of frames were used to characterize knowledge in the audit process. The first level of frames provided knowledge about global concerns for the audit planning process (e.g., management background and audit history). The second level of frames gives knowledge about the specific client environment (e.g., organization and manuals). The third level of frames summarized information on internal control functions (e.g., purchasing). Kelly also made use of rules in the IF-THEN form.

Representing Uncertainty   Three of the expert systems developed in accounting use an uncertainty factor. Dungan (1983) and Hansen and Messier (1985a), in the context of AL/X, use an estimate of uncertainty in each rule. Michaelsen (1984) circumvents the uncertainty factor in EMYCIN by using a factor of 1.0 with each rule.

4.5.2   Inference Engine

If an expert system shell is used, then the inference engine generally is either backward chaining or forward chaining. In accounting ESs the goal normally is known and a backward-chaining approach is used to solve the problem. Dungan (1983) and Hansen and Messier (1985a) use the backward-chaining methodology embedded in AL/X. Michaelsen (1984) uses the backward-chaining inference engine in EMYCIN.

If a computer programming language is used, then the language can be used to define a general inference engine approach. For example, in Munakata and O'Leary (1985), the inference engine is the execution of a sequence of Prolog procedures. Kelly uses both forward- and backward-chaining rules.

4.6   RELATIONSHIP OF THE ACCOUNTING ESs TO EACH OTHER

Judging the extent of similarity of the accounting ESs to each other or to ESs in other disciplines has received little or no attention in the accounting literature. However, there are at least three dimensions on which to examine the similarity of the ESs: generic tasks, functional areas, and language/shell.

Some of the systems are related to each other based on the generic task they perform. For example, AUDITOR, EDP AUDITOR, and TAXADVISOR are diagnosis systems. Accordingly, these systems will use similar knowledge bases and inference engines.

Some of the systems are related to each other based on their functional similarity. For example, AUDITOR and EDP AUDITOR are auditing problems and thus are similar in terms of knowledge base and inference engine.

Another basis of similarity is the language or shell used to program the problem. To a certain extent this is a function of the functional area of application. For example, the audit ESs (AUDITOR and EDP AUDITOR) were written using AL/X. As noted, both audit ESs were based on diagnosis problems. As a result, it is not surprising that the same shell could be used in each system. Since they use the same shell, the inference engine and knowledge base are likely to be similar.

4.7   RELATIONSHIP OF THE ACCOUNTING ESs TO OTHER ESs

Two of the best known ESs are the mineral exploration system PROS-PECTOR (Duda and Gaschnig 1981) and the medical system MYCIN (Buchanan and Shortliffe 1984). PROSPECTOR was developed to diagnose sites for potential mineral deposits. AL/X is based on PROSPECTOR and was developed to diagnose the underlying causes of oil platform shutdowns. MYCIN was developed to diagnose human illness. EMYCIN has evolved from MYCIN into an ES shell for general diagnosis purposes.

Two of the audit ESs used AL/X, and a tax accounting ES used EMY-

CIN to diagnose the appropriate tax plan. The ability of the accounting ES developers to design these accounting systems using these ES shells suggests that these accounting problems have a structure somewhat similar to the mineral exploration and medical diagnosis problems. In particular, it is likely that diagnostic-based problems such as those encountered in auditing are very similar to diagnostic-based problems from other disciplines.

However, this does not mean that all accounting problems are directly analogous to mineral exploration and medical diagnosis problems. For example, not all generic tasks of scheduling or design-based problems are accommodated as easily by using these shells. This is partially verified by the lack of use of EMYCIN and AL/X in these other types of generic tasks in the accounting ESs developed to date.

4.8 LIMITATIONS OF ES IN ACCOUNTING

There are a number of limitations associated with ESs in accounting. These limitations derive from ESs in general as applied to accounting and ESs in the accounting domain.

4.8.1 General Limitations of ESs

The current general limitations of ESs include the following development problems (Messier and Hansen 1983).

- A substantial effort is required to build an expert system.
- The size of the knowledge base is limited by current technology.
- The development of expert systems must cope with the current languages, since computers are unable to understand natural language.
- The development of an expert system requires an expert to spend time developing and debugging the system.

The general limitations of ESs also include problems with the current systems (McDermott 1984).

- The systems do not have a general knowledge to fall back on if the specific knowledge is insufficient.
- The systems do not learn from their experience.
- The systems often provide a trace of the decision. However, often this is not a satisfactory explanation of the decision.
- The systems have little knowledge of their own scope and limitations.

Recent efforts in ESs have relied on specific knowledge about the particular domain. Thus the lack of a general knowledge base suggests that current ESs are limited to problems that can be decomposed so that specific knowledge can be used effectively.

The need for the specific knowledge base indicates the importance of the expert. The system is only as good as the expert from whom the knowledge is derived and the ability of the systems personnel to determine the knowledge base from the expert.

4.8.2   Accounting-Specific Limitations of ESs

The accounting-specific limitations of ESs derive from the application of ESs to accounting. The primary limitations derive from changes in the knowledge base, which can occur in at least five ways.

First, the rule-making bodies that affect accounting (e.g., the SEC, FASB, and IRS) are likely to make rapid changes in the knowledge base. This is exemplified by recent proposed changes in the tax code and SEC compliance requirements. Second, the knowledge in the functional accounting discipline is likely to be subject to periodic revision. Third, company policy may lead to changes in the rule base of expert systems of internal auditors, for example. Fourth, the EDP auditor's knowledge base is subject to the technological changes of computers. Fifth, if the system contains information on management, the industry, or the economy (see Kelly 1984), then the system will require periodic updating as this information changes.

4.8.3   AI/ESs in Accounting Are DSSs

Another limitation of AI/ES in accounting is that the systems that have been developed to date are decision support systems (DSSs) and not independent systems. That is, in the applications discussed previously the systems were designed to support the decision making of an experienced user — not replace the decision maker or provide support for the neophyte decision maker. This is a characteristic not only of accounting ESs but of most ESs (Bonczek, Holsapple, and Whinston 1984). However, the example of the sorcerer's apprentice may suggest that at least in the near future the focus will be on the experienced user not the neophyte.

4.9   EXTENSIONS

This section briefly discusses some extensions in the area of accounting AI/ES. These applications come from two sources: (1) related disciplines and (2) functional areas for which few systems have been developed.

4.9.1   Related Applications

There are some ESs that have been developed in other disciplines that can be useful in accounting. For example, accounting firms schedule employees to meet client needs. There have been two ESs that schedule employees: ISIS (Fox and Smith 1984; and Glover, McMillan, and Glover 1984).

A set of related potential applications is found in the legal profession. Sergot (1982) discusses some possibilities of representing the law using AI.

4.9.2   Areas for Which Few or No Systems Have Been Developed

It is apparent from this review that there are only a few applications developed in most of the functional areas of accounting (see Table 4.3). In addition, there are no applications in the financial/SEC accounting area. This suggests that there is room for further applications in each of these

TABLE 4.3
FUNCTIONAL ACCOUNTING APPLICATIONS OF AI/ES

I.   Auditing
    A.   External Auditing
        1.   Braun (1983) — Determine the importance of analytic review information in the audit process
        2.   Dungan (1983) — Assessing adequacy of allowance for bad debts
        3.   Dillard and Mutchler (1984) — Analysis of the auditor's opinion process
        4.   Dillard and Mutchler (1984) — Auditor's analysis of going concern decisions
        5.   Kelly (1984) — Audit planning process
        6.   Meservy (1984) — Analysis of internal controls
        7.   Bailey et al. (1985) — Designing, analyzing, and evaluating internal control systems
        8.   Biggs (1985) — Auditor's analysis of going concern decisions
        9.   Willingham and Wright (1985) — Loan evaluation system

    B.   Internal Auditing
        Dillard, Ramakrishna, and Chandrasekaran (1983) — Analysis of the fairness and reasonableness of contract prices

    C.   EDP Auditing
        Hansen and Messier (1985a, 1985b) — Evaluate the reliability of computerized accounting systems

II. Management Accounting/Planning and Control Systems
    Reitman (1985) — Capital budgeting

III. Tax Accounting
    A.   McCarty (1977) — Tax implications of corporate reorganizations
    B.   Michaelsen (1982a, 1982b, 1984) — Estate tax planning

IV. Accounting Information Systems
    Munakata and O'Leary (1985) — Accounting financial reports

V.   Financial Accounting
    No known previous applications

functional areas. Elliot and Kielich (1985) discuss other potential applications.

4.10   CONCLUSION

This chapter has examined the current use of AI/ES in accounting and has outlined the primary functional areas of accounting and their relationship to generic tasks. Based on the information presented, accounting is a fruitful area for the application of AI/ES.

The primary characteristics of the accounting ES, TAXADVISOR, were analyzed and compared with the other systems using the same characteristics.

This chapter also analyzed the commercial and prototype expert systems in terms of their inference engines and knowledge bases. The accounting ESs were compared to each other and to ESs in other disciplines using generic task, function, and language/shell. The similarity was judged by the impact on inference engine and knowledge base. Finally, this chapter discussed the limitations of accounting ESs and some extensions of the current ESs.

ACKNOWLEDGMENTS

I particularly would like to thank Dr. Barry Silverman for his comments on an earlier version of this chapter. Also, I would like to thank the anonymous referees for their comments on an earlier version. Of course, any limitations remain due to the author.

REFERENCES

Arens, A.A., and Loebbecke, J.K. (1984), *Auditing: An Integrated Approach*, Englewood Cliffs, N.J.: Prentice-Hall.

Bailey, A.D., Duke, G.L., Gerlach, J., Ko, C., Meservy, R.D., Whinston, A.B. (1985), "TICOM and the Analysis of Internal Controls," *The Accounting Review*, 2:186, April.

Bedard, J., Gray, G., and Mock, T.J. (1984), "Decision Support Systems and Auditing," in *Advances in Accounting*, B. Schwartz, ed., Greenwich, Conn.: JAI Press.

Biggs, S. (1985), "Developing an Expert System for Going Concern Judgment," paper presented at the ORSA/TIMS Boston meeting.

Bonczek, R.H., Holsapple, C., and Whinston, A.B. (1984), "Developments in Decision Support Systems," *Advances in Computers*, 23:141–175.

Braun, H.M. (1983), "An Application of Expert Systems to Study the Decision Process Used by Analytic Review Information for Audit Decisions," Ph.D. dissertation proposal, University of Illinois.

Buchanan, B.G., and Shortliffe, E.H. (1984), *Rule-Based Expert Systems*, Reading, Mass.: Addison-Wesley.

Dillard, J.F., and Mutchler, J.F. (1984), "Knowledge Based Expert Systems in Auditing," working paper, Ohio State University, July.

Dillard, J.F., Ramakrishna, K., and Chandrasekaran, B. (1983), "Expert Systems for Price Analysis: A Feasibility Study," in *Federal Acquisition Research Symposium*, Williamsburg, Va.: U.S. Air Force, December.

Duda, R.O., and Gaschnig, J.G. (1981), "Knowledge-Based Expert Systems Come of Age," *Byte*, September, pp. 238–281.

Dungan, C. (1983), "A Model of an Audit Judgment in the Form of an Expert System," unpublished Ph.D. dissertation, University of Illinois.

Dungan, C. (1985), "Development of an Expert System in an Auditing Context," paper presented at the Boston ORSA/TIMS meeting.

Dungan, C., and Chandler, J. (1983), "Analysis of Audit Judgment Through an Expert System," faculty working paper no. 982, University of Illinois, November.

Elliot, R.K., and Kielich, J.A. (1985), "Expert Systems for Accountants," *Journal of Accountancy*, September.

Fox, M.S., and Smith, S.F. (1984), "ISIS — A Knowledge-Based System for Factory Scheduling," *Expert Systems Journal*, 1:25–49.

Glover, F., McMillan, C., and Glover, R. (1984), "A Heuristic Programming Approach to the Employee Scheduling Problem and Some Thoughts on 'Managerial Robots,' " *Journal of Operations Management*, 4 (2): 113–128.

Hansen, J.V., and Messier, W.F. (1982), "Expert Systems for Decision Support in EDP Auditing," *International Journal of Computer and Information Sciences*, 11:357–379.

Hansen, J.V., and Messier, W.F. (1985a), "A Knowledge-Based Expert System for Auditing Advanced Computer systems," working paper, University of Florida, January.

Hansen, J.V., and Messier, W.F. (1985b), "Some Results from Testing an Expert System for EDP Auditing," paper presented at the Boston ORSA/TIMS meeting.

Hayes-Roth, F., Waterman, D.A., and Lenat, D.B. (1983), *Building Expert Systems*, Reading, Mass.: Addison-Wesley.

Kelly, K.P. (1984), "Expert Problem Solving for the Audit Planning Process," unpublished Ph.D. dissertation, University of Pittsburgh.

Kieso, D.E., and Weygandt, J.J. (1983), *Intermediate Accounting*, New York: John Wiley & Sons.

Lewis, B., and Dhar, V. (1985), "Development of a Knowledge-based Expert System for Auditing," unpublished research proposal, University of Pittsburgh.

McCarty, L.T. (1977), "Reflections on TAXMAN: An Experiment in Artificial Intelligence and Legal Reasoning," *Harvard Law Review*, 90:827–893.

McDermott, J. (1984), "Background, Theory and Implementation of Expert Systems," paper presented at the CPMS Seminar on Expert Systems, December.

Meservy, R.D. (1984), "Auditing Internal Controls: A Computational Model of the Review Process," unpublished dissertation proposal, University of Minnesota, October.

Messier, W.F., and Hansen, J.V. (1983),; "Expert Systems in Auditing: A Framework and Review," *Proceedings of the University of Oklahoma Behavioral Research Conference.*

Michaelsen, R.H. (1982a), "A Knowledge-Based System for Individual Income and Transfer Tax Planning," unpublished Ph.D. dissertation, University of Illinois.

Michaelsen, R.H. (1982b), "Application of an Expert Computer System to Federal Tax Planning," *ACM-SIGART Newsletter*, 82 (October).

Michaelsen, R.H. (1984), "An Expert System for Federal Tax Planning," *Expert Systems*, 1:149–167.

Michaelsen, R.H., and Michie, D. (1983), "Expert Systems in Business," *Datamation*, 29:240–246.

Miller, R.K. (1984), *The 1984 Inventory of Expert Systems*, Madison, Ga.: SEAI Institute.

Munakata, T., and O'Leary, D. (1985), "A Prototype Business Expert System: A Case Study in Accounting," unpublished working paper, University of Southern California.

Peat, Marwick, Mitchell and Company (1985), *Peat Marwick Foundation Research Opportunities in Auditing Program*, interim report.

Ramakrishna, K., Dillard, J.F., Harrison, T.G., and Chandrasekaran, B. (1983), "An Intelligent Manual for Price Analysis," in *Federal Acquisition Research Symposium*, Williamsburg, Va.: U.S. Air Force, December.

Reitman, W. (1985), "Artificial Intelligence Meets Decision Support: A.I.-Based Decision Support Systems," unpublished presentation, Palladian Software.

Sergot, M. (1982), "Prospects for Representing the Law as Logic Programs," in K.L. Clark and S.A. Tarnland, eds., *Logic Programming*, London: Academic Press.

Willingham, J., and Wright, W. (1985), "Development of a Knowledge-based System for Auditing the Collectability of a Commercial Loan," paper presented at the Boston ORSA/TIMS meeting.

5

Fuzzy Knowledge in Rule-Based Systems

Thomas Whalen
Brian Schott
Nancy Green Hall
Fred Ganoe

This chapter presents some applications of a relatively new approach to rule-based systems, using approximate reasoning based on fuzzy linguistic variables. Section 5.1 introduces the concepts of fuzzy sets, fuzzy propositions, linguistic variables, fuzzy logic, and approximate reasoning, together with how these concepts apply to rule-based expert systems. The next four sections discuss particular fuzzy rule-based systems for management decision support. Section 5.2 discusses PRICE, a small rule-based decision support system designed to complement a business simulation game. Section 5.3 presents fINDex, an intelligent index to problem-solving techniques. The topic of Section 5.4 is FAULT, which diagnoses potential problems in financial accounting networks. Section 5.5 concerns FANFARE(S), another financial accounting application, which assesses a firm's overall liquidity position and compares possible causes for any deficiencies in liquidity. And Section 5.6 presents STRATAS-SIST, an expert system for strategic business planning. Finally, Section 5.7 presents concluding comments about the role of fuzzy rule-based systems in management decision support.

5.1 INTRODUCTION

The advantages of rule-based acquisition and representation of knowledge are amplified by a relatively new approach based on fuzzy sets (Zadeh 1965) and approximate reasoning (Prade 1983). In this approach, knowledge is represented by a collection of fuzzy production rules, which deduce the implications of the input data by means of a many-valued logic. The acquisition of knowledge via fuzzy rules is facilitated by the use of linguistic variables (Zadeh 1975a, 1975b, and 1975c; and Whalen and Schott 1985).

In contrast to traditional variables that take on numeric values, the values taken on by a linguistic variable are words or phrases from a quasi-natural language. The purpose of linguistic variables is to provide a linkage to the numerical/logical demands of the computer and the imprecise or uncertain facts and rules comprising most of our actual knowledge about the world and how to function in it. As a very simple example, the linguistic variable *age* may have the value *young* for one person, *very old* for another person, and *neither old nor very young* for a third. Other values that the linguistic variable *age* may take on include fuzzy numbers such as *around 25* or *roughly 35 to 40*, and crisp values such as *36 years and 56 days old*.

A linguistic variable of this type has a well-defined universe of discourse; in the case of *age* this universe consists of real numbers between 0 and 120 representing actual chronological ages. Corresponding to each syntactically legal word or phrase in the quasi-natural language is a fuzzy set of values (e.g., chronological ages) from the universe of discourse of the linguistic variable. (A *fuzzy set* is a set to which members of the universe of discourse may belong in varying degrees, as opposed to the all-or-nothing membership characteristic of conventional "crisp" sets.) When implementing a linguistic processing system on a computer it is convenient to sample the membership grade of each fuzzy set at the same fixed number of points in every universe of discourse. The fuzzy sets that define the semantic meanings of the linguistic variables are then represented by vectors; each element in a vector represents the degree to which one specific point in the universe of discourse belongs to the fuzzy set in question. Linguistic primitives such as *low, medium, high, unknown*, and *undefined* are generally provided to give the system an elementary expressive power (Wenstop 1980). In addition, a good system must also support the customized primitives and other features to tailor the system's language to the language appropriate to the application (Whalen and Schott 1985).

Another very important class of linguistic variables have no clearly defined underlying universe of discourse, but instead refer to concepts with no analogy in nonfuzzy mathematics. Examples of such variables include *beauty, stability*, and *liquidity*. Part of the power of the linguistic approach comes from its ability to represent the values of members of this second class of linguistic variable by the identical system of vectors used to represent linguistic variables with a well-defined metric universe of discourse. This allows the easy construction and use of mixed IF-THEN rules such as: "If *stability of country* is *at least lower medium* and *expected profit* is *around six figures*, then *attractiveness of investment* is *upper medium.*

Thus linguistic variables have the flexibility to handle knowledge at various levels of specificity or vagueness and in a natural and expressive vocabulary. A hard-and-fast rule such as "If *current liabilities* exceed *current assets*, then the firm is *insolvent*" can coexist with a more vague, but still useful, rule such as "If *current ratio* is *below medium* and *inventory* to *working capital* ratio is *high* and *cost of sales* to *inventory* ratio is *not high*, then *liquidity*, is *low.*"

The fuzziness of the rules also contributes to the overlap between their applicability. While overlap between the conditions in which conventional rules apply can present problems, overlap is a decided advantage for fuzzy rules. If the fuzzy knowledge base has rules specifying the consequences when X is *low*, when X is *medium*, and when X is *high*, then the computed consequence when X is actually *upper upper medium* will be a compromise between the consequences specified by the latter two rules.

Linguistic variables also give flexibility in the way data are input. Some data, such as dollar transaction amounts, are quite precise, but other data such as a firm's overall competitive position or liquidity are much fuzzier. Still other variables, such as the total cost of a long-range project, are quite fuzzy in the early planning stages and gradually become more precise as planning and implementation proceed. Fuzzy rule-based systems are well suited to this kind of environment, since any level of vagueness or specificity in the input data can be recognized and dealt with systematically.

5.2   PRICE

PRICE (Whalen and Schott 1983) is a decision support system (DSS) for student managers who are playing a management simulation game. In this game the manager has only one decision to make, setting the price for the single product of its firm for twelve decision periods. The simulation was developed by Ronald Frazer at Clarkson College (Frazer 1975). Four simulated firms compete in this exercise; each firm's profits are a function of the price it charges for the product and of the prices charged by the other three firms.

The assumed goal of each of the management teams is to maximize total profit over twelve periods of game play. In this game a simulated firm's market share from one period of play affects its level of demand in future periods. Relative price among the firms determines the changes in market share. Although the game itself has a distinct goal, the DSS, implemented in a fuzzy rule-based system mode is controlled by a data-driven, not a goal-driven, formalism.

5.2.1   Knowledge Engineering in PRICE: Expert Time

Because this DSS is supporting a goal-oriented decision, many principles from the decision/management sciences literature can be utilized to provide an initial "neophyte" system before expert input is requested. This approach often helps "break the ice" in a knowledge-engineering project, giving the expert a concrete starting point to critique and take exception to rather than a blank slate that the expert is expected to fill from scratch.

The knowledge engineering can be organized around the concepts of objective function definition, decision variables, uncontrollable variables, and constraints (Morris 1967). The goal of maximizing total profit suggests that the variable *profit* is fundamental. *Price* is the concrete decision variable around which the actual play of the game revolves, so it is the principal output from the decision support system. A very important intervening variable is *market share* since this influences future demand in conjunction with current relative prices. In addition, the winning strategy of the game depends on how strongly the goal of increasing market share is weighted relative to immediate profit taking; this is reflected in the DSS linguistic variable *share goal*. The demand levels and prices of competitors must also be considered. Consequently, variables such as *others' share* and *average price* are necessary components of the system.

Management literature suggests that the product life cycle is a critical determinant of decisions. In the present DSS, a related but simpler variable is important. The game is played for only twelve decision periods. The variable *time* provides a means of explicitly dealing with this time horizon concept.

In addition to having *time* as an explicit variable, it became clear during the knowledge-engineering process that each period's decision is made in terms of the relation between the company's current state and the desired or new state. Consequently, several of the variables show up in pairs. For example, we have *price* and *new price*, the price that will be set for the coming decision. Similarly, we have the pair *market share* and *market share goal*. Also, our competitors have market share goals; this has suggested the variables *others' share* and *others' share goal*.

The rules that are constructed in the PRICE system are of two general types. Some are absolute rules; others are relative or local rules. The absolute rules make statements about the absolute levels that the company achieves. The relative (local) rules are statements in terms of the levels of other variables in the data base. An example of a relative clause is, "If *share* is less than *others' share.*" An example of an absolute clause is, "If *time* is *not high.*"

The PRICE DSS also contains multiple-condition rules. The conditions may be joined by either ands or ors. Naturally, a rule that has multiple conditions connected by ands is more difficult to match than one connected by ors. The fuzzy nature of the logic system allows it to compute the overall degree to which the data match a multiple-condition rule, as a function of the degrees to which the individual conditions are matched wholly, partially, or not at all.

During Expert Time the expert is prompted first to give each IF condition, one at a time. After each IF condition is accepted, the expert is asked whether another IF condition is needed for the rule. If not, then the consequent clauses of the rule are requested. If there are several consequences, they are treated as if they were several individual rules, each of which updates a fuzzy variable in the data base.

5.2.2 DSS Operation: User Time

In the User Time aspect of the PRICE DSS, the primary activity of the student manager is to supply values for certain data base variables after each period of the game and then observe the change on other data base variables. The values of the observed variables suggest decisions. For example, at the beginning of the third round of play the user would be expected to indicate that the time is period 3. Although 3 is a scalar number and is known with certainty, *time* is stored in the data base as a fuzzy linguistic number (a vector). The chief reason for this is that the expert's knowledge about good strategy in the game does not extend to specific strategies for each consecutive period, but only general advice such as: "If *time* is *low* (i.e., early), then *price* should be below *others' new price.*" In order to store the value 3 in the linguistic variable *time*, the user would type TIME IS CRISP 3. The procedure CRISP (an APL monadic function developed for this purpose) converts the scalar 3 into a linguistic value that is fuzzily equivalent. Similarly, for other variables, during User Time, the user replaces the incumbent values of the variables with the newer environmental conditions and decision variables.

After all of these new values have been set by the user, the data base is updated according to the fuzzy rules. In order to determine the rule consequences, the user queries the data base for each of the important variables. For example, if the user wanted to know the price suggested by the rule base, he or she could type the word (command) PRICE. However, since the word PRICE requests a numerical vector (giving the compatibility between each particular dollar amount and the fuzzy set value of the linguistic variable *price*), another query is more common. The command LABEL PRICE produces a natural language linguistic representation of the value of *price*. LABEL is a procedure for linguistic approximation developed by Wenstop (1980). A typical output of the command LABEL PRICE might be *low to lower lower medium.*

If the data base values that have resulted from the execution of the rules are unsatisfactory, the user of the DSS can either change the previous environmental condition variables and reexecute the rule base or use the suggestions as a springboard to react against, even to the extent of doing the opposite.

5.3   fINDex

fINDex (Schott and Whalen 1983) is an interactive system designed to suggest appropriate techniques for forecasting future sales of commercial products. It is intended to be used early in a decision-making process involving some kind of business forecasting. The system provides an intelligent alternative to searching through a general purpose book or article on forecasting.

fINDex asks the user a flexible series of questions including questions about the type and quality of outputs that the user will require from the forecasting process and questions about the resources (e.g., time, money, and data) that can be made available as inputs to the forecasting process. Which questions are asked later in the dialogue depends on the answers given to earlier questions. The user may respond to a fINDex question either with an exact numeric value or with a linguistic description of the value; the latter may be as vague or as precise as the user's own current knowledge of the output requirement or input resource in question. This is desirable since some of the resources and requirements may be only vaguely known early in the process of structuring an originally ill-structured decision-making problem. If the user gives a vague answer to a question, the system will try additional questions about other variables in an attempt to settle on a short list of possible techniques. However, if the variable in question turns out to be especially critical to the decision, fINDex will eventually ask for additional information about it.

fINDex does not itself do any forecasting; instead, it applies the user's responses to a knowledge base of fuzzy IF-THEN rules in order to reduce a large array of possible forecasting techniques down to a fuzzy set of a few techniques that are highly possible given the user's needs and resources.

In general, the rules may be classified either as resource constraints, which specify the fuzzy minimum level of some resource at which a particular technique is possible, or as quality constraints, which specify the fuzzy maximum level of some measure of quality that a particular technique is capable of delivering. An example of a resource constraint is: "If available *long-term historical data* are *at least fair,* then *regression analysis* is possible." An example of a quality constraint referring to the same technique is: "If *medium-term accuracy* required is *at most good to very good,* then *regression analysis* is possible." The overall degree to which regression is inferred to be a member of the fuzzy set of possible techniques would be the minimum of its possibilities as evaluated by all of the rules referencing that technique.

Most previous fuzzy rule-based systems have been data driven rather than goal directed. These systems require the user to specify some value for each possible input variable; however, that value may be as vague as necessary to reflect how much or how little information is available. fINDex, in contrast, uses a hierarchical structure to implement a hybrid of data-driven and goal-directed methods. fINDex begins a problem-solving session by asking some powerful basic questions about the problem; this screens out forecasting techniques that are clearly irrelevant. The sequence of question in this phase is based on a general, but partial, knowledge about the structure specific to business forecasting problems of this class. Following this phase, fINDex asks a dynamically selected series of increasingly specific questions in order to converge on a short list of techniques to recommend for further consideration by the user. Upon request, the system can explain its reason for making a particular suggestion or its reason for requesting certain information from the user.

To demonstrate and validate fINDex, some straightforward examples of user sessions are described. The Appendix summarizes a session in which the user's answers to questions perfectly match the conditions for the technique of regression analysis. For example, the expert rule, "If the available *recent historical data* are *at least fair,* then *regression analysis* is possible," is just matched by the user response *fair* to the query about available recent historical data. The idealized responses shown in the Appendix provide some insight into how rapidly fINDex is able to eliminate inappropriate forecasting techniques from consideration.

Ironically, the first question posed by fINDex concerns the constraint variable *time available* (to produce the forecast). But since Chambers et al. (1983) did not explicitly discuss the time required for regression analysis, the prototype knowledge base lacks any rule relating time availability to the possibility of regression analysis. In the bench mark session, no user response was given to this question, equivalent to a user response of *unknown.*

After the user has given more concrete answers to the next two queries about the availability of *recent historical data* and *knowledge of structural relations*, fINDex is asked to give its reaction to the information received so far. The result is a table showing the membership of each technique in the fuzzy set of possible techniques, listed in descending order of possibility. Note that little has been eliminated yet; regression analysis is among several techniques that have a current possibility measure of 1.00.

At the same time that a reaction is printed out, fINDex also recomputes the sequence of questions to be asked. The next question, about the degree of *long-term accuracy* required in the forecast, still does not lead to a definitive answer; regression is just one of several strong candidates. The next two questions, regarding the availability of a *delphi coordinator* and a *panel of experts*, are not responded to by the user; if necessary, fIN-Dex could ask these questions again later. The user's response to the next question, about the *short-term accuracy* required, narrows the fuzzy set of candidates somewhat; and the final question, about *turning point identification* required, leaves regression analysis as the only remaining serious contender. Although the user responses in this bench mark session are artificial, it is heartening to see that fINDex did single out regression as the ideal technique after only five non-null responses, all drawn from the knowledge about selection of forecasting techniques summarized by Chambers et al. (1983).

Other validation tests of the fINDex system were done. Notable among these were two repetitions of the scenario in the Appendix with slightly different user responses. The user responses in one of the two comparison sessions were slightly more liberal and in the other the responses were slightly more limiting than the values given by Chambers for regression. For example, in the "liberalized" session the user indicated that the level of *recent historical data* available was *fair to good* rather than the response *fair* seen in the Appendix. The reactions of fINDex to the two test sessions were as predicted: the liberalized responses permitted more techniques to be recommended than in the control session, while in the restricted response session more techniques other than regression were eliminated at an earlier time than in the control session.

The benefits of this work are not limited to the area of conceptual and mathematical tools for business forecasting. The principles demonstrated can be readily extended to similar areas such as engineering design or public works planning, for which the conceptual tools are different but the nature of the problem of the initial choice of such tools is quite similar. On a more general level, the concept of an intelligent index based on approximate reasoning is offered to the information science community as a new perspective in its ongoing search for new and better ways to facilitate efficient and effective access to stored information of all kinds.

5.4   FAULT

FAULT (Whalen, Schott, and Ganoe 1982) is a prototype system that evaluates accounting line-items using judgmental assessments of financial ratios. Differences in the size and structure of various businesses make the dollar amounts of the accounting line-items difficult to interpret in isolation; thus financial analysts have developed dimensionless ratios that are easier to assess as acceptable, too high, or too low. The task of FAULT is to accept these qualitative assessments about ratios and deduce similar qualitative evaluations about the line-items.

Evaluating the performance and condition of an enterprise in order to identify problems and opportunities is the *raison d'être* of financial ratio analysis (Helfert 1967). An important trait of financial ratios is that they reflect not only financial performance, but also performance in such functional areas as production, marketing, and so forth. Furthermore, it is easier to assess the implications of a dimensionless ratio than it is to assess the implications of the dollar amount of an accounting line-item such as net profit or cost of goods sold, since the same dollar amount may be excellent for one firm in one situation but signal impending bankruptcy in another. Considerable expertise is still required to interpret the ratios, but the task is much more tractable than evaluating line-item dollar amounts *in vacuo*, especially for an outside analyst.

The role of ratio analysis in the overall view of the firm and its environment is illustrated in Figure 5.1. The firm and environment interact to produce results that are evaluated by the accounting systems. Accounting dollar values are summarized in ratios that can be evaluated to detect problems and to diagnose their causes. Management uses the information from this process as feedback in the organizational decision-making process. Our emphasis in this discussion is in the fault diagnosis block of Figure 5.1.

FAULT is a pilot-scale, fuzzy rule-based system that deduces qualitative linguistic assessments of the ten accounting line-items in Figure 5.2 (stock price, net income, owners' equity, tangible assets, taxes and interest, net operating income, operating expenses, gross profit, cost of goods sold, and sales) given qualitative linguistic assessments of the five financial indicator ratios – P:E, ROE, EP, OpM, and GPM (Price:Earnings, Return On Equity, Earning Power, Operating Margin, and Gross Profit Margin).

Financial data to demonstrate the FAULT model were obtained using PAVE (*P*lanning *A*nd *V*aluation of *E*nterprises), a strategic financial modeling system (Grawoig and Hubbard 1982). PAVE performs a simulation of the environment, firm, and ratio computation blocks of Figure 5.1 on the basis of characteristics of the firm and its environment, supplied to PAVE as inputs. PAVE's outputs include sets of financial statements and an assortment of indicator ratios. Data from this study came from runs of PAVE using a modification of the ECOFURN case published in Grawoig and Hubbard (1982). The five numeric ratios used in FAULT were obtained from PAVE simulation runs and subjectively assessed by an expert in financial analysis using a nine-point Likert scale: very low; low; lower lower medium; lower medium; medium; upper medium; upper upper medium; high; and very high. FAULT uses these assessments of the ratios to identify problematic line-items through the application of fuzzy rules developed for the purpose of financial diagnosis.

Table 5.1 shows the ten fuzzy rules that deduce linguistic assessments for the line-items, given the linguistic assessments of the ratios. The rules are represented as function calls that refer to the five rule frames in Table 5.2. The frames are used to analyze both ratios and differences; the actual rules are formed by binding the variables to the corres-

FIGURE 5.1
OVERALL BLOCK DIAGRAM OF FINANCIAL RATIO ANALYSIS

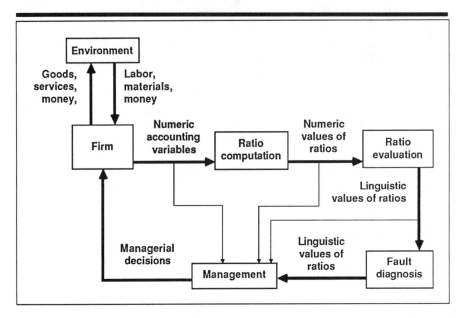

FIGURE 5.2
EXAMPLE NETWORK OF FINANCIAL RATIOS AND LINE-ITEMS

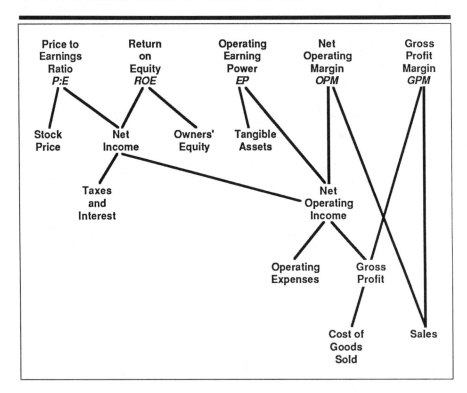

TABLE 5.1

FUZZY PRODUCTION RULES IN FAULT (Using the frames of Table 5.2)

NET INCOME = NUMDENOM($ROE, P{:}E$)

STOCK PRICE = NUM($P{:}E$, NET INCOME)

OWNERS' EQUITY = DENOM(ROE, NET INCOME)

OPERATING INCOME = NUM2(EP, OPM)

TANGIBLE ASSETS = DENOM(EP, OPERATING INCOME)

TAXES AND INTEREST = DENOM(NET INCOME, OPERATING INCOME)

GROSS PROFIT = NUM2(OPERATING INCOME, GPM)

OPERATING EXPENSES = DENOM(OPERATING INCOME, GROSS PROFIT)

SALES = DENOM2(OPM, GPM)

COST OF GOODS SOLD = DENOM(GROSS PROFIT, SALES)

TABLE 5.2

PRODUCTION RULE FRAMES FOR FINANCIAL ANALYSIS

NUM(RATIO, DENOM)

IF RATIO IS HIGH AND DENOM IS NOT LOW	THEN NUMA IS HIGH
IF RATIO IS LOW AND DENOM IS NOT HIGH	THEN NUMB IS LOW
IF RATIO IS MEDIUM AND DENOM IS MEDIUM	THEN NUMC IS MEDIUM
NUM IS NUMA AND NUMB AND NUMC	

DENOM(RATIO, NUM)

IF RATIO IS HIGH AND NUM IS NOT HIGH	THEN DENOMA IS LOW
IF RATIO IS LOW AND NUM IS NOT LOW	THEN DENOMB IS HIGH
IF RATIO IS MEDIUM AND NUM IS MEDIUM	THEN DENOMC IS MEDIUM
DENOM IS DENOMA AND DENOMB AND DENOMC	

NUM2(RATIO1, RATIO2)

IF RATIO1 EQUALS RATIO2	THEN NUM2 IS BETWEEN RATIO1 AND RATIO2

DENOM2(RATIO1, RATIO2)

IF RATIO1 EQUALS RATIO2	THEN DENOM2 IS ANTONYM BETWEEN (RATIO1 AND RATIO2)

NUMDENOM(RATION, RATIOD)

IF RATION EQUALS ANTONYM(RATIOD)	THEN NUMDENOM IS BETWEEN RATION AND ANTONYM(RATIOD)

---

ponding slots in the frames. In operation, a fuzzy rule evaluates the degree to which the actual assessment of each input variable in the IF clause matches the linguistic value hypothesized for that variable; the closer this match is, the higher the degree to which the THEN clause is to become effective.

Each line-item is assessed as close to the top of the network in Figure 5.2 as possible — that is, ratios are used as inputs whenever possible, and line-items assessed using ratios are used in preference to line-items assessed using other line-items. When the rules are executed in sequence, the result is a linguistic assessment for each of the ten line-items, derived entirely from the linguistic assessments of the five ratios.

The behavior of the fault diagnosis system was calibrated and validated using ratios derived from PAVE simulations, as follows. Starting from a set of PAVE inputs yielding acceptable performance, the cost of the goods sold by the firm was increased over a series of different scenarios by manipulating two PAVE inputs — direct materials cost and direct labor cost. This resulted in decreased profit performance in the outputs from PAVE. The five ratios were assessed for each scenario by an expert in financial analysis who was not informed of the inputs to PAVE or the relationships among the various scenarios. These assessments were then used as input to FAULT to determine its ability to detect the poor profit performance and correctly diagnose that the reason was excessive cost of goods sold. A similar analysis was performed manipulating operating expense rather than cost of goods sold.

Three illustrative PAVE outputs were selected to demonstrate the fuzzy fault diagnosis algorithm; they are presented in Parts A, B, and C of Table 5.3. In Part A inputs to PAVE were chosen to illustrate "near-normal" operation of the firm; in Part B the firm is suffering from elevated cost of goods sold; and in Part C the firm is suffering from elevated operating expenses. The numbers in Table 5.3 are the ratios and line items output from the PAVE simulation runs. The linguistic labels opposite the five ratios (P:E through GPM) were assigned judgmentally by the human expert, with *medium* representing the ideal value for a particular ratio. The linguistic labels opposite the ten accounting line-items, on the other hand, were automatically generated by FAULT, using only the linguistic assessments of the five ratios.

Note that when indicator variables are assessed by the human expert, the relationship between the numeric and linguistic values of any given ratio follows a simple pattern across the three runs. On the other hand, for line-items assessed by the FAULT system the relationship between the numeric and linguistic values is more variable. For example, the numeric value of *sales*, $526,714.00, is the same in all three scenarios, but it is linguistically assessed as *medium* in the first scenario, *very high* in the second scenario, and *upper medium* in the third because of the changes in the numeric values of the other variables. In general, the correct assessment of a dollar amount is much more context-sensitive than the assessment of a dimensionless ratio; it was for this reason that financial accountants developed the ratios originally.

Inspection of Table 5.3 reveals some important features. First, note the lack of an absolute standard in Part A of the table; it is difficult, and not very worthwhile, to build a PAVE scenario in which all ratios are simultaneously at the ideal *medium* value, so the output in Part A is characterized only as "near-normal operation." Also, the interconnections of a PAVE model, like those of a real firm, are not wholly captured

TABLE 5.3
RESULTS OF SIMULATION ANALYSIS

	Numeric Values	Linguistic Assessments
Part A: Near-Normal Operations		
RATIOS		
P:E	6.7%	Low
ROE	11.2%	Lower Medium
EP	21.9%	Medium
OPM	9.9%	Lower Medium
GPM	50.5%	Upper Medium
LINE-ITEMS		
NET INCOME	25,106	Upper Medium
STOCK PRICE	169,058	Low
OWNERS' EQUITY	225,106	Upper Medium
OPERATING INCOME	52,354	Medium to Lower Medium
TANGIBLE ASSETS	239,448	Medium
TAXES AND INTEREST	27,248	Lower Medium
GROSS PROFIT	266,098	Medium
OPERATING EXPENSES	213,744	Medium to Upper Medium
SALES	526,714	Medium
COST OF GOODS SOLD	260,615	Medium
Part B: High Cost of Goods Sold		
RATIOS		
P:E	19.7%	Upper Upper Medium
ROE	3.6%	Very Low
EP	9.4%	Very Low
OPM	4.0%	Very Low
GPM	44.5%	Low
LINE-ITEMS		
NET INCOME	7,530	Rather Low
STOCK PRICE	148,186	Upper Upper Medium
OWNERS' EQUITY	207,530	High
OPERATING INCOME	20,854	Very Low
TANGIBLE ASSETS	222,697	Unknown
TAXES AND INTEREST	13,329	Not High
GROSS PROFIT	234,604	Very Low
OPERATING EXPENSES	213,744	Unknown
SALES	526,714	Very High
COST OF GOODS SOLD	292,110	High

by the fuzzy network, which is only a useful approximation to an intractable complexity. Manipulating *cost of goods sold* in Part B and manipulating *operating expenses* in Part C cause repercussions on several other line-items, which greatly complicates the relationship between these variables and the financial indicator ratios. Thus the ratios in Parts B and C cast varying degrees of suspicion on a number of line-items in each case. The measure of success of the FAULT model is the degree to which the linguistic value of the correct line-item (*cost of goods sold* in Part B and *operating expenses* in Part C) is given a prominent place in the fuzzy set of suspected causes of the diagnosed problem.

TABLE 5.3 *(Cont.)*

	Numeric Values	Linguistic Assessments
Part C: High Operating Expenses		
RATIOS		
P:E	12.4%	Medium
ROE	5.9%	Low
EP	13.1%	Low
OPM	5.6%	Low
GPM	50.5%	Upper Medium
LINE-ITEMS		
NET INCOME	12,642	(Below Medium) but not Low
STOCK PRICE	156,593	Medium
OWNERS' EQUITY	212,642	High
OPERATING INCOME	29,759	Low
TANGIBLE ASSETS	227,089	Unknown
TAXES AND INTEREST	17,117	Not (More or less High)
GROSS PROFIT	266,098	Lower Medium
OPERATING EXPENSES	236,339	High
SALES	526,714	Upper Medium
COST OF GOODS SOLD	260,615	Upper Medium

5.5   FANFARE(S)

FANFARE(S) (Ganoe 1984) builds on the financial ratio analysis experience gained in developing FAULT. Phase I of the system accepts numeric financial ratios, converts these into tentative qualitative assessments by comparing them with published ratios from comparable firms, and presents these tentative assessments to the user to accept or modify. Phase II uses a collection of fuzzy rules to assess the firm's overall liquidity based on the qualitative assessments of the ratios. Finally, Phase III uses a second set of fuzzy rules to examine the causes of any liquidity problems discovered in Phase II; the results of this analysis is a fuzzy set of possible causes for a problem with liquidity in the firm. Figure 5.3 is a schematic representing the major system processes, which will now be elaborated.

5.5.1   Financial Ratios — Input Processing

Financial ratios comprise the input data for the diagnostic system as indicated in Figure 5.3. A subset of Miller's (1972) cause-and-effect ratios is used for liquidity assessment in the current prototype version of FANFARE(S). After the system has been successfully validated in this area of expertise, the scope of the system will be expanded by adding new ratios to the input lists and new rules to the knowledge base.

FIGURE 5.3
FINANCIAL DIAGNOSIS SYSTEM MODEL

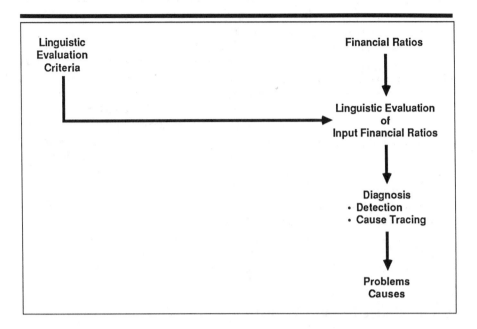

Initial processing of input financial ratios translates numeric values of ratios to linguistic assessments (e.g., a *current ratio* of 2.0 might be characterized linguistically as *medium*); this operation is termed "linguistic evaluation." FANFARE(S)' criteria for linguistic evaluation are based on empirically determined averages and frequency distributions of the numeric values of each ratio in the industry to which the firm in question belongs.

The FANFARE(S) inference engine is an approximate reasoning mechanism that derives diagnostic inferences from input evidence and the financial knowledge represented in rule-based systems. Fuzzy logic technology provides an appropriate analytical framework for the financial environment in which numbers are not always as precise as they appear, problem concepts are not crisp, and problems may have multiple interacting causes. Furthermore, the linguistic interface provided by fuzzy logic may prove to be a significant advantage in the human engineering aspects of the system.

5.5.2   Problem Detection System

Diagnosis is viewed here as a process of problem detection and cause determination. Financial ratio values are the evidence—the signs and symptoms—used by FANFARE(S) to analyze financial data for possible problems. The ability to synthesize inferences about conceptual problems from the evidence is the design objective for the system. Knowledge drives the expert system to its conclusions.

Cause-and-effect ratios derived from Miller (1972) provide evidence for both the detection and cause determination phases of financial analysis. Effect ratios obviously are symptomatic of problem existence, hence they are useful for detection. Complex relationships among both types of ratios are instrumental in cause determination. FANFARE(S) possesses knowledge of the relationships among the ratios with respect to liquidity.

Knowledge resides in FANFARE(S) in the form of a fuzzy rule-based system. Table 5.4 illustrates some sample rules that lead to a fuzzy linguistic rating value of liquidity. Each rule is evaluated, and the result is stored temporarily (e.g., in *Liq-A*). Ratings from all the rules are then combined linguistically into one overall liquidity value that determines whether or not illiquidity is to be considered a problem. A liquidity rating of *low*, for example, causes diagnosis routines to be invoked to find the source of the liquidity problem, whereas a value of *medium to upper medium* is not considered to be a problem.

5.5.3   Cause Diagnosis System

Knowledge for cause diagnosis is conceptually quite different from knowledge for problem detection, even though it is represented in the familiar rule format (see Table 5.5). Generation of cause hypotheses is an early step in various models of the problem diagnosis process. Miller (1972) recognized six possible causes of working capital inadequacy or illiquidity; three of these are programmed into the FANFARE(S) prototype as hypotheses to be investigated.

TABLE 5.4
PROBLEM DETECTION PRODUCTION RULES

IF	Current ratio is Low
THEN	Liq-A is not High
IF	Current Ratio is Below Medium
&	Inventory : Working Capital is High
&	Cost of Sales : Inventory is Not High
THEN	Liq-B is Low
IF	Current Ratio is Below Medium
&	Accounts Receivable : Working Capital is High
&	Collection Period is Not Low
THEN	Liq-C is Low

.
.
.

LIQUIDITY is Liq-A & Liq-B & Liq-C ...

TABLE 5.5
PRODUCTION RULE FOR CAUSE DIAGNOSIS

IF	Sales : Fixed Assets is Low
&	Fixed Assets : Net Worth is High
THEN	Cause is Excessive Fixed Assets is Possible

As implied by the conclusion in Table 5.5, each hypothesized cause of illiquidity receives a possibility rating commensurate with the amount of evidence in the data as determined by FANFARE(S)' knowledge. Cause diagnosis results are reported as shown in Table 5.6. Users must interpret liquidity detection and cause diagnosis ratings and exercise their judgments concerning appropriate courses of action.

5.6   STRATASSIST

STRATASSIST (Green 1984) is an innovative decision support system for the strategic planning decision process. It supports the generation of strategic alternatives using imprecise input data via fuzzy sets technology, specifically L-fuzzy mathematics. This allows the use of natural language descriptions rather than crisp numbers as input for computerized assistance to the alternative generation phase of the strategic planning decision processes.

Data acquisition for STRATASSIST is by means of a menu-driven interactive program that poses questions about the firm and its environment. User responses are natural language descriptions of the situation as the manager believes it to be. The questions are based upon Porter's *Competitive Strategy* (1980), in which he describes his theory of the competitive marketplace and strategic planning. Typical questions would include: How rapid is the growth rate of your industry? How high are the exit barriers in your industry? How concentrated is your buyer group? This prescriptive approach to data collection and analysis ensures consideration of much that might otherwise have been overlooked or dismissed as peripheral to the question. As an aid to planning managers, it may be more important that questions be asked than that they be answered.

The rule based approach to processing the information in the data base occurs by means of a fuzzy expert system whose fuzzy rules are

TABLE 5.6
CAUSE DIAGNOSIS REPORT

LIQUIDITY is Low.	
Cause Possibilitities	
Trade Receivables:	0.9
Excessive Fixed Assets:	0.2
Inventory:	0.1

based upon Porter's opinions. These rules relate characteristics of the firm and/or its environment to recommended strategies and strategic actions: for example, "If *exit barriers* are *at least more or less high*, then *strategic action* should be *avoid confrontation with competitors that may trigger bitter price cutting.*"

The inference engine measures the approximate degree to which the user data matches the value described by the expert, and it interprets this as the degree of truthfulness of the left-hand-side proposition of the rule. The inference engine then returns the right-hand-side conclusion to the user with an appropriate "possibility" rating ranging between zero and one, which is determined using the truthfulness of the left-hand-side proposition. If the user data match the expert description exactly (e.g. *exit barriers* are *more or less high*), then the conclusion is *Strategy/Strategic action* should be *C* (avoid confrontation...) with a possibility rating of 1. Variations in a value of *A* recorded in the data base will cause corresponding variations in the possibility rating assigned to the implication that the recommended strategy/strategic action should be *C*.

In a validation study, STRATASSIST was tested against a partial system, consisting only of the survey phase without the rule-based deductions, and against a simple review of Porter's theory without tie-in to the problem firm, using both regular MBA students and a group of Executive MBA students with at least ten years managerial experience each. STRATASSIST significantly improved the performance of the regular MBA students, but the Executive MBA students performed best with just the survey phase; these seasoned managers seemed to need the system's suggestions far less than the beginners in management did. Similar results have been reported in many other areas of expert system use; the beneficiaries of stored expertise are not the advanced specialists, but the average or neophyte practitioners.

5.7   CONCLUSION

The long-term goal of our research is to develop operational "apprentice" systems for management decision support. Continued work on the general problem of knowledge acquisition should eventually make possible a decision support system that can play the role of a smart apprentice. Like any good apprentice, it will come supplied with an initial knowledge base of common sense and general business background; at least as important, however, it will be prepared to learn more. It should be relatively easy for a manager to explain or demonstrate to the system how to complete a new task. A very important requirement is that the system must have sufficient knowledge about itself to recognize its limitations and request help when necessary; otherwise it could come to resemble the "sorcerer's apprentice" of legend, applying limited knowledge beyond its proper scope and thus conjuring up disaster.

REFERENCES

Chambers, J.C., Mullick, Sattinder, K., and Smith, D. D. (1983), "How to Choose the Right Forecasting Technique," in D.M. Dickson, ed., *Using Logical Techniques for Making Better Decisions*, New York: John Wiley & Sons.

Frazer, R.A. (1975), *Business Decision Simulation: A Time-Sharing Approach*, Reston, Va.: Reston Publishing Co.

Ganoe, F. J. (1984), "Knowledge-Based Support for Financial Analysis," *Proceedings of International Conference on Systems, Man and Cybernetics*, IEEE, pp. 229–233.

Grawoig, D.E., and Hubbard, C.L. (1982), *Strategic Financial Planning with Simulation*, New York: Petrocelli Books.

Green, N.L. (1984), "Interfacing Interactive Graphics with Fuzzy Production Rules in a DSS," *Proceedings of International Conference on Systems, Man and Cybernetics*, IEEE, pp. 226–228.

Helfert, E.A. (1967), *Techniques of Financial Analysis*, Homewood, Ill.: Richard Irwin.

Miller, D.E. (1972). *The Meaningful Interpretation of Financial Statements: The Cause-and-Effect Ratio Approach* (rev. ed.), New York: American Management Association.

Morris, W.T. (1967), "On the Art of Modeling," *Management Science*, 13:B707–B717.

Porter, M.E. (1980), *Competitive Strategy*, New York: The Free Press.

Prade, H. (1983), "Approximate and Plausible Reasoning: The State of the Art," Text for tutorial session preceding IFAC symposium on Fuzzy Information, Knowledge Representation and Decision Analysis, Marseille (France), July 18–21.

Schott, B. and Whalen, T. (1983), "fINDex, An Intelligent Index to Business Forecasting," *Proceedings of the International Conference on System, Man, and Cybernetics, IEEE,*, vol. 1, pp. 10–13.

Wenstop, F. (1980), "Quantitative Analysis with Linguistic Values," *Fuzzy Sets and Systems* 4:99–115.

Whalen, T. and Schott, B. (1983), "Decision Support with Fuzzy Production Systems," in P. Wang, ed., *Advances in Fuzzy Set Theory and Application*, New York: Plenum Press.

Whalen, T. and Schott, B. (1985), "Advances in Linguistic Processing," IEEE Conference on Languages for Automation.

Whalen, T., Schott, B., and Ganoe, F. (1982), "Fault Diagnosis in a Fuzzy Network," *Proceedings of the International Conference on Cybernetics & Society*, pp. 35–39.

Zadeh, L.A. (1965), "Fuzzy Sets," *Information and Control*, 8:338–353.

Zadeh, L.A. (1975a), "The Concept of a Linguistic Variable and its Application to Approximate Reasoning—I," *Information Science*, 8:199–249.

Zadeh, L.A. (1975b), "The Concept of a Linguistic Variable and its Application to Approximate Reasoning—II," *Information Science*, 8:301–357.

Zadeh, L.A. (1975c), "The Concept of a Linguistic Variable and its Application to Approximate Reasoning—III," *Information Science*, 9:43–80.

APPENDIX

SAMPLE fINDex EXECUTION SUMMARY

	Constraint query	User response
	time required	‹no response›
	recent historical data available	fair
	knowledge of structural relations available	very good

Possibility	Technique
1.00	delphi method
1.00	panel consensus
1.00	visionary forecast
1.00	historical analogy
1.00	moving average
1.00	exponential smoothing
1.00	X-11
1.00	trend projections
1.00	regression model
1.00	intention-to-buy surveys
1.00	leading indicator
0.35	Box-Jenkins
0.35	life-cycle analysis
0.02	econometric model
0.02	input-output model
0.02	diffusion index
0.00	market research
0.00	economic input-output model

	Constraint query	User response
	long-term accuracy required	low

Possibility	Technique
1.00	delphi method
1.00	panel consensus
1.00	visionary forecast
1.00	historical analogy
1.00	trend projections
1.00	regression model
0.35	life-cycle analysis
0.26	moving average
0.26	exponential smoothing
0.26	Box-Jenkins
0.26	X-11
0.26	intention-to-buy surveys
0.26	leading indicator
0.02	econometric model
0.02	input-output model
0.02	diffusion index
0.00	market research
0.00	economic input-output model

	Constraint query	User response
	delphi coordinator available	‹no response›
	panel of experts available	‹no response›
	short-term accuracy required	good to very good

Possibility	Technique
1.00	delphi method
1.00	trend projections
1.00	regression model
0.26	exponential smoothing
0.26	Box-Jenkins
0.26	X-11
0.02	econometric model
0.02	input-output model
0.01	moving average
0.01	intention-to-buy surveys
0.01	diffusion index
0.01	leading indicator
0.00	panel consensus
0.00	market research
0.00	economic input-output model
0.00	visionary forecast
0.00	historical analogy
0.00	life-cycle analysis

	Constraint query	User response
	turning point indentification required	very good

Possibility	Technique
1.00	regression model
0.35	delphi method
0.26	X-11
0.02	econometric model
0.01	Box-Jenkins
0.01	input-output model
0.01	intention-to-buy surveys
0.01	diffusion index
0.01	leading indicator
0.00	panel consensus
0.00	market research
0.00	economic input-output model
0.00	visionary forecast
0.00	historical analogy
0.00	moving average
0.00	exponential smoothing
0.00	trend projections
0.00	life-cycle analysis

6

Knowledge-Based Decision Support Systems for Military Procurement

Jesse F. Dillard
Kamesh Ramakrishna
B. Chandrasekaran

Artificial Intelligence (AI) technology is applied in constructing a prototype system to assist in price analysis decisions. The decision task is specified, and expert human behavior is represented and encoded into a computer system. The task is ascertained using in-depth interviews, verbal protocols, and available authoritative documentation. The resulting knowledge base is used to design the architecture of a prototype system. This decision support prototype system provides the basic structure for building intelligent expert computer systems in this and other related decisions situations. From a behavioral perspective, the findings provide a better understanding of how pricing decisions are actually made. From an implementation perspective, benefits accrue from:

1. Providing decision support within pricing situations
2. Providing audit trails of the actual decision process used by the price analyst, and
3. Providing a training tool for both formal settings and informal on-the-job situations.

From a research perspective, the study provides a basis for future AI system development and for gaining insight into expert decision-making behavior.

6.1 INTRODUCTION*

A prerequisite for developing expert systems is precise problem definition and specification. This requirement along with the need for adequate knowledge-base support make it difficult to construct fully-automated expert decision systems for many interesting but complex tasks. However, applying AI tools and methodology within these contexts can be fruitful. The utility of these undertakings can be enhanced by developing and applying a flexible architecture within a multi-tool environment (Kunz, Kehler, and Williams 1984). The objective of this project is to determine the applicability of AI tools to the price analysis task as carried out during the military procurement process. The research that follows is designed to complete the first stage of building an expert system based on expert price analysts decision-making behavior. The specific task studied is the determination of the "fairness and reasonableness" of a contractor's proposed price in government procurement actions. The result of the project is a knowledge-based decision support system implemented as an intelligent manual. The system is designed so that as problem specification evolves the system can be upgraded to include more automated decisions as well as to incorporate new automated data bases as they become available.

Section 6.2 discusses the phases of system development as they relate to their project, and Section 6.3 presents the system architecture for the intelligent manual. Sections 6.4, 6.5, and 6.6 briefly describe the task analysis of the pricing domain, identify the system requirements, and illustrate the prototype system. The final section provides a summary of the project.

6.2 SYSTEM DEVELOPMENT PHASES

Constructing knowledge-based AI systems is viewed as a three-stage process requiring many person-years of work. The first stage, and the one addressed here, is the specification of the task and the design of a system architecture based on the analysis. The result of the first stage is a knowledge-based decision support system. This stage is carried out by identifying the task and human experts within the area and representing the human knowledge in such a way that it can be understood and encoded into a computer system. The decision hierarchy, decision points, and linkages are identified. This results in a specific description of the task and the information processing that is required. The structure is encoded in an information organization program that represents, organizes, and links the decision frames or episodes. The prototype system contains one frame representing each decision required. This frame is linked to all other relevant frames, required data bases, and prior decision results.

*The work discussed here was supported by the United States Air Force Business Research Managment Center under Contract No. F33615-82-C-5114.

The ZOG system, a software system for organizing knowledge in this way, was chosen for use in this study because of the researchers' familiarity with the system and its availability (Robertson, Newell, and Ramakrishna 1977; Robertson, Newell, and McCracken 1979; and Ramakrishna 1981).

The resulting system provides a detailed description of the decision process. It identifies the types of data bases and prior information used and the sequence of use. It identifies the requisite analytic capabilities needed to carry out the task and the point at which they are utilized. It identifies the decisions that must be made in carrying out the task, their sequence, and their relationship to prior and/or future decisions. The resulting system is a detailed outline of the task. It provides a means for testing the proposed structure in on-line, interactive sessions with human experts. The intelligence in this first-stage system is the decision structure—its sequence, hierarchy, and component linkages, which provide the framework for building a sophisticated knowledge-based expert system. As is explained more fully later in the chapter, these tasks and their relationships are represented within an intelligent manual context.

The second stage in developing an AI system, which is not addressed in this research, modifies the structure constructed in the first phase through intensive testing with human experts and comparisons of predictions from historical cases. In effect, the first-stage results (i.e., the prototype system) are viewed as a set of hypotheses to be tested. As the structure is refined, it is also made more "intelligent." The first-stage system confronts the user with the decisions that must be made but requires that the user make the decision.[1] In the second stage, some of the intermediate decisions will begin to be made by the system. That is, all the steps will not have to be carried out by the user. The system will have the capability of inferring some of the needed results, thus relieving the decision maker of that responsibility. Prior work indicates that the requisite formal representation necessitates the implementation and encoding of decision heuristics as well as the availability of requisite data bases.[2]

The third stage in developing AI systems involves the construction of an expert system that contains extensive reasoning, learning, and language capabilities and that can be applied to more sophisticated pricing tasks.

In summary, the purpose of this research is to carry the design of an expert price analysis system through stage one. Expert behavior is iden-

---

[1] The decisions are broken down into their lowest components so that the decision maker makes many intermediate decisions required to arrive at the final decision. This is intelligence only in the sense that the intermediate decisions are aggregated, formated, and presented to the decision maker.

[2] System interfaces with requisite data bases and other decision support facilities can present a major impediment in constructing an AI system (Chandrasekaran, Dillard, and Ramakrishna 1983). It is also recognized that formal knowledge representation may be quite formidable; however, the first-stage results should provide a foundation for this task.

tified, encoded, and represented within a computer system. The prototype system constructed as part of stage one is designed to have the following capabilities:

1. On-line decision support
2. Interactive tutorial capabilities
3. Requisite decision documentation

6.3 INTELLIGENT MANUAL FOR THE PRICING TASK

An intelligent manual is a decision support system designed to provide assistance in task domains for which automated expert systems are not currently feasible because of limitations in problem specification, AI technology, and/or requisite automated data bases. The architecture of an intelligent manual has four components (see Figure 6.1):

1. *The Task Support System*: This component supports the basic task by providing an appropriate organization for the overall task. The organization is obtained from an analysis of how experts perform the task and is designed to support the expert's performance.

2. *The Guidance System*: This component provides explanation and guidance in performing the basic task. The structure of this component parallels the structure of the task support system so that a novice, on requesting help, is given the appropriate explanation and is guided to perform the appropriate activities.

3. *The Task Action System*: This component consists of the programs and tools (e.g., statistical analysis programs, text editors, learning curve programs, data bases, etc.) that are necessary for performing the analysis called for in the task support system. These programs can be invoked from the task support system (as well as the guidance system); the input data required by these programs is provided via the task support or guidance systems, and the generated output data is accessible from the task support or guidance systems.

4. *The External Interface System*: This component uses the results of the user's interaction with the previous three systems to generate appropriate output. For example, this system may generate a structured document that documents the user's decision (e.g., a price negotiation memorandum) or an audit trail report that specifies the actions performed by the user and the possible reasons for these actions. Many different kinds of output are possible, and all of them must be based on information gathered from the user's interaction with the other three components.

FIGURE 6.1
THE ARCHITECTURE OF AN INTELLIGENT MANUAL

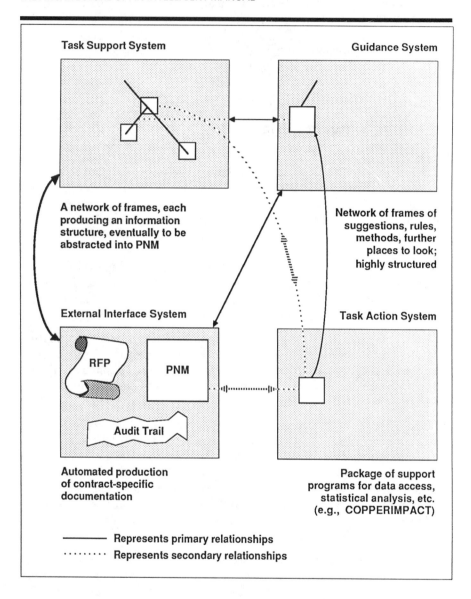

Task Support System

Guidance System

A network of frames, each producing an information structure, eventually to be abstracted into PNM

Network of frames of suggestions, rules, methods, further places to look; highly structured

External Interface System

Task Action System

RFP

PNM

Audit Trail

Automated production of contract-specific documentation

Package of support programs for data access, statistical analysis, etc. (e.g., COPPERIMPACT)

——— Represents primary relationships

········· Represents secondary relationships

6.4   PRICE ANALYSIS IN THE AIR FORCE

The primary buying functions in the United States Air Force (USAF) can be illustrated by three buying activities:

1. Systems Command central procurement (SC)
2. Logistics Command central procurement (LC)
3. Logistics Command base procurement[3] (base level)

The relevant characteristics of the three buying activities are summarized in Figure 6.2 and include:

- Type of analysis generally undertaken
- Type of procurement actions
- Type of accounting system encountered
- Availability of data
- Average number of procurement actions undertaken
- Average dollar value of actions
- Availability of support

The base level was selected as the area to focus expert system development for the following reasons:[4]

- Price analysis is the major method of analysis.
- Cost data generally are not available.
- Little assistance is currently available in terms of specialist support.
- Lack of contractor data available for cost analysis.
- Procedures are fairly standard.
- A relatively stable procurement environment exists.

It should be pointed out that the basic concepts of establishing "fair and reasonable" prices for procuring process inputs are similar for both the military and nonmilitary sectors. Thus, with some "demilitarization" the system appears to be applicable to a fairly wide range of private sector environments. The architecture appears to be applicable to a wide range of structured, expert decision situations.[5]

---

[3] Referred to as base-level pricing. It is recognized that there are some differences among different base-level procurement activities; however, the basic price analysis task is the same.

[4] See Chandrasekaran, Dillard, and Ramakrishna (1983) for a more complete comparison of the three buying activities.

[5] A project is currently underway using this architecture to construct a knowledge-based system for components of the independent auditor's audit opinion decision as it relates to an entity's financial statements.

FIGURE 6.2
SUMMARY OF PROCUREMENT ACTIVITY CHARACTERISTICS

Characteristic	SC	LC	Base Level
Analysis type	Cost analysis	Cost & price analysis	Price analysis
Procurement type	Large systems	Diverse, mostly spares	Varied
Accounting systems	Sophisticated but diverse	Unique, mostly standard	Nonstandard poorly developed
Pricing/costing data	Abundant and available	Generally available	Very little available
Number of actions	Very few	Moderate	Very high
Dollar value of actions	Very high	Varies	Low
Availability support	Specialist part of evaluation team	Specialist generally available	Little specialist support

6.5   TASK ANALYSIS OF THE PRICING DOMAIN

As stated previously, the task of interest in this study is the price analysis function as carried out by base-level procurement activities. The design feasibility of a related knowledge-based system is investigated by evaluating the following questions:

- What assistance can or should an expert system provide?
- What information, knowledge, and environment would have to be maintained in order to support an effective expert system that can be utilized by all buying activities?

The task analysis[6] was carried out through evaluation of authoritative government publications and in-depth interviews and protocol analysis of experts in the area of price analysis. Actual procurement cases were

---

[6] See Stephens, Dillard, and Bhaskar (1981) for a discussion of the relationship between expert system design and formal task analysis.

used to collect the empirical data. In some instances, the individual who had originally evaluated the case was asked to review and explain the process. These cases were also evaluated by personnel who had not previously seen the cases. The sessions ran from one to four hours depending on the availability of the expert and resulted in four to twelve case evaluations. Approximately ten experts were involved in this phase of the study.[7]

The remaining portions of this section characterize price analysis in the Air Force and identify system requirements.

*   *   *

An intelligent computer system designed to aid in price analysis must have the capabilities required to function within the procurement domain. Generally, there are three major functional entities involved: the user, the contractor, and the contracting officer. The user provides a set of technical specifications and a cost estimate of the proposed procurement. Based on the requirements set forth in the solicitation, the contractor submits a proposed price for providing the desired item or service. The contracting officer is responsible for taking the user's request, soliciting proposals, evaluating the proposals, establishing a negotiating position, carrying out the negotiations, and consummating a contract. Throughout this process, the contracting officer may require in-depth technical, pricing, or legal knowledge necessitating access to specialists in these areas.

The following discussion focuses on the portion of the procurement task related directly to price evaluation in establishing a negotiating position (ASPM 1975). The following activities are carried out in developing the objective price:

- Verification of user requirements
- Fact finding
- Price comparisons
- Exception comparisons

The bases for developing an objective price are the user's technical specifications and the required delivery schedule/period of performance. Next, the following fact finding activities are undertaken:

- Eliminate sources
- Evaluate prior buys
- Request and receipt of field reports
- Identify facilities to be provided by the government
- Identify relevant outside influences

---

[7] See Chandrasekaran, Dillard, and Ramakrishna (1983) for a more complete discussion.

- Evaluate time pressures
- Document objective development activities

As a result of fact finding, it is determined which of the following procedures is appropriate for establishing a government position:

- Competitive pricing
- Published catalog, market, or regulated pricing
- Prior quotes and prices for similar items
- Cost analysis

Once the government objective is established, the proposals/bids are evaluated in terms of this objective price, the prices proposed by the other contractors, and the exceptions taken by the contractors to the solicitation specifications.

Price analysis is defined generally as determination of a fair and reasonable price for the item being procured. The task may be as simple as comparing two numbers and choosing the smallest in a competitive pricing situation or as difficult as constructing a price based on full costs generated from engineering specifications. The information gathered during fact finding indicates which type of analysis is appropriate and provides data useful for carrying out the analysis.

As is the case with the overall procurement function, the price analysis function has access to specialist functions. For example, field personnel can provide information as to the level of compliance with Cost Accounting Standards Board (CASB) requirements and technical specialists can provide evaluations of proposed work processes and material and labor specifications. The system design problem is choosing which tasks to include as part of the price analysis function and which to treat as specialty areas to be called by the price analysis system when needed (Mittal, Chandrasekaran, and Smith 1979). Figure 6.3 displays our model of procurement and the role of price analysis in this context.

Price analysis, or the determination of a "fair and reasonable price," can be viewed as the task of *developing a government objective*. There are two general methods for developing this objective:

1. Determining the lowest price proposed in a truly competitive environment
2. Developing a price based on a knowledge-based analysis of the item

Figure 6.4 represents the model of price analysis underlying the prototype system. The analysis is restricted to those contracts meeting the technical, pricing, delivery, and legal specifications set forth in the purchase request. Contract evaluation employs one or more of the four classes of analytical methods shown in Figure 6.4. If there is a truly competitive situation, the analyst's task may be comparing two numbers and choosing the smaller of the two. Where there are two or more contracts,

FIGURE 6.3
THE PROCUREMENT CONTEXT OF PRICE ANALYSIS

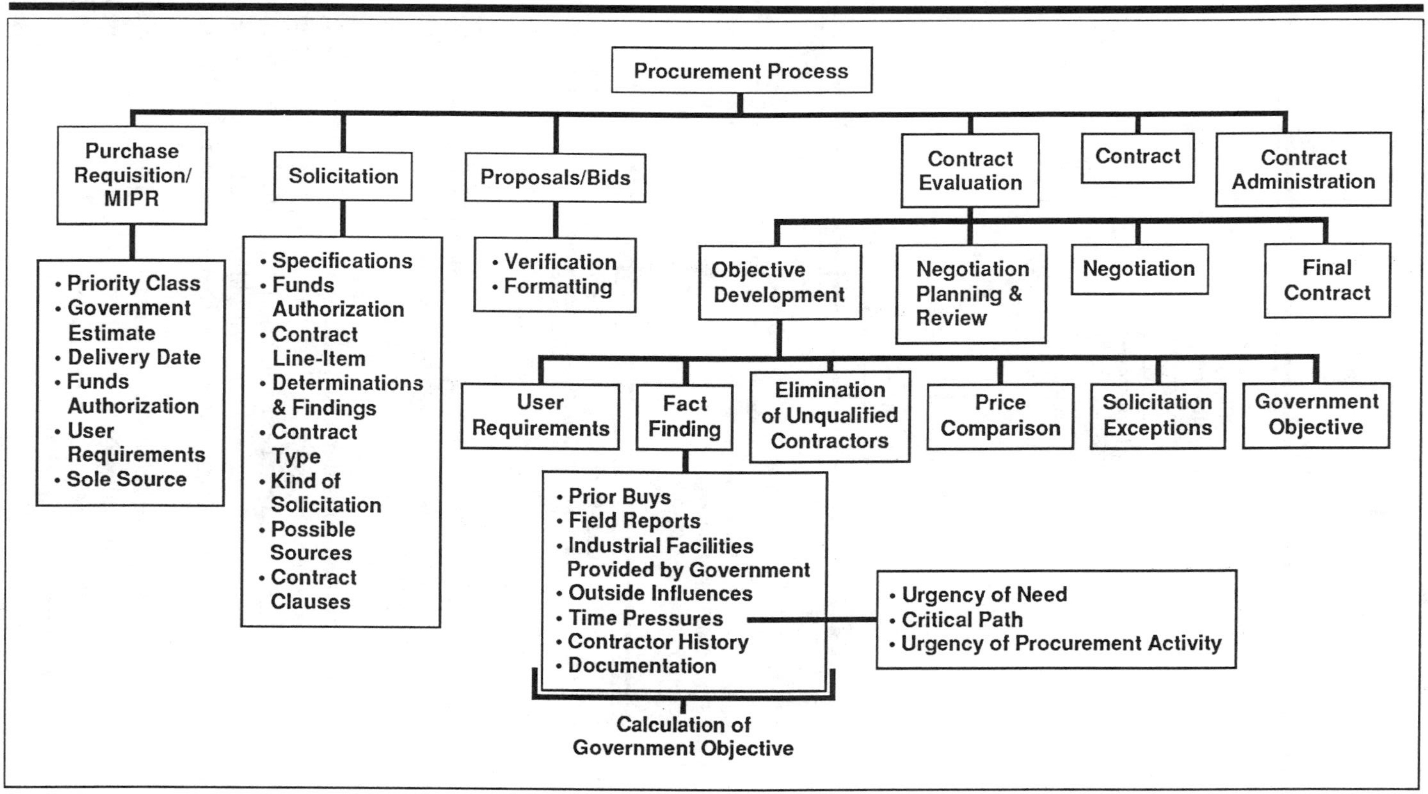

FIGURE 6.4
PRICE ANALYSIS PROCEDURES

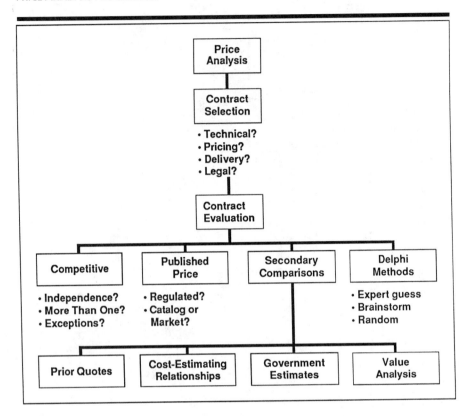

the task is one of determining if a competitive situation actually exists. That is, are the contractors independent; are there exceptions made to the purchase request? The competitive pricing method is the most preferred method.

The next method considered is published price. If there are no comparable contracts, then the price analysis consists of trying to determine and evaluate what price other customers are paying for the item. This consists of determining if there is an established market price. Are other customers purchasing the same item? Is there a valid price list or published catalog price? Is the price regulated?

The third method is secondary comparisons. This is generally the most complex and demanding of the methods. There are few, if any, market forces acting. Thus the price must be estimated or constructed from secondary information sources such as:

- Prior quotes for like items
- Cost-estimating relationships that have been developed for similar items

- Value analysis in which the value of the item is estimated by an evaluation of the technical and production specification

The Delphi methods are used when there is little available information for developing a price. In effect, a group of knowledgable people estimate what they think a reasonable price might be. This method is the least objective and the least desirable.

6.6 THE PROTOTYPE SYSTEM

The price analysis system is constructed on top of the ZOG system. ZOG has been described elsewhere (Robertson, Newell, and Ramakrishna 1977; and Robertson, Newell, and McCracken 1979) and has been applied in a number of different data base and project management situations (Fox and Palay 1979; Mantei and McCracken 1979; and Ramakrishna 1981).

ZOG is a large data base of information organized as a network of *frames*. A ZOG-user moves from frame to frame using the computer terminal to view the contents of a frame at a time. Frames are designed to be displayed on a single screen; by convention, every frame has a one-line *title* at the top of the screen, a few lines of *text* below the title, a set of numbered (or lettered) menu items of text called *selections*, and a line of ZOG commands called *global pads* at the bottom of the screen.

Frames are interconnected by the selections. When the user *selects* an item (by typing its number or letter, or in more advanced ZOG systems by touching the screen location of the item), ZOG "moves" the user to the frame "pointed to" by the selection. This new frame is now displayed on the screen, replacing the frame from which the selection was made. The new frame will have the same general format; it will usually contain new information and further selections that lead to more detailed information. Occasionally there may be "dead ends"—frames that have no selections and represent the task primitives. The frame network is a hierarchical information structure with extensive cross-referencing as well as mechanisms for moving directly from frames deep down in the hierarchy to frames much higher up. The network of frames is often termed a *ZOGnet*.

6.6.1 Task Support System

A ZOGnet is constructed for the task support system. As stated previously, the task support system provides the appropriate organization for the overall task and is designed to support expert performance. As illustrated in Figure 6.5, the frame format presents the user with the sequence of actions or subtasks that must be undertaken.

The title specifies the task being carried out. There is little or no text. The menu section presents the subtasks that must be addressed in

FIGURE 6.5
OBJECTIVE DEVELOPMENT

```
-------------------------------------------------------------------------
  Objective Development                                         Procd10


  U.  User Requirements    (Points to the requirements stated in the
                            purchase request.)


  F.  Fact Finding


  E.  Elimination of Unqualified Contracts


  C.  Contractor(s) Proposed Price Comparisons


  X.  Contractor(s) Exceptions to Solicitation Comparison


  G.  Government Objective


                                                              H.  Help
  edit   help   back   mark   return   zog   display   user   comment   goto   find
-------------------------------------------------------------------------
```

order to properly carry out the task. Selecting an option takes the user to another frame, which presents the elements that must be addressed in accomplishing the subtask. For example, if the user undertakes the fact-finding subtask, he or she selects "F" and goes to the frame shown in Figure 6.6, which represents the elements considered as part of the fact-finding activity.

Upon completing the associated subtasks, a review-action frame is presented. Figure 6.7 illustrates the frame for calculating the government objective when the user is asked to quantify the effects of the relevant components and provide a final estimate.

6.6.2   Guidance System

As illustrated in the prior discussion, the task support system is intended to guide the user through a series of questions that must be raised in a procurement situation. If the user cannot answer a particular question, the system decomposes the question into less complex questions. If at any point the user does not understand what is required, he or she will be directed to the guidance system, which is a tutorial explaining the necessary concepts and providing examples. Referring back to Figure 6.5, if the user does not understand what is meant by developing a government objective, he or she types "H" for help and is taken to the frame shown in

FIGURE 6.6
FACT FINDING

```
------------------------------------------------------------------------------

  Fact Finding                                                       Procd21

  P. Prior Buys

  F. Field Reports  (PA report, Audit report, Technical report)

  I. Industrial Facilities Provided by the Government

  O. Outside Influence

  T. Time Pressures

  D. Documentation of Fact Finding Activity


                                                                    H. Help
  edit    help    back    mark    return    zog    display    user    comment    goto    find
------------------------------------------------------------------------------
```

FIGURE 6.7
CALCULATING THE GOVERNMENT OBJECTIVE

```
------------------------------------------------------------------------------

  Calculating the Government Objective                               Procd300

  Item Number:
  Option Number:
  Basic Value:  Quality * Unit Price = _____
  Effect of Parameters Identified Below = _____
  Final Estimate = _____
  1. Time Pressure Effect: _____
  2. Outside Influence Effect: _____
  3. Reductions due to Use of Government Facilities: _____
  4. Profit Estimate: _____
  5. Unusual Overheads: _____
  Q. Quantity: _____
  U. Unit Price: _____


                                                                    H. Help
  edit    help    back    mark    return    zog    display    user    comment    goto    find
------------------------------------------------------------------------------
```

Figure 6.8. This is an information-guidance frame. The frame contains an *information* component that provides the user with information relevant to the task or issue being considered and an *option* component that indicates the next task(s) to be considered.

If the user continues in the contract comparison phase (e.g., selects option 2 in Figure 6.8), the frame shown in Figure 6.9 is called. This represents a decision-action frame for which there is an *action* component and a *decision* component in addition to an information and option component. The action component instructs the user to do something: "You must make the determination of the appropriate method of analysis to use on the contract(s) that survived the contract selection phase." The decision component specifies the question: "Which method is appropriate?" In this frame, the option component provides the user with the set of possible answers. If an alternative can be chosen at this point, the user is taken to a review-action frame.

If the user does not know how to choose a method, he or she selects "specify," which beings an explanation of competitive pricing[8] by calling the frame shown in Figure 6.10. This is a decision-option frame in which choosing an option results in a specific decision. If the user can make the decision, he or she is taken to a review-action frame. If not, additional help is available within the guidance system.

[8] This is the sequence specified by USAF guidelines.

FIGURE 6.8
INFORMATION-GUIDANCE FRAME

Price Analysis: Developing an Objective Price   **Pat100**

The goal of price analysis is to determine a "fair and reasonable" price to be used as the government objective. There are three ways to meet this goal:

1. **By developing an independent price for the item(s) to be procured**
2. **By determining a best (or lowest) price as offered by some contractor**
3. **By identifying a small set of offers that can be the basis for requesting a "best and final offer" from contractors**

This development is performed in two phases, described below.

1. **Contract Selection Phase**
2. **Contract Comparison Phase**

S. SPECIFY   E. EXAMPLE   L. LEARN

edit   help   back   mark   return   zog   display   user   comment   goto   find
---

FIGURE 6.9
DECISION-ACTION FRAME

```
-------------------------------------------------------------------------------------------------
Contract Comparison                                                                      Pat29

The second phase of the price analysis task is the contract comparison phase.
You must make the determination of the appropriate method of analysis to use on
the contract(s) that have survived in the contract selection phase.


                        WHICH METHOD IS APPROPRIATE?

1. Competitive pricing

2. Published price

3. Secondary comparisons (prior quotes, CER models, government
   estimates, and value analysis)

4. None Apply


S. SPECIFY          E. EXAMPLE          L. LEARN

edit   help   back   mark   return   zog   display   user   comment   goto   find
-------------------------------------------------------------------------------------------------
```

FIGURE 6.10
DECISION-OPTION FRAME

```
-------------------------------------------------------------------------------------------------
Competitive Pricing                                                                      Pat32

At this point, you must decide upon which method to use to analyze the contract.
If you have a competitive situation, then you simply accept the bid unless the
particular solicitation falls into some exception category.

                   DO YOU HAVE A COMPETITIVE SITUATION?


1. Yes


2. No



S. SPECIFY          E. EXAMPLE          L. LEARN

edit   help   back   mark   return   zog   display   user   comment   goto   find
-------------------------------------------------------------------------------------------------
```

FIGURE 6.11
A REVIEW-ACTION FRAME

```
-------------------------------------------------------------------------

Review Competitive                                                  Pat33

By claiming that a competitive situation exists, you are claiming that:

1.  At least two responsible offerers responded to the solicitation and passed
    the Contract Selection Phase.
2.  The offerers independently contended for the contract.


                    IS THE SITUATION COMPETITIVE?

1.  Continue
2.  Document (not a competitive situation)


S.  SPECIFY         E.  EXAMPLE         L.  LEARN

edit  help  back  next  mark  return  zog  display  user  comment  goto  find
-------------------------------------------------------------------------
```

Figure 6.11 is a review-action frame in which the user is asked to review the decision made in the previous frame. If the decision is confirmed, it is documented and the user is returned to the task support system. If not, the fact that the situation was determined not to be competitive is documented, and the user goes back to the guidance system where help was first requested (in this case, Figure 6.9) and evaluates the next alternative. Figure 6.12 illustrates the structure of the guidance system.

6.6.3 Task Action System

Selections and frames may have associated task actions that activate programs (or other entities) on behalf of the user. These task actions are executed when the frame is displayed or when a selection is made by the user, and they implement the connecting link between the task support system and the task action support system.

The previous example of a ZOG system is not a problem-solving or a problem-analysis system. It presents the underlying model of the domain that would help a user perform the task of price analyst without necessarily having the expertise or the training. However, it also performs another important function — it identifies the questions that an intelligent system must answer and is of use in identifying the information necessary to answer these questions. While some of this information must be obtained

FIGURE 6.12
STRUCTURE OF THE GUIDANCE SYSTEM

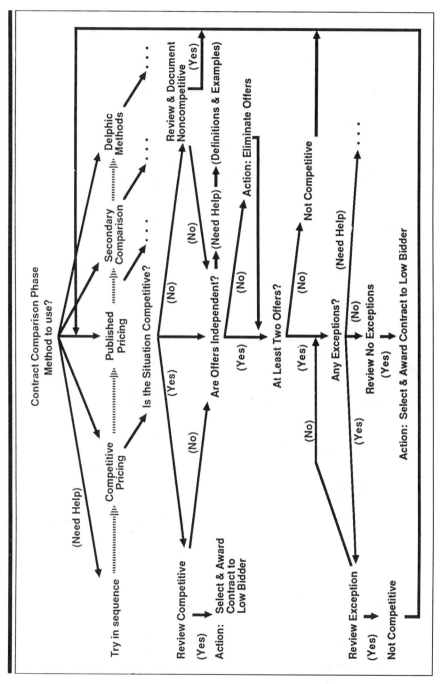

from the contract and some from knowledge of the regional and national economy, other information is unique to the contractor or contractors. All of this knowledge must be accessible to the intelligent manual in an appropriate representation. This requires that the kinds of information be identified and represented in the system.

6.7   CONCLUSION

In this study, AI technology has been applied in constructing a prototype system for price analysis within the government procurement environment. The price analyst's task has been identified using in-depth interviews, protocol analysis, and authoritative government publications. The process is described as a network of decision nodes that lead to the determination of a government price objective. This decision network has been translated into a ZOG-based computer system. The system architecture has four major components:

1. Task support system
2. Guidance system
3. Task action system
4. External interface system

The prototype system has undergone preliminary evaluation by government personnel.

The prototype system is the first stage in designing and building an expert system in this area. The "intelligence" contained in the system is the decision structure and the capability of guiding the user through the process. The next task is to begin to combine the decision nodes such that the system can carry out logical reasoning activities within the domain.

As more serious attempts are made at building and implementing AI systems in accounting and accounting-related areas, evaluation criteria are needed. The following questions have been proposed by Bobrow (1975) in his discussion of representation. They emphasize the need for addressing basic research issues in expert system design.

- How do objects and relationships in the world correspond to the units and relations encoded in the expert system?
- In what ways do the operations in the system correspond to actions in the world?
- How can system knowledge be used in mapping the world state?
- How can information be added to the system without further external input?
- How are units linked to provide access to appropriate knowledge?
- How are two structures compared for equality and similarity?
- What knowledge does a system have to have about its own structure and operation?

This study has established the real-world decision components and processes for the price analysis task and begins the process of translating them into an intelligent computer system. The resulting system illustrates that an intermediate stage in expert system development can yield a system that is useful in its own right.

REFERENCES

Armed Services Procurement Manual for Contract Pricing (ASPM Number 1), U.S. Army, 1975.

Bobrow, D.G. (1975), "Dimensions in Representation," in D.G. Bobrow and A. Collins, eds., *Representation and Understanding*, New York: Academic Press, pp. 1–33.

Chandrasekaran, B., Dillard, J.F., and Ramakrishna, K. (1983), "The Design of an Expert System For Contract Price Analysis," Phase III Technical Report, Department of Computer Science and Information Science, The Ohio State University, September.

Fox, M.S., and Palay, A.J. (1979), "The BROWSE System: An Introduction," in *Proceedings of the Annual Conference*, American Society for Information Science, Minneapolis, Minn., October.

Kunz, J.C., Kehler, T.P., and Williams, M.D., (1984), "Applications Development Using a Hybrid AI Development System," *The AI Magazine*, 5(3):41–54.

Mantei, M., McCracken, D.L. (1979), "Issue Analysis With ZOG, a Highly Interactive Man-Machine Interface," in *First International Symposium On Policy Analysis and Information Systems*, Duke University, Durham, N.C., June.

Mittal, S., Chandrasekaran, B., and Smith, J. (1979), "Overview of MDX—A System For Medical Diagnosis," in *Proceedings of the Third Annual Symposium on Computer Applications in Medical Care*, Washington, D.C.: Computer Applications in Medical Care, October.

Ramakrishna, K. (1981), *Schematization As An Aid To Organising Zog Information Nets*, Ph.D. dissertation, Computer Science Department, Carnegie-Mellon University, August.

Robertson, G., Newell, A., and McCracken, D. (1979), *The ZOG Approach To Man-Machine Communication*, Technical Report, Computer Science Department, Carnegie-Mellon University, October.

Robertson, G., Newell, A., and Ramakrishna, K. (1977), *Zog: A Man-Machine Communication Philosophy*, Technical Report, Computer Science Department, Carnegie-Mellon University, August.

Stephens, R.G., Dillard, J.F., and Bhaskar, R. (1981), "The Role Of Task Analysis In Understanding Problem Solving Behavior," *Instructional Science* 10:23–45.

7

Knowledge-Based Representation of System Acquisition Knowledge

Franz Hatfield
Thomas C. Varley
Dana A. Madalon

Considerable effort has been expended in applying quantitative analysis, in particular the methods of operations research and decision analysis, to the problem of planning acquisition strategies for major defense systems. While these approaches have been useful in developing an understanding of those parts of the problem that are amenable to quantification, they are not particularly useful in addressing the qualitative features of the problem. This chapter discusses some of the qualitative aspects of acquisition planning that should be addressed in designing an expert system for acquisition planning. It then describes features of a knowledge base and inferencing system that were developed to assist the acquisition planner in designing a strategy for the full-scale engineering development phase of a tactical missile.

*This research was partially funded by the Naval Material Command under contract MDA903-83-C-0482.

7.1 INTRODUCTION

The acquisition of major defense systems presents decision-making challenges of almost unimaginable complexity. These systems are usually characterized by high technology, long development times, and substantial investment. Defense officials are faced with the customary management problem of matching competing needs (defense requirements) to available resources (service budgets); however, this match must be made in the presence of unusual levels of uncertainty stemming from numerous factors such as technological immaturity, the prevailing sentiments of the administration and Congress, and changes in the perceived military threat.

Considerable effort has been expended over the years to model various aspects of the acquisition process using quantitative techniques. High-level notional models that depict key events and milestones in the life cycle of a major weapon system have been useful to planners in laying out acquisition strategies for particular systems (Cox and Hullander 1981). Other models have focused on specific aspects of the acquisition process such as the use of competition in procurement (Kratz 1983) or the employment of various contractual mechanisms including incentive contracting (Moore and Cozzolino 1978) and multiyear procurement (Henry, Frazier, and Dolan 1983).

While the approaches of operations research and decision analysis have yielded many significant insights, they have focused largely on elements of the process that are amenable to *quantification* and for the most part have ignored the *qualitative* aspects of the acquisition process.

Many of the factors that must be considered in developing an acquisition strategy are hard to assess in qualitative terms and frequently are not possible at all in quantitative terms. Some of the factors influencing acquisition strategy development include:

- Technological maturity
- Inventory requirements
- Government resources
- Contracting policy
- Political environment
- Urgency of need (schedule)
- Industrial environment
- Cost

Some of the factors that will influence the outcomes arising from acquisition planning in a particular instance are not even known in advance; and of those that are known, the nature and magnitude of their influence are not known with precision. Moreover, the inability to specify with precision the relationship between action (means) and objectives (ends) limits the application of more conventional decision-making paradigms to the acquisition strategy development problem. Differences in the perception of planning problem objectives and the existence of ambiguous domain concepts present two other barriers (see Hatfield and Madalon 1985).

Instead of formal models, there have emerged a number of heuristics (i.e., rules of thumb) that planners use in developing acquisition plans. Although heuristics are used, they are not universally agreed upon. A good case in point is the effect of introducing competition (e.g., through a second production source) into the acquisition process. The benefits of doing so continue to be hotly debated among the experts. Until some kind of consensus is reached, any expert system devised will be seen as inexpert by a large constituency of "experts" if they do not agree on certain basic assumptions and relationships.

In this chapter, we describe an application of expert system technology to the design of a partial strategy for the acquisition of a major weapon system. While the application is highly specific, the human cognitive processes associated with its solution are characteristic of many management planning problems. In Section 7.2 we discuss two key elements of acquisition strategy planning and suggest knowledge representation approaches for certain aspects of the problem. Section 7.3 illustrates how we have begun to represent this knowledge formally, and in the conclusion of this chapter, Section 7.4, we summarize the near-term and far-term benefits, as we see them, that arise from adopting a knowledge-based approach for this kind of application.

7.2   TWO FEATURES OF ACQUISITION STRATEGY PLANNING

Simply put, the purpose of an acquisition strategy is to define a set of acquisition *objectives* and prescribe a *plan* or set of actions for accomplishing those objectives. The limitations of previous analytic approaches and the opportunities afforded through expert system technology can be appreciated by examining acquisition objectives and acquisition plan creation in turn. Characteristics that should be embodied in an expert system for acquisition strategy planning can be gleaned by careful examination of these two elements. The following two sections discuss some of the features of acquisition planning that should be addressed in designing an expert system to aid the acquisition planner.

7.2.1   Acquisition Objectives

Frequently, acquisition objectives are multiple, not stated explicitly, ambiguous, competing, and change with time (often for good reason). Moreover, unlike less complex planning problems in which the planner is often guided by a series of established and readily attainable subgoals, the development of acquisition strategy almost always involves the mediation of competing objectives, values, and preferences across several individuals and/or organizations. The planner needs to use knowledge of the acquisition environment and process to assign importance to the various objectives, possibly order them, or perhaps treat them more as constraints. Traditional algorithmic approaches have failed to capture the richness of this mediation process, as a review of the extensive literature on group and consensus decision making makes evident. For a discussion of the limitations of algorithmic approaches in similar complex decision-making situations, see Tamashiro (1981).

Parallel processing and backtracking are alternative control structures that may be employed to solve problems characterized by multiple and competing objectives. An expert system for acquisition planning might be designed to pursue several objectives (or "goals" in a search space) simultaneously through parallel processing or to pursue one objective at a time, returning, if necessary, to a previous planning step by backtracking. The choice of strategy will depend on the particular planning applications. Both methods require a significant amount of recordkeeping to keep track of the multiple possibilities. In the case of parallel processing, all the ones being tried must be recorded; in the case of backtracking, all the ones not yet tried must be kept track of. However, the number of alternatives that are actually pursued can be significantly pruned when backtracking is guided by knowledge about which alternatives are more likely to prove fruitful. Work in the area of truth maintenance systems (Doyle 1979) is partly motivated by this concern for search efficiency. An expert system should utilize relevant knowledge so that early rejection of possibilities can be realized.

A key aspect of planning, also seen in acquisition strategy planning, is that planners not only reason at many levels of abstraction but move freely between them, that is, as a multidirectional process (Hayes-Roth and Hayes-Roth 1978). Another aspect is that planning is opportunistic. Goals that fit into a developing plan are integrated; related goals are clustered into subplans, similar to island driving (Paxton 1976) in which a problem solver finds part of a solution that is thought to be correct — an "island" — and extends the solution from there by looking at neighboring pieces of increasing size. Islands can represent subplans that can be linked by sequences of planning actions. For example, in planning the acquisition of advanced weaponry, it is often desirable to allow for the incorporation of more advanced technology should that technology become available prior to system fielding. Acquisition alternatives that will allow one to exploit emerging technologies will be kept in mind by the planner and possibly worked into a larger plan even though the apparent objectives emphasize mature technology.

This type of planning, opportunistic and multidirectional, contrasts with least-commitment planning, in which steps are refined only when there is evidence that they will not have to be abandoned later. It also contrasts with pure hierarchical planning (Sacerdoti 1984) in which plans are created in top-down fashion, each level representing a different level of abstraction and detail. In acquisition strategy planning, when it may be impossible to avoid interaction between plan steps and it is desirable to make the solution process transparent, constructive planning without backtracking may not only be impossible but undesirable as well. For example, if the level of system development required exceeds a certain threshold, it may be inadvisable to promise system delivery in less than y years; however, if operational requirements dictate delivery in x years where x is less than y, then x years must be considered as a constraint, thus throwing out the tentative constraint of y years, and some other means of mitigating technical risk must be devised. Neither least-commitment nor hierarchical planning alone would be adequate in addressing this sort of problem.

7.2.2 Acquisition Plan

From the perspective of the acquisition planner, the "slipperiness" of objectives may not be the major source of difficulty in formulating an acquisition strategy. Frequently of more importance is the fact that there is only a limited understanding of how a particular strategy will contribute to a set of acquisition objectives. For example, suppose your task is to develop a plan for traveling from San Francisco to Boston by road. Given a roadmap, the task would be easy because the set of existing roads establishes a clear connection between where you are and where you would like to go. This serves as the basis for laying out a precise strategy. However, without a roadmap and without the ability to recall the sequence of roads from memory, you would have difficulty performing your assignment.

An acquisition strategy can be viewed as a roadmap, but it is not always certain how the various milestones in the plan (i.e., cities on the map) are or should be connected because the relationship between ends and means is not always clear. In other words, there is not a good causal theory underlying some aspects of the acquisition process; whenever some evidence is uncovered that supports a cause-effect relationship, other evidence of a disconfirming nature frequently follows shortly thereafter. For example, the extent to which cost-incentive contracting leads to lower total acquisition costs remains unresolved (Kratz and Hatfield 1985).

It is perhaps not unusual for planners to be faced with various, perhaps quite dissimilar options that may or may not lend themselves to an easily established preference ordering. Sage and White (1984) have argued that people are able to evaluate alternative plans efficiently and effectively when a clear dominance pattern exists among alternatives. In searching for such a pattern, humans often employ a number of heuristics, including selective perception, perhaps ignoring information that, if explicitly considered, would preclude establishing a clear dominance structure. While this behavior may contribute to ease of plan selection, it may not result in choosing the best plan. An expert system could be effectively used to mitigate the deleterious effects of these heuristics by making very explicit the precise information and logic that is employed in deriving a particular plan.

An understanding of how specific actions will contribute to the accomplishment of one or more acquisition objectives is essential to the implementation of means-end analysis in an expert system. Means-end analysis seeks to reduce the difference between the current state of the problem and the goal state or solution, thereby ruling out directionless expansion of possible solutions. Means-ends analysis guides the generation of states in the problem space (Newell and Simon 1972). One drawback to the application of means-ends analysis in the context of acquisition strategy planning is that it can be inefficient when there are interacting subgoals, particularly if accomplishing one subgoal *precludes* accomplishing another. (Refer to the discussion on system development and delivery time given at the end of section 7.3.) The planner must then backtrack to the beginning of the problem to try subgoals in a different order. However, if the backtracking is dependency directed—that is, the inferential steps taken by a reasoning program are recorded using dependency records to link conclusions with the reasons behind them— then greater insight into the planning problem may result. Thus means-ends analysis, incorporated with the capability to provide a clear audit trail of the inferencing process and the logic behind the heuristics employed, would be desirable in an acquisition planning expert system. The acquisition expert system discussed in the next section, while it does not explicitly use means-end analysis to generate planning "states," does feature an audit trail capability.

The design of an acquisition strategy requires solution of a number of highly interacting and interdependent subproblems. When subproblems and respective subgoals are highly interactive, it is difficult to represent the knowledge required for their solution in a modular form (Simon 1969). Fodor (1983) has argued that most higher-level human problem-solving processes are nonmodular in nature. The success of many expert system applications has been due to the applicability of the linear assumption heuristic to the problem domain (Sussman 1973). The assumption is that subgoals are independent and thus can be sequentially achieved in an arbitrary order. However, in the case of acquisition strategy planning, the lack of modularity necessitates taking a more complex approach. Expert system developers have dealt with the problem of linear ordering of subproblems in various ways including: destructive reordering (see Sussman's [1975] HACKER planning system and Tate's [1975] INTERPLAN); constructive goal-regression (Waldinger 1977); and layering, which may have promise in representing acquisition strategy planning.

The lack of modularity in acquisition strategy development is reflected in Figure 7.1, which depicts a partial hierarchy of subproblems that must be solved in designing an acquisition strategy for the full-scale

FIGURE 7.1
SUBPROBLEMS IN DESIGNING AN FSED-PHASE ACQUISITION STRATEGY

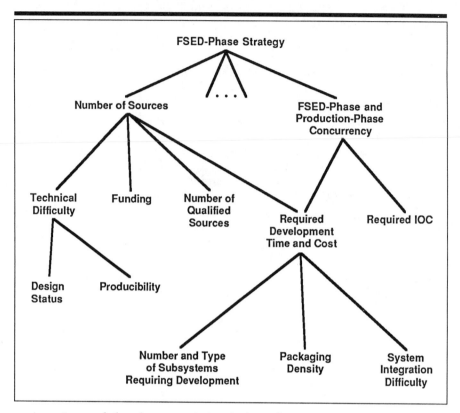

engineering and development (FSED) phase.* Two key subproblems are the number of sources (i.e., potential system producers) to carry through FSED and the degree of overlap (concurrency) between the production and FSED phases. The solution to the problem of determining the number of sources depends on the technical difficulty anticipated. This, in turn, is a function of: (1) the system design maturity and the ease with which the system can be produced in a manufacturing environment (in this regard, a second source might provide a hedge against the failure of the first source); (2) the level of funding available (multiple sources in FSED simply cost more than a single source, although there is some evidence to suggest that savings accrue in the following production and deployment phases of the acquisition cycle if multiple sources are used in FSED); (3) the anticipated FSED phase cost for a single source or multiple sources; and (4) the number of sources available that could realistically be expected to successfully produce the system.

*There are typically five phases in the acquisition of a major weapons system: concept exploration, demonstration and validation of concepts, full-scale engineering and development, production, and deployment.

The other major subproblem depicted in Figure 7.1 is the determination of FSED-phase and production-phase overlap. The solution to this subproblem depends on the anticipated development time that is determined essentially by the amount of work to be done and the time available before the first systems must be operational, that is, the initial operational capability (IOC) date.

The interaction and hence, the lack of modularity between the two subproblems depicted in Figure 7.1 occurs because more concurrency is generally assumed to incur greater development risk (which argues for multiple sources), but the greater development risk generally argues for less concurrency. A balance between development time and development risk must be achieved, and this is one area for which no successful algorithms exist. Another area of interaction is that the number of sources and the degree of concurrency both depend on the required development time and cost.

It may be possible to use a method similar to that developed by Hayes-Roth and Hayes-Roth (1978) in handling the complexity of acquisition planning that results from the lack of modularity. This method is to utilize a central blackboard upon which multiple experts or knowledge sources can interact. To accommodate the various factions that input and generate tentative decisions into the acquisition planning process (e.g., levels of management in the acquiring service, the Office of the Secretary of Defense, etc.), each knowledge source produces hypothetical plans or subplans that are posted on the blackboard in no particular order (i.e., asynchronously), as is typical of the way management planning occurs. The idea is to have knowledge sources viewed as independent modules of expertise, cooperatively solving a problem by posting hypotheses on a global data structure. The data structure, a blackboard, is accessed by all the knowledge sources through an established protocol. Since this technique creates a modular data structure, the knowledge sources need not address each other directly.

Layers could then be used to represent the overall planning process as depicted in Figure 7.2. A level representing the operational plan contains alternative plans and goals, while a meta-plan level is needed to capture a lot of the reasoning done before any tentative planning decisions are made. This level is necessary because it is possible for more than one acquisition planning strategy to be acceptable. A plan abstraction, useful for organizing all the elements of an operational plan, could be represented on another level as could the knowledge base. Execution plans, which schedule the planning decisions, would fill a final layer.

7.3   REPRESENTATION OF ACQUISITION KNOWLEDGE

A demonstration acquisition expert system (AES) was developed to test the usefulness of applying a knowledge-based approach to the problem of

FIGURE 7.2
DEPICTION OF THE ACQUISITION PLANNING PROCESS USING A BLACKBOARD AND
LAYERING APPROACH

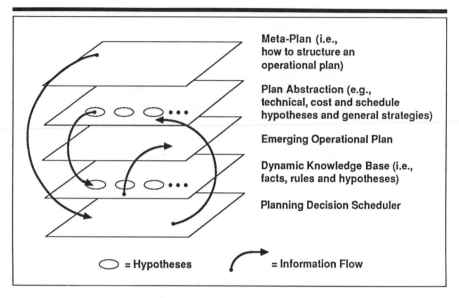

Meta-Plan (i.e.,
how to structure an
operational plan)

Plan Abstraction (e.g.,
technical, cost and schedule
hypotheses and general strategies)

Emerging Operational Plan

Dynamic Knowledge Base (i.e.,
facts, rules and hypotheses)

Planning Decision Scheduler

◯ = Hypotheses   = Information Flow

acquisition strategy development. While the resultant system does not
adequately address all the characteristics of acquisition planning described
in Section 7.2, it represents a first attempt to apply AI concepts to this
very complex problem domain. In its present state of development, AES
addresses principally the FSED phase of a tactical missile development.

The knowledge representation scheme used in AES consists of: a set
of frames with frame-slot-facet-value access paths; a set of production
rules; and forward and backward-chained, deductive inferencing processes (details are given in Hatfield 1985). Table 7.1 lists the nine key frames
comprising the frame system, and Figure 7.3 gives the slots, possible slot
values, and slot explanations for two frames — the FSED-PHASE and SYS-
TEM frames. Slots can be filled by the user as user-entered data or by the
system as inferred results. For example, the first six slots of the FSED-
PHASE frame are "derived by the system," and their possible values are
shown; the next two are intended to be filled by the user; and the last two
are filled by the system.

AES allows frame inheritance. For example, both the FSED-PHASE
and PROD-PHASE frames inherit default values from a generic ACQ-
PHASE frame. Demons are also implemented in AES. For example, the IF-
ADDED facet (not shown in Figure 7.3) of the NUMERICAL-RISK slot of
the SYSTEM frame activates functions to compute development cost and
development time.

Production rules are expressed in conjunctive-normal form,
whereby all the antecedent clauses (if-statements) must be satisfied be-

TABLE 7.1
ACQUISITION EXPERT SYSTEM FRAMES

Frame	Description of contents
PROGRAM	Program characteristics (e.g., production start date)
SYSTEM	Basic system characteristics (e.g., system type, operational concept, system users, and degree of technical challenge)
SUBSYS-DEVELOP	Information pertaining to the amount of development work required on the various subsystems
SYS-DEVELOP	Information pertaining to the current development status of the system as a whole (e.g., prototype, trade studies), and packaging and producibility issues
INDUST-BASE	Information pertaining to the industrial base (e.g., the number of qualified sources and industry experience)
POLIT-ENVIRON	Information pertaining to the political environment that might influence acquisition strategy development
FSED-PHASE	Programmatic, funding, schedule, and strategy information pertaining to the FSED phase
PROD-PHASE	Programmatic, funding, schedule, and strategy information pertaining to the production phase
COMPUTE-RISK	Used by the system to heuristically generate a numerical risk estimate

fore the conclusion (then-statement) is instantiated. Each clause in a rule consists of an object-attribute-value triple corresponding to a specified frame-slot-value access path. For example:

> If the FSED-phase objective is to start production as soon as possible,
> and the system technical challenge (complexity) is low,
> and the system concept is well established,
> then a concurrent strategy is acceptable

is encoded as:

> IF (FSED-PHASE OBJECTIVE START-PROD-ASAP)
> AND (SYSTEM TECH-CHALLENGE LOW)
> AND (SYSTEM CONCEPT ESTABLISHED)
> THEN (FSED-PHASE ACCEPT-ALTS CONCURRENT).

Figure 7.4 gives several other examples of existing rules and their explanations.

Statistical models are used in AES as well as frame and production rule formalisms. Different statistical models are used depending on whether the development constitutes a new design or a modification to an old design. System development cost is expressed using cost-estimating relationships (CERs), which relate cost to a heuristically derived measure of development risk. This measure is based on the amount of development work required across all the subsystems, the degree of

FIGURE 7.3
FRAME EXAMPLE

Frame: FSED-Phase	

Slot:	**Accept-Alts**
Possible Values: (Derived By The System) Concurrent End-to-end	
Explanation:	This slot, which lists acceptable alternatives, is normally filled by the program.

Slot:	**Inappr-Alts**
Possible Values: (Derived By The System) Concurrent End-to-end	
Explanation:	This slot is normally filled by the program.

Slot:	**Sources-desired**
Possible Values: (Derived By The System) Concurrent End-to-end	
Explanation:	This slot is normally filled by the program.

Slot:	**Sources-desired**
Possible Values: (Derived By The System) Single Multiple	
Explanation:	This slot is normally filled by the program based on risk characteristics of the system and program phase objectives. It does not reflect what is fiscally possible. See the SOURCES-AFFORD slot in this frame for the latter, system-derived information.

Slot:	**Sources-afford**
Possible Values: (Derived By The System) Single Multiple	
Explanation:	This slot is filled by the program based on an algorithm that compares the values in the AVAIL-DOLLARS slot and the DEVELOP-COST slot of this frame. If AVAIL-DOLLARS is at least 175% of DEVELOP-COST, then multiple sources are considered affordable.

Slot:	**Reqd-concurr**
Possible Values: (Derived By The System) Specified In Terms Of Months Of FSED-PHASE And Production-PHASE Overlap	
Explanation:	This slot is filled by the program based on an algorithm that compares the value placed in the PROD-START slot of the PROGRAM frame to the DEVELOP-TIME slot of this frame. If the DEVELOP-TIME is less than the PROD-START value, then no concurrency is required; otherwise, the amount of required overlap is computed as the value of Y where,

$$Y = \text{DEVELOP-TIME} - \text{PROD-START}$$

Slot:	Objective
Possible Values:	ENHANCE-MANTECH MIN-PROD-COST ENHANCE-SYS-RELIAB REACH-IOC-ASAP ENHANCE-INDUST-BASE ENHANCE-MULT-SOURCE-OPPO MIN-DEVELOP-COST MIN-TOTAL-COST OBTAIN-QUALITY-TDP REDUCE-DESIGN-RISK START-PROD-ASAP
Explanation:	This slot contains the major objectives set in each phase. While there may be several objectives to be achieved in a phase, it is best to enter the one or two most important at first, review the results generated, and then revise the objective list.

Slot:	Avail-dollars
Possible Values:	Specify In Millions Of 1980 Dollars
Explanation:	This slot contains the level of funding anticipated for the specific phase.

Slot:	Develop-time
Possible Values:	(Derived By The System) Specified In Terms Of Months
Explanation:	The system derives this result based upon the value assigned to the NUMERICAL-RISK slot in the SYSTEM frame. The number of months is computed according to the equation:

$$MONTHS = a \ (NUMERICAL\text{-}RISK) + b$$

Slot:	Develop-cost
Possible Values:	(Derived By The System) Specified In 1980 Dollars
Explanation:	The system derives this result based upon the value assigned to the NUMERICAL-RISK slot in the SYSTEM frame. The cost is computed according to the equation:

$$COST = a \ (NUMERICAL\text{-}RISK) + b$$

FIGURE 7.3 (Cont.)

Frame: System	
Slot:	Type
Possible Values:	Missiles
Explanation:	This slot contains information as to the type of weapon system to be developed and produced. The current knowledge base only contains information on tactical missiles.
Slot:	New-or-mod
Possible Values:	New Mod
Explanation:	Enter MOD if the system is a modification to an earlier system; otherwise, enter NEW. The default value is NEW.
Slot:	Concept
Possible Values:	Established Not-Firm
Explanation:	This slot contains information on how well the operational concept has been defined and accepted by the Service, OSD, the Congress, and other factions.
Slot:	Tech-challenge
Possible Values:	(Derived By The System) High Moderate Low
Explanation:	This slot is normally filled by the program based on slots in the SYS-DEVELOP frame.
Slot:	Numerical-risk
Possible Values:	(Derived By The System) Value Applies To Last Inferencing Run
Explanation:	The value in this slot is computed on the basis of the development work required in each of the subsystems (as entered by the user in the SUBSYS-DEVELOP frame) and a series of rules that map the qualitative description of required subsystem development into a risk index ranging from 1 to 9. A system with a numerical risk greater than 5 probably should not enter FSED and one greater than 3 should not enter production.
Slot:	Developers
Possible Values:	US-firm Foreign-firm
Explanation:	Enter here the nationality of the developing firm—foreign or U.S.
Slot:	Users
Possible Values:	US-forces For-forces US-and-for
Explanation:	This slot contains information on the services, both U.S. and foreign, that use the system.

FIGURE 7.4
EXAMPLES OF AES RULES

(RULE G00009
    (IF (INDUST-BASE NUMBER-SOURCES SINGLE-US)
      (SYSTEM CONCEPT ESTABLISHED)
      (PROD-PHASE OBJECTIVE MIN-PROD-COST))
    (THEN (PROD-PHASE ACCEPT-ALTS MULTIYEAR)))

EXPLANATION: When no other production source exists to provide cost competition, cost may be reduced by negotiating a multiyear contract. There is incentive for the producer to offer a lower price based on economies of scale (e.g., large lot material purchases) and a longer, more stable production period.

(RULE G00106
    (IF (SYS-DEVELOP PRODUCIBILITY NO-SIGNIF-ISSUES)
      (SYS-DEVELOᴰ STATUS FULL-SYS-PROTO))
    (THEN (SYSTEM TECH-CHALLENGE LOW)))

EXPLANATION: When production technology has already been developed and full system prototyping has been accomplished (i.e., packaging issues have been solved), the bulk of the technical challenge has been eliminated.

(RULE G00111
    (IF (FSED-PHASE SOURCES-DESIRED SINGLE)
      (SYSTEM TECH-CHALLENGE HIGH))
    (THEN (PROD-PHASE ACCEPT-ALTS LEADER-FOLLOWER)))

EXPLANATION: If only one source is desired (or mandated) through FSED and the technical challenge is high, but competition in production is desired, a leader-follower arrangement may be acceptable if the production quantity is sufficiently high.

miniaturization of components, and the extent of system integration required. Figure 7.5 depicts the logic involved in developing this numeric, but heuristically derived, measure of development risk. The rule numbers are indicated above each decision node. A similar approach is used to estimate development time.

AES employs a forward and backward-chained, deductive inferencing similar to that given in Winston and Horn (1981). The inferencing procedure is relatively straightforward and effective. After the user enters all known data by sequentially accessing all the frames, the system creates a list of facts (in object-attribute-value triples). These facts are then sequentially tested to determine if new conclusions can be instantiated; if so, these new facts are added to the fact list. After the first pass through the fact list, the process is iterated until no new conclusions can be instantiated. AES then adds all the new facts to the relevant frames where the user can inspect the results of the inferencing process. The system also

FIGURE 7.5
NUMERICAL-RISK VALUE COMPUTATION LOGIC

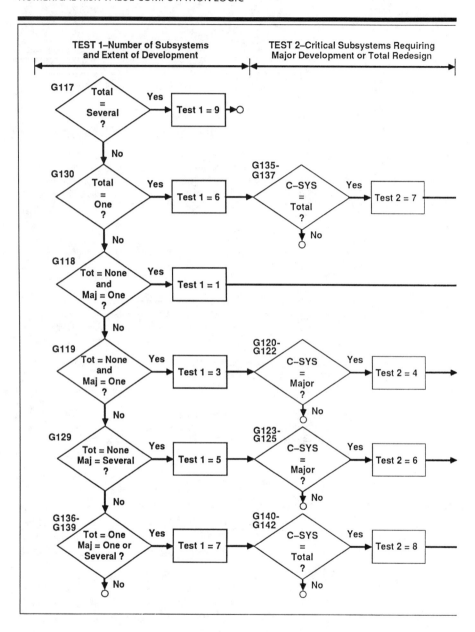

154

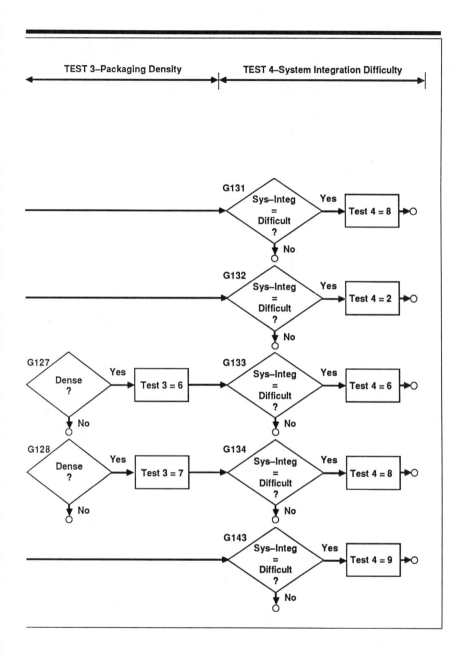

produces a listing of conclusions and an audit trail to give the user insight into the rationale of the system. Backward-chained inferencing is implemented in a straightforward fashion. The user specifies one or more hypotheses in the form of object-attribute-value triples, and the inference engine looks for facts or other rules to support the specified hypotheses. The inference engine employs standard recursion to search through the rule base to obtain other rules to instantiate the hypotheses and, if all else fails, queries the user for needed facts.

Figure 7.6 gives partial results from a sample session with AES. In Part A of Figure 7.6, the results of the forward-chained inferencing are given; Part B illustrates the audit trail results. Note that the first two rules have a frame-slot access path of COMPUTE-RISK TESTX. These relate to the numerical-risk computation. As shown in Figure 7.5 previously, there are four separate tests that are used to heuristically derive a numerical index of development risk. The final value assigned to the NUMERICAL-RISK slot, achieved by TEST2 since TEST3 and TEST4 did not revise TEST2's result, is "4." This is used to generate the values for the DEVELOP-COST and DEVELOP-TIME slots using the estimating relationships discussed previously.

Another interesting and insightful feature of AES is its ability to highlight potential conflict. Figures 7.7 and 7.8 depict two lines of reasoning. The first has led the system to conclude that concurrent development and production phases are required. The second line of reasoning has led to the conclusion that a concurrent strategy is *not* appropriate due to the acquisition-phase objective and the perceived high risk associated with the development effort. The resolution of this conflicting advice is either to allow the initial operational capability (IOC) date to slip beyond 40 months or to suffer the consequences of a poor technical data package (i.e., run into producibility problems later on). In the present acquisition example, the explicit representation of this conflict is specifically desired since it fundamentally shows that there is no workable solution to the problem as it currently stands. However, it does show the explicit tradeoff that must be made. This example illustrates that AES does not have an explicit conflict resolution strategy and that in some instances (notably non-real-time applications) this is a desirable property for an expert system to have, particularly one that is performing a management planning function.

7.4 CONCLUSION

As we see them, the key near-term benefits afforded by expert system technology in enhancing our understanding of acquisition planning are the explicit representation of problem assumptions and the inferential process plus the explicit statement of acquisition objectives. The representation of the inferential process is especially important when the re-

FIGURE 7.6
AES OUTPUT

CONCLUSIONS

RULE G00119 DEDUCES – – –
      (COMPUTE-RISK TEST1 3)

RULE G00121 DEDUCES – – –
      (COMPUTE-RISK TEST2 4)

RULE G00106 DEDUCES – – –
      (SYSTEM TECH-CHALLENGE LOW)

RULE G00049 DEDUCES – – –
      (FSED-PHASE ACCEPT-ALTS CONCURRENT)

RULE G00029 DEDUCES – – –
      (FSED-PHASE SOURCES-DESIRED MULTIPLE)

A. Example Inferencing Results

AUDIT TRAIL

(FSED-PHASE SOURCES-DESIRED MULTIPLE) – – –DEMONSTRATED BY:
(INDUST-BASE NUMBER-SOURCES SINGLE-US)
(FSED-PHASE OBJECTIVE ENHANCE-MULT-SOURCE-OPPO)

(FSED-PHASE ACCEPT-ALTS CONCURRENT) – – – DEMONSTRATED BY:
(SYSTEM CONCEPT ESTABLISHED)
(SYSTEM TECH-CHALLENGE LOW)

(SYSTEM TECH-CHALLENGE LOW) – – –DEMONSTRATED BY:
(SYS-DEVELOP PRODUCIBILITY NO-SIGNIF-ISSUES)
(SYS-DEVELOP STATUS FULL-SYS-PROTO)

(COMPUTE-RISK TEST2 4) – – –DEMONSTRATED BY:
(SUBSYS-DEVELOP GUIDANCE MAJOR)
(COMPUTE-RISK TEST1 3)

(COMPUTE-RISK TEST1 3) – – –DEMONSTRATED BY:
(COMPUTE-RISK SUBS-TOTAL NONE)
(COMPUTE-RISK SUBS-MAJOR ONE)

B. Example Audit Trail Results

---

lationship between ends and means is unclear, as previously discussed. The representation of a set of planning objectives and the ways in which they might conflict is critical if there are multiple and competing objectives present.

In the future, expert system technology may also contribute to acquisition understanding in a much more powerful role. There is merit in committing to memory (whether human or machine memory) the kinds of tradeoffs faced by experts and the solutions determined. If solutions are

FIGURE 7.7
LOGIC LEADING TO CONCURENCY RECOMMENDATION

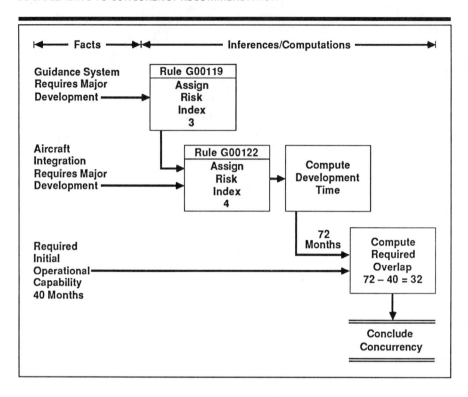

FIGURE 7.8
LOGIC LEADING TO NONCONCURRENCY RECOMMENDATION

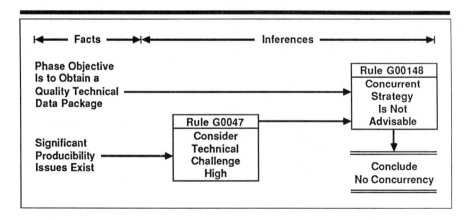

unworkable, they must at some point be corrected or their associated plans will presumably fail. The truly advanced expert system could react to a failed plan by associating that plan with the problem's parameters, noting the failure, and developing a causal theory underlying the failure. If we also commit to memory the correct solution, then presumably we have learned something. A future expert system could maintain a historical record of problem characteristics and solutions with the ultimate goal of generating a more general representation (i.e., a new rule, based upon numerous, similar experiences). Some of these solutions would be judged workable or unworkable in light of subsequent experience; some unworkable solutions, if "recognized" as such in time, would never have the chance of being vindicated in actual experience — they would just be unworkable in the eyes of the relevant experts. An expert system imbued with the capability to examine this historical record and essentially learn from it would truly satisfy a key objective of artificial intelligence research, that is, the extension of human knowledge. We recognize that this is still several years away.

It is highly unlikely that expert systems technology will ever replace strategic planners, not only because of the complexity of the management planning process itself but also because of the reluctance of top management to delegate this function to a machine. Indeed, the goal of developing the application discussed in this chapter was not to replace acquisition strategists but to begin to formalize some of the principles that have been guiding acquisition strategy planning over the past 30 years or so. There could be large economic benefits resulting from this research — better problem understanding should lead to better acquisition planning, which would mean better national defense for less. However, the means to accomplish this is not so much to develop a program that captures human expertise as it now exists, but to enhance problem understanding and create new knowledge through use of the technology itself.

REFERENCES

Cox, L.W., and Hullander, R.A. (1981), "Feasibility and Development Study for a System Acquisition Strategy Model," Technical Report TR-1375, Arlington, Va.: The Analytic Sciences Corporation.

Doyle, J. (1979), "A Truth Maintenance System," *Artificial Intelligence*, Vol. 24.

Fodor, J.A. (1983), *The Modularity of Mind*, Cambridge, Mass.: MIT Press.

Hatfield, F. (1985), *Acquisition Expert System (AES) Tutorial*, Technical Report TR-5031-1, Arlington, Va.: The Analytic Sciences Corporation.

Hatfield, F., and Madalon, D.A. (1985), "Heuristics and Algorithms — Why an Artificial Intelligence Approach Can Be Useful in Analyzing Acquisition Management Problems," *Proceedings of the 1985 Federal Acquisition Research Symposium*, Defense Systems Management College, Fort Belvoir, Va.

Hayes-Roth, B. (1980), "Human Planning Processes," Report No. R-2670–ONR, Santa Monica, Calif.: Rand Corp.

Hayes-Roth, B., and Hayes-Roth, F. (1978), "Cognitive Processes in Planning," Report No. R-2366, ONR–Santa Monica, Calif.: Rand Corp.

Henry, F.J., Frazier, T.P., and Dolan, M. (1983), "Analysis of Cancellation and Termination Aspects of Multiyear Procurement," Technical Report, Bethesda, Md.: Booz-Allen and Hamilton, Inc.

Kratz, L.A. (1983), "Dual Source Procurement: An Empirical Investigation," EM-223-WA, Arlington, Va.: The Analytic Sciences Corporation.

Kratz, L.A., and Hatfield, F. (1985), "Analysis of SDI Cost Reduction Initiatives—Interim Report," Technical Report TR-4614-6-1, Arlington, Va: The Analytic Sciences Corporation, pp. 2–6.

Moore, W.F., and Cozzolino, J.M. (1978), "More Effective Cost Incentive Contracts Through Risk Reduction," *Defense Management Journal*, July, pp. 12–17.

Newell, A., and Simon, H.A. (1972), *Human Problem Solving*, Englewood Cliffs, N.J.: Prentice-Hall.

Paxton, W.H. (1976), "A Framework for Language Understanding," SRI Technical Note 131, Menlo Park, Calif.: AI Center, SRI International, Inc.

Sacerdoti, E.D. (1974), "Planning in a Hierarchy of Abstraction Spaces," *Artificial Intelligence*, 5(2): pp. 115–135.

Sage, A.P., and White, C.C. (1984), "Ariadne: A Knowledge Based Interactive System for Planning and Decision Support," *IEEE Transactions on Systems Man and Cybernetics*, 14(1): January/February.

Simon, H. (1969), *The Science of the Artificial*, Cambridge, Mass.: MIT Press.

Sussman, G.J. (1973), "A Computational Model of Skill Acquisition," AI Technical Report 297, Cambridge, Mass.: AI Laboratory, MIT.

Tamashiro, H.Y. (1981), *Problem Solving Heuristics in International Politics*, Ph.D. dissertation, The Ohio State University, Columbus, OH.

Tate, A. (1975), "Interacting Goals and Their Use," *Proceedings IJCAI 4*.

Waldinger, R. (1977), "Achieving Several Goals Simultaneously," in E.W. Elcock and D. Michie, eds., *Machine Intelligence, 8*, New York: Halstead/Wiley.

Winston, P.H. (1977), *Artificial Intelligence*, Reading, Mass.: Addison-Wesley.

Winston, P.H., and Horn, B.K.P. (1981), *LISP*, Reading, Mass.: Addison-Wesley.

EXPERT SYSTEMS

By contrast to the preceding section of this book, the authors in Part III uniformly seem to feel their expert systems hold potential to actually replace human supervisors and managers at various tasks and jobs. There are several possible explanations for this difference, a few of which might be:

1. *Smallness of the Sample* — The difference might simply be an entirely arbitrary one. There are almost certainly ES practitioners in accounting and procurement attempting to replace personnel, while other AI practitioners in operations management probably exist who are only attempting expert support systems.

2. *Different Types of Topics Addressed* — There is potentially an inclination in the accounting and procurement chapters of Part II to focus on economic factors, market forces, and/or legal variables, all of which tend to be highly dynamic and/or fairly difficult to structure and define. The operations management chapters in Part III focus somewhat more, although not totally, upon engineering considerations that exhibit recurring patterns and behaviors.

3. *Historical Differences by Field*—The auditing, accounting, and procurement fields have tended to gravitate toward management information systems as their principal form of automation. The logical extension of this trend is an expert support system. Operations, on the other hand, historically relied more heavily on operations research methods, algorithmic techniques, and automatic control software. ES practitioners in operations management might very well tend to see ES technology as the final answer to overcoming the automation obstacles previously encountered.

4. *Cognitive Modeling and Understanding*—Chapter 9, and to some extent Chapter 3 in Part I, base the potential to replace humans on the fact that the practitioners are attempting to model how the humans think. Thus cognitive modeling is used as a design guide for the AI/ES effort. The subject of cognitive modeling is addressed here and is more fully explored in Part V of this book.

Whatever your opinion on the ability to actually replace operations management or supervisory personnel, the two chapters offer an interesting array of knowledge-engineering techniques. Even though the three authors of these two chapters discuss expert systems, they differ in the precise types of expert knowledge acquisition, representations, and inferencing techniques being exploited. In particular,

1. Chapter 8 explores operations or production planning using an exclusively rule-based technique. Rule-based representation is felt to be sufficient, and an off-the-shelf inference engine is utilized.

2. Chapter 9 examines the traditional resource allocation problem using military resources as the example domain. A working expert system is described that makes optimal resource allocation decisions. (The reader will hopefully not view this chapter as a commentary on the internal warfare in the operation divisions of many organizations). This chapter explains a custom-designed inference engine that makes use of computation networks, resource allocation trees, and heuristic values to direct search, traversal, and pruning of the tree so as to select the best allocation path. The authors utilize a case-oriented, rule-induction approach for developing their knowledge base, and they devote a substantial amount of space to evaluating how well the individual heuristics and rules work for the cases addressed.

As different as these approaches are they still only reflect a relatively small portion of the AI/ES tool kit. The ES field has yet to determine which techniques for acquisition, representation, or inferencing are precisely correct for any given application. However, the careful reader may be able to cull several insights from the differences encountered in these chapters.

8

The Conceptual Design for a Knowledge-Based System as Applied to the Production Planning Process

Peter Duchessi

This chapter describes the conceptual design for a knowledge-based system as applied to the production planning problem. The system searches a state-space composed of partial production plans to arrive at a feasible final production plan. Production rules are used to solve the problem. The rules establish decision variable values and guide the search process.

8.1 INTRODUCTION

In recent years, expert systems or knowledge-based systems have become the fastest growing branch of artificial intelligence. These programs employ an expert's knowledge to simulate human consulting and problem solving in a specialized domain. They are intended to improve human performance and to transfer knowledge to end users in the same domain. Expert systems have been developed for a number of diverse applications (Ennis 1983; Hayes-Roth, Waterman, and Lenat 1983; Michaelsen and Michie 1983; Nau 1983; Rich 1983; and Webster and Miner 1982).

As research on developing and implementing knowledge-based systems progresses, management and research staffs are beginning to apply this technology to improve manufacturing operations. Bourne and Fox (1984) describe how a rule-based approach can be used to enhance the automation of process planning. They indicate that much of the knowledge relating part descriptions to manufacturing operations may be represented as IF-THEN production rules. GARI is an expert system that plans a sequence of processing steps for machining mechanical parts (Descotte and Latcombe 1981). The system utilizes the production rule formalism for representing the knowledge required to generate machining plans. An explicit control strategy is used to resolve conflicting advice about processing steps.

Another system, ISIS, creates job-shop schedules (Bourne and Fox 1984; Fox 1983; and Fox et al. 1983). Because the scheduling task involves the consideration of constraints, such as availability of shared resources, much of ISIS's knowledge takes the form of constraints on schedule generation. The constraints reduce the solution space of partial schedules and guide the search process.

The result of this activity has been the development of methods for representing solution spaces, acquiring and structuring knowledge, and applying this knowledge to complex tasks in several production settings. Knowledge-based technology has been applied primarily to short-term planning and control of production activity on the shop floor. These systems address manufacturing and scheduling issues that are close to the production units of a factory. However, this chapter discusses concepts and techniques of knowledge engineering as they relate to the complex problem of production planning often termed aggregate production planning. These concepts and techniques are essential for applying knowledge-based technology at the top (production plan) end of a production planning system, rather than at the bottom (detailed schedules) end.

Elements integral to a knowledge-based system for aggregate production planning are depicted in Figure 8.1. They are data base, knowledge base, and inference engine. As input, a production planner would provide a forecast of marketing requirements for a given planning horizon and certain initial conditions including (1) beginning inventory and (2)

FIGURE 8.1
ELEMENTS OF A KNOWLEDGE-BASED SYSTEM FOR AGGREGATE PRODUCTION PLANNING

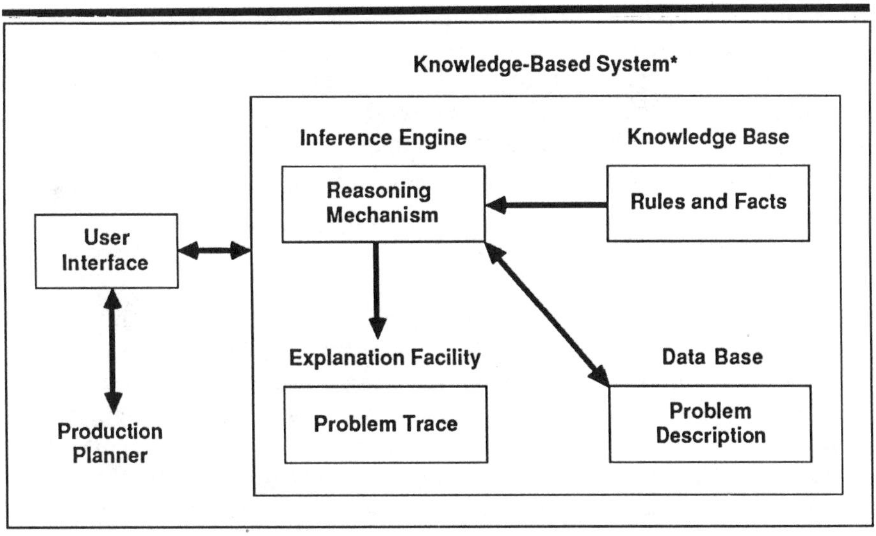

*Arrows indicate flow of knowledge during operation.

work force and production levels for the most recent period. The inference engine of the system uses rules and facts about production planning stored in the knowledge base to solve a particular planning problem described in the data base. The output is a production plan that satisfies the marketing requirements while staying within constraints that influence the plan. For each period of the planning horizon, the plan would provide production rates, work force requirements, inventory levels, overtime days, and values for other important decision variables. Moreover, a user interface assists in communicating with the system, and an explanation facility explains the logic used to obtain a final solution. These basic elements are used here to develop a knowledge-based system for a simple production planning problem for illustrative purposes. In addition, they may be used to develop larger systems for actual problems.

The following section provides an overview of the production planning problem and examines some of the issues involved in creating production plans. Moreover, it reviews some conventional techniques suggested for creating aggregate production plans. Next, an example production planning problem is presented followed by a description of an alternate approach to production planning that uses knowledge-based techniques. The example problem is intended to provide practical information for applying knowledge-based techniques to actual production planning problems. Finally, comments on the implication of this research are provided.

8.2 AGGREGATE PRODUCTION PLANNING

Aggregate production planning is the process of establishing production rates for individual products or broad product groups by time periods of usually a month for an extended planning horizon of six months or longer. A broad objective is to satisfy demand for each period without violating certain financial, policy, and production capacity constraints of the organization. More specific objectives include:

- Maintain a specified level of employment while minimizing labor costs
- Maintain a specified level of inventory while minimizing inventory costs.

The decision variables are interrelated. For example, maintaining a high rate of production increases production efficiency but also increases inventory investment. Thus, when selecting appropriate combinations of production rates, work force levels, and inventory levels to respond to demand, a production planner is faced with a number of tradeoffs in attempting to optimize the total system performance. Normally, system performance is measured by the costs associated with production, inventory, and work force.

A number of pure strategies may be employed to meet aggregate demand. These include:

- Varying the work force size by hiring and laying off employees as demand fluctuates
- Maintaining a stable work force but varying output through overtime and short time
- Maintaining a stable work force and allowing inventory to absorb fluctuations in demand

A mixed strategy, that is, a combination of several pure strategies, may also be used to absorb demand. The determination of an acceptable plan is not a trivial problem due to the large set of decision variables and constraints that may be considered.

A number of conventional techniques are available as decision tools for production planning. Linear decision rules developed by Holt et al. (1953) determine optimal production and work force levels. A number of linear programming models have been formulated that determine optimal inventory, production, and work force levels. However, a major drawback of these models is the assumption of fixed cost and production relationships. For example, the cost functions of the linear decision rules are quadratic, and the linear programming models are restricted to linear cost functions only. Jones (1967) describes a heuristic approach that is dependent on work force and production decision rules. A search procedure is used to evaluate the parameters for these rules in order to minimize a cost function that reflects a particular firm's cost structure. A search decision rule developed by Taubert (1968) employs an aggregate planning cost model and computer-based search techniques to obtain near-optimal results. Although actual cost functions can be modeled which may be more complex than those of the linear decision rules and linear programming models, there is no guarantee that either technique will produce an optimal solution. Lee and Khumawala (1974) demonstrate a simulation model that determines the effect on a firm of various production planning decisions. The model has been used to compare several production planning models including those previously discussed. Model validation and managerial acceptance are key factors that may impede implementation and continuous use of such a model.

Despite the large amount of quality work in this area, none of these analytical techniques have been applied in industry on a broad scale. A number of reasons postulated for this are:

- Excessive data requirements and mathematical complexity of some models
- Simplifying assumptions of some models
- Large set of decision variable values

The first item requires that input data must be generated and maintained and that managers are knowledgable about the mathematical technique. If the solution process is not well understood, a manager must exercise a great deal of faith to accept the results. The second item indicates that current techniques are handicapped by the simplifying assumptions required to make the problem mathematically tractable. According to Mellichamp and Love (1978), the third item may be the most important factor limiting the application of these models. The authors argue that a large set of decision variable values that change each period is inconsistent with a management goal of a stable schedule.

Almost all organizations have developed a set of planning rules or guidelines based on their experience with and knowledge of scheduling and manufacturing processes (Fogarty and Hoffman 1983). For example, the production rate should not be changed more than 25 percent between two periods, and the work force should not be changed more than four times over twelve months. As explained by Fogarty and Hoffman (1983), similar rules are applied in a trial-and-error method in which a number of partial or complete plans are generated and compared before a satisfactory plan is accepted.

Bowman (1963) explains that managers make good decisions in their production planning due to their awareness of and sensitivity to the production system. He suggests that inconsistency in decision making rather than biased decision making is responsible for poor managerial performance. Using data from past production planning decisions, Bowman uses multiple regression analysis to estimate equations similar to those of the linear decision rules. The advantage of this approach is that it strives for consistency in operations.

Capturing management expertise to develop a knowledge-based system that can be used by a production planner to develop an aggregate production plan is the approach that is proposed here. For each period of the production plan, the system would determine the value of each decision variable under consideration. There are a number of reasons for doing this. One of them is that the conventional methods do not allow for a mathematical model that is representative of the prototype situation. The following is an example of one of several policies used by an established manufacturing organization for developing a production plan.

> If it becomes clear three months prior to the final month that the target inventory cannot be achieved, then production in the last two months can fall below the lowest allowable limit. However, if production in the last two months of the year is below the lower limit, and stockouts occur in the first three months of the following year as normal increases in production are scheduled, then adjust the target inventory upward and adjust the last two months of production to ensure that stockouts are avoided and the lower production limit is not exceeded.

There is no easy way to represent this procedure with current techniques. However, a knowledge-based system can incorporate this information as IF-THEN production rules to enhance the process of generating production plans. A knowledge-based system has several other advantages. It would help overcome the cognitive limits of manual planning efforts, and it would ensure the consistent application of planning rules and guidelines. Another advantage is that it incorporates the fundamental data, constraints, planning rules, and heuristics actually used by managers to develop production plans. Additionally, explanatory facilities such as those of the Mycin system (Hayes-Roth, Waterman, and Lenat 1983) can be used to explain the logic used by the system to obtain its results. These factors suggest that the approach would have strong intuitive appeal to management.

8.3   AN EXAMPLE PRODUCTION PLANNING PROBLEM

Given a demand forecast, the primary task of production planning is to set production rates that satisfy demand, keep production relatively stable, raise or lower inventories or backlogs as desired, and minimize the relevant cost over the planning horizon. In the process a number of organizational constraints are considered in arriving at a suitable production plan.

The following information pertains to a highly simplified production planning problem:

Period	Demand	Days
1	2000	20
2	8000	15
3	9500	20

The rate of production and ending inventory for the period immediately preceding the first period of the plan is 300 units per day and 1000 units, respectively. The production rate is limited to increases of 50 units per day across each period, and stockouts are not allowed. A stockout occurs when the computed value for ending inventory is less than zero. Only one day of overtime is permitted for each period. If a stockout occurs, an additional day of overtime is preferred before an increase in production is considered. Production rates, overtime, and beginning and ending inventories are to be determined for just the first three periods of the planning horizon. The example problem is intended to clarify and organize the presentation of pertinent knowledge-engineering concepts and techniques discussed in the remaining part of this chapter.

8.4 STATE-SPACE REPRESENTATION FOR PRODUCTION PLANNING

One appropriate problem-solving formulation for production planning is state-space search (Gardner 1981). The state-space is composed of states that represent partial production plans. It consists of all the alternative partial plans that might exist from an empty plan to a complete plan that contains the values of the decision variables for all periods covered by the planning horizon. The empty plan represents the initial state. A complete plan that satisfies the problem's constraints at the least cost or at the most reasonable cost represents the goal state. Each plan may consist of production rates, ending inventories, work force levels, and period costs for a finite number of periods. User-supplied marketing requirements and available production days are associated with each period. Operators, represented as production rules, are used to solve the problem. They describe how the data about the problem is manipulated to accomplish the goal state. Rules are used to set production rates and to compute the values of other decision variables, including size of inventories, work force requirements, and related costs. Additionally, the application of rules to a plan results in the creation of new and more complete plans. The production rules generate alternative partial production plans in a forward direction until a final, feasible plan has been formulated.

Figure 8.2 illustrates a portion of the state-space for the example production planning problem. For each state displayed in Figure 8.2, only production rates and overtime days are listed. Other items (e.g., inventory values) have been excluded from each state in order to simplify the presentation. The initial state is an empty plan that does not contain any values. Goal states are complete plans that satisfy certain conditions, such as production, overtime, and inventory constraints. The remaining states are all the partial plans that exist from the empty plan to a complete plan.

The combinatorial nature of the state-space is a function of the number of decision variables and the range of allowable values that are

FIGURE 8.2
PARTIAL STATE-SPACE LISTING ONLY PRODUCTION RATES AND OVERTIME DAYS FOR
EXAMPLE PROBLEM

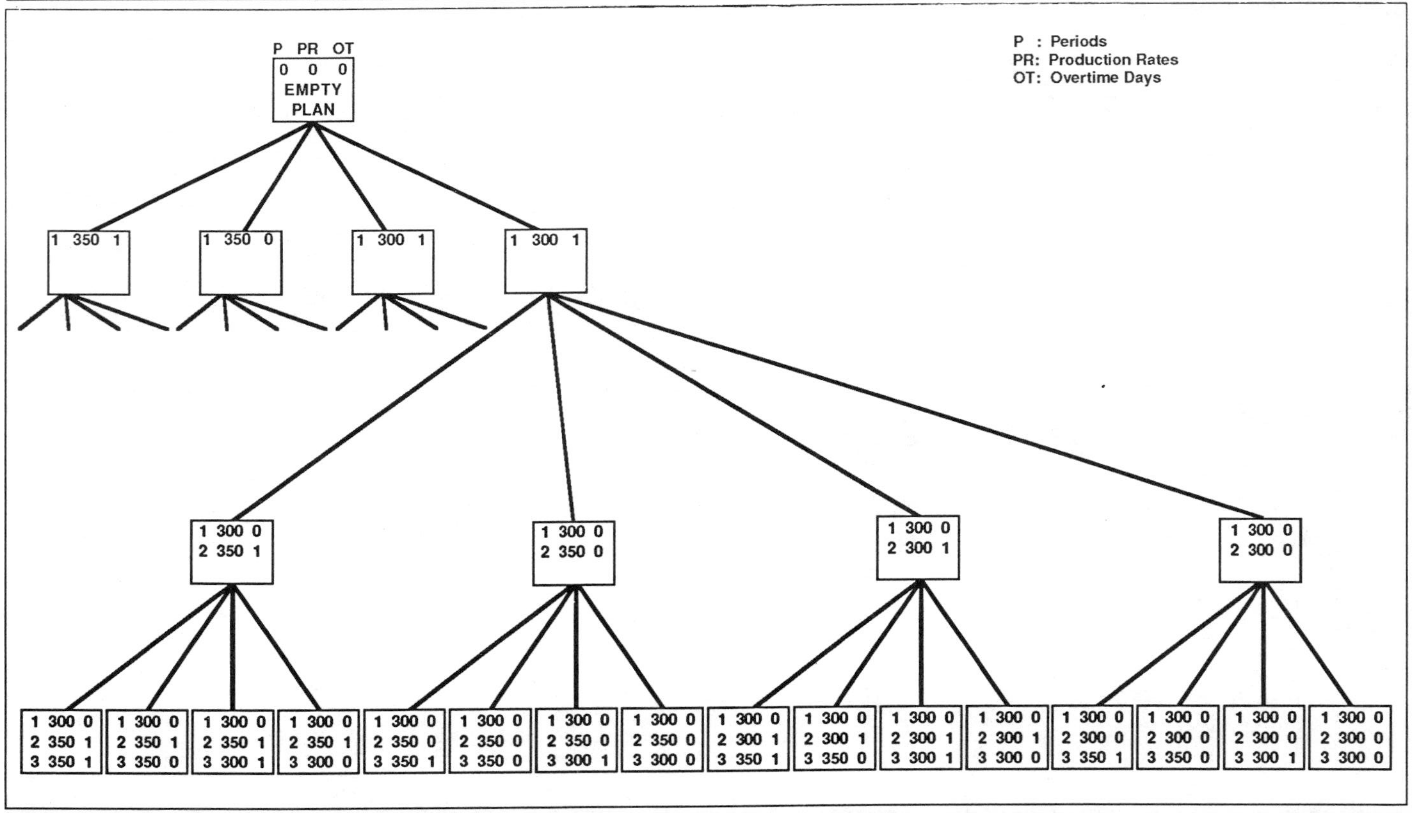

considered for each variable. For instance, if the production rate for any period can be any number between some minimum amount (e.g., 300 units per day) and some maximum amount (e.g., 800 units per day), the number of plans generated and evaluated quickly becomes overwhelming. However, production managers generally plan in terms of discrete production rates that change from period to period by some fixed amount. Therefore, a limited set of production rates, for instance, say 300, 350, 400, 450, 500, 550, 600, 650, 700, 750, and 800, would be more representative of the range of values actually considered.

8.5 DESIGN OF A KNOWLEDGE-BASED SYSTEM FOR PRODUCTION PLANNING

Generally, knowledge-based systems search a problem space in attempting to arrive at a final state. Production systems provide a means to structure the search process (Davis and King 1977; and Waterman and Hayes-Roth 1978). A production system provides the basic framework for a knowledge-based production planning system (see Figure 8.1). They typically consist of three main components: a data base, a knowledge base, and an inference engine. The data base contains a collection of elements that describe the problem constructed by the system from facts supplied by the user or inferred from the knowledge base during execution. The knowledge base is composed of conditional statements referred to as production rules. Each rule consists of (1) a situation, or left-hand side (LHS), representing some pattern that describes data base elements and (2) an action, or right-hand side (RHS), that modifies the data base when the data matches the pattern. The LHS typically contains several elements linked by the logical connectives AND and OR, and the RHS consists of several verb phrases that specify the actions to be taken. The rules are usually in the form of IF-THEN constructs: IF situation THEN action. They embody an expert's knowledge and are responsible for much of the system's knowledge. The inference engine contains general problem-solving knowledge. It organizes and controls the steps required to solve a problem. Generally, the inference engine reasons about problems in either a forward direction to arrive at a goal state from a set of initial facts or in a backward direction to verify a selected goal from a set of supporting facts. These inferencing methods are sometimes used together. For example, Hearsay-II uses both techniques (Erman et al. 1980).

The data base and knowledge base of a production system for the example problem are displayed in Figures 8.3 and 8.4, respectively. Figure 8.5 provides detailed explanations of the items in the data base and knowledge base. The data base contains elements describing entities associated with a plan. For instance, marketing requirements and regular-time production days are described by MKT-REQS and DAYS elements, respectively. The contents of the data base change as rules are applied to

FIGURE 8.3
DATA BASE FOR EXAMPLE AGGREGATE PRODUCTION PLANNING PROBLEM

Row	Data Base		
	(MKT-REQS ^PERIOD 1 ^DEMAND 2000)	(MKT-REQS ^PERIOD 2 ^DEMAND 8000)	(MKT-REQS ^PERIOD 3 ^DEMAND 9500)
	(DAYS ^PERIOD 1 ^QUANTITY 20)	(DAYS ^PERIOD 2 ^QUANTITY 15)	(DAYS ^PERIOD 3 ^QUANTITY 20)
1	(PRODUCTION-RATE ^PERIOD START ^QUANTITY 300)	(INVENTORY ^PERIOD START ^QUANTITY 1000)	
2	(AGGREGATE-PLAN ^PERIOD 1 ^STATUS ACTIVE ^PRD-RAT 300 ^OVR-TIM 0 ^BEG-INV 1000 ^END-INV nil)		
3	(AGGREGATE-PLAN ^PERIOD 1 ^STATUS ACTIVE ^PRD-RAT 300 ^OVR-TIM 0 ^BEG-INV 1000 ^END-INV 5000)		
4	(AGGREGATE-PLAN ^PERIOD 1 ^STATUS NOT-ACTIVE ^PRD-RAT 300 ^OVR-TIM 0 ^BEG-INV 1000 ^END-INV 5000)	(AGGREGATE-PLAN ^PERIOD 2 ^STATUS ACTIVE ^PRD-RAT 300 ^OVR-TIM 0 ^BEG-INV 5000 ^END-INV nil)	
5	(AGGREGATE-PLAN ^PERIOD 1 ^STATUS NOT-ACTIVE ^PRD-RAT 300 ^OVR-TIM 0 ^BEG-INV 1000 ^END-INV 5000)	(AGGREGATE-PLAN ^PERIOD 2 ^STATUS ACTIVE ^PRD-RAT 300 ^OVR-TIM 0 ^BEG-INV 5000 ^END-INV 1500)	

```
(INCREMENT
  ^PERIOD 1
  ^STATUS ACTIVE)



(INCREMENT
  ^PERIOD 1
  ^STATUS ACTIVE)



(INCREMENT                    (INCREMENT
  ^PERIOD 1                     ^PERIOD 2
  ^STATUS ACTIVE)               ^STATUS ACTIVE)



(INCREMENT                    (INCREMENT
  ^PERIOD 1                     ^PERIOD 2
  ^STATUS ACTIVE)               ^STATUS ACTIVE)
```

FIGURE 8.3 (Cont.)

Row	Data Base		
6	(AGGREGATE-PLAN ^PERIOD 1 ^STATUS NOT-ACTIVE ^PRD-RAT 300 ^OVR-TIM 0 ^BEG-INV 1000 ^END-INV 5000)	(AGGREGATE-PLAN ^PERIOD 2 ^STATUS NOT-ACTIVE ^PRD-RAT 300 ^OVR-TIM 0 ^BEG-INV 5000 ^END-INV 1500)	(AGGREGATE-PLAN ^PERIOD 3 ^STATUS ACTIVE ^PRD-RAT 300 ^OVR-TIM 0 ^BEG-INV 1500 ^END-INV nil)
7	(AGGREGATE-PLAN ^PERIOD 1 ^STATUS NOT-ACTIVE ^PRD-RAT 300 ^OVR-TIM 0 ^BEG-INV 1000 ^END-INV 5000)	(AGGREGATE-PLAN ^PERIOD 2 ^STATUS NOT-ACTIVE ^PRD-RAT 300 ^OVR-TIM 0 ^BEG-INV 5000 ^END-INV 1500)	(AGGREGATE-PLAN ^PERIOD 3 ^STATUS ACTIVE ^PRD-RAT 300 ^OVR-TIM 0 ^BEG-INV 1500 ^END-INV -2000)
8	(AGGREGATE-PLAN ^PERIOD 1 ^STATUS NOT-ACTIVE ^PRD-RAT 300 ^OVR-TIM 0 ^BEG-INV 1000 ^END-INV 5000)	(AGGREGATE-PLAN ^PERIOD 2 ^STATUS NOT-ACTIVE ^PRD-RAT 300 ^OVR-TIM 0 ^BEG-INV 500 ^END-INV 1500)	(AGGREGATE-PLAN ^PERIOD 3 ^STATUS ACTIVE ^PRD-RAT 300 ^OVR-TIM 1 ^BEG-INV 1500 ^END-INV nil)
9	(AGGREGATE-PLAN ^PERIOD 1 ^STATUS NOT-ACTIVE ^PRD-RAT 300 ^OVR-TIM 0 ^BEG-INV 1000 ^END-INV 5000)	(AGGREGATE-PLAN ^PERIOD 2 ^STATUS NOT-ACTIVE ^PRD-RAT 300 ^OVR-TIM 0 ^BEG-INV 500 ^END-INV 1500)	(AGGREGATE-PLAN ^PERIOD 3 ^STATUS ACTIVE ^PRD-RAT 300 ^OVR-TIM 1 ^BEG-INV 1500 ^END-INV -1700)
10	(AGGREGATE-PLAN ^PERIOD 1 ^STATUS NOT-ACTIVE ^PRD-RAT 300 ^OVR-TIM 0 ^BEG-INV 1000 ^END-INV 5000)	(AGGREGATE-PLAN ^PERIOD 2 ^STATUS NOT-ACTIVE ^PRD-RAT 300 ^OVR-TIM 0 ^BEG-INV 1000 ^END-INV 1500)	(AGGREGATE-PLAN ^PERIOD 3 ^STATUS ACTIVE ^PRD-RAT 350 ^OVR-TIM 0 ^BEG-INV 1500 ^END-INV nil)
11	(AGGREGATE-PLAN ^PERIOD 1 ^STATUS NOT-ACTIVE ^PRD-RAT 300 ^OVR-TIM 0 ^BEG-INV 1000 ^END-INV 5000)	(AGGREGATE-PLAN ^PERIOD 2 ^STATUS NOT-ACTIVE ^PRD-RAT 300 ^OVR-TIM 0 ^BEG-INV 1000 ^END-INV 1500)	(AGGREGATE-PLAN ^PERIOD 3 ^STATUS ACTIVE ^PRD-RAT 350 ^OVR-TIM 0 ^BEG-INV 1500 ^END-INV -1000)

```
(INCREMENT              (INCREMENT              (INCREMENT
  ^PERIOD 1               ^PERIOD 2               ^PERIOD 3
  ^STATUS ACTIVE)         ^STATUS ACTIVE)         ^STATUS ACTIVE)


(INCREMENT              (INCREMENT              (INCREMENT
  ^PERIOD 1               ^PERIOD 2               ^PERIOD 3
  ^STATUS ACTIVE)         ^STATUS ACTIVE)         ^STATUS ACTIVE)


(INCREMENT              (INCREMENT              (INCREMENT
  ^PERIOD 1               ^PERIOD 2               ^PERIOD 3
  ^STATUS ACTIVE)         ^STATUS ACTIVE)         ^STATUS ACTIVE)


(INCREMENT              (INCREMENT              (INCREMENT
  ^PERIOD 1               ^PERIOD 2               ^PERIOD 3
  ^STATUS ACTIVE)         ^STATUS ACTIVE)         ^STATUS ACTIVE)


(INCREMENT              (INCREMENT              (INCREMENT
  ^PERIOD 1               ^PERIOD 2               ^PERIOD 3
  ^STATUS ACTIVE)         ^STATUS ACTIVE)         ^STATUS NOT-ACTIVE)


(INCREMENT              (INCREMENT              (INCREMENT
  ^PERIOD 1               ^PERIOD 2               ^PERIOD 3
  ^STATUS ACTIVE)         ^STATUS ACTIVE)         ^STATUS NOT-ACTIVE)
```

FIGURE 8.3 (*Cont.*)

Row	Data Base		

12 (AGGREGATE-PLAN   (AGGREGATE-PLAN   (AGGREGATE-PLAN
    ^PERIOD 1   ^PERIOD 2   ^PERIOD 3
    ^STATUS NOT-ACTIVE ^STATUS ACTIVE ^STATUS ACTIVE
    ^PRD-RAT 300   ^PRD-RAT 300   ^PRD-RAT 350
    ^OVR-TIM 0   ^OVR-TIM 0   ^OVR-TIM 1
    ^BEG-INV 1000   ^BEG-INV 500   ^BEG-INV 1500
    ^END-INV 5000)   ^END-INV 1500)   ^END-INV nil)

13 (AGGREGATE-PLAN   (AGGREGATE-PLAN   (AGGREGATE-PLAN
    ^PERIOD 1   ^PERIOD 2   ^PERIOD 3
    ^STATUS NOT-ACTIVE ^STATUS NOT-ACTIVE ^STATUS ACTIVE
    ^PRD-RAT 300   ^PRD-RAT 300   ^PRD-RAT 350
    ^OVR-TIM 0   ^OVR-TIM 0   ^OVR-TIM 1
    ^BEG-INV 1000   ^BEG-INV 500   ^BEG-INV 1500
    ^END-INV 5000)   ^END-INV 1500)   ^END-INV -650)

14 (AGGREGATE-PLAN   (AGGREGATE-PLAN
    ^PERIOD 1   ^PERIOD 2
    ^STATUS NOT-ACTIVE ^STATUS NOT-ACTIVE
    ^PRD-RAT 300   ^PRD-RAT 300
    ^OVR-TIM 0   ^OVR-TIM 0
    ^BEG-INV 1000   ^BEG-INV 1000
    ^END-INV 5000)   ^END-INV 1500)

15 (AGGREGATE-PLAN   (AGGREGATE-PLAN
    ^PERIOD 1   ^PERIOD 2
    ^STATUS NOT-ACTIVE ^STATUS ACTIVE
    ^PRD-RAT 300   ^PRD-RAT 350
    ^OVR-TIM 0   ^OVR-TIM 0
    ^BEG-INV 1000   ^BEG-INV 1000
    ^END-INV 5000)   ^END-INV nil)

16 (AGGREGATE-PLAN   (AGGREGATE-PLAN
    ^PERIOD 1   ^PERIOD 2
    ^STATUS NOT-ACTIVE ^STATUS ACTIVE
    ^PRD-RAT 300   ^PRD-RAT 350
    ^OVR-TIM 0   ^OVR-TIM 0
    ^BEG-INV 1000   ^BEG-INV 1000
    ^END-INV 5000)   ^END-INV 2250)

17 (AGGREGATE-PLAN   (AGGREGATE-PLAN   (AGGREGATE-PLAN
    ^PERIOD 1   ^PERIOD 2   ^PERIOD 3
    ^STATUS NOT-ACTIVE ^STATUS NOT-ACTIVE ^STATUS ACTIVE
    ^PRD-RAT 300   ^PRD-RAT 350   ^PRD-RAT 350
    ^OVR-TIM 0   ^OVR-TIM 0   ^OVR-TIM 0
    ^BEG-INV 1000   ^BEG-INV 1000   ^BEG-INV 2250
    ^END-INV 5000)   ^END-INV 2250)   ^END-INV nil)

```
(INCREMENT              (INCREMENT              (INCREMENT
  ^PERIOD 1               ^PERIOD 2               ^PERIOD 3
  ^STATUS ACTIVE)         ^STATUS ACTIVE)         ^STATUS NOT-ACTIVE)



(INCREMENT              (INCREMENT              (INCREMENT
  ^PERIOD 1               ^PERIOD 2               ^PERIOD 3
  ^STATUS ACTIVE)         ^STATUS ACTIVE)         ^STATUS NOT-ACTIVE)



(INCREMENT              (INCREMENT
  ^PERIOD 1               ^PERIOD 2
  ^STATUS ACTIVE)         ^STATUS ACTIVE)



(INCREMENT              (INCREMENT
  ^PERIOD 1               ^PERIOD 2
  ^STATUS ACTIVE)         ^STATUS NOT-ACTIVE)



(INCREMENT              (INCREMENT
  ^PERIOD 1               ^PERIOD 2
  ^STATUS ACTIVE)         ^STATUS NOT-ACTIVE)



(INCREMENT              (INCREMENT              (INCREMENT
  ^PERIOD 1               ^PERIOD 2               ^PERIOD 3
  ^STATUS ACTIVE)         ^STATUS NOT-ACTIVE)     ^STATUS ACTIVE)
```

FIGURE 8.3 (*Cont.*)

Row	Data Base		
18	(AGGREGATE-PLAN ^PERIOD 1 ^STATUS NOT-ACTIVE ^PRD-RAT 300 ^OVR-TIM 0 ^BEG-INV 1000 ^END-INV 5000)	(AGGREGATE-PLAN ^PERIOD 2 ^STATUS NOT-ACTIVE ^PRD-RAT 350 ^OVR-TIM 0 ^BEG-INV 1000 ^END-INV 2250)	(AGGREGATE-PLAN ^PERIOD 3 ^STATUS ACTIVE ^PRD-RAT 350 ^OVR-TIM 0 ^BEG-INV 2250 ^END-INV -250)
19	(AGGREGATE-PLAN ^PERIOD 1 ^STATUS NOT-ACTIVE ^PRD-RAT 300 ^OVR-TIM 0 ^BEG-INV 1000 ^END-INV 5000)	(AGGREGATE-PLAN ^PERIOD 2 ^STATUS NOT-ACTIVE ^PRD-RAT 350 ^OVR-TIM 0 ^BEG-INV 1000 ^END-INV 2250)	(AGGREGATE-PLAN ^PERIOD 3 ^STATUS ACTIVE ^PRD-RAT 350 ^OVR-TIM 1 ^BEG-INV 2250 ^END-INV nil)
20	(AGGREGATE-PLAN ^PERIOD 1 ^STATUS NOT-ACTIVE ^PRD-RAT 300 ^OVR-TIM 0 ^BEG-INV 1000 ^END-INV 5000)	(AGGREGATE-PLAN ^PERIOD 2 ^STATUS NOT-ACTIVE ^PRD-RAT 350 ^OVR-TIM 0 ^BEG-INV 1000 ^END-INV 2250)	(AGGREGATE-PLAN ^PERIOD 3 ^STATUS ACTIVE ^PRD-RAT 350 ^OVR-TIM 1 ^BEG-INV 2250 ^END-INV 100)

it. Data base elements are removed, modified, and added as a production plan is being developed. At any point in time, the contents of the data base describe the current state of the problem. The knowledge base for the example problem consists of ten production rules. The situation part of a rule is separated from the action part by the symbol→. The situation consists of one element or a conjunction of several elements, and the action specifies one or more actions to perform. The rules determine decision variable values, test for and act on infeasible conditions, and perform a depth-first search with backtracking of the state-space to arrive at a solution.

8.6   OPS5 PRODUCTION SYSTEM LANGUAGE

OPS5 is one of several programming languages known as production systems (Forgy 1981). It is used to develop a production system for the example problem. OPS5 provides a single global data base called *working memory*. Production rules are stored in a separate memory called *production*

(INCREMENT	(INCREMENT	(INCREMENT
^PERIOD 1	^PERIOD 2	^PERIOD 3
^STATUS ACTIVE)	^STATUS NOT-ACTIVE)	^STATUS ACTIVE)
(INCREMENT	(INCREMENT	(INCREMENT
^PERIOD 1	^PERIOD 2	^PERIOD 2
^STATUS ACTIVE)	^STATUS NOT-ACTIVE)	^STATUS ACTIVE)
(INCREMENT	(INCREMENT	(INCREMENT
^PERIOD 1	^PERIOD 2	^PERIOD 3
^STATUS ACTIVE)	^STATUS NOT-ACTIVE)	^STATUS ACTIVE)

memory. The elements appearing in working memory and production memory consist of objects with associated attribute-value pairs. For instance, in this representation, marketing requirements of 2000 units in period 1 are described by an object name (i.e., MKT-REQS) followed by several attribute-value pairs (i.e., ^PERIOD 1 and ^QUANTITY 2000), with everything enclosed in parentheses. Attributes are distinguished by being preceded by the symbol ^. The complete statement for the element just described would be (MKT-REQS ^PERIOD 1 ^QUANTITY 2000). Attribute values may be numbers, symbols, or variables. Variables are used to specify values at various levels. They are preceded by the character < and end with the character >. For instance, $<x>$, $<y>$, and $<z1>$ are legitimate representations.

Production rules consist of an open parenthesis, the symbol P, a name, the LHS of the production, the symbol →, the RHS, and a close parenthesis. The following is typical of the rules in the OPS5 production system for the example problem. The rule is used to compute ending inventory. The text after the semicolons offers a more detailed explanation.

```
(P RULE-1                              (MAKE AGGREGATE-PLAN
  (PRODUCTION-RATE                       ^PERIOD (COMPUTE ( ⟨x1 ⟩ + 1))
    ^PERIOD START                        ^STATUS ACTIVE
    ^QUANTITY ⟨x1 ⟩)                     ^PRD-RAT ⟨x2 ⟩
  (INVENTORY                             ^OVR-TIM ⟨x3 ⟩
    ^PERIOD START                        ^BEG-INV ⟨x5 ⟩
    ^QUANTITY ⟨x2 ⟩)                     ^END-INV nil)
-->                                    (MAKE INCREMENT
  (REMOVE 1)                             ^PERIOD (COMPUTE ( ⟨x1 ⟩ + 1))
  (REMOVE 2)                             ^STATUS ACTIVE))
  (MAKE AGGREGATE-PLAN
    ^PERIOD 1                        (P RULE-4
    ^STATUS ACTIVE                     (AGGREGATE-PLAN
    ^PRD-RAT ⟨x1⟩                        ^PERIOD ⟨x1 ⟩
    ^OVR-TIM 0                           ^STATUS ACTIVE
    ^BEG-INV ⟨x2 ⟩                       ^PRD-RAT ⟨x2 ⟩
    ^END-INV nil)                        ^OVR-TIM { ⟨x3 ⟩⟨ 1}
  (MAKE INCREMENT                        ^BEG-INV ⟨x4 ⟩
    ^PERIOD 1                            ^END-INV { ⟨x5 ⟩ ⟨0})
    ^STATUS ACTIVE))               -->
                                       (MODIFY 1
(P RULE-2                                ^OVR-TIM (COMPUTE ⟨x3 ⟩ + 1)
  (AGGREGATE-PLAN                        ^END-INV nil))
    ^PERIOD ⟨x1 ⟩
    ^STATUS ACTIVE                   (P RULE-5
    ^PRD-RAT  ⟨x2 ⟩                    (AGGREGATE-PLAN
    ^OVR-TIM  ⟨x3 ⟩                      ^PERIOD ⟨x1 ⟩
    ^BEG-INV  ⟨x4 ⟩                      ^STATUS ACTIVE
    ^END-INV nil)                        ^PRD-RAT ⟨x2 ⟩
  (MKT-REQS                              ^OVR-TIM 1
    ^PERIOD ⟨x1⟩                         ^BEG-INV ⟨x3 ⟩
    ^DEMAND⟨x5 ⟩)                        ^END-INV { ⟨x4 ⟩⟨0})
  (DAYS                               (INCREMENT
    ^PERIOD ⟨x1⟩                         ^PERIOD ⟨x1 ⟩
    ^QUANTITY ⟨ x6⟩)                     ^STATUS ACTIVE)
-->                                 -->
  (MODIFY 1                            (MODIFY 1
    ^END-INV (COMPUTE                     ^PRD-RAT (COMPUTE ( ⟨x2 ⟩ + 50) )
(( ⟨x2 ⟩ * ( ⟨ x3 ⟩ + ⟨ x6 ⟩ ))       ^OVR-TIM 0
+ ⟨x4 ⟩ – ⟨ x5 ⟩ ))))                  ^END-INV nil)
                                       (MODIFY 2
(P RULE-3                                ^STATUS NOT-ACTIVE))
  (AGGREGATE-PLAN
    ^PERIOD  ⟨x1 ⟩                   (P RULE-6
    ^STATUS ACTIVE                     (AGGREGATE-PLAN
    ^PRD-RAT ⟨x2 ⟩                       ^PERIOD ⟨x1 ⟩
    ^OVR-TIM ⟨x3 ⟩                       ^STATUS ACTIVE
    ^BEG-INV ⟨x4 ⟩                       ^PRD-RAT ⟨x2 ⟩
    ^END-INV { ⟨x5 ⟩) = 0})             ^OVR-TIM 1
-->                                      ^BEG-INV ⟨x3 ⟩
  (MODIFY 1                              ^END-INV { ⟨x4 ⟩⟨0 })
    ^STATUS NOT-ACTIVE)
```

```
(INCREMENT
  ^PERIOD ⟨x1⟩
  ^STATUS NOT-ACTIVE)
-->
  (REMOVE 1)
  (REMOVE 2)

(P RULE-7
  (AGGREGATE-PLAN
    ^PERIOD ⟨x1⟩
    ^STATUS NOT-ACTIVE
    ^PRD-RAT ⟨x2⟩
    ^OVR-TIM ⟨x3⟩
    ^BEG-INV ⟨x4⟩
    ^END-INV {⟨x5⟩} = 0 })
  (INCREMENT
    ^PERIOD ⟨x1⟩
    ^STATUS ACTIVE)
- (AGGREGATE-PLAN
    ^PERIOD { ⟨x6⟩ ⟨⟨x1⟩ }
    ^END-INV nil)
-->
  (MODIFY 1
    ^STATUS ACTIVE
    ^PRD-RAT (COMPUTE
( ⟨x2⟩ + 50 ))
    ^END-INV nil)
  (MODIFY 2
    ^STATUS NOT-ACTIVE))

(P RULE-8
  (AGGREGATE-PLAN
    ^PERIOD ⟨x1⟩
    ^STATUS NOT-ACTIVE
    ^PRD-RAT ⟨x2⟩
    ^OVR-TIM ⟨x3⟩
    ^BEG-INV ⟨x4⟩
    ^END-INV {⟨x5⟩} = 0 })
  (INCREMENT
    ^PERIOD ⟨x1⟩
    ^STATUS NOT-ACTIVE)
-->
  (REMOVE 1)
  (REMOVE 2))

(P RULE-9
  (AGGREGATE-PLAN
    ^PERIOD 1
    ^STATUS NOT-ACTIVE
    ^PRD-RAT ⟨x1⟩
    ^OVR-TIM ⟨x2⟩
```

```
    ^BEG-INV ⟨x3⟩
    ^END-INV {⟨x4⟩} = 0 })
  (AGGREGATE-PLAN
    ^PERIOD 2
    ^STATUS NOT-ACTIVE
    ^PRD-RAT ⟨x5⟩
    ^OVR-TIM ⟨x6⟩
    ^BEG-INV ⟨x7⟩
    ^END-INV {⟨x8⟩} = 0 })

  (AGGREGATE-PLAN
    ^PERIOD 3
    ^STATUS ACTIVE
    ^PRD-RAT ⟨x9⟩
    ^OVR-TIM ⟨x10⟩
    ^BEG-INV ⟨x11⟩
    ^END-INV { ⟨x12⟩ } = 0 })
-->
  (WRITE (CRLF) (TABTO 49) BEGINNING
(TABTO 65) ENDING)
  (WRITE (CRLF) (TABTO 4) PERIOD
(TABTO 27) RATE (TABTO 36) OVERTIME
(TABTO 49) INVENTORY (TABTO 63)
INVENTORY)
  (WRITE (CRLF) (TABTO 7) 1 (TABTO 27)
⟨x1⟩ (TABTO 40) ⟨x2⟩ (TABTO 52) ⟨x3⟩
(TABTO 66) ⟨x4⟩ )
  (WRITE (CRLF) (TABTO 7) 2 (TABTO 27)
⟨x5⟩ (TABTO 40) ⟨x6⟩ (TABTO 52 ⟨x7⟩
(TABTO 66) ⟨x8⟩ )
  (WRITE (CRLF) (TABTO 7) 3 (TABTO 27)
⟨x9⟩ (TABTO 40) ⟨x10⟩ (TABTO 52)
⟨x11⟩ (TABTO 66) ⟨x12⟩ )
  (HALT))

(P RULE-10
  (MKT-REGS
    ^PERIOD ⟨x7⟩
    ^DEMAND ⟨x8⟩ )
- (AGGREGATE-PLAN
    ^PERIOD ⟨x1⟩
    ^STATUS ⟨x2⟩
    ^PRD-RAT ⟨x3⟩
    ^OVR-TIM ⟨x4⟩
    ^BEG-INV ⟨x5⟩
    ^END-INV ⟨x6⟩ )
- (PRODUCTION-RATE)
- (INVENTORY)
-->
  (WRITE (CRLF) FAILURE)
  (HALT))
```

FIGURE 8.5
DESCRIPTION OF DATA BASE AND KNOWLEDGE BASE FOR EXAMPLE PROBLEMS

Data Base

Elements	Element Names	Attributes	Acronym Interpretations	Example Values	Description
MKT-REQS ^PERIOD ^DEMAND	MKT-REQS	PERIOD DEMAND	Marketing Requirements	1,2,3* 2000,8000,9500**	Represents the marketing requirements for a certain period
DAYS ^PERIOD ^QUANTITY	DAYS	PERIOD QUANTITY		1,2,3* 20,15,20**	Represents the quantity of regular time production days for a certain period
PRODUCTION-RATE ^PERIOD ^QUANTITY	PRODUCTION-RATE	PERIOD QUANTITY		START 300**	Represents the starting production rate for the production plan
INVENTORY ^PERIOD ^QUANTITY	INVENTORY	PERIOD QUANTITY		START 1000**	Represents the starting inventory for the production plan
AGGREGATE-PLAN ^PERIOD ^STATUS ^PRD-RAT ^OVR-TIM ^BEG-INV ^END-INV	AGGREGATE-PLAN	PERIOD STATUS PRD-RAT OVR-TIM BEG-INV END-INV	Production Rate Overtime Beginning Inventory Ending Inventory	1,2,3* ACTIVE, NOT-ACTIVE 300,350** 0,1** 500–5000** nil, –2000–5000**	Represents a certain period of the production plan
INCREMENT ^PERIOD ^STATUS	INCREMENT	PERIOD STATUS		1,2,3,** ACTIVE, NOT-ACTIVE	Represents whether the production rate of a certain period can be increased

*Values may be any positive integer value
**Values may be any real number

Knowledge Base

Form	Description
situation	Situation or left-hand side (LHS) contains a conjunction of several
↑	elements, and the action of right-hand side (RHS) consists of several
action	actions that modify the data base.

LHS Operators	Description
<	Less than
>	Greater than
<=	Less than or equal
>=	Greater than or equal
–	Negation
{ }	Allows specifying restrictions on variable binding

Actions	Description
MAKE	Creates and adds a new element to the data base
MODIFY	Changes one or more parts of an existing element in the data base
REMOVE	Removes elements from the data base
WRITE	Types information on a terminal

Functions	Descriptions
COMPUTE	Allows OPS5 to do arithmetic
CRLF	Returns the end-of-line symbol
TABTO	Writes in a specified column

Variables	Descriptions
⟨x1⟩, ⟨x2⟩, ..., ⟨x12⟩	All variables are preceded by the character ⟨ and end with the character ⟩

```
(P rule-2                          ; IF
  (AGGREGATE-PLAN                  ; the aggregate production plan
   ^PERIOD <x1>                    ; has a certain period
   ^STATUS ACTIVE                  ; which is active
   ^PRD-RAT <x2>                   ; has a certain production rate
   ^OVR-TIM <x3>                   ; has a certain number of available
                                   ;   overtime days
   ^BEG-INV <x4>                   ; has a certain beginning inventory
   ^END-INV nil)                   ; has no ending inventory
  (MKT-REQS                        ; And marketing requirements
   ^PERIOD <x1>                    ; of the same period
   ^DEMAND <x2>                    ; are a certain quantity
  (DAYS                            ; And regular time days
   ^PERIOD <x1>                    ; of the same period
   ^QUANTITY <x6>                  ; are a certain quantity
-->
  (MODIFY 1                        ; THEN modify the value of
   ^END-INV (COMPUTE               ; ending inventory
             (((<x2>*              ; by computing
               (<x3>+              ; a new value
              <x6>))+              ; that replaces the nil value
              <x4>-<x5>))))
```

Patterns in the LHS of production rules are descriptions of working memory elements. They are matched against working memory elements to determine the appropriateness of a rule. As the LHS is matched, variables are bound to attribute values. OPS5 provides a number of operators that influence the matching process. Several of the operators are particularly important: the prefix operators, ‹, ›, ‹ =, and › =, and the brackets, {}. The brackets allow specifying some restrictions on a value and binding a variable to the value that meets the restrictions. For instance, END-INV{ <x> = 0} would match any value greater than or equal to zero and bind the variable <x> to it. LHS patterns may be preceded by the negation operator –. A negated element will match if there is no element in working memory to match the non-negated element. The OPS5 rule interpreter controls the matching process and resolves conflicts when more than one rule matches the data.

A rule having patterns that match has its RHS modify the data base. The most important actions are MAKE, MODIFY, REMOVE, and WRITE. MAKE creates and adds a new element in working memory. For instance, (MAKE INCREMENT P̂ERIOD 1 ŜTATUS ACTIVE) would add the element (INCREMENT P̂ERIOD 1 ŜTATUS ACTIVE) to working memory. MODIFY changes one or more parts of any existing element. A number immediately following the action MODIFY identifies the element matched by the pattern of the LHS to be modified. For instance, if (INCREMENT P̂ERIOD 1 ŜTATUS ACTIVE) is the first LHS element of a rule, executing the action (MODIFY 1 ŜTATUS NOT-ACTIVE) would change the current value of STATUS to NOT-ACTIVE. The action (RE-

MOVE 1) deletes from working memory the element matched by the first pattern of the LHS. Finally, WRITE types information on a terminal. For instance, (WRITE FINAL SOLUTION (CRLF)) would write on the terminal FINAL SOLUTION and would start a new line. CRLF is a function that returns the end-of-line symbol. The function TABTO causes the WRITE action to move to a specified column. Another function, COMPUTE, ALLOWS OPS5 to do arithmetic.

OPS5 is used here to demonstrate a knowledge-based system for the example problem considered. The system runs on a VAX 11/780 with UNIX.

8.7   KNOWLEDGE REPRESENTATION FOR PRODUCTION PLANNING

In developing a knowledge-based system for production planning, a variety of knowledge must be represented so that it can be used effectively during the problem-solving process. One method for acquiring the requisite knowledge begins by having an experienced production planner solve a variety of production planning problems. By analyzing the process that a production planner uses in developing a number of actual plans, the plan's major entities and their interrelationships, production rules, and relevant problem-solving strategies are determined. Both typical and atypical planning problems should be solved so that the knowledge obtained is representative of a wide range of planning problems. Several knowledge representation schemes are available for representing the knowledge. The most prominent are production rule formalisms, network structures, and frame-based structures (Nilsson 1980; and Rich 1983). System properties, including representational adequacy and inferential efficiency, are impacted by the choice of a representation scheme (Rich 1983). The primary source of domain-specific knowledge for a production planning system are production rules. The rules represent the procedural knowledge required to build production plans and to search the state-space of partial plans.

The data base for the example problem contains items that are described by means of a data structure that is a collection of attributes and associated values. Marketing requirements, regular time production days, starting production rate, starting inventory, and the production plan may be described by several attributes. For instance, marketing requirements (i.e., MKT-REQS elements) have two attributes, PERIOD and DEMAND, to describe separate periods and their associated demand. Regular time production days, (i.e., DAYS elements) have two attributes, PERIOD and QUANTITY, to describe separate periods and the quantity of regular time days available for each period. There is one element of each type for each of the three periods of the example problem's planning horizon. The preceding period's production rate and its inventory (i.e., PRODUCTION-

RATE and INVENTORY elements) are also described by ˆPERIOD and QUANTITY attributes. For each of these elements, the attribute PERIOD has a value of START, indicating that the quantity associated with each is a starting value. For each period of the planning horizon, there is an aggregate production plan (i.e., AGGREGATE-PLAN) element described by PERIOD, STATUS, PRD-RAT, OVR-TIM, BEG-INV, and END-INV attributes. When the attribute STATUS has the value ACTIVE, the production system attempts to determine values for the other attributes. When it has the value NOT-ACTIVE, the attributes PRD-RAT, OVR-TIM, BEG-INV, and END-INV attributes. When the attribute STATUS has the value ACTIVE, the production system attempts to determine values for the other attributes. When it has the value NOT-ACTIVE, the attributes PRD-RAT, OVR-TIM, BEG-INV, and END-INV (representing production rate, overtime days, beginning inventory, and ending inventory, respectively) have been assigned feasible values. Associated with each period of the aggregate production plan is an increment (i.e., INCREMENT) element described by two attributes, PERIOD and STATUS. When the attribute STATUS has the value ACTIVE, the production rate of the associated period can be incremented by 50. When it has the value NOT-ACTIVE, no additions to the production rate are permitted. Attribute values are supplied by the user or are generated by the production rules. For instance, the starting production rate element (i.e., PRODUCTION-RATE ˆPERIOD START ˆQUANTITY 300) is supplied by a user during an input session.

The situation of each production rule is compared with the state description in the data base. The situation that agrees with the current state description has its action modify the data base to bring about some desired result. The rules embody the knowledge required to build a production plan for the three-period planning horizon of the example problem. RULE-1 adds to the data base and activates both the first period of the production plan and its associated increment element. Although they are removed from the data base by RULE-1, the production rate and inventory elements for the preceding period supply values for the production rate and beginning inventory for the first period of the production plan. The ending inventory for a certain period is determined by RULE-2. For an active period, it computes an ending inventory to replace the nil value based on the period's production rate, overtime days, beginning inventory, and knowledge of its marketing requirements and regular time production days. If the ending inventory of a period is greater than or equal to zero, RULE-3 deactivates the current period, adds to the data base, and activates the next period of the plan and its associated increment element. However, if an active period with no overtime has an ending inventory less than zero, RULE-4 adds one day of overtime to the plan and replaces the current inventory value with nil. When overtime has been considered, ending inventory is less than zero, and an increment can be made to the production rate, RULE-5 increments the current production rate by

50, resets overtime, and replaces the current inventory value with nil. RULE-6 removes from the data base active periods and their associated increment elements, which have considered use of overtime and increments to the production rate but have ending inventories less than zero. By doing so, it initiates the first step of a backtracking procedure. If the previous period's increment element is active, indicating that the production rate can be increased by 50, then RULE-7 activates the preceding period, increments the production rate by 50, and replaces the current value of ending inventory with nil. If the preceding period's increment element is not active, then RULE-8 continues the backtracking process by removing the next most recent period and its associated increment element from the data base. RULE-9 describes certain conditions that the final solution should meet. For the example problem, these conditions specify that each of the three periods have an ending inventory greater than or equal to zero. It also writes this solution on a screen. If there is no solution, RULE-10 halts execution and writes that the system failed.

To illustrate the application of these rules to the example problem, the ten rule knowledge base is applied to a data base that initially contains MKT-REQS, DAYS, PRODUCTION-RATE, and INVENTORY elements. Modifications made to the data base are provided in rows 1 through 20 of Figure 8.3. Each row represents the data base at any point in time. Rows 1 through 20 trace changes made to the data base each time a rule executes. For instance, RULE-1 executes first, deleting the starting production rate and inventory, and adding the first period of the aggregate production plan and its associated increment element to the data base. Next, RULE-2 executes, computing a value for ending inventory that replaces the nil value. Since the ending inventory for the current period is greater than zero (i.e., no stockout), RULE-3 executes, advancing the plan an additional period by deactivating the current period and adding another period and its associated increment element to the data base. As long as there are no stockouts, RULE-2 and RULE-3 repeatedly execute. If a stockout should occur, as it does in period 3 (row 7 of the data base), overtime is used to make up the deficit. RULE-4 executes adding one day of overtime to the current period. Next, RULE-2 executes computing a new ending inventory. Because an additional day of overtime does not eliminate the stockout, RULE-5 executes incrementing the production rate by 50, resetting overtime,and deactivating the status of the increment element. Again, RULE-2 executes, recomputing ending inventory at the higher production rate. Because neither an additional day of overtime nor increasing the production rate eliminates the stockout, the system backtracks to determine whether increases in production in a preceding period will eliminate the stockout in period 3. RULE-6 executes, deleting all elements related to the current period. Because the increment element of period 2 is active, indicating that it is feasible to increment the production rate of that period, RULE-7 executes, incrementing the production rate by 50 and deactivating its associated increment element. Otherwise,

FIGURE 8.6
PATHS SEARCHED FOR EXAMPLE AGGREGATE PRODUCTION PLANNING PROBLEM

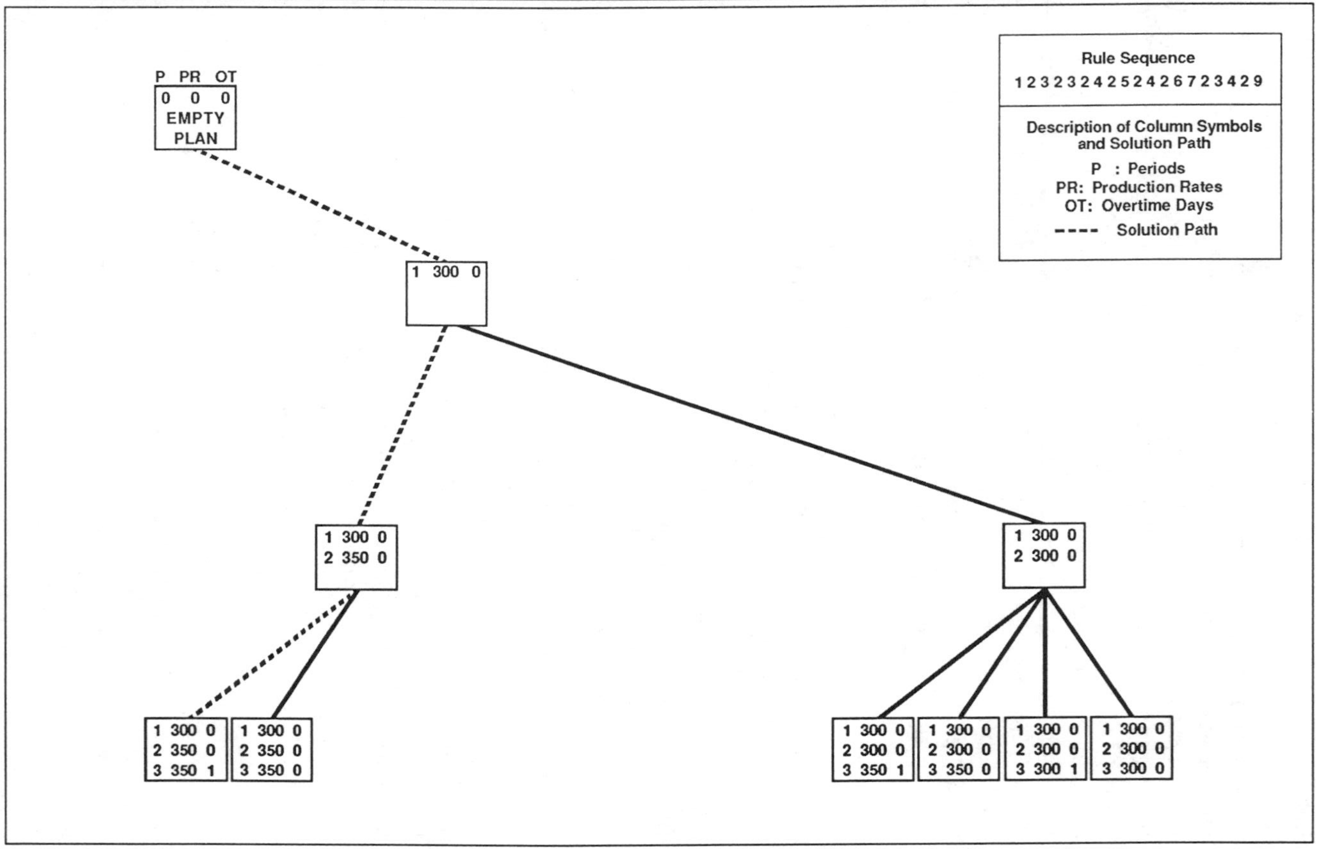

RULE-8 would have executed, continuing the backtracking process by deleting all elements related to the period. Together RULE-6, RULE-7, and RULE-8 execute one simple backtracking strategy. If the ending inventory, as computed by RULE-2 at a new production rate, is greater than or equal to zero, RULE-3 executes, continuing the depth-first search. Production rules are applied to the data base until either RULE-9 is executed, indicating that a complete, feasible plan has been obtained, or RULE-10 is executed, indicating that the system is unable to arrive at a solution. The LHS of RULE-9 identifies a final solution in row 20 of the data base — an ending inventory greater than or equal to zero for each of the three periods.

Only the right-hand side of the state-space is searched to arrive at this solution. The solution path and the sequence of rules that executed are provided at the bottom of Figure 8.6.

8.8   SEARCH MECHANISMS FOR PRODUCTION PLANNING

A number of techniques exist for searching the state-space of partial plans (Nilsson 1980; and Rich 1983). These techniques make explicit only a part of the state-space to arrive at a final solution. A general-purpose search strategy, such as depth-first with backtracking, hill-climbing, or best-first, can be used to decide in which direction the search is to continue. Rules that govern the search are embedded in the inference engine. These rules select the partial plan from which to generate new partial plans. For the example problem, if the ending inventory of an active period is greater than or equal to zero, RULE-3 executes a depth-first search by adding another period and its associated increment element to the data base. As long as an active period's ending inventory meets this condition, RULE-3 repeatedly executes and a production plan is quickly developed. When the ending inventory of an active period is less than zero, an additional day of overtime and an increase in production of 50 are considered, respectively. When neither of these measures work, RULE-6, RULE-7, and RULE-8 execute the backtracking process. RULE-6 eliminates all elements associated with the current period. If permissible, RULE-7 executes, activating the previous period and incrementing its production rate by 50. Otherwise, RULE-8 executes removing the next most recent period's elements.

Although not considered in the example problem in order to simplify the illustration, cost would be one factor on which to base a search. For instance, once feasible values for decision variables for a period are generated, the cost associated with each of them is computed by an actual cost function. These costs are combined with the costs of preceding periods to develop a total cost for the current plan for purposes of evaluation with alternate plans. One method for evaluating the overall quality of the system's solutions would be to have an experienced production planner scrutinize each solution. A system that consistently produces low-cost solutions without violating constraints would be evaluated favorably.

Alone, the general-purpose strategies are not very efficient. However, by coupling one of these strategies with a constraint satisfaction method, gains in efficiency can be made. A major advantage of incorporating constraints into the reasoning process is a reduction in the number of plans evaluated. Plans not satisfying constraints are pruned from the state-space.

Production rules that post constraints in the data base may be used to represent certain operating restrictions that influence the production plan. The rules post constraints that are applicable to a specific period or that are applicable to several periods. As an example of the former, consider the following: the ending inventory for only period 1 must be at least 10 percent of that period's marketing requirements. For the example problem, a production rule for posting this constraint in the data base is:

```
(P RULE-X
 (AGGREGATE-PLAN
   ^PERIOD 1
   ^STATUS  ACTIVE
   ^PRD-RAT <x1>
   ^OVR-TIM <x2>
   ^BEG-INV <x3>
   ^END-INV nil )
 (MKT-REQS
   ^PERIOD 1
   ^DEMAND <x4>)
→
   (MAKE CONSTRAINT
   ^PERIOD 1
   ^TYPE MIN-INV
   ^VALUE COMPUTE (.10 * <x4>))))
```

To test the feasibility of the ending inventory for period 1, a constraint term would be incorporated into the LHS of another rule. For example, to base the test on some minimum inventory value rather than on zero, as done in the example problem, the situation part of RULE-3 in Figure 8.4 would be modified as follows:

```
(P RULE-3
 (CONSTRAINT
   ^PERIOD <x1>
   ^TYPE MIN-INV
   ^VALUE <x2>)

 (AGGREGATE-PLAN
   ^PERIOD x1
   ^STATUS ACTIVE
   ^PRD-RAT <x3>
   ^OVR-TIM <x4>
   ^BEG-INV <x5>
   ^END-INV {<x6> > <x2>})
```

If the ending inventory for the active period exceeds the minimum value (i.e., the value bound to the variable $<x2>$, then an additional period is added to the plan. Otherwise, a search for a feasible solution is initiated. Additional rules may be used to establish minimum and/or maximum levels for other decision variables and to ensure that constraints on these variables are not violated. Posted constraints specific to the current period are removed from the data base after all relevant variables have received feasible values. Those constraints that pertain to more than a single period remain active until no longer needed.

In addition to the constraint satisfaction method presented here, heuristic knowledge can be used to further focus the search. Heuristic information could be incorporated as a heuristic function or as production rules. Heuristic functions associate measures of desirability with problem states to guide the search in the most favorable direction. Nilsson (1980), Rendell (1983), and Rich (1983) describe a number of issues related to the development and use of such functions. Heuristic information in the form of production rules can also select a promising direction. As an example consider the following: if the marketing requirements for the next three periods are increasing, then for the succeeding period only plans with production rates that are equal to or greater than that of the current period should be considered. This information can be encoded as production rules.

8.9 CONCLUSION

A description of the aggregate production planning process and of the important decision variables and constraints that are involved has been provided to elaborate the task domain. Knowledge-engineering concepts pertinent to the development of an expert system for production planning that have been discussed include:

- Representation of the state-space
- Production system design
- Production rule representation of relevant domain knowledge
- Techniques for searching the state-space of partial plans
- Integration of constraints into the solution process to reduce the size of the state-space
- Use of heuristic problem-solving techniques to guide the search toward a final production plan

While the example problem presented in this chapter involves only ten production rules and the consideration of only two decision variables (i.e., production rate and overtime), the technique has sufficient flexibility to expand the number of rules and variables representative of a real-life production planning problem. For an actual problem, other options may have to be considered, such as use of short time, subcontracting, and backlogging. Moreover, the process of making adjustments to production rates would be more complicated than the one used by the example problem, which was to increment the production rate by only 50 when a stockout occurred. For instance, to develop a production plan for fluctuating demand would require a more sophisticated means of adjusting production rates. Additionally, constraint posting as described in this chapter would have to be expanded to capture the variety of operating restrictions that influence a production plan. For instance, factors related to physical, financial, and political realities that impact the plan could be encoded as production rules. The degree to which any of these problem characteristics are present determines the level of difficulty associated with solving a particular production planning problem. Moreover, the level of difficulty determines the size of the state-space, number of production rules written, and other system characteristics. For instance, a more complex problem would require a greater number of production rules.

The task of applying expert system technology to production planning has uncovered several areas requiring additional research. These include:

- Extension of knowledge representation techniques to include the uncertainty in a marketing forecast
- Expansion of initial prototype to include a more generic set of decision variables

The contribution made by this chapter is not that of trying to solve the definitive production planning problem, but rather it is to demonstrate the use of knowledge-based systems techniques on the problem of capturing management expertise and sensitivities to improve consistency in the decision-making process. Knowledge-based systems have the potential to develop powerful problem-solving systems and to gain managerial acceptance because they employ ongoing practices encoded in a rule base and have explanatory facilities. This chapter represents a step toward the realization of this potential as it relates to production planning.

In summary, a production system provides a suitable framework for a knowledge-based system for aggregate production planning. The data base consists of items, described by attributes and associated values, for representing state knowledge. Rules required to solve the problem are stored in a rule base. The rules consist of situation-action pairs that may be expressed as IF-THEN statements. If the situation in the left-hand side of a rule is satisfied, then the right-hand side of the rule is activated to change the contents of the data base in some prescribed way. Once the values of the decision variables for a given period are determined, rules embedded in the inference engine evaluate potential plans and select a partial plan to pursue based on a standard search technique. Constraint satisfaction and heuristic rules, coupled with a standard search technique, are used to efficiently arrive at a feasible final plan.

REFERENCES

Bourne, D.A., and Fox, M.S. (1984), "Autonomous Manufacturing: Automating The Job-Shop," *Computer*, 17(September):76–86.

Bowman, E.H. (1963), "Consistency and Optimality in Managerial Decision Making," *Management Science*, 9(January):310–321.

Davis, R., and King, J. (1977), "An Overview of Production Systems," in E.W. Elcock and D. Michie, *Machine Intelligence 8*, New York: John Wiley and Sons.

Descotte, Y., and Latcombe, J-C. (1981), "GARI: A Problem Solver that Plans How to Machine Mechanical Parts," *Proceedings Seventh International Joint Conference of Artificial Intelligence*, pp. 300–332.

Ennis, S.P. (1983), "Expert Systems An Emerging Computer Technology," *Oil And Gas Journal*, 81(July):184–188.

Erman, L.D., Hayes-Roth, F., Lesser, V.R., and Reddy, D.R. (1980), "The Hearsay-II Speech-Understanding System: Integrating Knowledge to Resolve Uncertainty," *Computing Surveys*, 12(June):213–253.

Fogarty, D.W., and Hoffman, T.R. (1983), *Production And Inventory Management*, Cincinnati, Ohio: South-West Publishing.

Forgy, C.L. (1981), *OPS5 User's Manual*, Department of Computer Science, Carnegie-Mellon University.

Fox, M.S. (1983), "Constraint Directed Search: A Case Study of Job Shop Scheduling," Ph.D. Dissertation, Technical Report, CMU-RI-TR-83-22, Robotics Institute, Carnegie-Mellon University, Pittsburg, Pa.

Fox, M.S., Allen, B., Smith, S., and Strohm, G. (1983), "ISIS: A Constraint Directed Approach to Job-Shop Scheduling," *Proceedings IEEE-CS Conference Trends and Applications*, National Bureau of Standards, Washington, D.C., Technical Report, CMU-RI-TR-83-3, Robotics Institute, Carnegie-Mellon University, Pittsburg, Pa.

Gardner, A.L. (1980), "Search: An Over," *AI Magazine*, 1(Winter):2–6.

Hayes-Roth, F., Waterman, D.A., and Lenat, D.B. (1983), *Building Expert Systems*, Reading, Mass.: Addison-Wesley.

Holt, C.C., Modigliani, F., Muth, J.F., and Simon, H. (1953), "A Linear Decision Rule for Production and Employment Scheduling," *Management Science*, 1(October):1–30.

Jones, C.H. (1967), "Parametric Production Planning," *Management Science*, 13(July):843–866.

Lee, W.B., and Khumawala, B.M. (1974), "Simulation Testing of Aggregate Production Planning Models in an Implementation Methodology," *Management Science*, 20(February):903–911.

Mellichamp, J.M., and Love, R.M. (1978), "Production Switching Heuristics For the Aggregate Planning Problem," *Management Science*, 24(August):1242–1251.

Michaelsen, R., and Michie, D. (1983), "Expert Systems In Business," *Datamation*, 29(November):240–246.

Nau, D.S. (1983), "Expert Computer Systems," *Computer*, 16(February):63–85.

Nilsson, N.J. (1980), *Principles of Artificial Intelligence*, Palo Alto, Calif.: Tioga Publishing.

Rendell, L.A. (1983), "Toward a Unified Approach For Conceptual Knowledge Acquisition," *AI Magazine*, 9(Winter):19–27.

Rich, E. (1983), *Artificial Intelligence*, New York: McGraw-Hill.

Taubert, W.H. (1968), "A Search Decision Rule For The Aggregate Scheduling Problem," *Management Science*, 14(February):B343–B359.

Waterman, D.A., and Hayes-Roth, F. (1978), "An Overview of Pattern-Directed Inference Systems," in D.A. Waterman and F. Hayes-Roth, eds., *Pattern Directed Inference Systems*, New York: Academic Press.

Webster, R., and Miner, L. (1982), "Expert Systems Programming Problem-Solving," *Technology*, 2(January-February):62–73.

9

Resource Allocation by an Expert System

James R. Slagle
Henry Hamburger

An expert consultant system for resource allocation has been implemented at the Naval Research Laboratory. This system, Battle, combines two important tools of artificial intelligence to generate improved resource allocation plans for the Marine Integrated Fire and Air Support System (MIFASS) based on information provided by a user. First, the effectiveness of each individual resource for accomplishing each prospective task is computed using a computation network similar to the networks of PROSPECTOR. The networks used in Battle are generalized to allow nonprobabilistic reasoning and to use a criterion called *merit* for efficient direction of information acquisition. After the calculation of individual effectiveness values, a resource allocation tree is constructed to determine good allocation plans for the set of resources. The individual effectiveness values are used to direct the traversal and pruning of this allocation tree and to select the best allocation plans. This method of search succeeds in finding a globally optimal resource allocation plan.

9.1 INTRODUCTION

Resource allocation is a task that is interesting to all levels of management. Strategic considerations by top management require the evaluation of alternative investments of capital or other company resources. Middle managers must consider how best to use the resources that are currently at their disposal. Operational managers must quickly reallocate resources in response to changing conditions to restore, maintain, or improve production efficiency.

Resource allocation problems can be addressed by managers at all levels using a four step process: (1) define goals, (2) define critical success factors for each goal, (3) define plans for allocating resources to achieve each success factor, and (4) evaluate the relative effectiveness of each possible allocation. Steps 1 and 2 are generic to virtually all management problems (Rockart 1979). Steps 3 and 4 are specific to resource allocation tasks. To accomplish step 3, ideally we would examine all possible combinations of resources and tasks. For many typical problems this is not possible; there are either too many possibilities (e.g., for strategic problems), or there is not enough time to evaluate them all (e.g., for operational problems). To complete step 4 we would additionally need to gather all pertinent facts about the current problem in order to make an informed evaluation. This too, may be impractical if many details must be considered or if time is critical.

However, using techniques from the field of artificial intelligence, systems can be designed that have four advantages over more traditional types of systems. First, they efficiently generate only those alternatives that have a possibility of being better than solutions already discovered. This allows the consideration of many more potential plans than could be generated by manual means. Second, they rapidly converge on the optimal solution. Rapid convergence makes it possible to address time-constrained problems since the system can be stopped at any time with assurances that the best allocation plan generated so far will be close to the best possible solution. Third, they reason with default assumptions in the absence of complete information. Finally, they request data about the most critical factors first. Reasoning with defaults and asking questions intelligently also contribute to getting an initial solution that is close to optimal and to the generation of successively better alternatives as more data become available.

This chapter reports on such a system: a computer-based expert system designed for resource allocation problems. We will describe one version of it called Battle, developed for the United States Marine Corps. The resource allocation problem addressed by this system is an operational one that involves deciding what resources (i.e., weapons) are appropriate for each task (i.e., destruction of a particular target); but the principles would apply equally well to problems of allocating personnel to tasks or positions or to decisions concerning capital commitment.

The remainder of this chapter will consider the Battle system in more detail. We will discuss the problem, the details of the implementation, the achievements of the existing system, and then note some areas for further improvement.

9.2 THE PROBLEM

The objective of the Battle system is to improve the Marine Integrated Fire and Air Support System (MIFASS) by providing recommendations for the allocation of a set of weapons to a set of targets. The key to the MIFASS concept is the forward observer (FO) equipped with a digital communications terminal with burst communication to "provide for the establishment of fire and air support centers to plan, integrate, direct, and coordinate the fires of supporting arms" (MTACCS 1981). The information provided by the FO can be used by Battle for its allocation task.

The resource allocation task is addressed by Battle in two phases. The first phase is the analysis of the effectiveness of allocating each resource to each feasible task. For the specific problem addressed here, this is the effectiveness of a weapon against a target—that is, the expected proportion of the target that would be destroyed if the weapon were fired at it. Effectiveness is the final output of a complex calculation that uses 55 factors of the weapon, target, and battlefield situation. Some examples of the factors used by Battle are:

- Range and position
- Personnel readiness
- Counterfire ability
- Resupply
- Ammunition status
- Number of tubes per group
- Maintenance status

The second phase uses individual effectiveness results from phase 1 to evaluate composite allocations or plans. A plan may call for all available resources (weapons) or any subset of them to be used, and it may have several allocated to the same task (i.e., firing at the same target). The basis for evaluation of a plan is the probabilistic expectation of its total effectiveness. For an application such as analysis of capital investment, effectiveness might be measured by return on investment. For the Battle application, effectiveness is measured by the reduction in target value. A plan that maximizes this quantity will be called *optimal*. The possible plans can be regarded as constituting a tree, but one that in typical circumstances is too large to be constructed and examined exhaustively.

To provide intelligent recommendations, Battle must acquire reliable information of two kinds. It first must have knowledge of the generally applicable expertise in the subject matter. This includes information about what factors determine how effective each kind of resource is when applied to various kinds of tasks and functional relationships among these factors. Second, the system must obtain information that is specific to the current problem from a user at the decision center. Under some circumstances the user may wish to direct what information is given to the system, and in other situations the user may want the system to ask about whatever it currently considers to be the most critical facts.

9.3   OVERVIEW OF THE BATTLE IMPLEMENTATION

Battle was programmed for a Digital Equipment Corporation (DEC) VAX 11/780 using the FRANZ LISP dialect of Lisp. Development required approximately five person-years over a two-and-one-half-year period. The first phase of the Battle algorithm, as described earlier, is the computation of the effectiveness of each resource (weapon) on each task (target). Battle moves significantly beyond the capabilities of its predecessor, MIFASS, by the range of battlefield factors it considers. The current MIFASS implementation does take into account some restrictions directly related to the weapon and target, notably fire time, fire zones, and the availability of ammunition. However, it ignores other important aspects of the situation, such as the combat readiness of personnel, resupply possibilities for various resources, and weather, which can be decisive factors in a military engagement. At best, MIFASS has default values for these factors, but the factors do not have constant values in real battlefield situations, and the variations have important effects.

To overcome these limitations, Battle uses a computation network constructed with rules specified by a military expert to propagate information through a data base. Every factor specified by the expert can play a role in the determination of the effectiveness of each weapon against each target. The network is a generalization of the inference networks of PROSPECTOR (Duda et al 1979). Like a PROSPECTOR network, it propagates information. However, it is more general by allowing forms of information other than probabilities, inferencing about an unlimited number of objects (the weapons and targets), and permitting the classification of those objects into types. In addition, a procedure called the *merit system* minimizes the amount of work and time required to enter the highly relevant information.

The second phase uses the evaluations of effectiveness of each resource for each task along with user-supplied task values to evaluate complete allocation plans. The original MIFASS algorithm, developed at Oklahoma State University (1975–77), sought good allocation plans by optimizing on successive resources (Case and Thibault 1976, 1977). However, to ensure an optimal allocation plan, it is necessary to solve the allocation problem as a whole, allowing for the possibility that the generally most effective resources may not always be allocated to the most valuable tasks. It must also be possible for two or more resources to be allocated to the same task.

The technique of successive individual allocation may seem intuitively sound, so it may be worth a brief digression to show its weakness. A qualitative example with just two resources and two tasks suffices to make the point. Suppose that one resource is effective on either task, but slightly more so on the first task. The tasks are of equal value. The other resource, although ineffective on the second task, is almost as effective as the first resource on the first task. Successive individual allocation will lead to an inferior allocation plan because the first resource will be allocated to the first task.

To find the plan with maximum effectiveness, one could compute the effectiveness for every possible plan. Battle can find an optimal plan without looking at all possible plans because it uses a pruning algorithm to eliminate plans with less than maximum effectiveness. The user can specify how many of the best plans should be kept by Battle as it proceeds. A plan is dropped from consideration if there are this specific number of plans that are demonstrably as effective. Notice that if the number specified is 1, then Battle will provide an optimal plan. The search method used by Battle is a pruned traversal of an allocation tree. Each node in the tree represents the choice, for a particular resource, among the $t + 1$ possibilities: being allocated to any of the t tasks or remaining unallocated. The way in which we have organized this tree enables the search to gain particular benefit from the pruning method it employs.

The importance of pruning is suggested by the size of the allocation tree, which is $(t + 1)^r$, where r is the number of resources. Exhaustive search of such a tree would be impractical for values of t and r that might characterize a complex resource allocation problem. Even with pruning, a substantial portion of the tree must be explored. Whether the computation time involved turns out to be a practical problem will depend on the implementation and on the complexity of the application. Accurate results, as emphasized here, may turn out to be more important than the time saved.

The user of Battle may choose to have an optimal plan generated or a plan that has less than the maximum effectiveness, that is, suboptimal. The tradeoff is the degree of optimality of the plan versus the time required for computation. For example, the optimum solution for the allocation of 8 weapons to 17 targets, in our research setting, took 11 minutes 43 seconds. A suboptimal allocation that was nevertheless 98 percent as effective as the optimal plan consumed 6.75 seconds.

In addition to considering very many factors in the first phase and assuring optimality in the second phase, Battle also takes into consideration many human factors. This results in the following advantages for the user listed on p. 200.

- Allows user control of information input
- Uses simple commands
- Allows easy error recovery
- Warns user of potential errors
- Provides interactive assistance

9.4 DATA BASE AND COMPUTATION NETWORK

The computation of the effectiveness of each resource on each task in phase 1 is carried out by a computation network directing the flow of information through a data base. These two principal, interrelated aspects of this part of Battle—the data base and the computation network—are described in turn.

9.4.1 The Data Base

The data base holds information about the various battlefield units. For present purposes, there are two broad categories of such units: the weapon units (resources), belonging to the friendly side, and the target units (places to allocate resources to), belonging to the enemy side. There is information in the data base not only about individual units but also about weapon-target pairs—for example, the distance between the two units. Each datum in the data base is a triple. For example, the datum (size, (E6), 15000) represents an assertion that the size of some enemy unit, E6, say an oil depot, is 15000 m^2. In this and following examples, selected from data in Battle, unit identifiers are given as E or F (for enemy or friendly), followed by a number.

The form of a datum is similar to the classical relational format (<attribute>, <object>, <value>). It differs, however, since the second element is not simply an object but a list of objects that in the previous example happens to have just one element. An example with a two-object list is (can-reach, (F7, E23), 0.9) that represents a subjective probability of 0.9 that the weapons of unit F7 can reach target E23. The term *attribute* seems inappropriate for the first element of the triple, when the second element is a list with more than one object. We will therefore call the first element of the datum a *datum function*. Each datum thus takes the form (<datum-function>, <object-list>, <value>).

The use of the term *datum function* is suggested by the possibility of writing the datum in the functional form size(E6) = 15000. Use of the functional form, size(E6), provides a way to refer to a possibly unknown value. The object E6 in the object list can appropriately be called an *argument*, and we will from here on call the object list an *argument list*. We shall also have occasion to refer to an object list as a *context*. The terminology also applies to two-object lists for two-argument functions such as can-reach.

Before leaving the subject of datum functions, it is worth noting that a predicate is a special datum function, one whose values are chosen from the set {true, false}. By analogy, a function such as can-reach, whose values are subjective probabilities that something is true, can be termed a *probabilistic predicate.*

9.4.2 The Computation Network

The computation network, as noted, is intimately related to the data base. It determines how certain values are computed to update the data base. Before describing this use of the network, let us examine its structure. The computation network has a set of nodes and a set of directed links between nodes. Each link connects two nodes, called the (direct) *antecedent* and the *consequent.* A node may be the antecedent of zero, one, or more other nodes and may be the consequent of zero, one, or more other nodes. When there is a sequence of links such that the consequent of each link is the antecedent of the next, we say that the antecedent of the first link and the consequent of the last are the indirect antecedent and the indirect consequent. We will assume that the network is acyclic, meaning that no node may be its own indirect consequent. A node that has no consequents is called a *top node,* and one that has no antecedents is called a *bottom node.*

Each node in the network has several kinds of information associated with it. Of particular importance in the specification of a node are its datum function, already introduced, and its assignment function. These two functions are used together in the updating process, as will be seen in the following discussion. The assignment function specifies relationships that must be maintained among data values in the data base. (Recall that the value is the third element of a datum.) Therefore, when one value changes, other values must also change to keep the assignment functions satisfied. These new changes, in turn, require changes in other data, via other assignment functions. In this way the effects of new information can be propagated through the data base.

A detailed example of a node should help clarify the foregoing. Our example will be a top node. Before discussing the example, we provide some perspective on the role of the node that is to be described.

The objective in phase 1 is to compute sound values for the effectiveness of each weapon unit against each target unit. This translates into determining values for those data whose datum function is effectiveness, such as (effectiveness, (F5, E13), 0.4). The military decision maker is typically unable to provide, directly and instantaneously, reliable estimates for all the effectiveness values. However, a military expert can specify in advance on what kinds of things effectiveness depends. For example, the distance from the weapon to the target should be neither too large nor too small in comparison to the range of the weapon, and the weapon unit should be well matched to the target. Values of these data may depend in turn on other characteristics of the weapon and the target, considered either jointly or separately, as well as aspects of the general situation.

In the computation network, such knowledge of relationships is represented by nodes and the links that connect them. In particular, consider a node EFF1, whose datum function is effectiveness. There is such a node in the network, and its assignment function has three arguments, corresponding to the three nodes with links directed to it. These three nodes have datum functions called max-range-ok, min-range-ok, and good-match. The assignment function of EFF1 is the product function for three variables, that is, f, where $f(x,y,z) = xyz$.

Now suppose that Battle is to compute the effectiveness of weapon unit F5 against target E13 by applying f to the values max-range-ok (F5, E13), min-range-ok (F5, E13), and good-match (F5, E13). These three values would be looked up in the data base and multiplied together.

Notice that the assignment function at node EFF1 is used for updating effectiveness not only for the particular objects F5 and E13 but for other weapons and targets as well. The domain of applicability of the node need not be all weapons and targets, however. Each node has a domain constraint that specifies what contexts it applies to according to their types.

A second example will show some other possibilities. Let there be a node, AMM1, with a one-argument datum function called has-ample-ammunition. Suppose that the assignment function of this node is g, where $g(x,y) = 1 - (1 - x)(1 - y)$. The presence of two arguments in this assignment function signals the existence of two antecedent nodes, while the function g itself is a model for combining the probabilities of two independent events, either of which ensures the occurrence of some third event. An *event* for us consists of a probabilistic predicate together with a specific list of arguments for it.

Since AMM1 has to do with having ample ammunition, one might reasonably expect its two antecedent nodes, RES1 and DEP1, to concern the existence of active resupply lines and the existence of an ammunition depot. Therefore let the one-argument datum functions on these antecedent nodes be has-resupply and has-ammo-depot. The assignment function, g, of AMM1 determines the probability of being amply supplied by computing the probabilistic "or" function on these two antecedent nodes.

So far we have mentioned three nodes but no data. We now introduce three data, one corresponding to each node and all with the same context, namely E9, a particular enemy unit. First, let the data base contain (has-ample-ammunition, (E9), 0.9), signifying that Battle currently contains 0.9 as the probability that E9 has ample ammunition. In addition, corresponding to the antecedent nodes, suppose that the data base contains (has-resupply, (E9), 0.5) and (has-ammo-depot, (E9), 0.8). If the probability of E9 having an ammunitions depot were to drop, possibly as a result of a bombardment whose results could not be observed, the user may request that has-ammo-depot(E9) be decreased to 0.6. This change leads Battle to examine consequents of node DEP1, including our example consequent AMM1. Using g, the assignment function of AMM1, has-ample-ammunition(E9) is set to $1 - (1 - 0.5)(1 - 0.6) = 0.8$. This new information is then propagated appropriately, beginning with the updating of data associated with the consequent nodes of AMM1.

9.4.3 A More Careful Treatment

In this section we introduce systematic terminology, still interspersed with examples but no longer relying on them. We begin with the objects on which Battle operates and then return to datum functions and assignment functions.

Unit — Units are the basic objects about which Battle reasons. A unit is either a weapon system that may attack only a single target at a time or a target area that may be the subject of an attack.

Side — There are two sides, called friendly and enemy. Every unit is either a friendly unit or an enemy unit. Every friendly unit is a weapon unit, while enemy units (called *targets*) may be weapons, other items such as vehicles or command posts, or combinations thereof.

Type — Types are a partition of the units with similar weapons or functions. No type may include both friendly and enemy units, so the side of a type is well defined. This use of the word *type* is derived from the notion of a data type.

Context — A list of units, containing no more than one unit from each side, is called a *context*.

Match — A unit is said to match a type if the unit is a member of that type. A context matches a list of types (with at most one type from each side) if each unit of the context matches the corresponding type. One weapon possessed by the friendlies is 105-mm artillery. These are clustered together in batteries generally consisting of six weapons that always fire together. A battery of them is considered to be a unit. Such a unit is of the type called friendly-art105. The unit itself will have a name like F34.

Using these definitions we can now be more precise about some other aspects of Battle.

Datum function — A datum function is a function whose domain is a set of contexts. A context is in the domain of a datum function if it matches one of the domain constraints of that datum function. Any set of numbers can be the codomain of a datum function.

Domain constraint — A domain constraint is a list of types, containing at most one type from each side. Positions in the list correspond to argument positions of a datum function.

As noted in the definitions, the domain of a datum function is specified by types, that is, subsets of the friendly and enemy units represented in Battle. On the other hand, the codomain of a datum function is typically not a type as we have defined it, but a set more like the classical notion of a data type. If the datum function is a probabilistic predicate, for example, then the codomain is the set of real numbers between 0 and 1.

Data base — The data base is the set of all data. Each datum is a triple consisting of a datum function, a context that is in the domain of the datum function, and the value of the datum function for that context. In the implementation, a datum function receives a permissible context (list of objects) and returns the associated value by looking it up in the data base.

The relationship between the data and the network can now be clarified. Recall that a node has a datum function and one domain constraint, and a datum has a datum function and a context. A node represents a datum when their datum functions are the same and the datum's context matches the node's domain constraint. The same datum function may appear on several nodes with different domain constraints, representing different sets of data. The domain of the datum function is the union of the sets specified by different domain constraints.

Nodes with the same datum function but different domain constraints mean the same thing in the real world. For example, "can-reach" always means the ability to deliver destructive force to a target. The reason for having different nodes with the same datum function is that different assignment functions (for updating) may be appropriate for different types of units. For example, with aircraft, but not with artillery, the ability to reach a target hinges on the availability of fuel. Thus a fuel supply node is an antecedent of any node with the datum function can-reach and a domain constraint that specifies an aircraft as the friendly unit, whereas a node with that same datum function but with a friendly artillery type in its domain constraint would have no antecedent dealing with fuel supply.

Each node on the computation network has an associated default value that its datum function returns when no specific information has been supplied. This default value must belong to the codomain of the datum function.

Here are some examples of nodes whose datum functions apply to two-, one-, and zero-element contexts respectively. The name of the datum function is given first, followed by an appropriate domain constraint. These two items together determine a node. The name of the node is given next, formed by concatenating the function name and the various elements of the domain constraint in appropriate order. The codomain of the datum function, a possible context for the datum function, and a default value are given next. In the second example the datum function is not a probabilistic predicate, since its codomain is not probability.

1. can-reach
   (friendly-art 105, enemy-art122)
   art105-can-reach-art122
   probability
   (F7, E23)
   0.9
2. size-of
   (enemy-oil-depot)
   size-of-enemy-oil-depot
   positive real number
   (E6)
   10000
3. it-is-raining
   ()
   it-is-raining
   probability
   ()
   0.2

Now that we have described the representational aspects of the computation network, we turn to inference. We intend that Battle be able to infer the value of a consequent datum from the values of antecedent data. To this end, we must first extend the definition of the antecedent-consequent relation between nodes to apply to the data represented by those nodes. We will then discuss the mechanics of inference.

When the nodes representing two data are the consequent and the antecedent of a link and when the context of the first datum contains every unit in the context of the second, we say that the data are each other's (direct) consequent and antecedent, respectively. We extend this definition to indirect consequents and antecedents of data similarly. Every unit in the context of the antecedent datum must appear in the context of the consequent datum.

Recall that in addition to its datum function each nonbottom node also has an assignment function whose arguments correspond to the antecedents of the node. The assignment function accepts as arguments precisely the values mandated by the respective codomains of the datum functions of its antecedents. In turn its set of possible values is just the codomain of the datum function on its own node. The following definition specifies how an assignment function updates the value of a datum.

Assignment — Assignment is the change of the value part of a datum by applying the assignment function of its node to the values of its direct antecedent data.

Propagation — Propagation is a sequence of assignments, beginning with any datum and proceeding to its indirect consequents. More precisely, propagation has the effect of assigning that datum and propagating its direct consequent data.

Connections between nodes are specified by experts based on their specific domain knowledge. Nevertheless, it is possible to make some general technical comments on node relationships. To do so we use the ideas of context length and relevance, as follows. Since a context is a list, it has a length, so we may speak of it as being long or short. Generally speaking, a datum with a short context will be relevant to more contexts than a datum with a long context. More precisely, a datum can be relevant only to a context of which its own context is a subset. From information about a unit, we may infer information about that unit's interaction with any unit of the opposite side. From information about the battlefield in general — data with empty contexts — we may infer information about any units or combinations of units on the battlefield.

Although the previous example concerns data, a corresponding point can be made about connections among nodes. If two nodes are the antecedent and consequent of a link, then the domain constraint of the antecedent node must be a subset of the domain constraint of the consequent node. This requirement ensures that when Battle does an assignment, it will not use narrowly applicable information to draw broadly applicable conclusions. Note in particular that the requirement does not rule out the most common case, in which the antecedent and consequent have the same domain constraint.

Having explored the structure of the network and how to use assignment functions, let us turn to the question of what functions are used. Battle supplies the expert with a variety of prepackaged assignment functions as an aid in setting up the network. Included are probabilistic versions of "and," "or," and "not," each of which is restricted to probabilities on both the input and output side. The simplest of them is "not," which has one argument $not(x) = 1 - x$. The "and" and "or" functions may take any number of arguments. The "and" function returns the product of its arguments. The "or" function may be defined by "and" and "not." Apply "not" to each argument, form the product ("and") of the results, and apply "not" to that product.

Battle also provides a facility for constructing assignment functions from a family called *evidence functions*. These functions make assignments with the subjective Bayesian method described by Duda et al. (1981). An evidence function makes use of estimates of the prior probability of its node and the conditional probabilities of its node, given the truth or falsity of each antecedent.

An important feature of the evidence functions is that certain truth or certain falsity of an antecedent does not necessarily lead to certainty about whether the consequent is true. This is desirable behavior for the function to have if in reality the antecedent has minor influence on the consequent. Such minor influence cannot be represented with either "and" or "or." For "or," the truth of any antecedent must always lead to the truth of the consequent. For "and," the falsity of any antecedent must always lead to the falsity of the consequent.

Despite their flexibility, system-defined assignment functions will not be appropriate for some nodes. This will be the case, for instance, whenever any of the input or output values is not a probability. To deal with this, Battle allows for the possibility of new kinds of functions specified by the expert. The programming work associated with such specification is minimal.

9.5   AN EXAMPLE FROM BATTLE

The Battle system has a computation network that was designed to decide the effectiveness of a particular type of weapon (e.g., 105-mm artillery) against a particular type of target (e.g., an oil depot). For various artillery weapons against various artillery targets, our expert, Marine Corps Major Edward Lucke, constructed a set of similar computation networks, each representing a subnetwork of the required network.

Each top node in the Battle network represents the effectiveness of a particular weapon type against a particular target type. In the artillery versus artillery subnetworks, a top node is a conjunction of three other nodes. The target must be within the maximum range of the weapon, it must be outside the minimum range of the weapon, and there must otherwise be a good match. A good match must include superior firepower of the friendly unit. An evidence function assigns a value to the good-match datum function. Superior firepower is computed by an expert-defined assignment function, mor, that compares the number of artillery pieces (tubes) possessed by both sides. These "number of tubes" nodes are bottom nodes, having no antecedents in the network. In all, there are 55 datum functions and 671 nodes.

9.6   ENTERING INFORMATION FOR A
PARTICULAR DECISION

To use the system, one first enters data relevant to a particular decision. If such data is already present, the user may wish to augment or alter it. One straightforward mode of data entry is called *volunteer*. The volunteer mode is initiated by a user who wishes to enter some particular datum. The datum may correspond to any node. After it is entered, propagation is done, potentially altering all data for which that datum is a direct or indirect antecedent.

In the questioning mode, on the other hand, Battle directs a dialog with the user. When entering the questioning mode, the user must specify a friendly unit, an enemy unit, or both as a context. Battle then proceeds to select questions, each one based on a datum function with arguments chosen from the user-supplied context. There will be a way to choose arguments from the context, consistent with the domain constraint of the datum function. The user may answer the question that is formed in this way either by providing a value, thereby completing a datum to be entered into the data base, or by refusing to answer.

An important design decision about the questioning mode is how Battle chooses a datum function for its next question to the user. To improve the efficiency of data entry, the question should have the best combination of being easy to answer and influential on the final decision. For this purpose we have devised the merit system (Slagle and Halpern 1982; Slagle and Gaynor 1983; and Hamburger and Slagle 1983). The question selected by the merit system is not invariably posed to the user. If the answer to that question has already been supplied to the data base by the user, then, understandably, Battle does not ask it, no matter whether the answer was supplied voluntarily or completed under questioning. Battle will also suppress a question that was previously asked and that the user refused to answer. At a more general level, the expert may have declared as unaskable a particular datum function and hence all questions associated with it. All other datum functions and questions are askable. A refused or unaskable question may ultimately be answered internally with the use of its assignment function and antecedent nodes.

The merit system proposes a question that will be put to the user if that question meets certain requirements. The merit system bases its choice of what question to propose next on a combination of two factors: how easy it will be to get an answer and how useful an answer is likely to be in reaching a decision. *Usefulness* here means, in effect, influence on the top node that is associated with the context that the user has specified.

The first step in understanding how these ideas are implemented is to look at the self-merit. *Self-merit* is the expected variability in the value part (third element) of a datum per unit of cost to get a new value. For example, weather would have a high self-merit. The cost is the difficulty of providing an answer. The scale or unit of cost does not matter, so long as the various costs are consistent with each other. Cost is presumably higher for questioning the user than for making an internal computation to get a new value. Also, among internal computations, one could let cost be proportional to the number of antecedents, other things being equal. However, these recommendations need not be followed. Indeed, costs are included in Battle only indirectly, via the self-merits, and these are at the disposal of the expert. The expert specifies a self-merit for each node.

In addition to self-merits, Battle also requires specification of a link-merit function on each link connecting an antecedent node to its consequent node. Roughly, the idea of a link merit is to transmit estimates of variability, that is, to provide a means of computing the variability of a consequent, given the variability of its antecedent. The link merit is computed by formally differentiating the assignment function. The merit system operates on a single top node, specifically the one that concerns effectiveness of a particular friendly weapon against a particular enemy target. The weapon and target are those specified in the current context picked by the user.

Given a top node and a context that has both a weapon and a target, Battle selects a node on which to base its question. This node will be an indirect antecedent of the given top node and will have maximal merit. The corresponding question that is formed will therefore have the best combination of being easy to answer and influential to the top node. After checking its askability and related matters mentioned previously, Battle asks the user to specify a value for the corresponding datum function in the specified context. After the user responds, merits are recalculated, and another most meritorious unasked question is again selected. If the merit of the next question that can be asked is less than a cut-off value specified by the user, Battle will stop questioning the user.

A more formal presentation of the merit system follows. Given a context, each relevant datum function together with that context determines a question. We speak of antecedent and consequent relations between questions whenever these relations hold between the corresponding nodes. An antecedent question will be called a subquestion of its consequent question. Let G be a top question and let its subquestions be G_i, for $i = 1,...,$ degree (G). Each subquestion G_i may itself have subquestions designated G_{ij}, for $j = 1,...,$ degree (G_i). Additional subscripts show successive subquestion levels. The merit of the question $G_{ij...st}$ on the top question G, is defined by the partial derivative

$$\frac{|\partial V(G)|}{|\partial C(G_{ij....st})|}$$

where $V(G)$ is the value of the top question and $C(G_{ij...st})$ is the cost of getting an answer to the question $G_{ij...st}$. Absolute value is used because increases and decreases in value are equally important. The amount of change is the determining factor.

The merit has been expressed as a derivative relating the value $V(G)$ of a top question to the cost $C(G_{ij...st})$ of asking a question that is its direct or indirect antecedent. The chain rule may be used to express the derivative as

$$\frac{|\delta V(G)|}{|\delta C(G_{ij....st})|} = \frac{|\delta V(G)|}{|\delta V(G_i)|} \frac{\delta V(G_i)}{\delta V(G_{ij})} \cdots \frac{\delta V(G_{ij....st})}{\delta V(G_{ij....st})} \frac{\partial V(G_{ij....st})|}{\partial C(G_{ij....st})|}$$

All factors except the last in this expansion have a similar form. These factors, called link merits, are computed by Battle using link-merit functions. The last factor expresses the ability to change $V(G_{ij...st})$ per unit cost applied in expansion of $G_{ij...st}$. This is precisely the definition of self-merit.

The procedure for selecting a question with maximal merit is as follows. Battle starts at the top node determined by the user's choice of context and examines all subquestions of that question. A merit value is calculated for each subquestion, and a subquestion with the merit value of greatest absolute value is selected, with ties being broken arbitrarily. If that subquestion is askable and has not been previously asked, it is asked. If the user answers the question, this response is propagated through the network to the top node, and the question is marked as answered. If the user decides to skip the question, this refusal is recorded, and the subquestions of that question are made available for questioning. After the user's response has been processed, the whole process is repeated, selecting the most meritorious of the remaining questions.

Merit values allow Battle to question the user about the battlefield in an intelligent manner. This algorithm always asks the most important questions first. Focusing on the important issues saves user time that would be wasted by classical depth-first traversal of a network. We have compared merit with the J^* algorithm used by PROSPECTOR by generating the values of two antecedents of a single node over a range of 26 probabilities; J^* never chose the more meritorious antecedent. See (Slagle and Gaynor 1983) for more detail.

9.7 THE ALLOCATION TREE

In the Battle system, each top node of the computation network represents the effectiveness of one type of friendly weapon (e.g., 105-mm artillery) against one type of target (e.g., an oil depot or a 122-mm artillery unit). Effectiveness is the ratio of expected destruction to total destruction and hence lies between zero and one. Targets may be composites of more than one type, for example, a camp containing both an oil depot and a 122-mm artillery unit. To calculate the effectiveness of one friendly unit against the composite target, we use a weighted average of the effectiveness of the friendly against each target component. To calculate the effectiveness of massing several friendly units against a single target, we take the complement of the product of the complements of the individual effectiveness numbers, corresponding to independent effectivenesses of the weapons.

Once an effectiveness value on a particular target has been determined, it is multiplied by its value to get the expected destruction. It is now possible to compute the total destruction by the allocation plan under consideration. It is just the sum of the values of expected destruction against all the various targets to be fired on.

To explore all the possible allocation plans, so that an optimal can be selected for a battlefield, we introduce a weapon allocation tree. Each level on the tree corresponds to the deployment of a different weapon, so that the number of levels on the tree is equal to the number of weapons in the situation. The degree of the tree is one greater than the total number of targets. This is because at each node of the tree there is one link for each target, corresponding to using the weapon against that target, and one other link, corresponding to not using the weapon. Each possible allocation plan of the weapons corresponds to a path from the root of the allocation tree to a given leaf. Massing of several weapons on a single target — often an important possibility — is represented by a path that for some i includes the ith link at each of several nodes on the path.

Battle will produce a number of best allocation plans, k, where k is chosen by the user. The presentation of multiple plans allows the user to override Battle's ranking of the options. As each of the first k leaves is encountered on the allocation tree, the corresponding allocation plan is added to a tentative solution list. Once this list reaches its full length, k, it remains full. Alteration of this list occurs thereafter only by substituting a new plan for an older one with lower expected total destruction. This list is used in pruning.

The number of leaves of an allocation tree for w weapons and t targets is $(t + 1)w$. This is too large to traverse for realistic fire support situations, so we prune the tree during its traversal. Pruning occurs if a partial plan cannot be completed to outrank one or more of the best plans so far. Therefore there is no pruning until k complete plans have entered the tentative solution list.

The pruning algorithm requires, for each type of weapon, the specification of a fighting capacity — the maximum destruction by that weapon type against any target in any circumstance. To see if a partial allocation plan should be pruned, its expected destruction is added to the combined fighting capacities of the weapons remaining to be used in completing that partial plan. If this sum does not exceed the expected destruction from the least destructive of the k complete plans currently on the tentative solution list, no attempt is made to complete the partial plan. It results in a substantial savings of time during the traversal. The weapons and targets are each ordered in decreasing value to maximize the expected amount of pruning.

9.8   FINDINGS

The Battle program has been exercised on an 8-weapon versus 17-target scenario, constructed with the advice of a Marine Corps artillery expert.

The expert judged the allocation plans generated by Battle against his expertise and found the plans to be acceptable solutions for the destruction of the targets. Therefore Battle has demonstrated face validity. It appears to do what it was designed to do. We will show Battle operating on a changing scenario later in this section.

We also examined the operation of Battle in a descriptive experiment, by timing the production of optimal assignment plans. The CPU time required for additional assignment plans is illustrated in Figure 9.1. The data points represent the average of 2 runs for the allocation of 8 weapons against 17 targets for the requested number of plans increasing from 1 to 25 plans. The maximum time to generate 25 plans was under 18 seconds. The required CPU time for increasing the number of plans increases at a decreasing rate.

9.8.1 Scenario

We will now present a scaled-down scenario to illustrate how the Battle system incorporates acquired information to modify its allocation plans. The situation shown in Figure 9.2 was presented to Battle. The dotted arrows show the preferred solution selected by Battle. The targets are: T1, a fixed target whose value is 40; T2, a 122-mm battery, with value = 60; T3, a 130-mm battery, with value = 70; T4, a 152-mm battery, with value

FIGURE 9.1
THE CPU TIME TO COMPUTE VARIOUS NUMBERS OF WEAPON-TARGET ASSIGNMENT PLANS FOR AN 8-WEAPON 17-TARGET SCENARIO

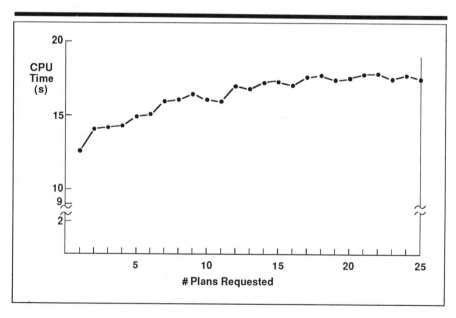

= 75; and T5, a fixed target valued at 100. The friendly units are: F1, a 155-mm battery; F2, an 8-in battery; F3, a 105-mm battery; and two mortars, F4-60 mm and F5-81 mm. Note that F3 and F5, are massed on target T1. We see that F4 is not allocated because all targets are out of range of its mortars.

In Figure 9.3, the friendly units have advanced to the northeast. T1 is now within firing range of F4, and F4 joins both F3 and F5 in massing on the target. In addition, the firepower of F1 has been switched from T3 to T5, a more valuable target that has just come into range.

Next in Figure 9.4, the target T1 has been neutralized by F3 and F5. Simultaneously, a new threat, T6, has appeared. The allocation plan chosen by Battle uses no massing and leaves both mortars (F4, F5) idle because they are out of range. Also F2 has been changed from T2 to T6 since it is the more valuable target of the two.

The unit positions remain unchanged in Figure 9.5. Intelligence reports, however, have recently discovered that T2 is not a 122-mm artillery piece, but an important mobile rocket launcher. Battle redirects both F1 and F2 to mass on T2. The two mortars, F4 and F5, again are idle because they are out of range. If the mortars are moved into position, as in Figure 9.6, Battle will include them in its fire plan. In addition, when target T4 moves into range for F3, that weapon is switched from T3 to T4.

After some pounding from F1, F2, F4, and F5, intelligence reports that T2 has lost its rocket-launching capacity. Its priority value is lowered, since it is no longer absolutely necessary to destroy it. None of the other units has moved or changed, but the allocation plan illustrated in Figure 9.7 has changed from Figure 9.6. There is no longer massing on T2. Each friendly weapon has been allocated to a different target.

Finally, through use of its questioning mechanism, Battle has determined that T5 is not an appropriate target for artillery fire. This information updates the effectiveness of F1 on T5, and as Figure 9.8 shows, F1 is reallocated to T6. A further reallocation of F2 from T6 to T2 is performed to optimize the allocation plan.

This limited scenario has demonstrated the weapon allocation for maximum expected total destruction to the enemy targets as range and value of targets changed from moment to moment.

9.8.2   Limitations of Battle

Since Battle is a demonstration project for the use of artificial intelligence techniques for the weapons allocation problem and similar resource allocation problems, there are some things it cannot do. The limitations include:

- It uses only static descriptions of resources; it does not simulate the changes that occur when used (e.g., does not automatically update fuel or ammunition usage as the battle goes on).

FIGURE 9.2
THE WEAPON-TARGET ASSIGNMENT FOR A 5-WEAPON 5-TARGET ASSIGNMENT
SCENARIO. TWO OF THE WEAPONS ARE MASSED ON ONE OF THE TARGETS, AND
ANOTHER WEAPON IS NOT USED.

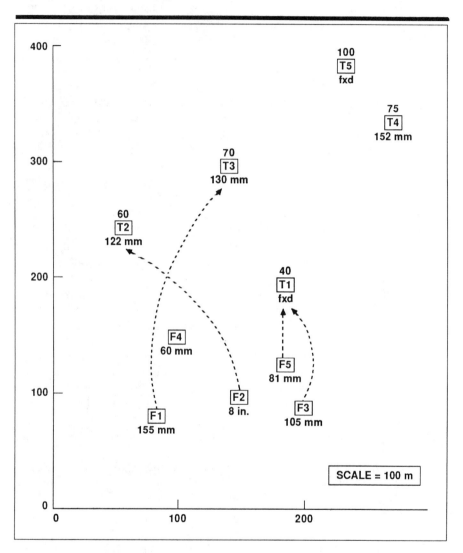

- It does not consider resource interactions when computing effectiveness and therefore will not schedule resource use to maximize this effectiveness (e.g., weapons effectiveness may depend on whether other weapons are being fired simultaneously at the same target).

FIGURE 9.3
THE REVISED WEAPON-TARGET ASSIGNMENTS AFTER AN ADVANCE OF FRIENDLY UNITS

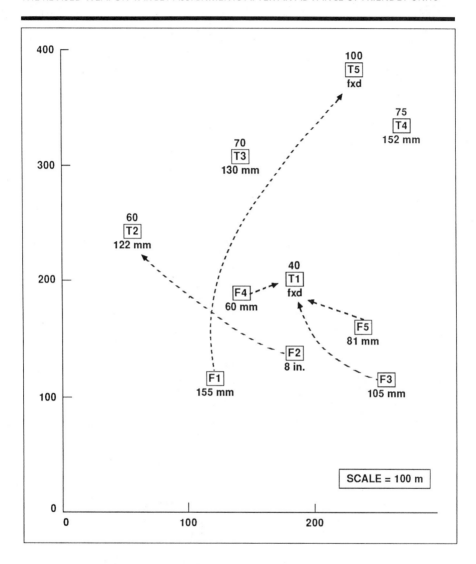

- It does not consider that resources may be used in different ways on different tasks with varying degrees of effectiveness (e.g., a given weapon may have different munition or fuse types that may be more or less effective on different targets).

Battle can be extended to overcome these limitations, and we are now engaged in such extensions.

FIGURE 9.4
AFTER NEUTRALIZATION OF T1, THE SYSTEM REDIRECTS THE WEAPONS THAT WERE USED ON IT. ALSO, A NEW TARGET DRAWS FIRE.

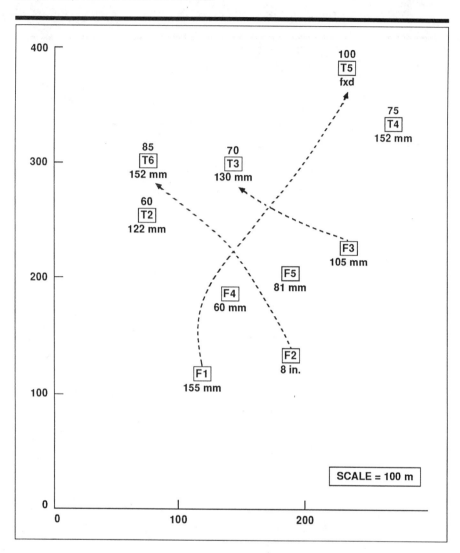

FIGURE 9.5
THE EFFECT ON WEAPON ASSIGNMENT OF A CHANGE IN TARGET VALUE

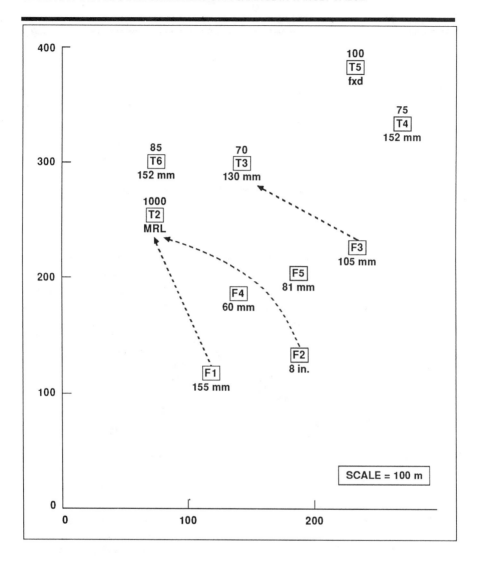

217

FIGURE 9.6
THE ASSIGNMENT AFTER MORTAR UNITS F4 AND F5 HAVE MOVED WITHIN RANGE OF
TARGET T2 AND AFTER T4 HAS COME CLOSER TO F3

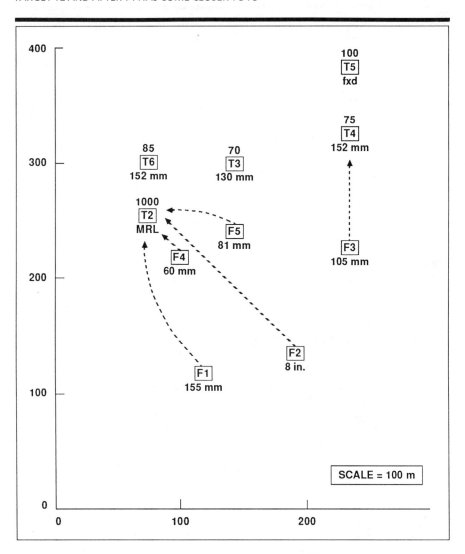

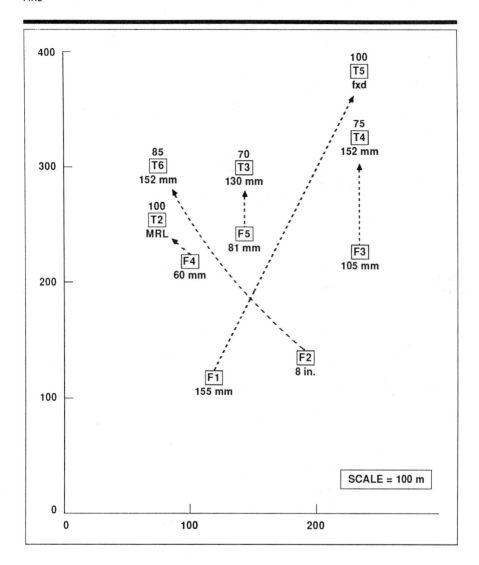

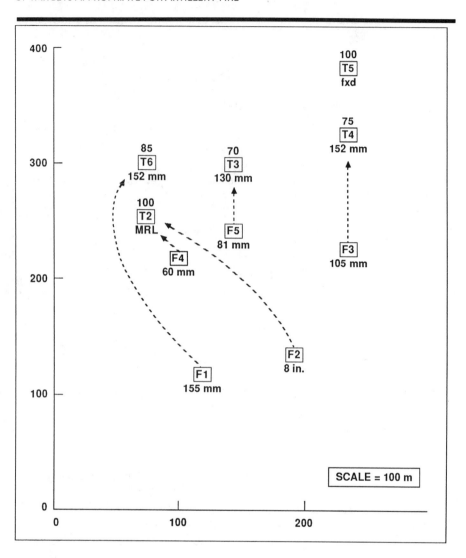

9.9   CONCLUSION

This report has presented Battle, an expert consultant system using artificial intelligence techniques to provide optimal and suboptimal resource allocation (weapon-target assignment) plans. Battle provides a dynamic user interface with simple commands, error warning, easy error recovery, and interactive user assistance. For example, the user may ask questions about resources (weapons) or tasks (targets) with *qw* or *qt* commands, or the user may modify the position, type, or value of a resource (friendly weapon) or task (target) with the commands *mf* or *mt*. Other similar commands exist to aid the user interaction with the system.

Battle has several features worth noting:

1. The applicability of this approach extends beyond the particular problem solved by the Battle system.

2. Battle uses a pruned tree–searching algorithm to generate and select the best allocation plans. Optimal allocation plans are found for real problems in a reasonable amount of time.

3. Data for the tree-searching algorithms are generated by an inferencing system. Effectiveness values for individual weapons against the various targets are determined by a computation.

4. Merit values are used to intelligently direct the acquisition of information.

Battle has shown the viability of application of artificial intelligence techniques to resource allocation. Other tasks, such as assigning individuals to jobs in an organization, capital investment decisions, or allocating scarce inventory items to production projects, may be amenable to similar approaches.

An extension and expansion of Battle, the Marine Artillery Consultant (MAC) with its general inference engine (GENIE), is currently being developed at the Navy Center for Applied Research in Artificial Intelligence. In GENIE, we are extending the inference engine to allow greater flexibility. The most important feature is the generalization of contexts from the present maximum of two elements, typically a weapon and a target, in Battle, to an arbitrary number of ordered elements in GENIE. For example, contexts of air power are available to back up an infantry unit, or an attack against a target can relate three distinct battlefield units and therefore correspond to a three-element context. In the latter case, the corresponding datum function should have three arguments.

We are also exploring the use of genetic algorithms (Holland 1975) in place of searching the weapon allocation tree. Such algorithms may speed up the generation of allocation plans and converge on a reasonable plan more quickly than searching the allocation tree, especially for large allocation problems. Finally, an alternative, more uniform system might include the present tree-searching algorithm or the genetic algorithm as the assignment function for a new top node to the system. The multitude of nodes that serve as top nodes for individual inference networks would all feed into a single supernode. The value assigned to this node would be a list of the k best allocation plans. Such a uniform network would allow naturally for the selection of questions with the merit system from any of the individual networks that now exist.

In some circumstances of importance to the Marine Corps, calls for fire on individual targets can be handled one at a time. For this class of situations, we are able to retain the phase 1 computations intact, and to simplify the algorithm in phase 2. Decision-theoretic analysis eliminates from consideration all but a handful of the weapon combinations, even if many weapons are available. The analysis, an algorithm based on it, and a proof that the algorithm yields optimal results are all provided in Hamburger and Slagle (1983).

ACKNOWLEDGMENTS

We thank Dan Hoey and Richie Cantone for their help and Paul Krueger (University of Minnesota) for help in preparing the manuscript. This project was funded by grants from the Office of Naval Research, Code 200, and Naval Ocean Systems Center/the Office of Naval Technology.

REFERENCES

Case, K.E., and Thibault, H.C. (1976), "A Heuristic Allocation Algorithm for Conventional Weapons for the Marine Integrated Fire and Air Support System," School of Industrial Engineering and Management, Oklahoma State University, Stillwater, Oklahoma, July.

Case, K.E., and Thibault, H.C. (1977), "A Heuristic Allocation Algorithm With Extensions for Conventional Weapons for the Marine Integrated Fire and Air Support System," School of Industrial Engineering and Management, Oklahoma State University, Stillwater, Oklahoma, September.

Duda, R.O., Hart, P.E., Konolige, K., and Nilsson, N.J. (1981), "Subjective Bayesian Methods for Rule-based Inference Systems," National Computer Conference, 1976; reprinted in B.L. Webber and N.J. Nilsson, eds., *Readings in Artificial Intelligence*, Palo Alto, Calif.: Tioga Publishing Company.

Duda, R.O., Hart, P.E., Konolige, K., and Reboh, R. (1979), "A Computer-based Consultant for Mineral Exploration," Menlo Park, Calif.: Artificial Intelligence Center, SRI International, September.

Hamburger, H. and Slagle, J.R. (1983), "Responding to a Call for Fire," Technical Report, Navy Center for Applied Research in Artificial Intelligence, Washington D.C.

Holland, J.H. (1975), *Adaptation in Natural and Artificial Systems*, Ann Arbor: University of Michigan Press.

"Marine Tactical Command and Control Systems (MTACCS), Master Plan," U.S. Marine Corps, Washington, D.C., March.

Rockart, J.F. (1979), "Chief Executives Define Their Own Data Needs," *Harvard Business Review*, March–April, pp. 81–93.

Slagle, J.R., and Halpern, E.H. (1982), "An Intelligent Control Strategy for Expert Consultant Systems," NRL Memorandum Report 4789, April.

Slagle, J.R., and Gaynor, M.W. (1983), "Expert System Consultation Control Strategy," Proc. AAAI-83, Washington, D.C. Aug. 22–24.

INTEGRATING EXPERT SYSTEMS INTO THE BUSINESS ENVIRONMENT

In the past decade business has exhibited a voracious appetite for office automation, factory automation, and other forms of automation. By now a certain degree of saturation has set in. Businesses have settled on the hardware and software they want, and they have put these into active use. With so much "sunk cost" there is a natural tendency to reject any change that represents a "black box" that cannot fit into and/or utilize the existing automation products. Embedded AI/ES is the logical escape hatch if ESS technology is to truly penetrate the business marketplace. It provides a way for software vendors to sell a new version of their product, while letting the business community access ES technology within the context of software with which they are already familiar.

Embedded AI/ES is an exciting development that suggests ES/AI will make the transition from a few maverick or stand-alone applications to an institutionalized capability available on a widespread and integrated basis. If every office and business automation environment includes a set of embedded and integrated AI/ES tools, then ES will become a mere extension of the spreadsheet, the data base management system, or the microcomputer. That is the plan of the fifth generation of computing systems. However, it appears that the market will not wait — embedded AI is occurring right now.

While Parts II and III of this book included a number of specific applications, Part IV focuses upon the opportunities, challenges, and obstacles to embedding *generic* ES in automated business environments. It does not address the topic of integrating a completed ES application into a user's world. Rather, the integration topic explored here is the one originally raised in Chapter 1, which indicated that AI would only be successful to the extent it could directly incorporate the user's preferred information stimulus-response channels.

Chapter 8 was a useful lead-in to this part of the book since it dealt with incorporating a generic ES capability into an already highly automated factory and control center environment. The five chapters of Part IV broaden that concern to the office place. Specifically, the treatment of this subject provided here touches on a variety of issues ranging from ESS to pure AI, from hardware to software, from teamwide coordination systems to one-person support, and from simple spreadsheet extensions to complete workstation environments. In short, an extensive exploration of the state-of-the-embedded-ES practice is provided.

At the same time, there are some important topics not covered here, for want of time and space. For example, the natural language field is not directly addressed in any major way. Neither is the relatively recent phenomenon of commercially available financial expert system shells. Despite these and similar gaps in the coverage, these chapters collectively constitute a useful and important statement on the integration/embedding topic. In particular, the following topics are addressed:

1. Chapter 10 looks at a quite fundamental obstacle, that of getting the computer to extract information from reports and documents designed for human consumption. This chapter shows the difficulties as well as the potential and describes an intelligent parser that potentially could be embedded in any user's microcomputer.

2. Chapter 11 is a thorough treatment of an attempt to embed rule-based reasoning in a spreadsheet system. The goals are fairly important; the spreadsheet subject should be familiar to almost every business-oriented reader; and the reader is exposed to an entire knowledge-engineering process, including the problem of obtaining user evaluations of the result.

3. Chapter 12 is a logical followup to Chapter 11 as it extends the reader's scope to a totally integrated environment. That is, rather than embedding ES technology in just a spreadsheet, this chapter explains how it is being embedded together with a spreadsheet, a data base management system, a graphics package, and other business software. The synergistic effects of the combined capability are explored.

4. Chapter 13 advances to the next logical step and offers a hint of what the fifth generation might be like. In particular, this chapter offers a fascinating description of a complete business workstation designed to assist team-oriented projects and groups.

5. Chapter 14 concludes this topic with a survey of the issues associated with integration and embedding AI into other capabilities. This chapter is relatively broad in scope, and it returns the reader to the ESS subject and issue in general. The authors add a number of interesting insights not previously addressed, particularly in the areas of uncertainty management in expert systems.

10

Data Bridges

Richard Roth

When AI techniques are considered, it is usually in the context of large-scale dedicated functions interacting with humans. This fails to consider a much simpler but critical application of these techniques. Furthermore, expert systems assume the availability of sufficient data sources; falling into disuse when data are not available in the proper form.

A *data bridge* is any computer function that has the primary job of converting information from one computer application to another, usually between different computers. When the original data are intended for human consumption, as in the form of a printed report, techniques ranging from natural language recognition to rule-based processing can be used to reengineer the data to be machine usable. This allows feeding reports from corporate data bases into personal computers for local analysis. Even when the original data are accessible across machine boundaries, the processing used to create reports adds implicit knowledge. For that, and other reasons, working with the derived report often has distinct advantages over working with raw data.

10.1   INTRODUCTION

Using computers as a corporate management tool usually results in heavy use of computer-generated information originating at lower levels of the organization. As small computers play an ever-increasing role, a key characteristic of their success—their independence from conventional MIS constraints—becomes a limiting factor. This is because the small machines are not directly tied into the corporate computer network; they are usually treated as outsiders, with limited access to information.

Moving information between machines initially seems to be the old problem of incompatibility of data formats that has plagued EDP shops ever since there was more than one computer manufacturer. However, if one is intent on finding both the immediate solution for today's user and on laying the groundwork for more transparent intercomputer networks, a whole new dimension of the problem opens up.

Much of the data available are not directly usable. The gap exists because management use of operational data, whether by managers or expert systems, requires not just machine-readable data, it also requires that the data be application understandable.

10.1.1   Introducing the Case Study

A better way to understand this problem is to follow the development of a specific system. This case study is about a system recently placed in use.

The user is the corporate controller who gets status reports on all the corporate cash funds from a dozen different bank computers. The reports are provided via standard time-sharing services and are down-loaded to the controller's personal computer. The data from the reports are combined and loaded into a data base that tracks investments. Then it is used by an expert system that helps the controller maximize return on short-term investments (see Figure 10.1).

FIGURE 10.1
USING REPORTS FOR DATA SOURCE VIA A DATA BRIDGE

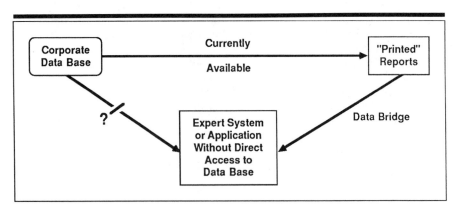

The crucial gap is between the bank computers and the controller's machine. This gap exists because the cash fund activity is available only as a report designed for human consumption.

10.2 WHY A DATA BRIDGE?

The data bridge approach to moving data, especially when working from reports rather than raw data, can be questioned as an inefficient approach. The argument is based on the improved effectiveness of working directly with the raw data base, especially when the raw data base is really a well-structured corporate data base. Our experience has shown significant reasons why working with derived data has major advantages over directly accessing the original data source (Roth 1984).

There are two guiding rules that justify use of a data bridge:

1. Using currently available reports is inexpensive.
2. Existing applications have built-in knowledge.

10.2.1 No Other Alternative

There are many situations in which data are maintained on one computer but are available to other machines only as the result of producing reports. These reports can be sent to another machine using a standard communications line, the second machine can act only as a "dump" terminal and has no direct access to the actual data base. This situation often exists when the data base is the result of a time-sharing service, but it can occur even within an organization.

10.2.2 Depth of Analysis

From an AI perspective, the most interesting aspect of using a derived data source is the implicit knowledge incorporated in the derived data. The process of building an application that accesses the corporate data base to produce a report requires an analysis to define the uses and goals of the report. This analysis affects a transfer of knowledge into the application that is used each time a report is created. If the user went directly to the corporate data base for data, even if the data are directly accessible, the implicit analysis would be lost. Depending on the reason for using the data, the implicit analysis can be more significant than the effort required to reprocess the report into machine-understandable form.

10.2.3 Massive Investment of Time and Resources

Building an application that provides a straight-through link from the corporate data base to a personal computer, especially where implicit knowledge exists, requires duplicating some of the cost and effort that went into producing the current application used for reporting. Depending on the access of the new user to this information and programming, a fair amount of the original effort must be duplicated.

This is especially true when the original application is "owned" by the MIS or DP department of the company, and the new user is in another management group. The underlying conflict in this situation was instrumental in introducing the use of PCs into corporate management and is detrimental to the sharing of resources needed to reengineer that application.

10.2.4   User Experience and Familiarity

There is something very important to be said for user level of comfort. When a user is familiar with a report, working with the report has major advantages over a more logical and efficient, but unfamiliar, process. This is especially important when a corporate manager, without heavy computer experience, must have access to data that are not currently available with a user-friendly access means, such as a fourth-generation data management language (Martin 1985).

10.2.5   Cost and Reconfiguration for Direct Machine Tie-Ins

The alternative to a data bridge is a direct tie to the data source. This requires building a communication facility, with access rights to the data base. It means building functions to allow users to connect to the data base and access the data they need. But most of all, it means getting the data center and management group responsible for the company operation to commit to providing and supporting direct-user access to the data they maintain. The nature of the resource needs and political issues makes this sort of solution to the problem a major decision at a corporate policy level. Even if this access means "only" setting up organizational channels, management inertia can be significant.

10.2.6   The Case Study — The Data Source Considered

Our corporate controller is caught by the worst condition of unavailable data — a "public" data source. Since the data come from another company as part of a standard service, just getting the data via a communications line is a relatively new feature. Unless an automated bridge is available, the data must be retyped. This problem is compounded by the complexity of the reports, the volume of the data, and the need for extreme accuracy (see Figure 10.2). This task has yet to be widely computerized because of these restrictions.

FIGURE 10.2
TYPICAL BANK CASH STATEMENT

```
                        Last National Bank
                     Balance Reporting System
                      Report for Fancy Clothes
                      Prepared: Dec 16, 1984
                       for data as of 12/13/84
```

Bank Name Account Name Account Number	Ledger Balance Total Credits One-Day Float	Collected Balance Total Debits Two-Day Float	Avail Balance Total Float Over Two Days
Local Bank 012-234567	40,354,345.93 23,456,456.45 12,345,657.34	40,354,345.93 23,456,456.45 12,345,657.34	40,354,345.93 23,456,456.45 12,345,657.34

Do You Wish to Look at Detail Credits/Debits ? (Y Or N) --- Y

Credit Amount	Credit Description
30,007,234.45	Incoming Money Transfer Ref.: 76554872.94
10,007,234.45	56754872.94
7,876,234.54	Check Deposit Package
2,007,233.45	Incoming Money Transfer Ref.: 76556772.94

Debit Amount	Debit Description
53,007,235.45	Debit adjustment for Location #24
247,234.45	Preauthorized Debit
56,345.45	Preauthorized Debit
200.12	Check Paid #1234
123.45	#1245
441.34	#1246

10.3   WHY AI TECHNOLOGY?

At first glance, there seems to be no reason conventional programming techniques cannot handle this type of problem. The catch is that the complexity, number, and variability of the situations a data bridge must handle require a more effective approach.

The problem is twofold. First, the reports themselves are not easy to read. Second, the data producers are rarely responsive to the need for detailed information or to the form and variations of the data.

The combined effect is that there is no clear definition for the range of formats that the reports may contain, nor is there control or warning over changes in report formats. In addition, since a data bridge is often part of a software system, the reports it must handle can vary between users.

Manually programming the reports for a specific project requires a clear definition of the reports at the very least. Since this information is rarely available, normal programming of the report translators would result in an unacceptable number of cases that would need manual intervention. Even allowing for the exceptions, normal programming of a single parser takes a fair amount of programming time, and most systems will have a dozen or more reports that must be handled. This makes initial production of the parsers for any real system a significant programming task. When the maintenance problem is added, as a result of the suppliers of the software having no control over the report suppliers, the effort required to produce and maintain the report parsers using normal programming techniques makes such an approach impractical. The solution is to develop a smart parser that can recognize key characteristics from a report.

There are a number of aspects that can be attacked using AI techniques. Handling report titles, descriptions, and exception messages have characteristics of a natural language understanding system. Techniques of rule-based systems can be used in recognizing the sections of a report and determining how to map the values into the output format, depending on different report situations.

10.3.1   The Case Study — Actual Results of Regular Programming

Examining the initial efforts at hard coding of reports in our case study shows the results of normal programming on a real set of reports. They are a typical example of bank statements. For most of the reports, even the project leader (who is an accountant, experienced in their use), had a problem finding the needed information. The reports available had only the data appropriate to those accounts held by the customers who helped in the development of the system, and so only the format of a report needed by this data was shown. In addition, the banks were not responsive to requests for details about the full formats of these reports. There were over 100 report formats to be supported.

The effort at manual programming was based on using a library of report-processing routines. This allowed a parser to be programmed in 8 to 16 employee-hours. Since there are over 100 reports, even this high level of programming productivity (by software engineering standards) made production of the parsers a significant programming task.

A set of second-generation hard-coded parsers was built using an interactive LISP system with some smart recognizers. This decreased production time for a parser to 4 to 8 employee-hours. Since this still required a programmer, it was only a minor improvement. Any major new report formats also require a senior programmer to code new recognizers. To make the system practical, the highest programmer skill required would have to be a so-called power user, indicating a nonprogrammer

FIGURE 10.3
REFINEMENT OF HARD CODED PARSER

Stage 1:
- Senior programmer
- High-level language
- 40 employee-hours per report

Stage 2:
- Junior programmer
- High-level language
- 8 to 16 employee-hours per report

Stage 3:
- Junior programmer
- Lisp with simple smart recognizers
- 8 to 16 employee-hours per report

Stage 4: Minimum goal
- Power user
- Rule-based parser
- 1 hour per report

Stage 5: Ultimate goal
- End user
- Self-directed recognizer
- Automatic

who is skilled enough to write Lotus 1-2-3 macro's or use a sophisticated data base manager. This would probably be an assistant to the controller or the installer of the controller's personal computer. In addition, to make the system practical, the allowable time for such a user to define a report would have to be under one hour (see Figure 10.3).

10.4 DATA BRIDGE FUNCTIONAL NEEDS

By outlining the needed functions for an operational data bridge, we can apply AI techniques to best advantage. A data bridge consists of a sequence of recognizers followed by translation functions for each recognized situation. When the situations are well defined and of a small number, standard computer techniques, such as finite state machines and simple IF/THEN/ELSE tests, can be used.

Actual uses require extension of basic techniques in two directions: (1) ability to distinguish potentially ambiguous cases and (2) easy expansion of defining or converting rules. Beyond functional needs are the operational requirements of underlying structures that are efficient in execution speed and storage size.

The most useful techniques have been found in the AI categories of:

Rule-based expert systems
Natural language understanding
Pattern recognition
Computer vision systems

In the case of each of these AI fields, the goals are different than in data bridging, and so the techniques must be molded to fit the differing needs.

The most useful concepts have been those leading to effective knowledge representations. There are two major knowledge functions required in a data bridge: (1) the feature selection criteria and (2) the translation criteria. Once representations have been defined for these, the operational functions fall in line rather quickly. When large classes of features can be grouped together, the commonality produces considerably improved results.

Effective techniques have been found in the frame/slot concept used in language and rule-based systems. The methods used to represent and execute rules (from rule-based systems concepts) have proved useful (Winston 1984). The disambiguity rules used in natural language processing have been helpful, but the context normally found in natural language text is missing from numerical reports, and so many of the techniques do not apply. Use of natural language techniques for the recognition of unexpected error messages or special case indicators (such as "No data available for this date") could prove very useful. The normal techniques for computer vision pattern recognition rely on the uniformity of the data source (the visual scanner), and so they do not apply.

The problem that has yet to be solved when dealing with numeric reports is the defining of a proper context that can be derived as the underlying structure. If this could be accomplished, then fully automatic data recognition would be possible, given only generic descriptions of the target data.

In lieu of a self-directed recognizer, user-constructed rules were used. These are based on the concept of the play script with cues to trigger data recognizers and detailed targets to fire the extracting of data. This works well once the script has been written, but does require user interaction to produce each script. This is practical when a data bridge is used repeatedly on the same format reports over an extended period of time.

10.5   BUILDING A REAL DATA BRIDGE

The goal of an effective data bridge is to be totally transparent to the user — just another step in a sequence of operations. Yet the current state of the technology requires capturing a description of each report that can be used repeatedly.

In fact, there are two levels of expected user: (1) the actual user of the application and (2) the installer who sets up the application. Since the corporate controller is the user and the system will probably be sold through a packaged system vendor or vertical applications reseller (VAR), the definition of a report typically will be done by a more technically proficient user. However, from a practical perspective, the less sophisticated the interaction needed to define the report, the wider the potential application of the system.

FIGURE 10.4
REPORT REPROCESSING SYSTEM

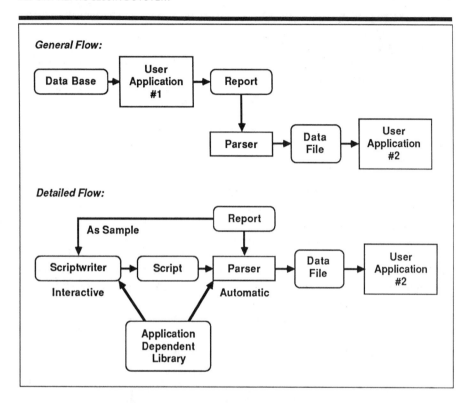

Once the description is built, each time a report must be processed by an application, the report description is used to process the report into a form the application can use (see Figure 10.4). This two-step process maximizes the transparent aspect of day-to-day operations, while the technology is developed for more automatic operation.

10.5.1   Report Representation Via a Script

The analogy that has been developed is that of a play script, with cues as to what is to be found at various places in a report. The data items that are required by the application are called *targets*. These are extracted as their associated cues are found.

Given a well-defined script and a clean report, the parsing engine (see Figure 10.5) looks for cues and then related targets following "conversion" and "output" action rules. Thus the engine works its way through a report finding the needed data.

The division of the recognizing function into cue and target has the dual purpose of making the process faster and matching the user's view of

FIGURE 10.5
DRIVING PARSER ENGINE

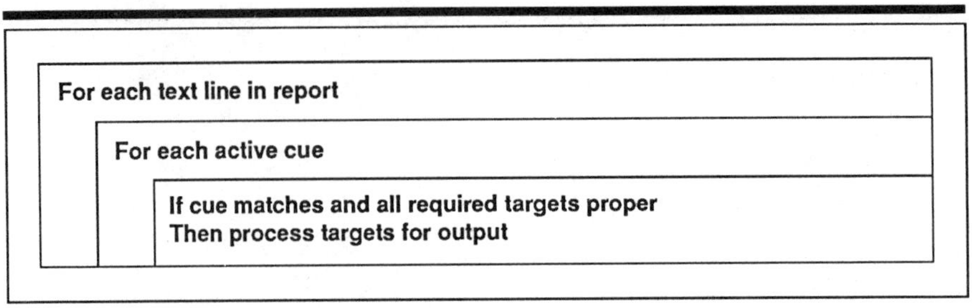

```
For each text line in report

    For each active cue

        If cue matches and all required targets proper
        Then process targets for output
```

data. By making any cue tied to a simple pattern match on a single text line, the matching engine was able to avoid extended paths of comparing data and backtracking on partial failure. This is a typical bottleneck for any powerful string matcher (Griswold, Poage, and Polonsky 1971).

This approach was developed from studying the average reader's approach to reading a report. It was clear that data are normally perceived as a target of the search, while titles and page breaks are only cues toward that goal. This user-oriented approach is key. For if the scriptwriter is to be used by a non-computer-oriented user, it must be compatible with the user's mental processes.

This system went through a number of paths before the current choice was made. An earlier product (ONESHOT, from Dataviz of Norwalk, Connecticut by this author) used a simple pattern-matching scheme that was not powerful enough to handle complex reports, such as in the case study. User feedback from the simpler scheme used in ONESHOT led to the more general techniques used in this design. It became clear, as the whole project proceeded, that any approach that was modeled after the user's perception of the data reading process would be more effective.

10.5.2 The Real World Intrudes

The real world starts intruding when one tries to put the script and a real report together in a production environment. The "cleanliness" of a report is fortunately obtainable on a fairly regular basis, since current telecommunications systems are reasonably reliable, especially when used during off-peak hours with automatic dialing systems. By preprocessing the report for garbage characters and standard line format, the parser can expect a consistent quality of report.

The completeness of the script is critical in this approach. Yet this is the hardest aspect of the system to guarantee. The cue/target approach allows removing the sequence-dependent nature of many reports, in the

FIGURE 10.6
TYPICAL BANK CASH STATEMENT MARKED FOR CUES/TARGETS

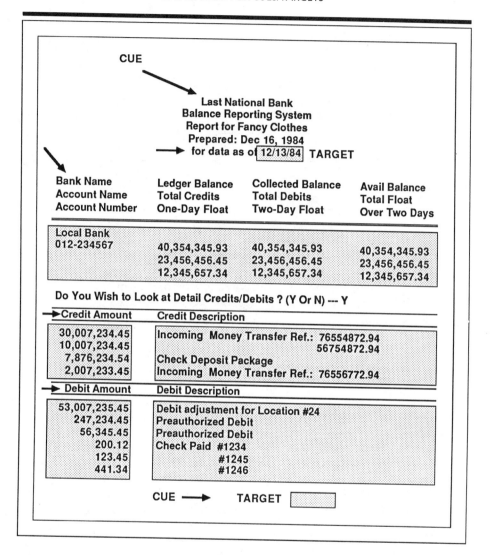

process simplifying the report description process. The one area of early concern was the reliability of correctness of simple matching schemes that ignored the normal header, title, body sequence in a report and relied solely on the localized cue/target region. This work has shown that the nature of most reports, combined with the two-dimensional cross-check provided by the simple verification of target data types, gives highly accurate data output.

It was found that the use of clear (to the user), well-defined data types, although complex, allow the user to easily indicate what is expected in simple terms. A date is a good example of such a data type. There are many normal date forms: MM-DD-YY, MM/DD/YY, Mon Day, Year, and so forth. The month can be numeric or spelled with three letters or fully; the year can be two digits (86) or four (1986). Yet from the user's perspective, these are all dates. Introducing such atomic elements can greatly reduce the complexity of the user interaction.

By making these elements intrinsic concepts for the user, the report description can be simplified. For example, truly sequence-dependent sections can be handled. This is done with the basic concept of a repeating section. This starts with a cue like any other, but then applies the target rules repeatedly until they fail to match or an end cue is found. The standard columnar report can be handled this way, as can considerably more complex repeating sequences.

When parts of a report are sequence dependent, a frame concept is used, to allow nesting report features. This allows looking only for certain features once others are found. The parser allows conditioning cues as enabled/disabled from other cues. The case of two similar sections (see Figure 10.6 – cue starting 'Credit' vs. cue starting 'Debit') can be easily handled this way. The repeating and frame concepts are related in use and implementation.

User Output Requirements.   The final part of any report script is what must be done with the data. The approach taken has relied on the application specific need for the system, where any one application has relatively few data output forms. This allows setting up the system for a specific application with predefined output names.

The user sets up a report by just selecting the name to be associated with a specific data item plucked from the report. The name invokes a function that does the proper output processing, as in SNOBOL (Griswold, Poage, and Polonsky 1971). Similarly a predefined set of data conversions (e.g., dates or dollar amounts) are supplied. An advanced facility may be eventually provided to set up these definitions for the applications builder. These routines can be seen in Figure 10.4 as the block labeled "application dependent library."

10.5.3   Producing the Script

Having an experienced analyst produce the script only partly solves the problem, since a complete report description is not generally available. This introduces a problem of its own, namely tying up a highly trained person to build and maintain the scripts, one of the originally stated problems. An effective solution has been to build a tool (the scriptwriter) that allows a fairly knowledgable user to build a script using feedback showing how the script handles the report.

The scriptwriter was subsequently produced to match the parsing engine. It is an on-screen interactive tool that shows a sample report on the screen and allows highlighting sections using the cursor and indicating the characteristics of these details. The interactive nature of the system shows the effect of a script directly at description time.

10.5.4   Processing a Report through the Engine

Processing a report, once the script has been written, now becomes a fairly straightforward problem consisting of structured sets of rule–consequent action groups. Usually the rule results in an output record of data in the needed format. Occasionally, intermediate data values must be calculated or data conversions applied, such as normal written date styles to julian date.

In the process cycle, each cue has a rule to define its location, how to recognize it, and a list of targets associated with it. When a cue is found, the related targets are triggered. Each triggered target gets its own recognition rules tested, and only if all targets that are marked "required" are proper is the cue fired. When a cue gets fired, all the associated targets are fully processed using extraction rules, optional conversion rules, and, finally, output rules. In addition, a cue can execute special control directives that activate or deactivate frames.

10.6   CASE STUDY IMPLEMENTATION

The system described here is intended for daily use as part of dedicated applications and to be a system-building tool for application builders. To meet this need, the implementation has to be as robust as possible in a product sense. It must meet basic speed requirements, although high-speed operation is not required of the batch operation of the parser.

This system has the text and list manipulation needs that have made LISP the language of choice for many AI systems. However, since the system must run on a personal computer (usually an IBM PC/XT), the limitation of the hardware requires the high-activity primitives to have a more efficient implementation. This balancing was done by using a LISP interpreter written in C language and by writing in C the primitives that handled data conversions, file operations, and user interfacing when speed was required (Betz 1984, 1985).

The parser engine was built using LISP property lists (Wilensky 1984), so that each cue was defined as a list with properties for such functions as: required, match test, and target extract rule. The value of each property is either a true-false flag or the actual sequence of operations to accomplish the goal.

10.6.1   Conventional Programming Escapes

As with any AI application, the report processor tends to do a central group of operations well and tends to do poorly outside this group. Since the parser must handle any report thrown at it, it allows for handling special cases by programming rules or actions directly in the underlying LISP language. These special cases are usually canned into a library function and entered into the scriptwriter's operation keyword dictionary. This way they are made transparent to the user defining a report.

10.6.2   Case Study Status

The system described in the case study was delivered to the system installation group in mid-summer 1985. They have been using and evaluating the system with an eye toward both the effectiveness of the techniques and the actual implementation.

The basic system is proving its usefulness, although the user response time of the interactive scriptwriter is proving to be a stumbling block. Since this is part of a commercial system, perceived speed is of key importance, even though the actual gain in productivity is more than expected. The speed of the parser has never been questioned because of both its off-line mode of operation and the effectiveness of the cue/target division in cutting off invalid matches very quickly.

Possible alternatives for improving the speed of the system are either recoding the interactive sections from LISP to the high-level language C or using a LISP compiler. The custom LISP used makes the latter choice not quite as simple as does the primitive nature of LISP environments for the IBM personal computer.

10.7   DESCRIBING A REPORT: FORMAT VERSUS CONTENT

The most complex problem has been putting into proper perspective the conceptual frame of reference of the user trying to describe a report. The user looks at a report for data items. He or she does not see the report as a set of feature details, such as heading and descriptions. Rather, he or she uses the detail as an implicit means of finding the needed data. The scriptwriter and the scripts required have had to be designed so the scripts were produced with a minimum of effort on the part of the user.

A repeating section is a good example of how a visually simple form can be very hard for the user to describe and the program to recognize. The start of a repeat is usually a simple title that can be recognized by specific words, as in the title starting "Division," in Figure 10.7. The end of a section is shown as a simple total bar, on the line before the total line. The general case is usually trickier, since there may not be a total; or for a longer report there may be a subtotal and new title at each page break, all

FIGURE 10.7
REPEATING SECTION

Division	Salesman	Quarter	Sales
Eastern	JL	First	12,345.67
	GH	First	23,456.78
		Second	N/A
		Third	12,345.67
		Salesman Total	35,802.45
		Division Total	48,148.12
Western	KH	First	12,345.67
	TY	Second	23,456.89
		Division Total	35,802.45
Total Sales			83,950.57

of which must be ignored until the final end of the repeating section. In this example, the two leftmost columns implicitly carry down until a new entry appears or a total appears in the third column. Note also the different uses of the word TOTAL in the third column.

This is basically an automatic pattern recognition problem in a two-dimensional space, not all that different from a vision problem. Unfortunately for this work, vision-oriented systems are geared toward having regular data representations at each point.

Work is in progress to enhance the automatic recognition ability of the scriptwriter and, if successful, even the parser. A learning-by-example technique seems promising to allow the user to quickly show the scriptwriter program what is of value in a report. Ideally, a more self-directed context-oriented approach will lead to more complete results. This work is based on the premise that reports (at least for a general range of applications) have common formats, enough so that context rules can be developed. If this can be done, scripts need only qualify the report category and indicate output operations.

10.8 DATA BRIDGES—THEIR POTENTIALS

10.8.1 Analytical Use of Available Data— The Starting Point

This effort was started when it was recognized how much of the analysis done on personal computers used in management is based on data re-keyed from printed reports—reports that were originally computer generated. This whole field of data bridges has developed from solving the simple problem of reducing the waste and errors implicit in the human step.

10.8.2 Feeding Expert Systems

One area of "fully" AI systems that has proved itself to be financially justifiable is the whole concept of expert systems. By carefully limiting the expert domain to areas of limited but complex knowledge, expert systems have been able to produce impressive cost savings and productivity improvements.

The limiting factor to expert systems use tends to be availability of information. This takes two forms: (1) the original knowledge structure base on which the expert system is built and (2) the steady stream of new information needed to keep the system current and growing. While the first is always required, the second depends on the type of expert provided by the system. Since the most useful of expert systems are those that fill in when a human expert is not available and those that must use data sources intended for human consumption, the availability of a data bridge opens new applications for expert system use.

10.8.3 Creating New Applications Potentials

The availability of data in machine-understandable form allows tying disjointed applications together to create unified functions. The gap for many applications relates to the way the separate applications were originally constructed. Since each application expected a human element to be present, there is no provision for extracting the information in an intermediate form. In addition, the lack of suitable common formats have tended to limit designers from predesigning such features into the system.

10.8.4 Extended Use of Other
AI Technologies

Just as data bridges can provide a new source of data for expert systems, so can data bridges complement other AI areas. An example is the rapidly dropping cost on OCR/text reading systems. The need to convert the raw text data into the machine-usable format has thus far limited these readers to input of basic textual material.

10.9 CONCLUSION

This chapter proposes a new form of AI system—that of the Data Bridge. This kind of system provides a pragmatic missing link to allow a system integrator to create more functional computer systems by knitting together existing components without recreating each component part. This chapter also shows how AI technologies are needed to make such a system practical and gives some insights into the problems that arise in such a system, through a description of work in progress.

REFERENCES

Betz, B. (1984), "XLISP: An Experimental Object Oriented Language," unpublished work available from the author.

Betz, B. (1985), "An XLISP Tutorial," *BYTE* 10 (March): 221–236.

Griswold, R.E., Poage, J.F., and Polonsky, I.P. (1971), *The SNOBOL 4 Programming Language*, Englewood Cliffs, N.J.: Prentice-Hall.

Martin, J. (1985), *Fourth-Generation Languages*, Englewood Cliffs, N.J.: Prentice-Hall.

Roth, R.L. (1984), "Making Connections in the Shadow of the Mainframe," *Computerworld* 18 (42): 9–16.

Wilensky, R. (1984), *LISPcraft*, New York: W.W. Norton & Co.

Winston, P.H. (1984), *Artificial Intelligence*, 2nd ed., Reading, Mass.: Addison-Wesley.

11

Looking at Worksheet Modeling through Expert System Eyes

Kenneth J. Fordyce

Increasing software quality and productivity requires tools to enhance end-user computing and reduce the workload of data processing professionals. Presently software professionals are looking toward the expert system field to provide such tools. This chapter describes one such tool, Automated Ledger Book (ALB), and reviews some of the other work to integrate expert systems into decision support tools.

ALB is a worksheet model generator with five enhancements based on an equation manipulating expert system and a natural language interface built by the authors in APL/APL2. The new functions are equation ordering, reversibility, calculation explanation, variable breakdown, and plain English queries against the model data. ALB enables the user to build and run worksheet type models in high school algebraic notation and English, without regard to equation order or specification of calculated and input variables. Solving sets of algebraic and conditional equations, ALB adjusts itself to input, responding to unlimited "what ifs." When challenged, ALB provides the rationale for its conclusions.

11.1   INTRODUCTION

Increasing software quality and productivity requires tools to enhance end-user computing and reduce the workload of data processing professionals. This need has made the role of the artificial intelligence (AI) fields of expert systems (ES) and natural language interfaces (NLI) in decision support systems (DSS) an important question to the academic and business communities. This chapter undertakes five tasks: (1) it establishes a framework for understanding enhancements to decision support tools, (2) it briefly reviews some of the other work being done to integrate AI into decision support tools, (3) it describes five enhancements to worksheet modeling software based on expert system and natural language interface techniques as they work in Automated Ledger Book (ALB), (4) it outlines some of the basic techniques used in an equation-manipulating expert system developed by the authors in APL/APL2 for ALB, and (5) it summarizes the results of a user survey to evaluate the five enhancements.

11.2   COGNITIVE SUPPORT

The purpose of DSS is to improve the effectiveness of decision makers by providing them tools to reduce the distortion caused by information processing limitations. This decision support can be divided into two categories: organizational and cognitive.

Organizational support concentrates on improving the collection and transmission of the information required for decision making (Cats-Baril 1982). It consists of developing an organizationwide information system based on a set of contingencies to switch information from one organization to another, to involve certain organizational units in the decision-making process and to exclude others, and to establish redundant sources of information and communication. Examples are (1) the rerouting, switching, and delaying of information (depending on the content of the message) to avoid overload and (2) the development of incentives and structure to minimize distortion.

Cognitive support is defined in Cats-Baril (1982) as the support provided by a system to a single user to help him or her structure problems, check assumptions, develop recommendations, and so forth. Cognitive support concentrates on improving the decision maker's ability to process information and does not address the reliability of the relevant information. It can be divided into the categories of indexing, computation, process support, display information, and documentation. A detailed description of each cognitive limitation can be found in Cats-Baril (1982).

Indexing support provides the user with data storage and retrieval capabilities. Examples are the U.S. Census data books, stock market data bases, and sales histories. It helps overcome the following cognitive limitations: limited memory, concreteness, salience, availability, misperception of frequency, and selective perception.

Computational support provides the user with algebraic and data manipulation capabilities. Examples are a hand-held calculator, abacus, and slide rule. It helps overcome the following cognitive limitations: limited computational ability, high complexity, sequential processing, inconsistency, conservatism, and stress.

Process or procedural support provides the user with an explanation of the relevant decision rules, "normative heuristics, or models and decision processes." Examples are a consultant or expert and a policy manual. It helps overcome the following cognitive limitations: schema, habit, misconception of uncertainty and chance, feedback errors (logical fallacies, hindsight, irrelevant learning structures), and stress.

Display/representational support provides the user with different ways to display and format the information. Examples are graphics packages and physical models. It helps with the following cognitive limitations: functional fixedness, data presentation, dependence on task characteristics, scale effects, and cognitive style.

Documentation of work provides the user with the ability to document the problem analysis work done for future reference by himself or herself or by others. Examples are a log of the work done on a system and a description of a model. This support could be considered a special case of process support. Due to its importance, it is listed separately.

A natural way to classify decision support systems is by the quality of each kind of cognitive support provided to the user. An example grade sheet (Cats-Baril 1982) is:

Type/Quality	None	Low	Medium	High
Indexing				
Computation				
Process				
Representation				
Documentation				

11.3   WORKSHEETS AND WORKSHEET MODELS

A worksheet is a tabular display of data portraying the status of a business, or portion of a business, or the potential status of a business under certain assumptions. Some data are obtained by observing the business environment; other data are calculated from the observed data.

Francesco di Marco Datini (circa 1335–1410), a famous Pratese merchant-banker, used worksheets to monitor a business that made him one of the richest men of his time (Bursk 1962). Datini branch managers were required to regularly send a copy of the balance sheet to headquarters. The income statement and the first portion of the balance sheet of the Barcelona branch on January 31, 1399 is shown in Figure 11.1.

FIGURE 11.1
EXAMPLE OF EARLY USE OF WORKSHEETS (BURSK 1962)

Francesco di Marco Datini & Co. in Barcelona
Balance Sheets on January 31, 1399

Assets

Explanation	Barcelonese Currency						Per Cent of total
	L.	s.	d.	L.	s.	d.	
CASH AT BANK AND HAND							
Cash on hand............	18	17	2				.1
Deposits accounts........	1,242	9	8				8.2
Special account.........	440	0	0				2.9
				1,701	6	10	11.2
RECEIVABLES							
Local tradesman for goods sold...........	4,841	14	10				31.9
Local customers for exchange............	2.192	19	4				14.5
Local customers for insurance............	99	17	11				.7
				7,134	12	1	47.1

Statement of Profit and Loss
July 11, 1397 — January 31, 1399
(in Barcelonese Currency)

	L.	s.	d.
Profits on trade (Pro di mercatantie)..........	689	11	5
Profits on foreign exchange (Pro di cambio)....	262	4	0
Credit balance of merchandise expense (Spese di mercatanie).................	133	13	7
Total of gross profits.................	1,085	9	0

Deduct expenses:	L.	s.	d.
Rent for eighteen months	60	0	0
Unrecoverable accounts	3	8	0
Convoy expenses (guidaggio).............	67	12	0
Living expenses......................	106	1	5
Depreciation on office equipment	16	17	0
Reserve for unpaid taxes and other accruals (riserbo di spese di lelede a pagare e altrespese)..........	80	0	0
Total of gross expenses	333	18	5
Net income......................	751	10	7

With the development of matrices by Arthur Caley in the middle nineteenth century (Newman 1956), worksheets took on a different look.

The worksheet now consists of m rows and n columns. The basic unit of the worksheet is the cell. Each cell is identified by its row and column position. A cell can be a label, a number, or a value to be calculated from an equation.

Problems amenable to worksheet modeling are those that can be defined by a set of continuous algebraic equations and noncontinuous conditional/logic equations across two dimensions. PROFIT = REVENUE – EXPENSE is an example of a continuous algebraic equation. An example of a noncontinuous conditional/logic equation is: BONUS equals 2,000 if PROFIT is greater than 100,000, else BONUS equals 0. One dimension (often rows) usually represents categories of information or variables. Examples are revenue, profit, sales, and costs. The second dimension (often columns) usually represents some natural way to organize the information. Examples are time, cases, products, and business units.

Most of the equations describe relationships between variables (rows) within a case (column), which is repeated across most cases (columns). These are intracolumn calculations. For example, the equation PROFIT = REVENUE – TOTAL EXPENSE might be repeated for each product. There are usually a smaller number of equations across cases or columns. These are intercolumn calculations. For example, TOTAL PROFIT equals the sum of the profits for each product.

11.3.1   The Application of Computers to Worksheet Modeling

The first application of computers to worksheet modeling showed the following typical sequence of events:

1. The financial planner would describe in detail his model to the programmer.

2. The programmer would write a specific application program for the financial planner in a third-generation programming language such as Fortran, COBOL, or BASIC.

3. Each time the program was run the financial planner or programmer would enter values for the same set of variables, and the output from the program would be a standard printed report.

4. Any changes described by the financial planner required modifications of the code by the programmer.

In this mode of operation, the programming effort was large and specific to the immediate problem; the output was inflexible, only the programmer could "harness" the computer; the backlog of requests made to the programmer was large; and many people still did things manually.

To overcome these negative features, a number of groups began work to develop worksheet modeling software packages in the late 1960s and early 1970s. The original intent of worksheet modeling software was to enable non–data-processing professionals to quickly make worksheet models operational on a computer with minimal professional assistance. Worksheet modeling software initially had three principal functions:

1. Ease of use by non–computer programmers
2. Worksheet data entry, storage, update, and display
3. Specification and execution of simple forward calculations

Worksheet modeling software's purpose was to improve the effectiveness of the decision maker by providing cognitive support. It did not provide any organizational support.

Using the cognitive support grade sheet presented in the last section, the early worksheet modeling software packages would receive the following score:

Type/Quality	None	Low	Medium	High
Indexing		X		
Computation			X	
Process	X			
Representation		X		
Documentation		X		

The early work to develop worksheet modeling software has resulted in two major types of commercial worksheet modeling software presently available. The two types are financial planning languages (e.g., Execucom's IFPS) and electronic spreadsheets (e.g., LOTUS 1.2.3).

11.3.2   Present Enhancements to Worksheet Modeling Software

For the past five years enhancements to worksheet modeling software have focused on providing new functions or on "tidying up" existing functions, as opposed to enhancing the basic functions of ease of use, data entry, and calculations. These enhancements are referred to as "session manager" or "integration" enhancements.

According to Sanger (1984), typical enhancements made to worksheet modeling software over the past few years include:

1. Increasing the size of the model that can be built and run
2. Allowing variable width columns
3. Easy access to column formatting and labeling

4. Report titles

5. Easy access to graph routines

6. Windowing to permit different segments of the model to be presented on the screen at the same time

7. Full-screen data entry

8. Consolidation across several worksheet models

9. Access to data bases, generation of data bases, and sophisticated data base retrieval

10. Access to statistical analysis routines

11. Network communication

12. Distributed processing

The integration type of enhancement has concentrated on providing the worksheet modeling software user easy access to additional functions for observation recording (e.g., better access to data bases) and information display (e.g., graphics). A little work has been done to improve the interface (e.g., full-screen data entry). These enhancements have substantially improved the cognitive support provided by worksheet modeling software. The present generation of worksheet modeling software would receive the following score for cognitive support (an X represents the original score, a # represents the new score):

Type/Quality	None	Low	Medium	High
Indexing		X	#	
Computation			X	
Process	X			
Representation		X	#	
Documentation		X		

With the exception of goal seeking (described in the next section), no enhancements are commercially available to improve the original calculation function. No enhancements are available to provide process and documentation support for model building and interpretation (Sandberg-Diment 1984). These two areas appear to be fruitful ground for expert system–based enhancements to worksheet modeling software.

11.3.3   Review of Enhancements to Basic Worksheet Modeling Software Functions

The earliest enhancement commercially available in some worksheet modeling software packages to assist with calculations is goal seeking. Goal seeking relies on a numerical analysis estimation technique to find the value of one variable, which generates a specified value of another value. For example, given the equation: PROFIT = REVENUE − EXPENSE, PROFIT = 100, REVENUE = 150, then goal seeking would estimate EXPENSE to be 50. Goal seeking has been a feature of most mainframe financial planning languages (FPL) since 1980 (*IFPS Tutorial* 1980).

Another enhancement provided with most FPL is "nonprocedural" modeling. With this aid the user may enter the equations in any order without penalty.

In April 1983 a similar, but more advanced, set of features was incorporated into a microcomputer software package for scientific and engineering work. It is called TK SOLVER (Chopsky 1983).

Research work in this area includes:

Sigi Lichtenthal (1984), manager of strategic plans and planning systems IBM Americas/Far East headquarters, put a limited interactive algebraic reversal module into his UNIMOD planning system in 1984.

M. Emden (1985) has proposed that spreadsheets are a subset of logic programming.

Donald Kosy and Ben Wise (1984) of Carnegie-Mellon University have recently begun work on an experimental worksheet model generator that will be able to review and evaluate a model's underlying structure. It attempts to explain why a value went up or down. This system is called a Reason-Orientated Modeling Environment (ROME).

The TIMS Management Science Roundtable (*OR/MS TODAY* 1984) commissioned two original reports to be written on the topic "Spreadsheet Modeling as a Stepping-Stone." One report was written by Samuel Bodily, and the second was written by Linus Shrage and Kevin Cunningham. Both reports are available from TIMS Business Office, 290 Westminster St., Providence, Rhode Island 02903.

David Farewell (1984) has recently proposed that the prerequisite for flexible use of models in a DSS is a mechanism(s) to maintain internal consistency. For example, if TOTAL COST = FIXED COST + VARIABLE COST, then you do not want to display values of 10 for FIXED COST, 20 for VARIABLE COST, and 5 for TOTAL COST, since 10 + 20 does not equal 5. Mr. Farewell has identified six mechanisms for maintaining internal consistency. The three pertinent to this chapter are: (1) model functional reversal—processing variables either as input or output depending on the user specification, (2) total passthrough—recalculation of variables given a change in value of any one variable, and (3) model judgment—use of models with different variable relationships between variables.

At the APL85 conference Fred Appleyard and Roger Hui (1985) illustrated some constructs necessary for a nonprocedural modeling language based in APL.

The use of expert systems to provide more intelligent interfaces to statistical packages is being seriously investigated. These improved interfaces would provide guidance, interpretation, and instruction on strategies for data analysis to the user (Gale 1985; Hahn 1985; and King 1983).

In the area of natural language interfaces, Robert Blanning (1985) has built a small prototype to investigate a natural language interface to drive worksheet models.

11.4   EXPERT SYSTEM–BASED ENHANCEMENTS TO WORKSHEET MODELING SOFTWARE

What can expert systems bring to worksheet modeling software? Expert systems (Sullivan and Fordyce 1987, 1985a) permit the information system builder to move process or problem domain knowledge from the expert into the computer. This can result in making information available about policy or procedure, about relationships between data elements, about which algorithms or data sets to access, and about techniques to analyze the problem.

The expertise a worksheet model builder brings to the problem consists of:

1. The knowledge of the relationships between elements of the model (elements are variables, relationship are equations) and the values for noncalculated variables.

2. The ability to move the relationships from words to equations, to identify key elements, and to eliminate unimportant elements.

3. The ability to manipulate equations. In addition to data (values for variables), the equations in a worksheet model contain important information. These equations represent the activities of a business in terms of quantitative relationships among variables. They are a type of knowledge base. The ability to manipulate the equations can provide additional insight into the model.

In ALB we concentrated on enhancements to worksheet modeling based on an expert system to help with the third category: manipulating equations. The expert system that provides the new enhancements or functions is called equation manipulating expert system (EMES). EMES provides the user four enhancements: equation ordering, reversibility, calculation explanation, and variable breakdown. This kind of enhancement is best suited to existing expert system techniques because this type of expertise is well defined (Kulikowski and Weiss 1985). Additionally, the ability to manipulate equations would be a prerequisite to work on the other two types of worksheet modeling expertise.

In ALB we also provided the user an improved interface to the model data. We used a natural language interface (NLI) to permit the user to make plain English queries against the model data (Sullivan and Fordyce 1982).

The enhancements of equation ordering, reversibility, calculation explanation, variable breakdown, and plain English queries generate the following revised score card (an X is the original score, a $\#$ is the change in score due to the integration enhancements, and a * is the change in score due to expert system–based enhancements):

Type/Quality	None	Low	Medium	High
Indexing		X	# *	
Computation			X	*
Process	X	*		
Representation		X	#	
Documentation		X	*	

11.4.1 Description of the Expert System–Based and Natural Language Interface–Based Enhancements as They Work in ALB

We will use the following example to illustrate the additional functions provided by the EMES and the NLI as incorporated into ALB. It is written in APL/APL2. It uses a Boolean array–based inferencing algorithm (Sullivan and Fordyce 1985b, 1985c). The next section outlines how EMES works.

Suppose a farm manager wants to calculate profit and cost ratio for three crops (apples, corn, and beans). Profit is a function of revenue and expense. Cost ratio is a function of expense and sales. Revenue is a function of units sold and price. Expense is a function of seed cost, fertilizer cost, labor cost, depreciation, and property taxes. Figure 11.2 lists all the variables and equations as they would be provided to ALB in the "build model activity."

Variables are divided into two categories:

1. Input or independent variables are those not defined by an equation. In the farm crop problem, PROD, SOLD, PRICE, SEED, FERT, LABOR, MACHD, and TAX are input variables.

2. Output, dependent, or calculated variables are those defined by an equation. In the farm problem, REVEN, VCOST, FCOST, EXPEN, PROFT, and RATIO are output variables.

In ALB's "run model activity," data are entered, calculations requested, calculation results posted, and calculation explanations requested. The full-screen worksheet interface is automatically generated from the model description provided by the user during the build model activity.

Figures 11.3 and 11.4 contain an example of initial data input and calculation with ALB for the farm crop problem. A value is entered for each input variable, and then ALB calculates each output variable. This activity is called *forward calculation.*

FIGURE 11.2
EXAMPLE OF ALB'S MODELING LANGUAGE

Variable Description	Variable Name	Equation (if any)*
Product name	PROD	
Profit	PROFT	REVEN – EXPEN <-------- eq 1
Cost ratio	RATIO	EXPEN / SOLD <-------- eq 2
Units sold	SOLD	
Price per unit	PRICE	
Revenue	REVEN	SOLD x PRICE <-------- eq 3
Seed cost	SEED	
Fertilizer cost	FERT	
Labor cost	LABOR	
Variable cost	VCOST	SEED + FERT + LABOR <- eq 4
Machine depreciation	MACHD	
Property tax	TAX	
Fixed cost	FCOST	MACHD + TAX <-------- eq 5
Total expense	EXPEN	VCOST + FCOST <-------- eq 6

*This column is blank if the variable is an input or independent variable; it contains an equation if the variable is a calculated, output, or dependent variable.

FIGURE 11.3
EXAMPLE OF INITIAL DATA INPUT IN ALB

Variable Description*	Columns**		
	1	2	3
Product name	APPLE	CORN	BEAN
Profit			
Cost ratio			
Units sold	9000	5000	1000
Price per unit	.1	.2	2.0
Revenue			
Seed cost	200	300	500
Fertilizer cost	100	100	200
Labor cost	300	200	800
Variable cost			
Machine depreciation	0	400	100
Property tax	100	100	100
Fixed cost			
Total expense			

*The variable description is posted by ALB. It is identical to the variable description provided by the user in model formulation.
**Each column is a particular value for the variable. In this problem, there is one column for each product. After the user is finished entering data, ALB tries to calculate as many blank cells as possible. Cells that cannot be calculated are left blank.

256

FIGURE 11.4
EXAMPLE OF FORWARD CALCULATION IN ALB

	Columns		
Variable Description	**1**	**2**	**3**
Product name*	APPLE	CORN	BEAN
Profit*	200	−100	300
Cost ratio	.077	.220	1.70
Units sold	9000	5000	1000
Price per unit	.1	.2	2.0
Revenue*	900	1000	2000
Seed cost	200	300	500
Fertilizer cost	100	100	200
Labor cost	300	200	800
Variable cost*	600	600	1500
Machine depreciation	0	400	100
Property tax	100	100	100
Fixed cost*	100	500	200
Total expense*	700	1100	1700

*Indicates cells for which ALB calculated a value.

Although the present sequence of equations for the farm crop model may be quite natural for the user, the equation set cannot be solved in its present sequence. For example, PROFT cannot be calculated because REVEN is defined after the PROFT equation. ALB would know to execute the equations in the following order:

Equation 3	REVEN = SOLD x PRICE
Equation 4	VCOST = SEED + FERT + LABOR
Equation 5	FCOST = MACHD + TAX
Equation 6	EXPEN = VCOST + FCOST
Equation 1	PROFT = REVEN − EXPEN
Equation 2	RATIO = EXPEN / SOLD

More importantly, the user may request to see the equation order at any time. This function is called *equation ordering*.

In forward calculation mode, ALB calculates each output variable. Alternatively, the user of ALB may wish to calculate one or more input variables from the output variables. Suppose the user wants to calculate PROFT, SOLD, PRICE, MACHD, and FCOST based on REVEN, EXPEN, RATIO, SEED, FERT, LABOR, VCOST, and TAX. Note that SOLD and PRICE, although written as input variables, are left undetermined. Additionally, the user wants the revenue for each product to be increased by $300. The user conveys this request by blanking out the PROFT, SOLD,

FIGURE 11.5
EXAMPLE OF REQUEST TO CALCULATE PROFT, SOLD, PRICE, MACHD, AND FCOST, WHEN
REVENUE IS CHANGED TO 1200, 1300,2300†

	Columns		
Variable Description	**1**	**2**	**3**
Product name	APPLE	CORN	BEAN
Profit			
Cost ratio	.077	.220	1.70
Units sold			
Price per unit			
Revenue (*new values)	*1200	*1300	*2300
Seed cost	200	300	500
Fertilizer cost	100	100	200
Labor cost	300	200	800
Variable cost	600	600	1500
Machine depreciation			
Property tax	100	100	100
Fixed cost			
Total expense	700	1100	1700

†ALB tries to calculate each blank cell.

PRICE, MACHD, and FCOST rows and inputting 1200, 1300, and 2300 to
the revenue row (see Figure 11.5).

ALB would manipulate the equations by reordering and reversing
(solving an equation for what usually would be considered an input variable) to find PROFT, SOLD, PRICE, MACHD, and FCOST in the following manner:

Solve equation 4 for VCOST	VCOST = SEED + FERT + LABOR
Solve equation 6 for FCOST	FCOST = EXPEN - VCOST
Solve equation 5 for MACHD	MACHD = FCOST - TAX
Solve equation 1 for PROFT	PROFT = REVEN - EXPEN
Solve equation 2 for SOLD	SOLD = EXPEN / RATIO
Solve equation 3 for PRICE	PRICE = PRICE / SOLD

Note that some equations can be used in their original form (e.g., equation 5) and others must be reversed (e.g., equation 1 is now used to calculate PRICE instead of REVEN). The calculations are carried out and
posted to the screen as shown in Figure 11.6.

Figure 11.6 is an example of the function called *reversibility*. ALB
will develop and execute a set of instructions to calculate as many blank

FIGURE 11.6
DISPLAY OF CALCULATED VALUES FOR PROFT, SOLD, PRICE, MACHD, AND FCOST, WHEN
REVENUE IS CHANGED TO 1200, 1300, 2300·

Variable Description	Columns		
	1	2	3
Product name	APPLE	CORN	BEAN
Profit	500	200	600 ----|
Cost ratio	.077	.220	1.70 |
Units sold	9000	5000	1000 ----|
Price per unit	.133	.26	2.30 ----|
Revenue (*new values)	*1200	*1300	*2300 |
Seed cost	200	300	500 |
Fertilizer cost	100	100	200 |
Labor cost	300	200	800 |
Variable cost	600	600	1500 ----|
Machine depreciation	0	400	100 ----|
Property tax	100	100	100 |
Fixed cost	100	500	200 ----|
Total expense	700	1100	1700 |

----Indicates cells for which ALB calculated a value.

cells as possible and maintain data integrity. Data integrity is lost when the worksheet contains conflicting data. For example, if a value of 100 is posted for PROFT, 50 for REVEN, and 10 for EXPEN, then the displayed data are in conflict with the equation: PROFT = REVEN − EXPEN (50 minus 10 does not equal 100). Cells that cannot be calculated are left blank. There are in excess of 200 possible unique requests a user could make for this farm crop example.

Once the new form of the equation is created, ALB incorporates it into its executable code. In the farm crop example, ALB generated the SOLD = EXPEN / RATIO version of equation 6 to satisfy the user request. This version of equation 6 is now saved for future use. ALB has modified itself to efficiently handle this condition.

When requested ALB will provide an explanation for any calculation carried out, therefore the user is always in control of the model. It will present a portion appropriate to a specific variable or the entire calculation sequence. This function is called *calculation explanation*. Figure 11.7 contains the explanation a user would receive from ALB if they "challenged" the calculation of PRICE for apples. Figure 11.8 contains the explanations if the user asked about the entire set of calculations.

A key task in effectively using a model is understanding the relationships between variables via the model equations. ALB provides two

FIGURE 11.7
RESPONSE TO CHALLENGE OF APPLE PRICE CALCULATION

THIS VARIABLE IS NORMALLY AN INPUT VARIABLE.
IN THIS CASE IT IS A VARIABLE TO BE CALCULATED.
IT WAS CALCULATED FROM THE ROOT EQUATION
REVENUE = SOLD X PRICE
IN THE FORM
PRICE = REVENUE / SOLD   WHERE
                                          REVENUE = 1200
                                          SOLD   = 9000
                                          PRICE   = .133

FIGURE 11.8
RESPONSE TO QUESTION ABOUT ALL CALCULATIONS

SOLVE EQUATION 4 FOR VCOST	VCOST = SEED + FERT + LABOR	(FORWARD)
SOLVE EQUATION 6 FOR FCOST	FCOST = EXPEN − VCOST	(REVERSE)
SOLVE EQUATION 5 FOR MACHD	MACHD = FCOST − TAX	(REVERSE)
SOLVE EQUATION 1 FOR PROFT	PROFT = REVEN − EXPEN	(FORWARD)
SOLVE EQUATION 2 FOR SOLD	SOLD = EXPEN / RATIO	(REVERSE)
SOLVE EQUATION 3 FOR PRICE	PRICE = REVEN / SOLD	(REVERSE)

types of equation analysis to help with this task. They are called *variable breakdown* and *variable breakup*. For example, it can identify which variables impact profit, as shown in Figure 11.9 (variable breakdown), or which variables are impacted by the variable VCOST, as shown in Figure 11.10 (variable breakup).

One end-product of building a worksheet model is a data base consisting of the original and calculated data (Figure 11.4 contains an example worksheet data base). Often the user wants to look only at selected portions of the model data. The natural language interface enables the user to select portions of the model data with queries made in English. For example, the user could enter either of the following requests to obtain the same desired information:

1. Show me the best two products by profit.
2. Give me the top two based on profit.

The natural language interface would provide the following display as shown in Figure 11.11.

FIGURE 11.9
BREAKDOWN OF THE VARIABLE PROFT

PROFT = REVEN − EXPEN
REVEN = SOLD x PRICE
EXPEN = VCOST + FCOST
VCOST = SEED + FERT + LABOR
FCOST = MACHD + TAX

PROFIT IS A FUNCTION OF:
SOLD   PRICE   SEED   FERT   LABOR   MACHD   TAX

PROFT = (SOLD x PRICE) − ((SEED + FERT + LABOR) + (MACHD + TAX))

FIGURE 11.10
BREAKUP OF THE VARIABLE VCOST

EXPEN = VCOST + FCOST
PROFT = REVEN − EXPEN
RATIO = EXPEN / SOLD

VCOST IMPACTS:
EXPEN   PROFT   RATIO

FIGURE 11.11
EXAMPLE OF THE NATURAL LANGUAGE QUERY ENHANCEMENT

		Columns	
Variable Description	**1**	**2**	**3**
Product name	APPLE	BEAN	
Profit	200	300	

ALB is able to identify and process simultaneous equations. An example of a simultaneous equation set is:

$$BONUS = .2 \times PROFT$$
$$PROFT = REVEN − (EXPEN + BONUS)$$

Additionally, ALB will handle conditional logic (e.g., maximum, minimum, if-then-else), special functions (e.g., mortgage payments, sine, cosine, and ln), and intercolumn calculations (e.g., sales this quarter = sales last quarter $\times$ 1.1).

The additional functions provided by EMES give the user additional flexibility in building and using a worksheet model. Additionally, the user is provided important insights into the relationships between variables he or she would at best find very time consuming to generate, at worst impossible to generate. Just as worksheet modeling packages such as LOTUS 1.2.3 lessened user dependence on programmers, enhancements such as those in ALB will lessen user dependence on "skilled equation manipulators" and reduce the chance of error due to a faulty analysis.

11.4.2   Outline of the Equation Manipulating Expert System

The equation manipulating expert system (EMES) is written in APL/APL2. It uses a Boolean array–based inferencing algorithm (Sullivan and Fordyce 1985b, 1985c). The algorithm is described in detail in the December 1985 issue of *APL Quote Quad*. EMES is described in detail in "An Equation Manipulating Expert System in APL/APL2" (Sullivan and Fordyce 1985d).

There are four major groups of functions in EMES: model examine, solution, calculation explanation, and variable analysis. "Model examine" takes in the list of variables and equations in the model and generates a small file of information characterizing the model. This information is used by the other three groups. "Solution" takes in the data inputted by the user, determines how to calculate as many unknown variables as possible, and generates the needed form for each equation. It also generates a log of its activity, which is used by calculation explanation. "Calculation explanation" responds to a user request about how a variable was calculated. "Variable analysis" provides the user information about which variables directly or indirectly influence a specified variable. In the following sections each group is described briefly, and the associated code is listed.

Model Examine   After the ALB user is done building his or her model, a list of the variables and equations are passed to the group of functions called *model examine*. This group builds a small data base with pertinent information about the variables and equations. This information is used by the other groups. Let's use an area, volume, perimeter model to illustrate the work done by this group. The variables and equations in the model are:

```
Variables              Equations
---------------------------------------------
LN
WD
AREA                   AREA = LN x WD (eq. 1)
HT
VOL                    VOL = HT x AREA (eq. 2)
PERM                   PERM = 2 x LN + 2 x WD (eq. 3)
```

The model examine function would carry out the following operations on this set of equations:

Step 1 — Place parentheses into the equations to indicate implied operation. The perimeter equation would become:

$$PERM = (2 \times LN) + (2 \times WD).$$

Step 2 — Establish an almost Boolean matrix indicating which variables are in which equations (one row for each variable; one column for each equation). A 1 indicates the variable is an input member of the equation, a 2 says it is the output variable, and a 0 indicates it is not a member. For this example the matrix would be:

```
Variable       Equation
                1   2   3

----------------------------
LN        |     1   0   1
WD        |     1   0   1
AREA      |     2   1   0
HT        |     0   1   0
VOL       |     0   2   0
PERM      |     0   0   2
```

Step 3 — Establish the correct ordering for executing the equations in forward mode. In this example the correct order is equations 1, 3, and 2.

Step 4 — Identify equations that are simultaneous, or equations that access information from another column. There are no such equations in this example.

Solution *Solution* takes in the data inputted by the user and then determines how to calculate as many unknown variables as possible. An example set of data is:

```
  LN  =  unknown
  WD  =  20
AREA  =  unknown
  HT  =  5
 VOL  =  1000
PERM  =  unknown
```

Using this information, the information generated by model examine, and various rules about solving sets of equations and doing algebraic reversal, this group calculates as many unknown variables as possible. For this example, the solution process would be as follows:

Step 1—Generate a Boolean single column matrix that identifies which variables are known (indicated as a 1) and which are unknown (indicated as a 0). For this example, the Boolean matrix would be:

$$
\begin{array}{rcl}
LN & = & 0 \\
WD & = & 1 \\
AREA & = & 0 \\
HT & = & 1 \\
VOL & = & 1 \\
PERM & = & 0
\end{array}
$$

Step 2—For each equation, calculate the number of variables in the equation, the number of variables that are known and in the equation, and the difference between these two numbers. Order the columns based on the established order of execution for forward solution. For this problem, the data are:

		Equation		
		1	3	2
In	|	3	3	3
Known	|	1	1	2
Difference	|	2	2	1

Step 3—Execute the first equation (left to right) with a difference value of 0 or 1 that has not been executed. For this problem, equation 2 is chosen. Since the unknown variable is AREA, equation 2 is solved for AREA (AREA = VOL / HT).

Step 4—The known/unknown matrix is updated and becomes:

$$
\begin{array}{rcl}
LN & = & 0 \\
WD & = & 1 \\
AREA & = & 1 \\
HT & = & 1 \\
VOL & = & 1 \\
PERM & = & 0
\end{array}
$$

Step 5—Recalculate the difference information.

		Equation		
		1	3	2
In	|	3	3	3
Known	|	2	1	3
Difference	|	1	2	0

Step 6—Equation 1 is chosen to be executed. The unknown variable is LN, so equation 1 is solved for LN (LN = AREA / HT).

Steps 7 and 8—The known/unknown and difference information is updated and becomes:

```
         LN   =   1
         WD   =   1
       AREA   =   1
         HT   =   1
        VOL   =   1
       PERM   =   0
```

	Equation		
	1	3	2
In	3	3	3
Known	3	2	3
Difference	0	1	0

Step 9—Equation 3 is chosen, and PERM is calculated. This is the last step for this problem.

Calculation Explanation   *Calculation explanation* responds to a user request about how a variable was calculated. It accesses a log of activity kept by the solution group. An example of this log would be:

Number of Equation Executed	Variable Solved for	Form of Equation
3	AREA	AREA = VOL / HT
1	LN	LN = AREA / WD
2	PERM	PERM = (2 x WD) + (2 x LN)

Analysis of Variable   *Variable analysis* provides the user information about which variables directly or indirectly influence a specified variable. To get this information, it uses the Boolean matrix generated by the model examine group, which describes the makeup of the equations. This matrix was presented in the model examine section and is repeated here.

	Equation		
	1	2	3
LN	1	0	1
WD	1	0	1
AREA	2	1	0
HT	0	1	0
VOL	0	2	0
PERM	0	0	2

The procedure to determine which variables impact VOL is:

Step 1—Examine column two (the equation in which VOL is the output variable). There are two variables immediately impacting VOL. They are HT and AREA. HT is an input variable (not calculated from any equation), therefore no other variables are associated with VOL through HT. This is not true for AREA, which is a calculated variable.

Step 2—Examine column one (the equation in which AREA is the output variable). There are two variables immediately impacting AREA (LN and WD), and therefore indirectly impacting VOL. Since both LN and WD are input variables, our search ends here.

11.5 EVALUATION OF THE EXPERT SYSTEM–BASED ENHANCEMENTS

The impact of the enhancements described in the previous section on the user was evaluated by concentrating on two questions: (1) Was the enhancement used? and (2) Did the quality of the problem analysis improve when the enhancement was used? Question 2 was broken down into two parts: (a) Was the time to accomplish the analysis reduced? and (b) Was the quality of the analysis better?

To answer these questions a survey-interview of worksheet modeling software users was conducted. The survey-interview technique is one of the principal data collection methods in information systems. It was successfully used in a joint research effort between IBM San José Research Laboratory and the MIT Center of Information Systems Research to understand where computers can be used to support office work (Bullen 1982, 1983). David Isenberg (1985) used this technique to successfully gather information about how top executives think.

First, each survey-interview participant filled out a background questionnaire that collected information about prior or related experience with worksheet models and software. Next, each participant was given a one-half-hour introduction to ALB including hands-on training. Then each person used ALB to help solve one of two case study problems. Finally, each participant was interviewed about the use of the enhancements and their view on the value of the enhancements.

The 20 survey-interview participants were business professionals from IBM or the Marist College MBA and MPA programs. All the participants in this evaluation had experience with electronic spreadsheets (e.g., LOTUS 1.2.3) and financial problems similar to the case study they were asked to solve using ALB. The participants could be divided into two classes: (1) those with weak equation-manipulating ability and experience and (2) those with a strong equation-manipulating ability.

Questions about the use and value of the enhancements were grouped into six categories:

1. General satisfaction with ALB
2. The use and value of equation ordering
3. The use and value of reversibility
4. The use and value of calculation explanation
5. The use and value of variable breakdown
6. The use and value of natural language queries

The actual questions are provided in Appendix A. The responses are provided in Appendix B. The case studies are in Appendix C. A short summary of their responses follows.

All the additional enhancements or functions were used with the exception of the natural language query of worksheet data bases. For the limited kinds of queries users made in this session, the menu-driven approach was more appealing. Participants particularly found the explanation functions (calculation explanation and variable analysis) valuable (both efficiency and quality). Equation ordering was significantly more important to participants with weak equation-manipulating skills, than for those who were not weak. Reversibility was used but was scored as having minimal value. This is probably because the trial and error alternative could provide the same information and this was the method they used with their electronic spreadsheet package.

11.6   CONCLUSION

Expert systems are one of the key tools in moving DSS into the next step in the evolution from passive data storage to highly active systems that participate in the decision-making process. Figure 11.12 contains the hierarchy. The next step is called *Decision Support/Decision Simulation (DSIM)* (Sullivan and Fordyce 1985a). In DSIM, data are increasingly extended into more compact and useful information. DSIM combines traditional DSS, quantitative analysis, graphics and simulation, data base management and query, and expert systems to provide the decision maker with a more powerful decision aid.

FIGURE 11.12
MANAGEMENT SYSTEMS HIERARCHY

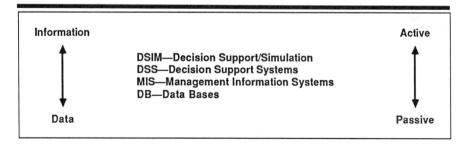

DSIM is not limited to answering the questions: What is the present status of some activity? or What if I change the value assigned to a variable in a model: DSIM is able to formulate alternatives, predict logical outcomes, and answer the question, "Why?"

Many of the new support systems are moving in the DSIM direction (Kosy and Wise 1984; Fox and Smith 1984; Brown et al. 1985; Bard 1985; Wiig 1985; Hagaman et al. 1985; and Duchessi 1985). This direction is also reflected in some of the latest expert system shells, languages, and consulting businesses. Examples include Inference Corporation's ART, Intellicorp's KEE, IBM's APL2, and many of the recent enhancements made to LISP and PROLOG.

Today's technology can and does measurably support the decision maker. Exploitation of AI in DSS/DSIM is largely a matter of implementation. It is academia's role to produce people capable of understanding, building, and using what technology provides. It is industry's role to develop and use the tools responsibly.

REFERENCES

Appleyard, F., and Hui, R. (1985), "Design: A Financial Modeling System," *Proceedings of the APL85 Conference*, ACM SIGAPL, 11 West 42nd St., New York, N.Y. May 12–16.

"Artificial Intelligence is Here," *Business Week*, July 9, 1984, pp. 54–62.

Bard, Y. (1985), "APLPIE – An APL Programmed Inference Engine," IBM Cambridge Scientific Center, Cambridge, Mass.

Blanning, R. (1983), "What is Happening in DSS," *Interfaces*, 13 (5): 71–80.

Blanning, R. (1984), "Expert Systems for Management: Possible Application Areas," *Transactions of Fourth International Conference on Decision Support Systems*, ed. R. Zmud, April.

Blanning, R. (1985), "A System for Natural Language Communication between a Decision Model and Its Users," Workshop in Artificial Intelligence in Economics and Management, Zurich, Switzerland, March.

Bonissone, P., and Johnson, H. (1984), "DELTA: An Expert System for Diesel Electric Locomotive Repair," Knowledge Base Systems Program and Flexible Automation Systems Program, Corporate Research and Development, General Electric Company, Schenectady, N.Y.

Brown, J., Cook, J., Groner, L., and Eusebi, E. (1985), "Logic Programming in APL2," IBM Santa Teresa Lab, San Jose, Calif.

Bullen, C., and Bennet, J. (1983), "Office Workstation Use by Administrative Managers and Professionals," *IBM Research Report 3890*, Yorktown Heights, N.Y., May.

Bullen, C., Bennet, J., and Carlson, E. (1982), "A Case Study of Office Workstation Use," *IBM Systems Journal*, 21 (3): 351–369.

Bursk, E., Clark, D., and Hidy, R., (1962), (eds.), *The World of Business*, vol. 1, New York: Simon and Schuster, pp. 81–87.

Cats-Baril, W. (1982), "Types of Support for Decision Making and Their Impact on the Design of Decision Support Systems," working paper, School of Business, University of Vermont, Burlington, Vermont.

Cercone, N., and McGalla, G. (1983), "Guest Editors' Introduction: Approaches to Knowledge Representation," *IEEE Computer*, 16 (10): 12–21.

Chopsky, J. (1983), "TK!SOLVER By Software Arts," *LIST*, October, pp. 28–34.

Duchessi, P. (1985), "The Conceptual Design of a Knowledge-Based System for Aggregate Planning," working paper, School of Business, SUNY at Albany, Albany, N.Y.

Dzielinski, B. (1983), "End User Scenarios," IBM National Accounts Division, Business Professional Marketing Support Department, 1133 Westchester Ave., White Plains, N.Y.

Emden, M. (1985), "Spreadsheets as a Subset of Logic Programming," working paper, University of Waterloo, Kitchner, Canada.

Farewell, D. (1984), "DSS Mechanisms for Judgmental Flexibility: An Exploratory Survey," *Journal of Management Information Systems*, 1 (2): 72–79.

Fox, M., and Bourne, D. (1984), "Autonomous Manufacturing: Automating the Job-Shop," *IEEE Computer*. 17 (9): 76–78.

Fox, M., and Smith, S. (1984), "ISIS—a Knowledge Based System for Factory Scheduling," *Expert Systems*, 1 (1): 25–50.

Gale, W. (1985), "Artificial Intelligence Research in Statistics," *The AI Magazine*, 2 (1): 72–75.

Gervarter, W. (1983), "Expert Systems: Limited But Powerful," *IEEE Spectrum*, August, pp. 39–45.

Gorry, G., and Krumland, R. (1982), "Artificial Intelligence Research and Decision Support Systems," in J. Bennet, ed., *Building Decision Support Systems*, Reading, Mass.: Addison-Wesley.

Hagaman, W. et al. (1985), "MEDCAT: An APL Program for Medical Diagnosis, Consultation, and Teaching," *Proceedings of the APL85 Conference*, ACM SIGAPL, 11 West 42nd St., New York, N.Y., May 12–16.

Hahn, G. (1985), "More Intelligent Statistical Software and Statistical Expert Systems: Future Directions," to be published in *American Statistician*, 39 (1): 36–56.

IFPS Tutorial (1980), EXECUCOM Systems Corp., P.O. Box 9758, Austin, Texas 78766.

Isenberg, D. (1985), "How Top Executives Think," *Transactions of Fifth International Conference on Decision Support Systems*, 290 Westminster St., Providence, R.I., April 1–4.

Keen, P. (1984), "A Walk Through Decision Support," keynote address for FCS-EPS users' group meeting, printed in *Computerworld*, January 14.

Keppel, E. (1985), "APL2 or LISP: Implementing Frames, a Knowledge Representation Scheme," IBM Germany Heidelberg Scientific Center, Tiergartenstrasse 15, D 6900 Heidelberg, FRG.

King, D. (1983), "An Expert System for Selecting Appropriate Statistical Analyses," *Transactions Third International Conference on Decision Support Systems*, ed. G. Huber, June.

King, D. (1985), "Bridging the 4th and 5th Generations: Linking Relational Databases with Expert Systems," *Fifth International Conference on Decision Support Systems*, ed. J. Elam, April.

King, W. (1984), "Decision Support Systems, Artificial Intelligence, and Expert Systems," *MIS Quarterly*, editor's comment, September, pp. iv–v.

Kosy, D., and Wise, B. (1984), "Self-Explanatory Financial Planning Models," *Proceedings of National Conference on Artificial Intelligence* (AAAI-84), Los Altos, Calif., William Kaufman, Inc., August, pp. 176–181.

Kulikowski, C., and Weiss, S. (1985), *A Practical Guide to Designing Expert Systems*, Totowa, N.J.: Rowman & Allanheld.

Lane, R. (1984), "Hybrid Systems for Decision Making," *Expert Systems*, 1 (1): 81.

Lee, R. (1985), "Database Inferencing for Decision Support," *Decision Support Systems*, 1 (1): 57–68.

Lembersky, M., and Chi, U. (1984), "Decision Simulators—Speed Implementation and Improve Operations," *Interfaces*, 14 (4): 1–15.

Lichtenthal, S. (1984), A/FE HQ division of IBM, to Kenneth Fordyce, 10 November 1984, personal files of Kenneth Fordyce, IBM, Poughkeepsie, N.Y.

LOTUS 1.2.3 User Manual (1983), Lotus Development Corporation, 161 First Street, Cambridge, Mass.

Luzi, A., and White, C. (1983), "The Audit-Concerns Model: An Extension of Auditing Theory Through Expert Systems Methodology," working paper.

Newman, J. (1956), *The World of Mathematics*, vol. 1, New York: Simon and Schuster, pp. 359–362.

OR/MS Today (1984), "Management Science Roundtable Awards Four Commissions," TIMS, 290 Westminster St., Providence, R.I., 11 (6): 13.

Sandberg-Diment, E. (1984), "Avoiding the Pitfalls of Spreadsheets: Documentation Should Be the First Step in Designing Any Application," *New York Times*, March 10, p. F19.

Sanger, D. (1984), "The Next Big Test for LOTUS," *New York Times*, February 13, p. D1.

Sanger, D. (1985), "Technology: The Next Goal Common Sense," *New York Times*, February 7, p. D2.

Schwartz, R.D. (1980), "Refocus and Resurgence in Artificial Intelligence." *IEEE Proceedings of the National Aerospace and Electronics Conference*, May.

Smith, D. (1981), "Perspectives: Computers, Tools, and People," working paper, IBM T.J. Watson Research Center, Yorktown Heights, N.Y.

Sullivan, G., and Fordyce, K. (1982), "A Natural Language Interface for Man-Machine Communication," IBM, H20/906, Poughkeepsie, N.Y.

Sullivan, G., and Fordyce, K. (1983), "A Decision Support System Paradigm," IBM, H20/906, Poughkeepsie, N.Y.

Sullivan, G., and Fordyce, K. (1984), "A Review of Expert Systems," IBM, H20/906, Poughkeepsie, N.Y.

Sullivan, G., and Fordyce, K. (1985a), "DSIM: One Outcome of Combining Artificial Intelligence and Decision Support Systems," *Transactions of the Fifth International Conference on Decision Support Systems* (DSS-85), 290 Westminster Street, Providence, R.I., April.

Sullivan, G., and Fordyce, K. (1985b), "AIDA: Artificial Intelligence Development Aids for APL," *Proceedings of the 1985 APL Conference*, May.

Sullivan, G., and Fordyce, K. (1985c), "A Boolean Array Based Algorithm in APL for Forward Chaining in Rule-Based Production Expert Systems," *APL Quote Quad*, 16 (3): 3–11.

Sullivan, G., and Fordyce, K. (1985d), "An Equation Manipulating Expert System in APL/APL2," IBM, H20/906, Poughkeepsie, N.Y.

Thimm, A. (1967), "The New Management Sciences and Managerial Behavior," *Personnel Journal*, 46 (7): 52–58.

Tversky, A., and Kahneman, D. (1979), "Judgment Under Uncertainty: Heuristics and Biases," *Science*, 85, September.

Watson, G. (1983), "Knowledge Base Management for Model Management Systems," working paper, Naval Post Graduate School, Monterey, Calif., June.

Wiederhold, G. (1984), "Knowledge and Database Management," *IEEE Software*, 1 (1): 63–74.

Wiig, K. (1984), "Will Artificial Intelligence Provide the Rebirth of Operations Research?" TIMS/ORSA Joint National Meeting, May.

Wiig, K. (1985), "The Artificial Intelligence Program at Arthur D. Little, Inc.," Arthur D. Little Decision Resources, Acorn Park, Cambridge, Mass., November.

Wiig, K., and Ernst, M. (1984), "Artificial Intelligence: The Near-Term Implications for Management," executive brief L840603, Arthur D. Little Decision Resources, Acorn Park, Cambridge, Mass., June.

Williams, T. (1985), "A Knowledge Based Investment Manager's Workstation," workshop in Artificial Intelligence in Economics and Management, Zurich, Switzerland, March.

Zivy, G. (1985), "The Role of Expert Systems in Producing Log Interpretation Software," *Expert Systems*, 1 (1): 57–64, 80.

Appendix A

Survey Questions on the Use and Value of the Enhancements

GENERAL SATISFACTION WITH ALB

1. How satisfied were you with ALB?
   a. Unsatisfied: ALB was difficult to learn, awkward to use, lacked necessary functions, etc.
   b. Neutral: ALB was usable, but nothing special.
   c. Satisfied: ALB met all the basic needs and more. It was easy to learn, easy to use, and its added functions were very helpful.
2. Did ALB enable you to carry out your case analysis faster?
   a. No: No reduction in time to complete analysis.
   b. Little: ALB reduced analysis time by 1–10%.
   c. Some: ALB reduced analysis time by 11–20%.
   d. Substantial: ALB reduced analysis time by more than 20%.
3. Do you think ALB improved the quality of your analysis?
   a. No: No improvement was made.
   b. Some: Some improvement was made.
   c. Substantial: A substantial improvement was made.
4. Comments on general satisfaction:

MODELING BUILDING AND EQUATION ORDERING

5. Were the equations initially inputted in the sequentially correct order (if the model was executed in the sequence it is written, it would function correctly)?
   a. No
   b. Yes

6. Were you aware the equations were or were not in the correct order?
   a. No
   b. Yes

7. Did you look at the correct equation order established by ALB?
   a. No
   b. Yes

8. How many times was the model structure changed after its initial generation?
   a. 0
   b. 1–4
   c. 5–8
   d. More than 8

9. How many different sets of numbers were run in the model ("what if" cases)?
   a. 1
   b. 2–6
   c. 6–12
   d. More than 12

10. Did the equation ordering enable you to carry out your case analysis faster?
    a. No: No reduction in time to complete analysis.
    b. Little: ALB reduced analysis time by 1–10%.
    c. Some: ALB reduced analysis time by 11–20%.
    d. Substantial: ALB reduced analysis time by more than 20%.

11. Did you think the equation ordering improved the quality of your analysis?
    a. No: No improvement was made.
    b. Some: Some improvement was made.
    c. Substantial: A substantial improvement was made.

12. Comments on equation ordering:

REVERSIBILITY

13. How often was reversibility used (having ALB solve for input variables; for example, solving the equation $A = L \times W$ for L)?
    a. 0
    b. 1–4

    c. 5–8

    d. More than 8

14. Would you reverse equations manually if ALB did not do it?

    a. No

    b. Probably not

    c. Occasionally

    d. Whenever needed

15. Did the reversibility enable you to carry out your case analysis faster?

    a. No: No reduction in time to complete analysis.

    b. Little: ALB reduced analysis time by 1–10%.

    c. Some: ALB reduced analysis time by 11–20%.

    d. Substantial: ALB reduced analysis time by more than 20%.

16. Did you think the reversibility improved the quality of your analysis?

    a. No: No improvement was made.

    b. Some: Some improvement was made.

    c. Substantial: A substantial improvement was made.

17. Comments on reversibility:

CALCULATION EXPLANATION

18. How often was the calculation explanation function used?

    a. 0

    b. 1–4

    c. 5–8

    d. More than 8

19. Did the calculation explanation enable you to carry out your case analysis faster?

    a. No: No reduction in time to complete analysis.

    b. Little: ALB reduced analysis time by 1–10%.

    c. Some: ALB reduced analysis time by 11–20%.

    d. Substantial: ALB reduced analysis time by more than 20%.

20. Did you think the calculation explanation improved the quality of your analysis?

    a. No: No improvement was made.

    b. Some: Some improvement was made.

    c. Substantial: A substantial improvement was made.

21. Comments on calculation explanation:

VARIABLE ANALYSIS

22. How often did you request a breakdown of a variable(s) to its input components?

    a. 0

    b. 1–4

    c. 5–8

    d. More than 8

23. Did the variable analysis enable you to carry out your case analysis faster?

    a. No: No reduction in time to complete analysis.

    b. Little: ALB reduced analysis time by 1–10%.

    c. Some: ALB reduced analysis time by 11–20%.

    d. Substantial: ALB reduced analysis time by more than 20%.

24. Did you think the variable analysis improved the quality of your analysis?

    a. No: No improvement was made.

    b. Some: Some improvement was made.

    c. Substantial: A substantial improvement was made.

25. Comments on the analysis of variable feature:

NATURAL LANGUAGE QUERY OF WORKSHEET DATA BASE

26. How many queries of the worksheet model data base did you make (query is defined as desiring to look at some subset of the worksheet data base satisfying a specified criteria)?

    a. 0

    b. 1–5

    c. 6–10

    d. More than 10

27. What percentage of the queries did you make using the natural language interface (NLI)?

    a. 0–5%

    b. 5–10%

    c. 11–20%

    d. 21–60%

    e. 61–100%

28. How often did the NLI handle your request correctly?

    a. 0–10%

    b. 11–40%

    c. 41–60%

    d. 61–80%

    e. 81–100%

29. Did the NLI enable you to carry out your case analysis faster?

    a. No: No reduction in time to complete analysis.

    b. Little: ALB reduced analysis time by 1–10%.

    c. Some: ALB reduced analysis time by 11–20%.

    d. Substantial: ALB reduced analysis time by more than 20%.

30. Did you think the NLI improved the quality of your analysis?
  a. No: No improvement was made.
  b. Some: Some improvement was made.
  c. Substantial: A substantial improvement was made.
31. Comments on the NLI feature:

Appendix B

Evaluation of Enhancements Data

An "0" indicates no response to the question.

GENERAL SATISFACTION WITH ALB

1	C	C	C	C	C	C	C	C	C	C	C	C	C	C	C	C	C	C	C	C	C
2	C	C	C	C	C	C	C	C	C	C	C	C	C	C	C	C	C	C	C	C	C
3	B	0	B	B	B	B	B	B	B	B	B	B	B	B	0	B	0	0	0	B	

All users were generally satisfied with ALB and thought it speeded their analysis. Participants often commented that the modeling language was easy to learn and the menu structure was easy to follow. Many participants thought ALB improved the quality of the analysis.

MODEL BUILDING AND EQUATION ORDERING

5	B	A	A	B	A	A	A	A	A	A	A	A	A	A	A	B	A	A	A	A	A
6	0	A	B	0	A	A	A	A	A	A	A	A	A	A	0	A	B	B	B	A	
7	0	A	A	0	A	A	A	A	A	A	A	A	A	A	0	A	A	A	A	A	
8	B	B	B	B	B	B	B	B	B	B	B	B	B	B	B	B	B	B	B	B	
9	B	B	B	B	B	B	B	B	B	B	B	B	B	B	B	B	B	B	B	B	
10	0	C	B	A	C	C	C	C	C	C	C	C	C	C	A	C	B	B	B	C	
11	0	A	A	A	B	B	B	B	B	B	B	B	B	B	A	B	A	A	A	B	

276

The equation ordering function was used by 17 of the participants. Of those 17, 13 were unaware that the equations were not in the proper sequence. Most of the participants felt equation ordering improved efficiency (speed of analysis), but the group was split about its impact on quality. The data below give the responses associated with equation manipulating ability.

		Equation Manipulating Ability	
		Weak	Not weak
Improve	no	0	7
Quality	yes	12	1

The most likely reason for this split was that participants with good skills in equation manipulation felt they could order the equations correctly without much effort for this size problem. Those without such skills felt the opposite.

REVERSIBILITY

13	B	B	B	B	B	B	B	B	B	B	B	B	B	B	B	B	B	B	B	B
14	B	A	A	A	A	A	A	A	A	A	A	A	A	A	A	A	A	A	A	A
15	B	B	B	B	C	C	C	C	C	C	C	C	C	C	B	C	B	B	B	C
16	A	A	A	A	B	B	B	B	A	A	A	A	B	A	A	B	A	A	A	B

All participants used reversibility, and no one thought they would do the algebraic reversals manually. Some participants thought the reversibility function improved efficiency.

Most participants did not think reversibility improved the quality of the analysis. A probable reason for this is that the same information provided by reversibility can also be obtained by trial and error. An example of trial and error is finding the LENGTH value, which provides an area of thirty when width is three, by trying different values for LENGTH. Users were familiar with the trial-and-error technique from their experience with electronic spreadsheets. Recalculations with ALB for this problem could be done six at a time with a three-second response time.

CALCULATION EXPLANATION

18	C	D	B	B	B	B	B	B	B	C	B	B	C	B	B	C	B	B	B	B
19	C	C	B	B	C	B	B	B	B	B	B	B	C	B	B	C	B	B	B	C
20	B	B	B	B	B	B	B	B	B	B	B	B	B	B	A	B	A	B	B	B

All participants used the calculation explanation function. With few exceptions, they thought it improved efficiency and quality. Many positive comments were made about this feature.

ANALYSIS OF VARIABLE

22	C	C	D	C	C	B	B	B	C	C	B	B	C	B	B	B	B	B	B	C
23	D	C	C	C	C	C	C	C	C	C	C	C	C	C	B	C	B	B	B	C
24	B	B	B	B	B	B	B	B	B	B	B	B	B	B	B	B	B	B	B	B

All participants used the analysis of variable function and thought it improved efficiency and quality. This feature received the highest grades of all functions for impact on efficiency and quality.

NATURAL LANGUAGE QUERY OF WORKSHEET DATA BASE

26	C	B	B	B	B	B	B	B	B	B	B	B	B	B	B	B	B	B	B	B
27	A	A	A	C	A	A	A	A	A	A	A	A	B	A	A	A	A	A	A	A
28	0	0	0	C	0	0	0	0	0	0	0	0	C	0	0	0	0	0	0	0
29	A	0	0	A	0	0	0	0	0	0	0	0	A	0	0	0	0	0	0	0
30	A	0	0	A	0	0	0	0	0	0	0	0	A	0	0	0	0	0	0	0

All participants made queries of the worksheet data base. With only a couple of exceptions, no one used the natural language interface to do it. Why?

Users made only one type of query — seeing the values associated with some subset of the variables in the model that fit on one screen. For the farm crop problem a typical query would be a request that just the values for product name, total expense, revenue, profit, and cost ratio be displayed as shown below.

	Columns		
Variable Name	1	2	3
Product name	APPLE	CORN	BEAN
Revenue	900	1000	2000
Total expense	700	1100	1700
Profit	200	-100	300
Cost ratio	.077	.220	1.70

Users never asked for selections based on some criteria such as products with profit greater than 100 or revenues greater than the revenue for APPLE. These kinds of comparisons could all be done visually.

To obtain a display of a certain subset of the variables using the natural language interface, the user had to type in a somewhat lengthy statement. An example is DISPLAY PRODUCT NAME REVENUE, TOTAL

PRICE, PROFIT, AND COST RATIO. To get the same display with the menu-driven query facility, the user only needed to place an X next to the variable he or she wanted to see.

```
Variable Name                      Put  X  if You  Want  the
                                   Field Displayed

---------------------------------------------------------------
Product name                        X
Units sold
Price per unit
Revenue                             X
Seed cost
Fertilizer cost
Labor cost
Variable cost
Machine depreciation
Property tax
Fixed cost                          X
Total expense                       X
Profit                              X
Cost ratio                          X
```

Since the second method does not require the user to type or remember the name of the variable requested, it is much more appealing.

Appendix C

Two Case Study Problems

CASE STUDY 1

A company is planning to introduce a new product and is interested in how well it will do in the first year. Initially there will be one office handling both administration and sales, but in quarter 3 a second sales branch will be opened.

Sales revenue is made up of two parts:

Branch 1 $10,000 in quarter 1 and growing linearly by 5 percent of that value per quarter.

Branch 2 $10,000 in quarter 3 and growing linearly by 3 percent of that value per quarter.

These values have already had cost of goods sold subtracted out.

Sales salaries will begin at $8,000 per quarter and in quarter 3 will increase by $3,000 because of the new sales branch.

Office expenses are projected to be $1,000 plus 5 percent of sales revenue.

Other expenses are projected to be $1,500 plus 2 percent of sales.

Sales promotion will be $500 per quarter.

Incentives will be paid as 5 percent of sales revenue.

You are the financial analyst:

1. Prepare a one-year outlook or plan based on the information provided, and explicitly identify all expense areas, calculate total expenses, revenue, and profit.

2. Evaluate the impact of the 5 percent increase in sales each quarter and a reduction of office expenses to 3 percent of sales revenue.

3. What if other expenses increase to 8 percent of sales revenue?

4. Evaluate the following options, which will increase profit by $1,000 per quarter: increased sales, with reduced expenses, and changes in incentives for salespersons.

See Figures 11.13 and 11.14 for possible models and calculations for this case study.

CASE STUDY 2

Market Research is evaluating the profitability of a new product over the next four years. Units sold are anticipated to be $50,000 increasing by 15 percent per year. The selling price of $8.50 increases 5 cents per year after the initial year. Variable costs per unit in the cost of goods sold are as follows:

> Raw material = $3.00
> Direct labor = $2.00
> Packaging = $0.50
> Distribution = $0.75

Inflation over the next three years is expected to be 3 percent.

Fixed costs involved in releasing the product fall into two categories:

> Factory = $25,000
> Other = $15,000

Administration feels that these costs can be held constant over the next four years.

The effective tax rate is 22 percent.

As the director of market research:

1. Prepare a one-year outlook or plan based on the information provided, and explicitly identify all expense areas, and calculate total expense, revenue, and profit.

2. Evaluate the impact of the 3 percent increase in sales each year and a $1.00 increase in price.

3. What if the inflation rate was 10 percent for each year?

4. Evaluate the following options, which will increase profit by $10,000 each year: increased sales, reduced expenses, increased prices, and reduced inflation rate.

See Figures 11.15 and 11.16 for possible models and calculations for this case study.

FIGURE 11.13
ONE POSSIBLE MODEL FOR CASE STUDY 1

Variable Description	Model Variable Name	Output Decimal Places	Formula or Equation
Quarter	Q	0	
Initial sales			
Branch 1	ISB1	0	
Branch 2	ISB2	0	
Growth in sales			
Branch 1	GSB1	2	
Branch 2	GSB2	2	
Sales for quarter			
Branch 1	SB1	0	ISB1 x (1 + (Q – 1) x GSB1)
Branch 2	SB2	0	ISB2 x (1 + (Q – 2) x GSB2)
Total sales	STOT	0	SB1 + SB2
Revenues			
Sales revenue	REVEN	0	STOT
Expenses			
Sales salaries			
Branch 1	SALB1	0	
Branch 2	SALB2	0	
Total salaries	SALTO	0	SALB1 + SALB2
Office expense	EXPOF	0	1000 + (.05 x STOT)
Other expense	EXPOT	0	1500 + (.02 x STOT)
Sales promotion	PROMO	0	
Incentives	INCEN	0	.05 x STOT
Total expense	TOTE	0	SALTO + EXPOF + EXPOT + PROMO + INCEN
Profit	PROFT	0	REVEN – TOTE

FIGURE 11.14
ONE POSSIBLE SET OF CALCULATIONS FOR CASE STUDY 1

Variable Description	Quarter			
	1	2	3	4
Initial sales				
Branch 1	10,000	10,000	10,000	10,000
Branch 2	0	0	10,000	10,000
Growth in sales				
Branch 1	.05	.05	.05	.05
Branch 2	.03	.03	.03	.03
Sales for quarter				
Branch 1	10,000	10,500	11,000	11,500
Branch 2	0	0	10,300	10,600
Total sales	10,000	10,500	21,300	22,100
Revenues				
Sales revenue	10,000	10,500	21,300	22,100
Expenses				
Sales salaries				
Branch 1	8,000	8,000	8,000	8,000
Branch 2	0	0	3,000	3,000
Total salaries	8,000	8,000	11,000	11,000
Office expense	1,500	1,525	2,065	2,105
Other expense	1,700	1,710	1,926	1,942
Sales promotion	500	500	500	500
Incentives	500	525	1,065	1,105
Total expense	12,200	12,260	16,556	16,652
Profit	−2,200	−1,760	4,744	5,448

FIGURE 11.15
ONE POSSIBLE MODEL FOR CASE STUDY 2

Variable Description	Model Variable Name	Output Decimal Places	Formula or Equation
Year	Y	0	
Revenue			
Base sales	BSALE	0	
Rate of increase for sales	SRATE	2	
Yearly sales	YSALE	0	BSALE x ((1 + SRATE) * (Y – 1))
Base selling price	BPRIC	2	
Yearly price inc	PRATE	2	
Yearly selling price	YPRIC	2	BPRIC + ((Y – 1) x PRATE)
Revenue	REVEN	0	YPRIC x YSALE
Expenses			
Base variable costs per unit sold			
Raw material	BRAWM	2	
Direct labor	BDIRC	2	
Packaging	BPACK	2	
Distribution	BDIST	2	
Yearly variable costs per unit			
Inflation rate	IRATE	2	
Raw material	YRAWM	2	BRAWM x ((1 + IRATE) * (Y – 1))
Direct labor	YDIRC	2	BDIRC x ((1 + IRATE) * (Y – 1))
Packaging	YPACK	2	BPACK x ((1 + IRATE) * (Y – 1))
Distribution	YDIST	2	BDIST x ((1 + IRATE) * (Y + 1))
Variable expense	VEXP	0	(YRAWM + YDIRC + YPACK + YDIST) x YSALE
Fixed costs			
Factory	FACT	0	
Other	OTHR	0	
Fixed expense	FEXP	0	FACT + OTHR
Total expense	TEXP	0	VEXP + FEXP
Profit			
Gross profit	GPROF	0	REVEN – TEXP
Tax rate	TAXER	2	
Taxes	TAXES	0	TAXER x GPROF
Net profit	NPROF	0	GPROF – TAXES

FIGURE 11.16
ONE POSSIBLE SET OF CALCULATIONS FOR CASE STUDY 2

Variable Description	Year			
	1	2	3	4
Revenue				
Base sales	50,000	50,000	50,000	50,000
Rate of increase for sales	.15	.15	.15	.15
Yearly sales	50,000	57,500	66,125	76,044
Base selling price	8.50	8.50	8.50	8.50
Yearly price inc	.50	.50	.50	.50
Yearly selling price	8.50	9.00	9.50	10.00
Total revenue	425,000	517,500	628,187	760,437
Expenses				
Base variable costs per unit sold				
Raw material	3.00	3.00	3.00	3.00
Direct labor	2.00	2.00	2.00	2.00
Packaging	.50	.50	.50	.50
Distribution	.75	.75	.75	.75
Yearly variable costs per unit				
Inflation rate	.03	.03	.03	.03
Raw material	3.00	3.09	3.18	3.28
Direct labor	2.00	2.06	2.12	2.19
Packaging	.50	.51	.53	.55
Distribution	.80	.82	.84	.87
Variable expense	314,784	372,861	441,654	523,139
Fixed costs				
Factory	25,000	25,000	25,000	25,000
Other	15,000	15,000	15,000	15,000
Fixed expense	40,000	40,000	40,000	40,000
Total expense	354,784	412,861	481,654	563,139
Profit				
Gross profit	70,216	104,639	146,533	197,298
Tax rate	.22	.22	.22	.22
Taxes	15,448	23,021	32,237	43,406
Net profit	54,769	81,618	114,296	153,892

12

Expert System Integration

Clyde W. Holsapple
Kar Yan Tam
Andrew B. Whinston

Traditional expert systems have a very narrow focus. They are only able to reason about problems for the purpose of reaching solutions or recommendations. This ability to reason is quite valuable but would be immensely more valuable if it were not separate from other knowledge-processing abilities. This chapter explains how expert system technology can be blended into the mainstream of business computing methods by eliminating the artificial barriers that have traditionally separated it from spreadsheet, data base management, and other business software. We describe a fundamentally new kind of expert system development tool that blends expert system facilities with all the usual business computing facilities, according to the principle of synergistic integration. The result is a vast new horizon of expert system possibilities.

12.1   INTRODUCTION

Chapter 1 aptly stressed the value of bringing an expert system into the "team" and suggested that it would be worthwhile (albeit cumbersome) for conventional expert system software to interface to external software. Some expert system construction kits have modest abilities to import data values from external software. But this semicompatibility of separate software packages is a far cry from integration, which takes a quantum leap beyond mere interfacing. As explained here, integration provides a comprehensive environment that makes all business-computing abilities (including expert system construction and consultation) available for use at any time — individually or in tandem.

This chapter begins with a brief review of knowledge management and synergistic integration (Section 12.2). Characteristics that tend to limit the widespread use of conventional expert system development tools in managerial applications are identified (Section 12.3). A method for synergistically integrating expert system technology into a more general knowledge management system is presented (Section 12.4) and illustrated for an inventory management application (Section 12.5). We conclude with an examination of implications of this new expert systems approach from the standpoints of decision support systems theory, application systems development, and knowledge worker usage.

12.2   INTEGRATED KNOWLEDGE MANAGEMENT

Today's managers can be characterized as knowledge workers. In the course of arriving at decisions, they may work with many kinds of knowledge in a variety of ways. Two of the more obvious kinds of knowledge are environmental and procedural (Bonczek, Holsapple, and Whinston 1981). The former consists of descriptive knowledge about the environment within which a decision is to be made. The latter refers to knowledge about how to accomplish various tasks pertinent to solving the decision problem. Each type of knowledge is susceptible to various computer-based representation techniques. For instance, environmental knowledge (sometimes called descriptive knowledge) might be represented as data base records, lines of text, spreadsheet cells, and values of variables. Procedural knowledge might be represented as prefabricated models, formula definitions in a spreadsheet, and sequences of programming language statements. The ways in which a particular fragment of knowledge can be processed are, of course, highly dependent on the technique used to represent it.

For nontrivial decision problems, there is no single knowledge representation technique that is superior to all others for managing all germane knowledge. As a result, various categories of generic software tools have arisen, each being oriented toward a particular knowledge representation/processing technique. It is frequently appropriate to employ knowledge management tools from multiple categories when working toward a decision. This may be accomplished directly by the knowledge worker or indirectly through the guise of an application system that uses multiple tools behind the scenes.

The problems of effectively coordinating multiple separate tools are well known. Even when their user interfaces and underlying file structures are compatible, user productivity is still impaired by such cumbersome requirements as switching back and forth among separate tools (or windows), "cutting and pasting" data from one tool into another, and importing/exporting data via intermediate files. These kinds of difficulties are largely overcome by a relatively new kind of software that includes multiple secondary tools within the confines of a single dominant tool (Holsapple and Whinston 1984). Examples of this nested approach to tool integration include Lotus 1-2-3, Symphony, and Framework. While they mitigate coordination difficulties, such systems have been properly criticized because their secondary components do not individually offer a level of functionality approaching stand-alone tools that address the same knowledge management tasks.

Full functionality and facile coordination can both be achieved through a distinctly different concept of integration. This synergistic integration effectively fuses capabilities of multiple tools into a single tool in such a way that the total effect is much greater than the sum of the component effects, and no component unduly constrains the operation of any other (Holsapple and Whinston 1984). Although each component can be used independently of the others, the components' functionalities are blended in such a way that there is no clear dividing line between components (Holsapple and Whinston 1983). A single operation can simultaneously exercise the functionalities of multiple components, resulting in knowledge management capabilities that are unattainable with separate tools or nested integration.

It is into this paradigm of synergistic integration that we introduce expert system techniques of knowledge representation and processing. The result is a tool that supports not only traditional expert system technology, but also drastically extends the conventional notions of rule-based expert systems. Through a synergistic integration that blends expert system functionalities with those of other components, many of the obstacles to effective use of expert system techniques in managerial settings are overcome. Moreover, many new knowledge management possibilities (involving automated reasoning) that do not exist in conventional business computing tools become available.

12.3 EXPERT SYSTEM DEVELOPMENT TOOLS

As explained in Chapter 1, an expert system (ES) is a computer-based consultant that draws upon application-specific expertise in the course of deriving, offering, and explaining advice about particular problems facing the system's end user. The expertise is typically represented as a set of rules. Each rule has a premise consisting of one or more conditions, a conclusion consisting of one or more actions, and an explanation. In addition to a rule set, an expert system must provide a language with which the user can ask for advice about specific problems. This language interface may be command-oriented, prompt-driven, menu-controlled or a natural language. Recall that the third essential constituent of any expert system is its inference engine, which is the software that infers advice from the rule-based expertise in response to some stated problem. This engine begins at some initial state that is descriptive of a problem and uses rules in an attempt to progress to a goal state that consists of desired advice (i.e., problem diagnosis, prognosis, or solution).

An expert system development tool (ESDT) is software that facilitates the construction and maintenance of expert systems by application developers. It consists of a rule management system for creating, manipulating, and analyzing a rule set's rules. It also provides a generalized inference engine that is invariant to the problem domain addressed by the rule sets on which it operates. The construction kits (sometimes called expert system shells) discussed in Chapter 1 are examples of conventional ESDTs. Such tools have two crucial characteristics that limit their effectiveness for building expert systems in managerial problem domains: their narrow focus and their limited flexibility in rule specification.

Because a conventional ESDT is strictly oriented toward reasoning, it does not enable the ES developer to make use of other knowledge management facilities that are so commonplace in supporting a knowledge worker's decision activities. Knowledge that is held in a data base, spreadsheet, program, or text is not readily accessible by an ES as it carries out a consultation. At best it can be extracted (usually a priori) into files with a format the inference engine can accept. The rules themselves are unable to directly reference pertinent knowledge in a convenient, flexible way. This is because conventional inference engines have to be designed solely for reasoning, not for data management, procedural modeling, spreadsheet processing, and so forth.

By itself, expert system reasoning ability is insufficient for many aspects of decision support. Similarly, data base management, spreadsheet, and other business computing abilities are individually inadequate for handling all aspects of decision support. The solution lies in *synergistically* integrating all of these abilities into a single piece of software. The full potential for managerial expert systems will only be realized to the extent that a new kind of ESDT appears — an ESDT with an inference engine that is able to directly do real data base management, spreadsheet processing, model execution, and so on.

Rule specification by traditional ESDTs is clearly not oriented toward the economical representation of managerial expertise. The capacity for numeric processing is typically rudimentary at best. Functions for both numeric and string transformations are frequently absent. Advanced conditional expressions (e.g., involving wildcard matching) normally are not supported in the premise of a rule. The conclusion of a rule is usually restricted to an assignment statement that the inference engine can use to modify the value of a single state variable, providing the premise is satisfied. The conclusion in a conventional rule cannot contain actions that do data base retrieval and updating, spreadsheet analysis, model execution, remote communications, graphics generation, and so forth.

One result of this inflexibility in rule specification is an unnecessarily large number of rules per rule set. That is, inherent limitations in the expressive power of traditional rule syntax often causes a fragment of expertise to be represented in multiple rules rather than a single rule. This kind of rule proliferation can have an adverse impact on the rule specification process and on inference efficiency. Beyond the productivity and efficiency problems, the inflexibility that results from an absence of synergy places a severe limit on the kinds of problems that can be effectively addressed by expert systems.

12.4   A NEW APPROACH TO EXPERT SYSTEMS

If the narrow focus and limited flexibility of traditional ESDTs can be overcome, then ES technology can become a much more valuable contributor to solving the knowledge management problems facing decision makers in corporate and governmental environments. To this end, we now introduce an ESDT that synergistically integrates expert system reasoning with other knowledge management abilities and provides unprecedented flexibility of rule specification. The result is not only a significant advance over conventional ESDT facilities, but also an important enhancement to the capabilities of present-day integrated software systems.

This new kind of ESDT is developed within the spirit of a very extensive software tool that is based entirely on the principle of synergistic integration. Called KnowledgeMan (Aarons 1984; and MDBS, Inc. 1983), this widely used software serves as a convenient starting point for specifying the nature of our new kind of expert system development tool. As a prelude to that specification, we briefly summarize some of the major KnowledgeMan characteristics that our new ESDT will inherit.

12.4.1   KnowledgeMan: An Overview

KnowledgeMan synergistically integrates a variety of basic knowledge representation and processing techniques into a single knowledge management tool (i.e., a single program). These include data management, ad hoc inquiry, statistical analyses, spreadsheet modeling, procedural modeling, forms management, business graphics, text processing, custom report generation, remote communication, and so forth. Each of these can be used independently of the others, or they can be used in conjunction with each other within a single command statement. Individually, each component ability is functionally at least comparable to stand-alone tools of the same genre. For instance, independent reviewers generally regard its data management abilities as greatly exceeding those of stand-alone data managers such as dBASE and R:base.

The data management portion of KnowledgeMan is a relational data base management system that maintains data in a tabular fashion. Each column of a table corresponds to a field. Each row of a table is a record consisting of a data value for each of the table's fields. Each field is also treated as a variable during KnowledgeMan execution. Its value at any moment is determined by the field value of the most recently accessed record in its table. Records can be accessed sequentially and/or randomly. There are extensive built-in security mechanisms.

KnowledgeMan provides a relational query language patterned along the lines of IBM's SQL (Structured Query Language) — the de facto standard for relational systems. With a single ad hoc command, a desired report based on data held in multiple tables can be produced. A query command can request dynamic sorting of the query output based on multiple fields and in any mixture of ascending/descending directions. It can also indicate that lines in the output report are to be grouped based on one or more fields, with statistics being reported for each group.

In a query command, a wide variety of conditions can be specified for the retrieval. For instance, the following query command produces a report showing the first name, last name, and salary (in thousands) for each employee in department 2, 7, or 9 whose salary exceeds $19,990 and whose last name begins with the letters "Tu."

```
SELECT FNAME,LNAME,SAL/1000 FROM EMPLOYEE
WHERE DNUM IN [2,7,9] & SAL>19990 & LNAME IN ["Tu*"]
```

The last part of this condition makes use of wildcard string matching. Any string of characters forms a valid match with the * wildcard symbol. Wildcard symbol matching and character class matching is also supported.

A statistics command is available that has the same basic form as a query command. Conditional statistical computation using data from multiple tables is fully supported. However, rather than displaying data values of all requested fields that satisfy stated conditions, this command displays statistics computed from those values. These statistics include sum, count, min, max, mean, standard deviation, and variance. The statistics are automatically preserved in variables that can be used in subsequent commands. For instance, a statistics command makes it very easy to get a report of all employees whose salaries are more than one standard deviation above the mean salary.

For governing screen I/O and printer output, KnowledgeMan has a built-in forms management capability, in addition to customary line-at-a-time input and output. Thus a single command is able to process an entire form at a time. A form is a rectangular area that is defined independently of the commands that utilize (e.g., display) it. When defining a form, the user can specify the placement of color blocks and/or form elements within it. A form element is either a literal (e.g., a title, a prompt) or a data input/output slot with values determined by a variable or expression.

For a data input slot, a mapping is specified to indicate where a data value is to be deposited when entered through the slot. For instance, if the slot is mapped into a field, then the entered data value becomes the new value of that field for a desired record in a table. Similarly, a mapping can be specified for an output slot to indicate where a data value is obtained for display through the slot. For instance, if a field is mapped to a slot, the value of that field in a desired record is output when the form is displayed.

Once a form has been defined there are various commands that enable it to be utilized: display a form on the console screen (PUTFORM), print a form, accept data through a form's input slots (GETFORM), clear a form from the screen, reset a form's slots, and so forth. Multiple forms can simultaneously appear on a console screen. They can be overlapped if desired and processing can be shifted among the forms as needed.

The integral programming language furnished in KnowledgeMan can be used to construct special procedural models or entire application systems. A variety of control structures are supported: while-do iteration, if-then-else, test-case, and parametric procedure invocation. Any KnowledgeMan command (e.g., for data management, statistics, inquiry, forms handling) can be invoked at any point within a KnowledgeMan program.

There is no limit on the number of variables that can be referenced within a program. Several variable types are supported, including: field variables, spreadsheet cells, statistical variables, working variables (both single-valued and arrays), and predefined environment and utility variables, which control various aspects of the operating environment. In addition to being used within normal programming commands, any of the foregoing variables can be used in data management, inquiry, statistics, spreadsheet, and form declaration commands.

The KnowledgeMan spreadsheet component supports the traditional spreadsheet processing commands. It also introduces four important new concepts: presentation styles, table access, defining a cell in terms of a program, and cell read/write security. A presentation style can be assigned to a cell or block of cells. It controls whether a cell's value will be visible or invisible, the cell's background and foreground colors, whether the cell value will be presented in reverse video, and whether it will blink. A cell's presentation style can be conditionally activated and deactivated.

As with conventional spreadsheets, a cell can be defined in terms of a constant or a formula involving other cells. In KnowledgeMan, a formula can also involve any of the various kinds of variables. Furthermore, a cell can be defined in terms of a data retrieval statement. This has several significant implications. It enables a spreadsheet to process data that is stored in data tables rather than spreadsheet cells. Multiple spreadsheets can therefore access the same data. This data can be created, maintained, and processed completely independently of the spreadsheets that access it by persons having no knowledge of or interest in spreadsheets.

Unlike other spreadsheet systems, a cell can also be defined in terms of an entire program that utilizes any of the procedural control structures cited earlier. Such a program can access large volumes of data from multiple tables in arriving at the cell's value. As a result, spreadsheet cells are not consumed by intermediate computations the results of which are of no direct interest. Furthermore, this allows very elaborate modeling to be accommodated within a spreadsheet context.

Just as with KnowledgeMan tables, both read and write security is provided for spreadsheet cell definitions. Read and/or write access codes can be assigned to any cell definition. A user can see a cell's definition only if the user's read access codes overlap the cell's read access codes. The user can change a cell's definition only if there is an overlap of the cell's and user's write access codes.

The KnowledgeMan business graphics component is quite versatile, supporting over a dozen types of graphs and allowing split-screen and superimposed graphics display. A single command will generate any desired graph from the output of an ad hoc query, a block of spreadsheet cells, an array, statistical results, or groups of working variables.

12.4.2 Integration of Expert System Construction and Consultation Abilities

Conceptually, the foregoing business computing capabilities provide a very good starting point for a new generation of ESDTs that go far beyond the conventional notions of a construction kit or shell. Ideally, this new kind of tool should possess all of the KnowledgeMan traits plus two additional capabilities: those of expert system construction and expert system consultation. Each would be integrated with the other capabilities according to the principle of synergy. This would result in an ESDT that allows each rule constructed for an expert system to reference objects (e.g., cells, fields, program variables, models, forms, graphs, etc.) used by any of the other integral capabilities. The synergy would also result not only in interactive consultation requests, but in the capacity for an expert system to be consulted by a spreadsheet, procedural model, textual passage, or another expert system.

In this way, the narrow focus and the inflexibility of conventional ESDTs can be overcome. The net effect is a single piece of software that actually goes beyond the scope of an ESDT. It can be used not only as a tool for developing more powerful expert systems, but also as an environment for consulting them. By blending the ability to reason with ordinary business computing abilities, there emerges an artificially intelligent environment of unprecedented power and versatility for addressing decision support needs.

12.4.3   Defining an Integral Rule Set

A rule set consists of the specific reasoning knowledge required to solve a particular type of problem. An integral rule set also is able to work with other kinds of knowledge represented in other ways (e.g., in a spreadsheet). As noted later, rule sets can be joined together implicitly in order to tackle problems that involve reasoning expertise from a number of areas. A syntax for defining integral rule sets follows. This syntax itself is of no special importance. The functionality that it conveys is what is significant.

```
RULE  SET<rule-set-name>READ<read-codes>
INITIALIZATION<commands>
GOAL<variable>
{RULE<rule-name>PRIORITY<priority-level>COST<action-cost>
    IF<condition>THEN<commands>
        CHANGES<variables>COMMENT<text>
}
·
·
·
COMPLETION<commands>
END
```

Here, there are five sections in a rule set declaration. The first section defines the name of the rule set <rule-set-name>, which is the unique identification tag of a rule set for purposes of both internal operation and external inspection/invocation. This section also provides security control mechanisms by allowing the creator of the rule set to specify the authority level for executing the rule set. The <read-codes> are optional in a sense that their omission implies that public access is allowed for consulting the rule set.

Unlike the first section, which is compulsory for any rule set, the INITIALIZATION section is optional. If the INITIALIZATION section is present, its commands are executed in sequence whenever the rule is invoked. Any sequence of valid KnowledgeMan-like commands can appear in this section. These commands may be performed to establish initial variable values by assignment, to retrieve additional information, to interact with an end user via forms and graphics, to perform computations for certain variables (e.g., via statistical, spreadsheet or other analysis), to establish communication links with other systems to initialize the memory state, and so on.

The mandatory GOAL section identifies the default variable, the value of which will be inferred when the rule set is invoked for consultation. Since there is no limitation on variables, it is permissible for a single consultation to seek the values of multiple variables. Like the INITIALIZATION section, the optional COMPLETION section consists of a list of any KnowledgeMan-like commands. These commands will be automatically executed as soon as reasoning with the expert system's rules is completed. Thus the developer has extensive flexibility in determining what happens to the results of a consultation.

The other section of a rule set definition contains the specification of individual rules. One or more individual rule definitions must be present. Each rule is given a unique name, an optional priority level, and an optional cost. The function of the priority level is to provide a measure of importance for the rule, while the relative processing cost of the rule's action is reflected by the action cost. These can affect the order in which pertinent rules are selected for consideration during backward chaining.

A rule's IF clause can consist of any logical expression such as those permitted in KnowledgeMan. That is, any logical expression that can appear in an SQL query can appear as a rule premise. It can involve any of the various kinds of variables and any of the extensive collection of built-in numeric, string, and logical functions that exist in KnowledgeMan. Additional functions could also be supported. For instance, there might be a general purpose function named EVAL having two arguments. The first is a KnowledgeMan-like command string (e.g., to perform a procedure), and the second is the name of a variable whose value upon execution of the command string will be returned as the function's value.

A rule's THEN clause consists of a sequence of actions (i.e., commands) that will be executed when the inference engine determines that the rule's premise is true. These can be any KnowledgeMan-like commands including not only traditional ES assignment statements, but also procedure invocation, rule set invocation, input statements, output statements, graphics, computations, data retrieval, and so forth. The CHANGES clause identifies variables with values that could be altered by the rule's action (i.e., those of interest for purposes of backward chaining). This optional clause is important because these variables may not be explicitly mentioned in the THEN clause. The optional COMMENT clause contains text that explains the nature of the rule. Implicit input rules exist for all condition variables in a rule set's rules.

12.4.4   Rule Set Invocation

A rule set can be invoked via the CONSULT command. The CONSULT command can be invoked interactively by an end user, via a macro, within a spreadsheet cell, during text processing, within a procedure, within the actions of rules in other rule sets, and so forth. The syntax is as follows:

```
CONSULT<rule-set-name>[TO SEEK<variable>]
```

This command causes the ESDT's inference engine to use a backward-chaining approach to inference. The optional SEEK clause is used if some variable other than the rule set's default goal variable is desired.

A variation of the CONSULT command is as follows:

```
CONSULT<rule-set-name>TO TEST<variable>
```

Here the rule set is used to determine the value of the variable, by means of forward chaining. This generative use of a rule set can be employed to test the implications of the present memory context. A variation of the generative usage of a rule set is:

```
CONSULT<rule-set-name>TO PERFORM<rule-name>,<rule-
name>,...
```

This will cause the rules to be executed in the indicated sequence.

12.5 AN EXAMPLE

The following example illustrates an expert system solution to a common operation's management problem that is faced by almost every inventory manager of a company — the reorder quantity problem. Questions such as "How much do we order for product X next month?" and "What will be the demand of product X in the next quarter of the year?" are two of the many routine questions posed by management.

In order to answer these questions, the manager should know the nature of product X and its relationships with other products. The nature of the product is an important issue that has to be considered by the analyst before a solution plan for the problem can be formulated. Also, the different physical structures of the products pose another dimension of constraint on the solution of the problem, especially in cases when mathematical techniques are used to abstract real-life problems into some "models." Since most of these models capture only a subset of all the features of a problem in the real-life situation, some of the solutions offered by these models may be mathematically sound but practically useless.

Failure to identify these "solution fallacies" may lead to poor decisions and eventually jeopardize global corporate operations. For example, an economic order quantity (EOQ) model predicts that the reorder quantity of oranges is 100,000 for the next order. However, there may not be enough space to hold 100,000 oranges with the current existing storage capacity. Or even though the warehouse has sufficient storage space to hold all the 100,000 oranges, a large portion may end up in spoilage due to the physical characteristics of oranges. To break down the 100,000 order into orders of smaller quantity is preferred in this case.

Moreover, we have to know whether product X is sold individually or sold in conjunction with other products. In the latter case, the relationships between product X and the other products must be considered. "Do the demands of the other products affect the demand of X?" "How many of X has to be sold in conjunction with each of the related products?" "What is the company's policy toward these products?" Questions such as these must be answered before we can proceed to solve the main problem. Using the integrated ESDT presented previously, we examine an example of how the reorder quantity problem is stated and processed.

Two rule sets, REORDER QUANTITY and PRODUCT DEMAND, are defined. For simplicity, all read codes are left blank in the two rule sets. When the inference engine executes the initialization section of REORDER QUANTITY (Figure 12.1), all the required data tables (Figure 12.2) are put in use and the user is prompted to input necessary parameters in an interactive manner. Once the identification of the product and the time frame have been made, the inference engine searches the FRE-QUANTITY table to see whether the corresponding reorder quantity of P in time T exists. If such a record is found, no inference is needed. Otherwise, the inference engine proceeds to use the rules in order to establish a reorder quantity. As the completion section shows, this derived quantity is attached as a new record in the FREQUANTITY data table and output via a form on the console screen (see Figure 12.3).

The default goal of the REORDER QUANTITY rule set is to determine the value of RQTY. There are two rules in REORDER QUANTITY, namely ROQ1 and ROQ2. An English translation of ROQ1 is if the reorder quantity of a product P in time T is not currently available and the user has not assigned a value to it in the initialization section, then get advice about the demand, retrieve the holding and replenishment costs of product P in time T, and perform the EOQ model to determine the reorder quantity for P. The second rule uses some heuristic other than the direct application of the EOQ model to solve the problem. ROQ2 states that if the reorder quantity of product P in time T is currently unavailable but P itself is a part of some other products, then use the same rule set (i.e., reorder quantity) to determine the reorder quantity of each of these products and then derive the reorder quantity of P in time T from these reorder quantities. Notice that statistical analysis of a newly generated table (MAINR) is employed to total up the reorder quantity.

The difference between the first and second rules is that ROQ1 applies to those situations in which the product sold by the company is independent from other products. Since no relationship with other products exists, we can directly apply the EOQ model to solve the problem. The second rule exists to handle cases in which products are interdependent and closely related. It takes into account the different relationships associated with the product. Here, a recursive method is used to determine the reorder quantities of all the products of which P is a part and from these derives the reorder quantity of P. The "part of" relationship is one of the many possible relationships that a product can have with other

FIGURE 12.1
REORDER QUANTITY RULE SET

```
rule set:  REORDER  QUANTITY

initialization:
    use FREQUANTITY; use FPARTS
    use FHOLDINGCOST; use FREPLENISHMENTCOST
    input P str with "PRODUCT CODE:"
    input T str with "TIME:"
    obtain record from FREQUANTITY  for PCODE = P & TIME =T
    if #FOUND then BREAK
      else RQTY = unknown
    endif

goal:   RQTY

rule:   ROQ1
if:   not known(RQTY)
then:   consult PRODUCT DEMAND
        obtain record from FHOLDINGCOST for PCODE = P
        obtain record from FREPLENISHMENTCOST for PCODE = P
        perform EOQ using RCOST, HCOST, PDEMAND, RQTY
changes:    RQTY
comment:   if the reorder quantity of a product P in time T is not available
  in the data base, then consult another rule set for the demand.  Obtain
  the holding cost and the replenishment cost of product P in time T from
  the data base.  Execute the EOQ model to determine the reorder quan-
  tity for P

rule:   ROQ2
if:   not known(RQTY) and
      eval(convert
      PCODE,TIME,FPARTS.PARTOF,RQUANTITY,FPARTS.NUMOFUNIT,
      FPARTS.FREQUANTITY where PARTOF = P,TIME = T,
      FREQUANTITY.PCODE = FPARTS.PCODE to  MAINR,#FOUND)
then:  obtain first from MAINR
       I = 1
       while I <= #CNT do
         consult REORDER QUANTITY
         if known (RQTY) then MAINR.RQUANTITY =  RQTY; endif
         I = I + 1
         obtain next from MAINR
       endwhile
       stat MAINR.RQUANTITY * MAINR.NUMOFUNIT from MAINR
       RQTY = #SUM
changes:    RQUANTITY
comment:    if the reorder quantity of a product P in time T is not known and P
  itself is a part of some other products, then ascertain the reorder quantities
  of these products and derive the reorder quantity for P from these values.

completion:
    putform ROQFORM
    tally ROQFORM
    attach 1 to FREQUANTITY
    PCODE = P; TIME =T; RQUANTITY = RQTY
end
```

FIGURE 12.2
TABLE DEFINITIONS

FREQUANTITY
  PCODE: str
  TIME: integer
  RQUANTITY: integer

FHOLDINGCOST
  PCODE: str
  HCOST: real

FPRODUCTDEMAND
  PCODE: str
  TIME: integer
  DEMAND: integer

REGTABLE
  TIME: integer
  DEMAND: integer

FPARTS
  PCODE: str
  PARTOF: str
  NUMOFUNIT: integer

FREPLENISHMENTCOST
  PCODE: str
  RCOST: real

MAINR
  PCODE: str
  TIME: integer
  PARTOF: str
  RQUANTITY : integer
  NUMOFUNIT: integer

MAIND
  PCODE: str
  TIME: str
  DEMAND: integer
  PARTOF: str
  NUMOFUNIT: integer

FIGURE 12.3
FORM DEFINITION

FORM ROQFORM　　　**AT 3,25 PUT "REORDER QUANTITY FORM"**

　　　　　　　　　　　AT 6,5 PUT "PRODUCT CODE:"

　　　　　　　　　　　AT 6,19 PUT P

　　　　　　　　　　　AT 8,13 PUT "TIME:"

　　　　　　　　　　　AT 8,19 PUT T

　　　　　　　　　　　AT 11,7 PUT "R-QUANTITY:"

　　　　　　　　　　　AT 11,19 PUT RQTY

ENDFORM

FIGURE 12.4
PRODUCT DEMAND RULE SET

```
rule set:  PRODUCT DEMAND

initialization
      use FPRODUCTDEMAND; use FPARTS
      obtain record from FPRODUCTDEMAND  for PCODE = P and TIME = T
      if #FOUND then BREAK
          else PDEMAND = unknown
      endif

goal:  PDEMAND

rule:  PD1
if:  not known(PDEMAND)
then:  convert TIME,DEMAND from PRODUCTDEMAND
          where FPRODUCTDEMAND.PCODE = P TO REGTABLE LAST 10
      perform REGRESS using REGTABLE,COEFF1,COEFF2,ERROR
changes: PDEMAND
comment:  if the demand of product P in time T is not known, then retrieve the most
      recent 10 sets of demand data and use a simple regression model to determine
      the relationship between demand and time and the corresponding error of the
      regression model.

rule:  PD2
if:  (COEFF 1<>0) and (ERROR < 0.1)
then:    perform PREDICTION using COEFF1,COEFF2,T,PDEMAND
changes:  PDEMAND
comment:  if the demand is not constant with time and the regression error is within
      tolerance, then use the regression line formed in PD1 to predict the demand of P
      in time T

rule:  PD3
if: COEFF1 = 0
then:  perform TWO-STANDARD-DEVIATIONS-TEST using
      REGTABLE,COEFF2,PERCENTIN
changes:  PERCENTIN
comment:  if the demand is constant with time, then use the two-standard-deviation
      tests to estimate the error of the regression model.
```

products in the real world. It is assumed that the inference engine can properly track variable values in recursive settings.

There is no restriction on where a particular rule set is invoked. Any rule set can be consulted directly by a user or indirectly by another rule set. In this example the second rule set, PRODUCT DEMAND (Figure 12.4), is consulted by the first rule set, REORDER QUANTITY. The initialization sequence puts the needed tables (Figure 12.2) in use. Similar to REORDER QUANTITY, a data base retrieval is conducted in the in-

```
rule: PD4
if: PERCENT-IN > 95
then: PDEMAND = COEFF2
changes: PDEMAND
comment: if the error estimated from PD3 is tolerable, then the demand of P is equal
   to the non-zero coefficient of the regression model.

rule: PD5
if:  not known (PDEMAND) and
     eval(convert  FPARTS.PCODE,FPRODUCTDEMAND.TIME,
     FPRODUCTDEMAND.DEMAND,FPARTS.PARTOF,FPARTS.NUMOFUNIT
     from FPARTS from FPRODUCTDEMAND
     where FPARTS.PARTOF= P,FPRODUCTDEMAND.TIME = T,
     FPARTS.PCODE = FPRODUCTDEMAND.PCODE to MAIND,
     #FOUND)
then:   obtain first from MAIND
     J = 1
     while J <= #CNT do
          consult PRODUCTDEMAND
          if known(PDEMAND) then MAIND.DEMAND = PDEMAND;endif
          J = J+1
          obtain next from MAIND
     endwhile
     stat MAIND.DEMAND * MAIND.NUMOFUNIT from MAIND
     PDEMAND = #SUM
changes:   PDEMAND
comment:   if the demand of P in time T is not known and P itself is a part of some other
   products, then recursively determine the demand of each product that P is a part of
   and use these values to determine the demand of P.
```

itialization section to determine whether the demand of product P in time T is currently available. Only when the demand is not available will the rules be invoked.

Obviously, the goal of this rule set is to determine the demand of P in time T, and it is stated in the goal section along with all the necessary constraints associated with it. Five rules, PD1, PD2, PD3, PD4, and PD5, are stated in the rule set. PD1 simply says that if the demand for product P in time T is not known, then retrieve the 10 most recent sets of demand data and store them in a table called REGTABLE; use this data as input to a simple regression model. PD2, PD3, and PD4 are rules that deal with the regression model in PD1.

PD2 is concerned with the dependence between demand and time and says that if the demand is not constant with time and the regression error is within tolerance, then use the regression line formed in PD1 to predict the demand in time T. PD3 also works on the result from PD1, and it deals with the case in which the demand of P is independent of time. It says that if the demand is constant with time, then use the two-standard-deviation test to estimate the error of the regression model. PD4 says that if the error from the two-standard-deviation test is tolerable, then use the regression line formed in PD1 to estimate the demand of P. One interesting observation is that we can collapse the four rules into one by putting PD2, PD3, and PD4 into the action part of PD1. Although this reduces the modularity of the rule set, it should enhance the performance of the inference engine.

The last rule of PRODUCT DEMAND is similar to ROQ2 in REORDER QUANTITY. It considers the case when the demand of a product depends on the demand of other products. Again, a recursive method is used to determine the demand of P by first determining the demand of each of the products of which P is a part. For both rules, ROQ2 and PD5, provisions should be made in the control of recursive calls in order to prevent circularity or infinite loops.

To fully deal with all the problems of reorder quantity would naturally require more extensive rule sets than those presented here. Nevertheless, this example serves to illustrate some of the interesting knowledge management possibilities provided by an integrated ESDT. A more detailed discussion of the possibilities appears in Holsapple and Whinston (1986).

12.6 CONCLUSION

The applicability and importance of artificial intelligence techniques for the decision support system (DSS) field was first described several years ago (Bonczek, Holsapple, and Whinston 1981a, 1981b, 1983). The form of meta-knowledge that deals with reasoning was identified as an important constituent of a DSS's knowledge system. It was shown how this knowledge about knowledge is crucial for the realization of a generalized problem processing system (GPPS) that can display intelligent behavior. The examination of such a problem processor has heretofore occurred on a conceptual or operational plane, rather than at an implementation level.

With the advent of KnowledgeMan, we have the first implementation of a high-level GPPS for building decision support systems. Coupling this with ESDT extensions along the lines introduced here, we have the basis for implementing a GPPS that can display artificially intelligent behavior via its integral inference engine. Guru, a new software package that meets these objectives has just been commercially released (MDBS, Inc. 1985). Decision support systems built with such a tool will come to be regarded as representatives of a fundamentally new generation of artificially intelligent decision support systems. The management of reasoning will come to be regarded as having the same degree of importance as managing environmental, procedural, and other kinds of knowledge for both DSS builders and the developers of application systems.

The vision of an ESDT as presented here reaches well beyond the traditional expert system development tools. It blends expert system functionalities with those of data base management, spreadsheet, graphics, programming, and so forth. It thereby allows the builder of expert systems to take advantage of all of these other approaches to knowledge representation and processing in the course of devising a rule set and designing the user language interface. This opens up entire new dimensions for thinking about expert systems and furnishes a much greater degree of flexibility in expert system design. It also results in expert systems with capabilities that far exceed traditional notions of what is possible for an ES.

The fusion of an ESDT with other knowledge management methods suggests a variety of research topics beyond those explored here. Although the implementation of the inference engine is based on the same principles as a stand-alone ESDT, certain economies may be realized by the ability of multiple components to share some of the same underlying code (e.g., expression evaluation code). There is also the topic of methodologies for rule design in this much "richer" setting. That is, the ES builder now has many more options for designing a rule set and the performance impact of alternative (but equivalent) rule set designs deserves study. Other topics for further investigation include the effective operation of multiple concurrent ES users (e.g., in a local area network environment) and parallel ES processing in the context of large decision problems.

REFERENCES

Aarons, R. (1984), "Wising Up with KnowledgeMan," *PC*, March 6.

Bonczek, R.H., Holsapple, C.W., and Whinston, A.B. (1981a), *Foundations of Decision Support Systems*, New York: Academic Press.

Bonczek, R.H., Holsapple, C.W., and Whinston, A.B. (1981b), "A Generalized Decision Support System Using Predicate Calculus and Network Data Base Management," *Operations Research*, March.

Bonczek, R.H., Holsapple, C.W., and Whinston, A.B. (1983), "Specification of Modeling Knowledge in Decision Support Systems," in H.G. Sol, ed., *Processes and Tools for Decision Support*, Amsterdam: North-Holland.

Guru Reference Manual, (1985), MDBS, Inc., Lafayette, Ind.

Holsapple, C.W., and Whinston, A.B. (1983), "Software Tools for Knowledge Fusion," *Computerworld*, April.

Holsapple, C.W., and Whinston, A.B. (1984), "Aspects of Integrated Software," *Proceedings of the 1984 National Computer Conference.*

Holsapple, C.W., and Whinston, A.B. (1986), *Manager's Guide to Expert Systems Using Guru*, Homewood, Ill.: Dow Jones-Irwin.

KnowledgeMan Reference Manual, (1983), MDBS, Inc., Lafayette, Ind.

13

Artificial Intelligence in Project Support

Brian Phillips
Jeff Staley
Eric Gold

The power of a workstation is normally used to enhance the design effectiveness of the individual user. However, project team members also spend much time on tasks that detract from the creative role. These tasks involve disseminating and acquiring project-related information, perhaps in meetings, perhaps by filling out forms or preparing reports. In the networked workstation environment, support tools can be developed to improve the management of information in a project. We are investigating the role that artificial intelligence can play in developing such tools. We describe our efforts in creating a project encyclopedia, a time management system, and a communication system. The encyclopedia is a structured repository of project information. To assist in managing time, a zoomable calendar interface to the temporal dimension of the encyclopedia has been developed. Eventually, automatic scheduling will be supported. The enhanced mailer is augmented by rules that can be used to filter and generate messages.

13.1 INTRODUCTION

Maintaining an efficient project team is a complex task. In a perfect world it would not be so. The problem to be solved would be fully circumscribed in advance, all participants would correctly understand their allotted tasks, and meet the specifications by the deadlines without need of further instruction or interaction. In reality, aspects of the problem are initially overlooked, misunderstandings occur, clarification and redesign are needed, and external events intrude. The ability of a group to respond to any of these forms of change depends on its ability to dynamically manage information. In the extreme, without access to and transfer of information an organization cannot respond to change.

Discord can be alleviated with good communication channels that enable questions to be promptly answered and information to be distributed to relevant parties in a timely manner. Even so, a project can go astray. Misunderstandings can lead to unwittingly following a wrong direction; with no cause to question the decision, it may be a while before the error is realized. It is easy for an affected party not to be updated either due to forgetfulness or to some change that placed him or her in the chain of information flow not being properly disseminated at an earlier time.

The situation may be becoming worse. New technologies — individual workstations and networking — make it possible for many computer-based projects to be physically widely distributed. This is the "electronic cottage" scenario. A distributed group has only the telephone and computer-mediated communication. Telephonic conversation, with the possibility of telephone tag, is often replaced by electronic mail. Real-time communication is lost and much of the information transfer is limited to textual material. Thus the physical and psychological communicative bandwidth of the distributed group is significantly narrower than that within a centralized group. With these limitations, how can the efficient progress of the project be maintained? How is a descent into anarchy to be avoided?

In this paper we are presenting an evolving experimental environment, the Intelligent Support Environment (ISE), in which the applicability and the effectiveness of some new technologies are being evaluated. The goal is to maintain the cohesion of a project by supporting communication among team members and their access to project information. Some of the technologies have to do with networked workstations, digitized speech, and optical character readers, but in particular we are interested in artificial intelligence (AI). Electronic equipment increases the volume of information accessible; intelligence is needed to prevent information overload.

The use of computers for transmitting information or for performing mundane tasks is now common. With these systems the "intelligence" remains in the human participants. The advent of AI ushers in an era in which it becomes possible to automate some judgmental activities.

Moreover, a project generates many kinds of information. AI has techniques for the computational representation of such complex and diverse information. Out of AI has also come integrated program development environments, the underlying mechanisms of which greatly assist us in developing an integrated support environment, rather than one that is a set of autonomous subsystems.

If we were to describe our AI developments out of the context of the other technologies we are using, the flavor of our ambitions would be lost; thus we focus on AI, but not to the exclusion of the other technologies employed. In fact, it is first necessary to build a considerable amount of structure that involves no AI. This dominates the present system, but we are at a point where AI-based techniques are increasingly present.

Our targeted environment is a team of professionals intent on creating some artifact, possibly hardware or software. We are thinking of groups with more than 10 members and less than 100. Each member generally has access to a high-performance workstation such as the Tektronix Magnolia [1] or 4404 AI Workstation on which we are developing ISE. However, we do not preclude members with less computing power, nor is it assumed that one has to be a trained computer scientist to utilize the system.

At present we can find many systems that perform some of the team support tasks in isolation. We believe that support systems will not achieve acceptance until many of these tasks are integrated. We are intent on creating a broad range of facilities for this reason.

We are building the system to mirror existing procedures, as new technology is generally accepted if it follows a familiar pattern. To this end we have interviewed a number of project managers within our own organization. Once the general framework is accepted, innovation becomes feasible.

Our aim is not the impossible one of completely automating all of the tasks we are studying. The system is an assistant that can be overridden.

13.2 THE FRAMEWORK FOR A SOLUTION

13.2.1 Team Support — Not Project Management or Design Tools

A project support system serves the needs of the entire team. We are not developing a "project management system," as that term is generally understood, that is, analysis and forecasting systems using numerical data (see Reimann and Waren 1985). Project management systems assist the

---

[1] Magnolia is an internally built and used personal workstation. It incorporates MC68000 processors and has a high-resolution screen and a three-button mouse. It supports UNIX 4.2 and the languages Smalltalk, LISP, and Prolog. The Magnolias are linked by Ethernet.

project leader. Such systems are not precluded from our environment; our interests simply lie elsewhere. Eventually we will consider developing or including symbolic decision support systems of the kind discussed by Bonczek, Holsapple, and Whinston (1981). We are not creating design tools. Our concern is with the information environment of a project not the task-dependent tools for VLSI design, programming, and so forth that are used to design the project product. The framework for our present system encompasses the communication and information needs of the team. Team members have to be able to find out what is happening in the project and be able to communicate efficiently.

13.2.2   Components of the System

The information needs can be handled by a *project encyclopedia*, an information base that contains the history and state of the project and a schedule of events. It has conceptual and temporal dimensions to capture the what and when of project evolution. The encyclopedia is not intended to be directly accessible. Rather task-specific interfaces will be offered. For example, a calendar gives a temporal view, or the history of some portion of the project can be traced to bring a new project member up to date. Eventually it may be possible to generate progress reports from the encyclopedia or for past projects to be studied for training. A *calendar system* is also needed to assist in coordinating the use of all time-restricted resources: people, rooms, and equipment. A *communication module* can reason about mail messages. Eventually we anticipate real and elapsed time communication channels over which text, voice, and pictures can be transmitted freely.

The completeness of the encyclopedia is crucial to the success of the system. The burden of entering information must be minimized. We are seeking as many ways as possible to reduce the manual effort involved. We are exploring optical character recognition techniques. Another idea is to automatically capture information from the communication channels and place it in the encyclopedia. To this end, we need to make the communication channels as attractive as possible to encourage their use, hence the planned support for text, voice, and graphics documents in both real-time and correspondence modes. Nevertheless, relevant information will be generated in informal, off-line situations such as at the coffee machine. Collecting this information is a future challenge. One hope is that the overall advantages offered by the system will make users willing to manually and separately enter such information to maintain the coverage.

13.2.3   A Design for Integration

The system covers a wide range of diverse activities. The tools should be made mutually accessible to permit them to be used conjointly. The

Apple Lisa environment illustrates the great increase in the effectiveness of an integrated system. The advanced programming environments on LISP Machines (Weinreb and Moon 1981) and in Smalltalk (Goldberg 1984) illustrate the power that comes from integrating the activities of the program development cycle. This level of integration is a goal of our system. It is also to be an open environment to permit new facilities to be added.

Metaphor   We characterize the system through an anthropomorphic "communicating object" metaphor. Objects are autonomous entities that are effective through their ability to communicate with other entities. Any object that knows of another object and the protocol for communicating with it can utilize the functionality of that object. We view people, program modules, resources, or meetings as objects. Of course, the range of interaction possible depends on the object. Objects that are human have a very wide range of capabilities. A conference room's capabilities are limited to queries about its size, its availability, its audio-visual equipment, and the like.

Implementation   The metaphor of communicating objects maps well onto our implementation language, Smalltalk [2]. The object-oriented nature of Smalltalk assists us in achieving our goal of integration. The message-passing form of interobject communication encourages modularity. The internal format of data is totally isolated from other objects of the system. New objects need only know the protocols of other objects, and any internal modification to an object is externally invisible.

13.3   SMALLTALK AND ITS ENVIRONMENT
13.3.1   Interfaces

Smalltalk is more than just a programming language for our system; its interface philosophy overtly influences our design. The Smalltalk environment provides approximations to many of the user interfaces we are developing, and we have created interfaces largely by modifying the

---

[2] Smalltalk is an object-oriented language. Instead of creating a procedure that controls system operation, the user creates an object (usually a data structure) and a set of methods (operations that transform and communicate with the object). Smalltalk programs create objects or send messages to other objects. Once received, messages result in the execution of a method.

Programmers do not create each object and its methods individually. Instead, classes of objects are defined. A class definition describes an object and the methods that it understands. Classes are structured hierarchically, and any class automatically inherits methods from its superclass.

As a result of this hierarchy and code inheritance, applications may be written by adapting previously constructed code to the task at hand. Much of the application code can be inherited from previously defined Smalltalk code. The programmer need only redefine differences by overriding the inappropriate code with customized code (Alexander and Freiling 1985).

Smalltalk system. We have built upon the menu, browser, and area selection facilities in Smalltalk.

Fixed Menus   A fixed menu is a group of items that are permanently displayed. A selection is made by moving the mouse cursor into the desired selection, "Person" in Figure 13.1, which becomes highlighted, and clicking a mouse button. Many of the options associated with the communications module have this form.

Pop-up Menus   Pop-up menus only appear in response to a mouse click in a window. The selections are window-dependent. In Figure 13.2, the pop-up menu (overlaying the second pane from the top left) contains actions pertinent to nodes in the project encyclopedia. A selection is made by clicking the mouse when the cursor is on the desired choice.

Browsers   A browser contains a system of menus. Figure 13.2 shows a browser for a project. This browser is a hierarchy of fixed menus such that selecting an item, starting from the left-most menu, causes sub-

FIGURE 13.1
COMMUNICATIONS DIRECTORY WITH FIXED MENU

Communications Directory: Outgoing			
-------------------------	-------------------------	-------------------------	
CRL	Systems	Ajit Prem	
Yale	Graphics	Allen Wirfs-Brock	
Tek	Design Environments	Angela Masotti	
Other	Artificial Intelligence	Balaji Krishnamurthy	
-------------------------	Secretaries	Brian Phillips	
	Summer Visitors	Chan Lee	
	Rick LeFaivre	Chip Schnarel	
	-------------------------	Dave Manicosy	
		Dave Meyer	
		David Sullivan	
		Dean Lee	
		Denise Ecklund	
		Earl Ecklund	
		Eric Gold	
		Erich Kaltofen	
Person	Subject	Media	Folder	Fred Tonge / Gus Helman
Form	Purpose	Request	Desc	Guy Cherry / Hoane Nguyen Kaltof
User defined	Action		Role	Hugh McLarty / Jack Gjovaag

FIGURE 13.2
PROJECT BROWSER AND POP-UP MENU

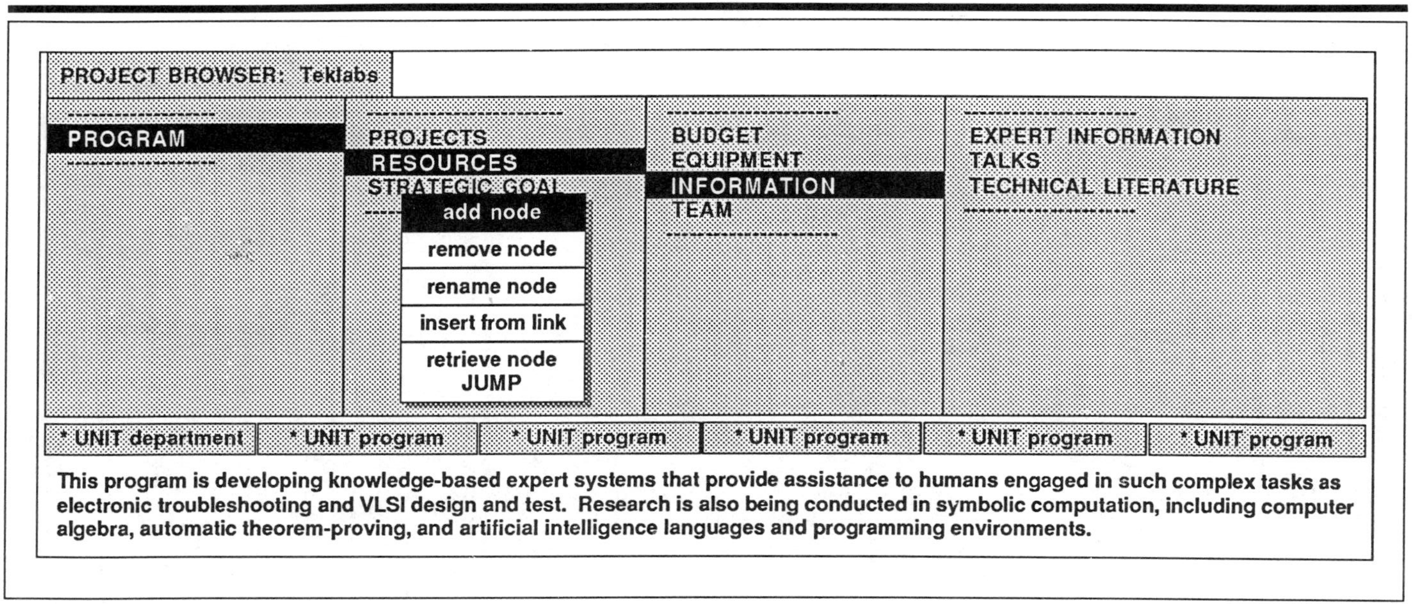

PROJECT BROWSER: Teklabs

PROGRAM

PROJECTS
RESOURCES
STRATEGIC GOAL

| add node |
| remove node |
| rename node |
| insert from link |
| retrieve node |
| JUMP |

BUDGET
EQUIPMENT
INFORMATION
TEAM

EXPERT INFORMATION
TALKS
TECHNICAL LITERATURE

* UNIT department   * UNIT program   * UNIT program   * UNIT program   * UNIT program   * UNIT program   * UNIT program

This program is developing knowledge-based expert systems that provide assistance to humans engaged in such complex tasks as electronic troubleshooting and VLSI design and test. Research is also being conducted in symbolic computation, including computer algebra, automatic theorem-proving, and artificial intelligence languages and programming environments.

311

ordinate choices to appear in the next window to the right. In the project browser shown, the information stored at a selected node can be retrieved and displayed in the lower pane.

Area Selection   Using the mouse, it is possible to select an area in a window by sweeping out a section of a window while a mouse button is depressed. The selection is highlighted. In Figure 13.3 the user has selected a time range in a calendar in this manner. The selection is part of the process of making a calendar entry. In the delineation for a day, Figure 13.3a, a period 1:00 to 3:00 p.m. is selected, shown as the black area in Figure 13.3b. An "empty" meeting is created, Figure 13.3c, which can then be annotated.

13.4   FACILITIES IN THE SYSTEMS AND A SCENARIO

13.4.1   An Overview of Facilities

The project encyclopedia is composed of objects and is built on top of a distributed file system. The physical organization of the encyclopedia is transparent to the user; only the logical structure is relevant to him or her. The logical structure is implemented as relations between objects (see Section 13.5). Many other parts of ISE access the encyclopedia, and a variety of tools are provided for viewing it.

Time is an omnipresent factor in a project. Accordingly, ISE offers facilities for managing time – the Intelligent Electronic Calendar (IEC).

FIGURE 13.3
SELECTING A TIME PERIOD IN THE CALENDAR

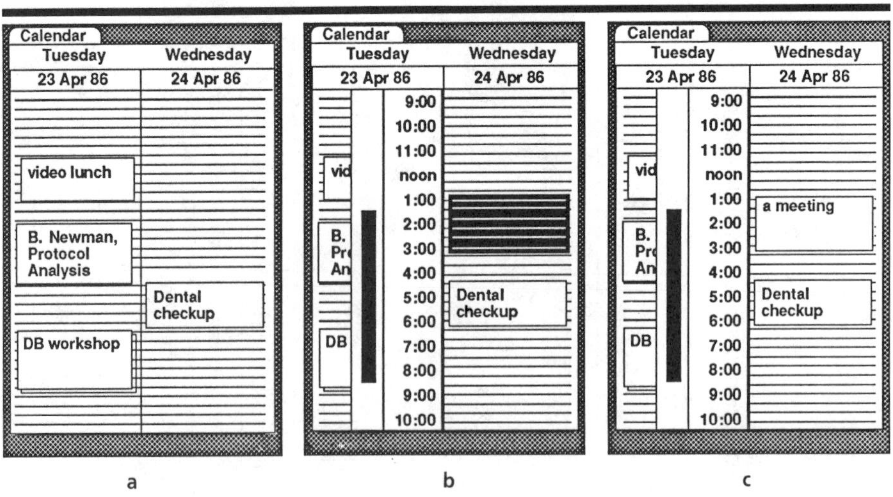

The IEC provides facilities to access the project encyclopedia, view multiple schedules, summarize a schedule, automatically schedule repetitive meetings, and automatically negotiate a meeting time. It is described in Section 13.6.

The communication module will eventually be a multimedia cocoon of services. At present the focus in on building an elapsed time communication system, an enhanced electronic mail system, described in Section 13.7. This module has the ability to evaluate rules, which allows it to filter and generate messages.

13.4.2   A Scenario

A consultant is visiting the project and is to give a talk. Room calendars can be examined to see when certain rooms are available. Similarly the calendars of concerned team members can be scanned to ensure that they have no conflict. Eventually, an automatic scheduling system would select the best time.

An announcement, including an abstract, must be mailed to members of the group. The mailer has default mailing lists for such eventualities. It also can be augmented with rules for some specific actions. For example, a member of another team may have requested to be included in all announcements concerning a specific topic. This request can be stored in a rule associated with the mailer to cause the name to be automatically added to the addresses when the topic is the subject of communication. A reminder should be sent out one day prior to the talk. An appropriate trigger can be placed in the calendar to cause this.

Someone may be mystified why such a topic is being discussed. To satisfy one's curiosity, use the project browser, Figure 13.2, ascend to the PROGRAM node then examine the projects of that program to see the relevance. There may also be a more direct path from the talk to a project, similar to the assignment arc that links a team member to a project.

Because of the high degree of integration of the component systems, there is often several ways to access information. For example, the abstract could have been accessed from a calendar entry for the talk.

13.5   THE PROJECT ENCYCLOPEDIA
13.5.1   The Role of the Encyclopedia

The encyclopedia is a structured repository for "all" project information. It is intended to be accessible by most, if not all, modules of the system. It is thus a basic integrating force in the system. At the present stage of development of ISE, it is a viewable information source and is used by the mail system and the calendar, as described in Sections 13.6 and 13.7.

The intention is that the encyclopedia should be integratable with other tools developed for the project environment. In his introduction to this text Silverman mentions that knowledge-based systems for management need to elicit evidence from many sources. In many cases, this is the very information that should be in the encyclopedia. The encyclopedia, then, could automatically feed a knowledge-based system. For the meantime, the encyclopedia is a manual reference source that can help locate needed data. This overcomes forgetfulness and removes the need to guess or to rummage through filing cabinets for relevant documents.

13.5.2   The Structure of the Encyclopedia

Information stored in the encyclopedia can be found in many formats in the physical environment of project team members. It exists as memoranda, notes on blackboards, in calendars, notebooks, and address books. Transferring this information to a computer offers the considerable advantage that links can be added to show relationships between information; in the paper environment no such associations can easily be represented.

Logically, then, the encyclopedia is a network of objects linked by labeled associations. As such, it can be considered a semantic network (e.g., Simmons 1973), a widely used form for knowledge representation in AI. It differs from other implementations in that it is implemented in a file system and in the granularity of the concepts represented by each node; usually the concept at a node is "primitive" (e.g., Schank 1977). It is impractical to reduce the large volume of project information to such a canonical level. For ISE we need to address the problem of "representation and reasoning in the large." Our encyclopedic nodes can contain units of any size, for example, a picture, a paragraph, or a digitally encoded conversation (cf Becker 1975). In addition there is the need to be able to relate abstract concepts to a more detailed explication. In Phillips (1978) representations and processes for abstraction and decomposition of complex concepts were presented. The notion relies on a set of primitive relations; a scheme is under development to allow for the definition and use of complex relations. The resulting representation scheme will allow complex nodes and arcs to be used in the project encyclopedia and have the mechanisms to reduce these structures to less abstract levels when needed.

Some localized parts of system knowledge (e.g., the rules for the mailer and the calendar) are in separate formal notations; these are discussed in Sections 13.6 and 13.7. Physically, the encyclopedia is a distributed file system, Hyperdata [3].

In Figure 13.4 we show a fragment of encyclopedic structure. It is displayed in a hyperdata graph browser and has been annotated with arc labels. A program has resources, a (strategic) goal, and projects. Projects

FIGURE 13.4
LOGICAL ASSOCIATIONS OF PROGRAMS AND PROJECTS

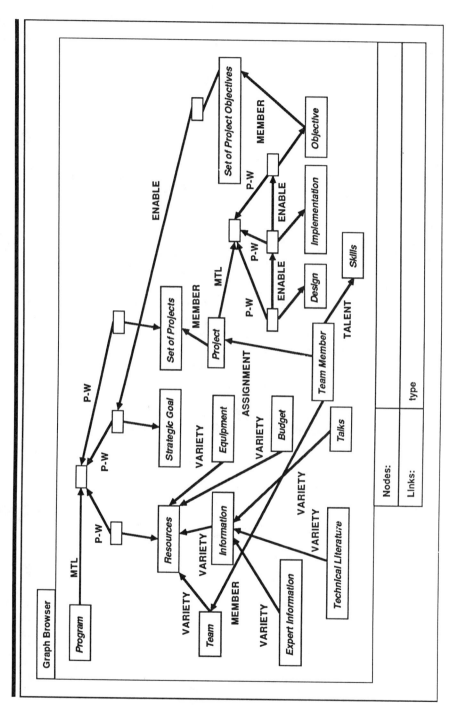

have a design that enables the implementation through which the objective is achieved. The set of objectives of a program's projects enable the strategic goal to be achieved. People, information, budget, and equipment are varieties of resources. Information comes from experts, the technical literature, and talks. Within the project schemata, there are links to the program resources, for example to the team members, assigned to it. For resource allocation, the skills of the team need to be represented. The ASSIGNMENT and TALENT relations are examples of complex relations; all others are primitive. With this representation, concepts can be viewed at different levels of detail. For example, a project can be viewed as a single concept or viewed more closely as the design, implementation, and objective structure; the MTL relation associates the levels. (Figure 13.4 represents abstract schema that are instantiated to describe actual programs and projects.)

Companies give an organizational and procedural framework for a project. A product follows a prescribed sequence of phases from concept to introduction. These phases are marked by events that must occur. This product development process is an important matrix for the encyclopedia. In some ways it is similar to the notion of a "script" (Schank and Abelson 1977) in AI systems. In Figure 13.5 we see a hypothetical product introduction process from Concept Phase to Production. This schemata provides an overall coherence to project activities. Various activities associated with the concept phase are shown in Figure 13.6. The schema of Figures 13.5 and 13.6 will be encoded in the formal representation system of the encyclopedia.

In conjunction with the mailer, the encyclopedia needs to represent dialogues among team members. The notion of conversations (Flores, 1981) is forming the basis for our representational system. A conversation is a network showing sequences of promises, requests, assertions, refusals, and so forth.

---

[3] A similar notion, called hypertext, is defined by Nelson (1981) as nonsequential writing; in a hypertext system a document consists of a collection of nodes that are connected by direct links. Links can also be used to interconnect related portions of separate documents, to attach annotations or margin notes to a portion of a document, and to associate multiple versions of a document. Nelson's Xanadu Hypertext System is intended to be an electronic repository for storage and publication of text, graphics, and other digital information.

Hypertextlike systems include NLS/AUGMENT (Englebart and English 1968), ZOG (Robertson et al. 1979), PIE (Goldstein and Bobrow 1981), and the Brown University system (Feiner, Nagy, and van Dam 1982).

The present hyperdata system (Delisle and Schwartz 1984) allows the nodes of a graph and its directory to be stored on any machine in a distributed network of workstations. When nodes are created, the user can specify which machine will be used for storage. Existing nodes can also be moved to another host machine. Attribute/value pairs can be associated with each node and also with each link. Operations are provided to traverse the graph subject to a Boolean expression composed from attribute/value pairs.

FIGURE 13.5
PRODUCT INTRODUCTION SCHEMA

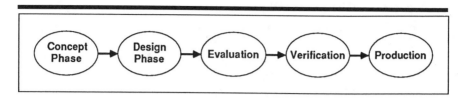

FIGURE 13.6
ASSOCIATIONS OF THE CONCEPT PHASE

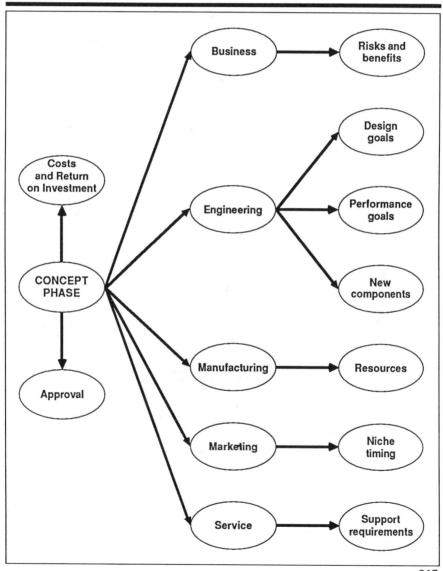

13.5.3   Accessing the Encyclopedia

The encyclopedia is not generally viewed directly. The structures shown in Figure 13.4 are not expected to be meaningful to the average user. It is expected that a user is performing a predefinable task, and hence an appropriate interface can be provided. This will guide him through the appropriate parts of the encyclopedia. A general interface is the project browser (Figure 13.2) that enables a topical hierarchical descent into the encyclopedia. The icons (small rectangles) at the top of the lower pane represent links to other nodes; selecting an icon gives access to the other node. This permits a user to move outside the hierarchical view imposed by the browser.

An example of another kind of interface to the encyclopedia is the calendar: a chronological access mechanism (see Figure 13.3).

13.5.4   Inference and the Encyclopedia

The graph structure of the encyclopedia allows the techniques of (1) spreading activation and (2) intersection (Quillian 1969) to be used. For example, in an experiment demonstrating the integrated use of the components of the system, a mailer passed to the encyclopedia information extracted from an incoming message about a forthcoming colloquium. To place the announcement, the encyclopedia needed to know the program with which it should be associated. The encyclopedia did this by noting the person who was assigned to host the visitor and seeking a path to the host's program.

The ability of the encyclopedia to represent and relate concepts at various levels of granularity will be used to control automatic reasoning. For text analysis, the plan is first to use keywords and abstract concepts to locate a context for a problem. Once the problem has been delimited, contextual constraints can be utilized as the concepts are expanded to the level of detail needed to carry out problem-solving inferencing (see Section 13.8.2).

13.6   THE INTELLIGENT ELECTRONIC CALENDAR (IEC)

13.6.1   The Importance of Time Management

Research has suggested that time management is ripe for automation (*Dun's Review* 1980; and Kincaid, Dupont, and Kaye 1985). Orciuch and Frost (1984) have developed an intelligent scheduling assistant for the manufacturing process. Kelley and Chapanis (1982) studied the manner in which professionals maintain their calendars and suggested that computerization would alleviate many of the current problems with the conventional paper-and-pencil system. Paper is not a permanent media; it is often lost or ruined. Paper calendars are difficult to maintain; changing information is often messy or impossible. They are difficult to share. They are inflexible in terms of time spans, hence several calendars are often required to completely meet the needs of a professional.

Additionally, we feel that the usual methods for scheduling a several-person meeting are unsatisfactory. In most cases these methods do not select the optimum time for the meeting. A meeting may be scheduled by making only one pass through the attendees, but, except for trivial cases, several passes would find a better solution. Or, when every attendee could not be contacted, a meeting may be scheduled at a default time.

We are resolving many of these problems with a computerized calendar system that keeps a permanent record of a person's schedule. Changing the information on an electronic calendar should be simple. A single calendar can cover different time spans: a day, a week, a month, or a year or more. An electronic calendar can share its information among a group of users, while respecting individual privacy. Moreover, an intelligent electronic calendar can automate much of the mundane scheduling needs for a person. It can automatically keep track of and schedule repetitive meetings. To schedule a meeting, a group of intelligent calendars can communicate to determine the most appropriate time for the meeting.

Several groups have studied natural language interfaces to a calendar system (e.g., Heidorn 1978; Kelley 1983). We do not preclude a natural language interface but feel that a graphical one is more appropriate. Thus, another goal is to develop an interface that has the graphical familiarity of a paper calendar (see Figure 13.7).

We feel that if these goals can be achieved, intelligent electronic calendars will become ubiquitous. Not just people, but all time-restricted resources, meeting rooms, audio-visual equipment, and so forth can be managed with an IEC.

13.6.2 Accessing the Encyclopedia via the Calendar

The repository of information for the ISE system is the project encyclopedia. The IEC stores its knowledge of schedules, meetings, dependencies, and rules for behavior there. The encyclopedia can be viewed through the Project Browser, which presents the contents in a topical fashion. The IEC can provide a temporal view onto the information contained within the encyclopedia.

This interface is useful for an information seeker who remembers approximately when the information was entered. For example, he or she might be interested in the minutes of a meeting that occurred toward the end of last month. He or she can scroll back to that time interval and inspect the meetings there. This interface is also an archiving device, allowing one to use the information for planning.

FIGURE 13.7
THE CALENDAR INTERFACE

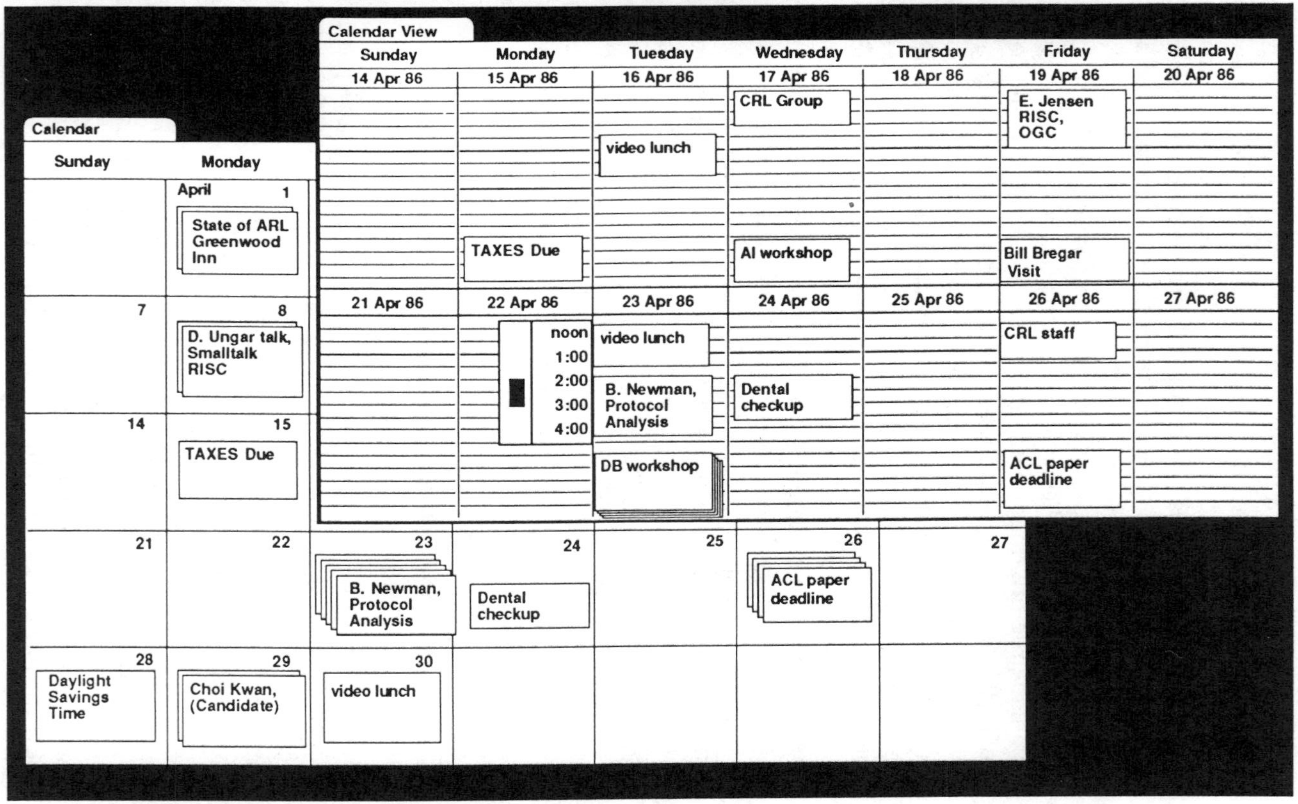

13.6.3 Facilities of IEC

This section describes the facilities that are planned for IEC.

Comparison with a Paper Calendar   Most people use a paper calendar to help organize and manage their schedules. By annotating a paper calendar, they can schedule meetings, note events, and scribble reminders to themselves. Paper calendars cover many time spans (e.g., a month, a week, a day, etc.). The tradeoff one makes in choosing one scale over another is the amount of detail available versus one's ability to overview. For example, a daily calendar is appropriate for planning the events of a day but is poor for quickly indicating how busy the next month will be. One solution is to maintain several calendars, each at a different scale. Then, one has the problem of having to enter some meetings on some calendars but not others. And worse is the problem of maintaining consistency among the calendars.

IEC is similar to a paper calendar; meetings can be scheduled, events can be noted, and reminders can be entered (see Figure 13.7). Additionally, any time-dependent item can be entered onto the calendar. For example, a user wants to send electronic mail one week from today. The user could enter the piece of mail for the day it is to be sent. The calendar automatically sends the mail at the correct time.

Unlike a paper calendar, an intelligent electronic calendar can be viewed on different scales. On each scale IEC will only display those events that are appropriate. Thus, when IEC is viewed at the day scale, all of the items for that day are shown in full. However, changing the scale changes the items that are seen. For example, when a month is viewed, monthly meetings, milestone meetings, and vacations would be displayed, but no reminders or daily meetings would be shown. Thus with one calendar many time spans can be covered, whether they be from one or two days to a year or more. In Figure 13.8a, April 23 through 26 have been selected in the monthly calendar for zooming, which produces the corresponding day views (Figure 13.8b).

Accessing Other Calendars   A person working at a remote site is often frustrated because he or she cannot access information that would be close at hand were he or she at the office. This tends to be community information, since this is less likely to be moved to a remote site. It could be the manager's schedule, the availability of a conference room, or the availability of shared equipment. For example, suppose a group member is at home in the evening adding some last minute touches to a presentation for the following day and decides to include some 35 mm transparencies to the talk, necessitating a room change. It is unlikely that the member could determine whether another is available. With remote ac-

FIGURE 13.8
ZOOMING IN THE CALENDAR

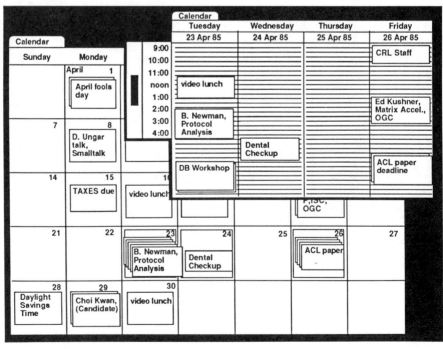

a

b

cess to an on-line IEC, the problem is solved. With the room's calendar on-line, he can determine that the room is available and then schedule it.

All intelligent calendars are available for perusal from anywhere within the system. However, access to a calendar should not be unconstrained. Even though anyone can communicate with any calendar, a calendar can restrict what may be seen. A room's calendar might be fairly cavalier with its permissions. A personal calendar should restrict who can view it and modify it. For example, a personal calendar might allow a third party to view only meetings that are common to the viewer and the owner of the calendar. Or it might allow the viewer to see all meetings in full with the exception of personal meetings that, although displayed, are not annotated. In spite of the restrictions, a viewer would still be able to get a feel for the person's schedule. It is important to realize that each intelligent calendar can be personalized. Whatever security restrictions the owner wishes must be codified. This is an important feature. Kelley and Chapanis (1982) found that personal concerns about privacy varied greatly; some were closely guarded, while others were quite free.

Repetitive Scheduling   Many meetings have a repetitive schedule. They can occur daily, every other week, or every second Monday. It would be unreasonable to expect the user to have to enter them individually. Hence the IEC allows the meetings to be specified once (called a *generator*), with a description of when it will occur. The IEC will then create repeated instances of the meeting. Each instance inherits the properties of its generator but can have its own annotation.

Consider the case in which there is a weekly group meeting to discuss the progress of a project. A single generator can describe the general properties of these weekly meetings. These would include descriptions of where it would be held, the group members who would typically attend, and that the subject is to discuss project progress. Once this generator is entered in the calendar, multiple instances would be created [4], each occurring a week apart. Every instance, a virtual copy (Section 13.7.2), inherits identical attributes from the generator. With time, some of these generated meetings might become individualized because of changes to them. For instance, a meeting's location might be changed or its purpose might be enlarged.

Meetings that can be automatically generated fall into two groups. For most, the cycle is based on time, as in the above example. A second group is irregular, triggered by particular events in the world. For example, a follow-up group meeting might need to occur one week following an occasional departmental meeting. When the IEC detects the appropriate departmental meeting, it will automatically schedule an instance

---

[4] These instances are not created ad infinitum, instead they are created as needed.

of the follow-up meeting for the following week. (See Section 13.7.3 for a discussion of external triggers.)

Multiperson Scheduling   One of the most difficult problems of scheduling a meeting is determining a mutually agreeable time for all of the attendees. When more than four or five persons are involved, it can become so difficult that a default time is often selected, which is seldom satisfactory to all. Moreover, the problem often becomes intractable when some of the attendees are not available for consultation. We plan for the IEC to have the ability to automatically schedule a meeting among a group of fellow IEC users.

To schedule the meeting, a user initiates the automatic scheduling by creating a meeting node on the calendar. In addition to the usual description (title, purpose, attendees, agenda, location, etc.) of the meeting, the user would include a general description of when the meeting should be scheduled, such as "beginning of next month," or "end of next week." He or she would indicate this time interval by graphically selecting the region on his or her calendar (see Figure 13.3). With this information, the user's IEC begins the process of negotiating with the other attendee's IECs, with the goal of finding a mutually agreeable time. If no common free slot is found, compromises will have to be made. Someone will have to reschedule another meeting, or one of the personal constraints will have to be waived.

A user's calendar cannot negotiate in a vacuum. If it is to schedule events for a user satisfactorily, it must have explicit guidelines as to how the user would like his or her schedule to be arranged. It must have knowledge about when the user likes to come and leave work, how long and important lunch is, what meetings are important, how busy particular weeks and/or days are, how important a balanced day and week are, and much other information particular to the user. This knowledge is coded as rules in the system.

13.6.4   Integration with Other Parts of the Project Support System

The calendar is not an autonomous system. It shares its world with the project encyclopedia and the communication system. The entire ISE system strives toward a level of integration that encourages synergism. In fact, much of the apparent intelligence comes about because the modules can communicate freely. The mailer modifies its behavior when a user is on a lengthy vacation. Only by communicating with the calendar system can the mailer determine when a person is scheduled to leave and return so that appropriate actions, such as redirecting mail, should occur.

The Mailer and Bulletin Boards   Events are often announced over an electronic bulletin board or through an electronic mail system. With conventional systems the user is burdened with the tedious task of retyping the information into the calendar system. The ISE system, however, permits convenient migration of information throughout the various modules. Thus it is quite simple for the communication system to have a meeting node scheduled by the calendar. Conversely, the calendar can easily have mail sent.

For example, suppose the user receives some electronic mail announcing an important group meeting. Instead of retyping the announcement onto the calendar, the user would simply ask the mailer to automatically enter the meeting onto the calendar. It then becomes the system's responsibility, not the user's, to transform the announcement into a meeting node on the calendar. Likewise, when a meeting is scheduled on the calendar, the system might decide that it is appropriate to mail a reminder to each of the attendees several days before the meeting is to occur.

We feel that this integration has the desirable effect of encouraging a trend toward more information being stored. By allowing convenient migration, information tends to be retained in its full form. With a paper calendar, only the briefest summary is usually recorded, but the ISE system enables the entire body of an announcement to be archived in the calendar with little effort.

13.7   THE COMMUNICATION SYSTEM
13.7.1   Group Issues

Importance of Communication   We met with many managers and executives before embarking on our system; most of them claimed that communicating or attempting to communicate was a major drain on their time. An important goal of our project is to reduce the time spent communicating and to increase the proportion of attempts that succeed.

The problem becomes worse when members of a group do not work at the same location. ISE also has the goal of allowing members of a group to work in remote locations and not incur communication problems.

Communication serves to keep members of a group informed about a project's progress; often this kind of communication is haphazard, and group members may not get all the information they need. Further goals are to organize all this information to facilitate access to it and to ensure this relevant information is sent to the appropriate people.

Societal Implications   By creating new styles of communication, we are in a position to tamper with the social structure of a group; it is important that we either do not change this structure or change it in a positive way. There are three types of social issues that we consider as we design the communication system: the effects of creating new lines of communication, the implications of certain types of messages, and the impact of group members working at remote locations.

Most groups are hierarchically organized. Currently, most communication takes place between people just one level above or below a group member on this tree structure. Our communication system presents the possibility of arbitrary links between any two members. We believe this to be positive; nevertheless, we must consider the effect on leadership and group decision making.

A number of studies indicate that the use of electronic mail does influence the way a group makes decisions (Turoff and Hiltz 1980, 1984). In general, decision making becomes more democratic; group members feel their input is more important but do not feel that their ideas are being evaluated as strongly as when they use more conventional types of communication.

Conklin and Reder (1984) argue that the way in which a message is sent makes an important social statement in a group. In some work groups, electronic mail is not appropriate for sending messages to superiors; in other organizations, it is perfectly acceptable. Conklin and Reder discuss situations in which problems in interorganizational communication occur when neither understands the other's etiquette. They recommend a consistent companywide policy. This, however, forces people to accept rules of communication that may not be best for their group. We propose a communication system that is aware of differences and can accommodate them. The idea is to encode the rules of communication in a group. We will see in later sections how this can be accomplished.

The last societal issue we deal with is the implications of our communication system for working at home or some other remote site. Indeed, this issue is an important motivation for the entire project. It is a goal of our project to facilitate the working at remote sites.

13.7.2   ETC Electronic Mailer

Because of the importance of communication, we have developed a communication system that is more than an electronic mailer; it is a communication assistant. The system is called elapsed time communication (ETC); it makes decisions about mail messages based on the topic, purpose, and other attributes of the message along with information about a group and project. ETC differs from other electronic mailers in that it is active. Other mailers take a message and deliver it, plain and simple; ETC can examine a letter, supply recipients, or modify the contents.

The ETC mailer consists of five components: a core mailer, communication directory, local reasoning system, rule generation system, and a distributed reasoning system. Each of these is described below.

Core Mailer   The core mailer provides the functionality of a typical electronic mailer. This includes creating, modifying, and examining messages along with the ability to set up mailing lists and aliases.

An ETC mail message contains information about the subject and recipient and indicates the purpose of the message, instructions on how to handle the message, information on when to send the message, and a description of the media used to deliver the message. Figure 13.9 shows an ETC mail message.

The core mailer does include a feature that is not found in other mailers. ETC provides a copying mechanism called *virtual copying* (Fahlman 1979). It is possible to create a copy such that the copy is automatically modified when the original is modified. One case in which such a feature is useful is mailing a message to many people and making an annotation for just one recipient. The sender can make a virtual copy of the original and make the appropriate annotations. The original remains unchanged by the copy's annotations, but if the original is changed, the copy will change also.

Communication Directory   The communication directory (see Figure 13.1) holds the information needed by the mailer. This component of the system works in conjunction with the project encyclopedia to gather and represent the knowledge needed to make informed decisions about mail messages. The information held by the communication directory includes names, electronic addresses, pointers to documents, the organization of groups, mailing lists, dates and authors of documents, possible purposes of messages, channels over which messages can be sent, and so forth.

Local Reasoning System   The local reasoning system makes decisions about messages based on knowledge about a group, their project, and information gleaned from other messages. This subsystem can make such decisions as who should receive a message, which messages are important, how to handle important messages, and how to handle special situations (e.g., a group member going on vacation). The local reasoning system can also make decisions such as who might be interested in reading a message about a particular topic, which messages a user wants to filter out, and how to file a particular message.

A user instructs the mailer on how to make these decisions by entering rules. For example, suppose a user wishes to forward all important messages to a secretary. To accomplish this, the user adds the following

FIGURE 13.9
AN ETC MAIL MESSAGE.

```
┌─────────────────────────────────┐
│  sample message                 │
├─────────────────────────────────┤
│  PERSON: Brian Phillips         │
│  SUBJECT: today's visitor       │
│  CHANNEL: email                 │
│  DESCRIPTION: important         │
│  PURPOSE: announce talk         │
│  FOLDER:                        │
│  REQUEST:                       │
│  FORM: scratch pad              │
│                                 │
│  Joe Franklin will speak today  │
│  at 3 p.m. in room 44.          │
└─────────────────────────────────┘
```

rule to the mailer's list of rules: "If the letter is important then forward it to the secretary."

Consider a more complex example. Suppose a group member is suddenly called out of town. Normally, electronic mail would collect while the worker was away, and the worker would be deluged with all the messages when he or she returned. Some of these messages would no longer be relevant, some of them should have been forwarded to other people in the worker's absence, and some people who did not know that the group member was out of town should have been notified of his or her absence.

The user could deal with problems by entering rules that specify how this situation should be handled. The user can enter rules to forward messages about particular subjects to other group members. If the purpose of a message is to announce a talk, then a rule could specify that the message be destroyed. Rules can be entered that specify when the sender of a message should be informed that the recipient is out of town. A very important message can be forwarded to a secretary of co-worker. A standard profile could be created in advance for such events and made effective with very little effort.

The local reasoning system is made up of a truth maintenance system (Doyle 1978; and Charniak, Riesbeck, and McDermott 1980). A truth maintenance system keeps track not only of what is true but why it is true. Such a system can undo the effects of a rule if the events that caused it to fire change. A rule parser takes rules as they are entered into the mailer and converts them to a representation that can be used by the truth maintenance system. Figure 13.10 shows some sample rules.

Distributed Reasoning System   Remote reasoning is accomplished in two ways: remote systems can share facts, and programs can be sent to other mailers for execution. Sometimes a fact needed by the local reasoning system resides at a remote knowledge base. In such cases, ETC can automatically create a message that asks a remote mailer to return that fact. The remote mailer responds, and the local reasoning system resumes. All this is done without human intervention.

Additionally, ETC allows programs to be sent for execution by remote mailers. To facilitate this, we have developed a language called mail control language (MCL). This permits the use of the knowledge present in

FIGURE 13.10
SAMPLE RULES

```
┌──────────────────────────────────────────────────────────────────────┐
│                                                                        │
│   ┌─────────────────┐                                                  │
│   │  ETC Events      │                                                 │
│   └─────────────────┴──────────────────────────────────────────────┐  │
│    - - - - - - - - - -                                              │  │
│     O Rule: "secretary" "Judy is secretary"  →  "Judy Comford"      │  │
│     O Rule: "secretary" "Angela is secretary"  →  "Angela Masotti"  │  │
│     O Rule: "secretary" "Ruth Ann is secretary"  →  "Ruth Ann Rose" │  │
│     O Rule: "secretary" "Lisa is secretary"→  "Lisa Wilson"         │  │
│     O Rule: "secretary"  →  "Eric Gold"                             │  │
│     O Rule: "Judy Comford"  →  "important"                          │  │
│     O Rule: "Angela Masotti"  →  "important" Annotations: "Angela Masotti" │
│     I Rule: "money owed"  →  "remove letter"                        │  │
│     I Rule: "on vacation" "announce meeting" "important" → "remove letter" │
│     I Rule: "verify message read" "message: opened"  →              │  │
│     I Rule: "on vacation" "request information"  →  "send to sender" │  │
│           [letter: = "vacation note"]                               │  │
│                                                                     │  │
│                                                                     │  │
└──────────────────────────────────────────────────────────────────────┘
```

the remote mailer along with the reasoning abilities and functionality associated with the remote mailer. Users can send MCL programs to remote mailers, mailers can send programs to other mailers, and other ISE components can send programs to either the mailer of the user of that component or other mailers in the system. MCL allows users to update remote data bases, retrieve information, make requests, give instructions or undo the actions of other messages.

13.7.3 Future Directions

Negotiation A problem arises when users enter rules that conflict with the rules of other users. What should happen if one user specifies that a message should be seen only by one named person but that person has a rule that would forward the message to some other person? What should happen if one person indicates that a message is important and should be rushed through the system but the rules that reside in the system specify that the message really is not very important? Our system will rely on a negotiation system to resolve such conflicts.

Triggers An automated communication system must decide when a message needs to be sent. This includes allowing the user to specify times and conditions for a message to be sent and also allowing the negotiation system and the action of the rules to trigger the sending of a message. A user, then, might specify that a message be sent at a particular date or that a message be sent out at regular intervals. For example, the user might specify that a reminder of a weekly meeting be sent unless the meeting has been canceled. This is similar to the scheduling of calendar events; thus ETC will work with the calendar to implement triggers.

Stereotyped Communication Many types of communication occur repeatedly with only minor differences. Consider the example of hiring a new employee. This involves communication between a secretary or manager and personnel, security, administration, and so forth. At our company, hiring a new employee requires over two dozen forms. Our system will replace this with a single form that contains information about the employee – information about how to create the multitude of forms and information about how the forms are to be handled. This latter type of information includes who is to receive a form, in which order to complete the forms, what to do about missing or incorrect information, any approvals that are required, what responses are expected from sending out the forms, and what to do if the responses are not received.

Conversations A *conversation* is a collection of messages that loosely relate to a topic and occur between some specified group of persons. An electronic conversation, then, is similar to a face-to-face conversation. A conversation is a much more natural unit of communication than a single message (Comer and Peterson 1984; and Flores 1981). Grouping messages into conversations allows users to gather and examine all messages that are part of a given conversation. More importantly, rules can apply to entire conversations rather than single messages. This results in a more powerful reasoning system.

13.8 NATURAL LANGUAGE PROCESSING

Natural language processing technology is used in the system as an interface methodology and for text analysis.

13.8.1 Natural Language Input

The ideal natural language interface would let any user, without any prior training, interact with a computer. It is one solution to our need to accommodate casual users. It is not a universal or ubiquitous solution; it complements the interfaces described in Section 13.3. Part of our experimentation is to find appropriate niches for the range of interface styles available in the system.

No natural language system offers complete coverage of a language. INGLISH [5] (INterface enGLISH) specifically addresses the problem of acquainting the user with the limitations of the coverage (Phillips and Nicholl 1986).

One potential use for INGLISH is in the acquisition of rules for the calendar and mailer. It is already being used for a comparable task in expert system development, that is, to acquire rules for troubleshooting (Phillips et al. 1986).

13.8.2 Natural Language Text Analysis

Much of the project information is in the form of natural language text. Consequently, text understanding/classification facilities are needed to link the information into the encyclopedia. Mail processing can also depend on the content of the message. The sender can enter a subject but may choose to defer to automatic classification. A recipient can write rules to filter incoming mail based on the topic of the message, which may not have been overtly indicated by the sender.

---

[5] INGLISH allows a user to create sentences either by menu selection, by typing, or by a mixture of the two. This allows the self-paced transition from menu-driven to a typed mode of interaction. In-line help is available. To assist the typist, automatic spelling correction, word completion, and automatic phrase completion are provided. INGLISH constrains users to create statements within a subset of English.

The volume of data in and passing through the system precludes, for the most part, detailed structural analyses (Schank and Abelson 1977; and Phillips 1978). Walker and Hobbs (1981) hand code the essential content of paragraphs of medical articles for retrieval by natural language queries. The labor intensiveness of this approach is justified by the permanence of the material and its large user community. We are choosing a keyword detection system. This approach, called *content analysis* (Stone et al. 1966), uses a topical thesaurus and selects a topic based on the density of keywords associated with topics. Later work (Kelly and Stone 1975) included limited context to disambiguate words. A pilot study to detect topics occurring in newspapers (DeWeese 1976) showed the promise of the technique.

Keyword analysis is clearly a crude technique. It is easy to see that it can be thwarted by the use of paraphrases, synonyms, euphemisms, and more. It is insensitive to negation; the presence of "not X" may be taken as an occurrence of "X." Nevertheless, in technical domains in which the style is more direct and does not use literary devices, the technique has greater credibility.

An Experiment   As an experiment we are attempting to automate the acquisition and classification by keyword of technical reports in our laboratory. The technical literature is an important resource in technical environments. Its choice as a first experiment was influenced by the availability of various computer science indexes that can form the basis

---

A statement can be entered as a sequence of menu selections using only the mouse. A mouse click brings up a menu of words and phrases that are valid extensions of the current sentence fragment. Once a selection is made from the menu using the mouse, the fragment is extended. This sequence can be repeated until the sentence is completed. Creating a sentence in this manner compares with the NLMENU system (Tennant, Ross, and Thompson 1983). Unlike NLMENU, keyboard entry is also possible with INGLISH. Gilfoil (1982) found that users prefer a command form of entry to menu-driven dialog as their experience increases. When typing, a user who is unsure of the coverage can invoke a menu, either by a mouse click or by typing a second space character, to find out what INGLISH expects next without aborting the current statement. Similarly, any unacceptable word causes the menu to appear, giving immediate feedback of a deviation and suggestions for correct continuation. A choice from the menu can be typed or selected using the mouse. INGLISH in fact allows all actions to be performed from the keyboard or with the mouse and for them to be freely intermingled. As only valid words are accepted, all completed sentences are well formed and can be translated into the internal representation.

This interface design alleviates the problem of coverage for designers and users of natural language interfaces. A natural language interface user composes his or her entries bearing in mind a model of the interface's capabilities. If the model is not accurate, the user's interactions will be error-prone. The user may exceed the coverage of the system and have the entry rejected. On the other hand, the user may form an overly conservative model of the system. An interface designer is confronted by many linguistic phenomena (e.g., noun groups, relative clauses, ambiguity, reference, ellipsis, anaphora, and paraphrases). Because of performance requirements or a lack of a theoretical understanding, many of these constructions will not be in the interface. The INGLISH design allows designers to rest more comfortably with the compromises they have made, knowing that users can systematically discover the coverage of the interface.

for the classification. Many journal articles also list keywords to help form the keyword vocabulary.

Our scheme is to use an optical character recognition system to capture the title, authorship, and abstract. This approach is part of our effort to reduce the manual burden of information capture. We are using an Oberon International OmniReader.

The abstract is searched for keywords to place the article into the hierarchical index. As a keyword may cue several domains, the choices are rank ordered and shown to the user, who can overrule the system if he or she so chooses.

A browser interface that follows the classification scheme is provided. A user can choose a conjunction of topical categories. Keywords are associated with each category in the index. These keywords are used to locate a list of matching titles, which in turn form a menu selection from which is produced the abstract.

A large volume of abstractless entries already exists on a VAX 11/780. We are presently remotely accessing that file from Magnolia through the UNIX "hunt" command. Later versions will store the index and articles in hypertext.

The literature index browser allows the creation of new entries in the index and cross-references to be added. As users can impose their own classification on an article, it will be possible to create a dynamic, personal index to a library.

Structural Text Analysis   In parallel with the keyword approach, we are developing a system that takes a structural analytic tack (Phillips and Hendler 1982; and Phillips 1984) that may eventually play a role in ISE.

13.9   CONCLUSION

13.9.1   User Acceptance

A user is likely to judge the system on his or her willingness to trust the decisions it makes as well as on the functionality it offers.

User Trust   A system that performs as much reasoning as the system we have described often makes a decision that the user would not have predicted. The question arises whether the user will accept such a system even if the actions of the system are appropriate for the situation. How would the user feel if he or she did not know who was going to receive a given message or how soon an important meeting would be scheduled? How would the user feel if he or she counted on the system to capture and store important information and the system decided the information was not important enough? Will the user trust the system? Should the user trust the system?

We believe that user acceptance depends on five factors: (1) whether the user can disable the reasoning mechanisms, (2) whether the user can undo any decisions made, (3) whether the user can tailor the decision-making process to his or her own needs, (4) whether the user can see and understand any decisions the system has made, and (5) whether the system is clever enough to make good decisions. Fortunately, we are laboring to create a system that meets each of these criteria. Once this is accomplished we expect the user to put as much trust and acceptance into our system as he or she would in a secretary and more acceptance into our system than he or she would into such conventional communication channels as the U.S. post office.

A user can decide not to utilize the reasoning facilities of the system; in this case the system degrades to a conventional (although easy to use and integrate) mailer, calendar, and data base. As the user comes to understand the reasoning capabilities of the system, he or she can add them to the functioning of the system.

Whenever possible, we have designed the system to make decisions while the user is working with the system. The system, then, makes decisions such as creating messages and scheduling meetings while the user is present to examine or modify these decisions. However, all decisions cannot be made in this way; some kinds of reasoning take too much time to be carried out while the user is waiting, and other decisions cannot be made while the user is present because of incomplete information present in the system. Even in these cases, the user can examine and approve any decisions at a later time.

As for the cleverness of the system, only time will tell.

Acceptable Functionality   Individual modules may be perceived as offering only marginal improvement over existing, familiar standard system modules. There is then little incentive to change to the new technology. Only when the collective gains from a number of systems reaches a convincing threshold do we expect users to voluntarily adopt our system. We also can hope that one of our modules may be overwhelmingly superior so as to entice a change.

We have no idea where this threshold lies. However, we ourselves are a captive, interested audience for our own developments and are the initial guinea pigs. Later we will inflict the system on our colleagues.

We are also aware that not all users are of equal diligence in maintaining those parts of the system that require individual effort (e.g., keeping a calendar up to date). The system itself imposes no penalty on the uncooperative. We foresee that peer pressure will be the factor that will operate on those that are remiss. The inconvenience for the majority, of not being able to rely on the automatic scheduling, for instance, will cause them to bring pressure to bear on the others.

Given all of these situations, testing the acceptability of the system will be an incremental, empirical, and informal process.

13.9.2 Enhancements

Once the basic environment is established and accepted, revolutionary enhancements become possible. The kind of interaction envisaged in Knoesphere (Lenat et al. 1983) for general encyclopedic knowledge is a direction to consider. The animated display of data, using constraint languages, as in Thinglab (Borning 1979) would considerably enhance the interface. The Media Room style of conversational interaction with large displays would be a useful extension of the system to conference room environments (Bolt 1985).

REFERENCES

Alexander, J.H., and Freiling, M.J. (1985), "Building an Expert System in Smalltalk-80®." *Systems & Software, 4* (April), 111–118.

ALL-IN-1: Office and Information Systems, (1984), Digital Equipment Corporation.

Becker, J.D. (1975), "The Phrasal Lexicon," *Conference on Theoretical Issues in Natural Language Processing,* Cambridge, Mass.

Bolt, R.A. (1985), "Conversing with Computers," *Technology Review,* 88 (February/March) 35–43.

Bonczek, R.H., Holsapple, C.W., and Whinston, A.B. (1981), *Foundations of Decision Support Systems.* Orlando, Fla.: Academic Press.

Borning, A. (1979), "Thinglab—A Constraint Oriented Simulation Laboratory," technical report (SSL-79-3), Palo Alto, Calif.: Xerox Palo Alto Research Center.

Burton, R.R. (1976), "Semantic Grammar: An Engineering Technique for Constructing Natural Language Understanding Systems," technical report (3453), Cambridge, Mass.: Bolt, Beranek, and Newman.

Charniak, E., Riesbeck, C., and McDermott, D. (1980), *Artificial Intelligence Programming,* Hillsdale, N.J.: Lawrence Erlbaum Associates.

Comer, D.E., and Peterson, L.L. (1984), "Conversation Based Mail," technical report (CSD-TR-465), West Lafayette, Ind.: Computer Science Department, Purdue University.

Conklin, N., and Reder, S. (1984), "The Economy of Communicative Work: A Channel Analysis of Electronic Mail Usage," *IEEE Conference on Office Automation,* New Orleans, La.

Delisle, N., and Schwartz, M. (1984), "Functional Requirements for a Hypertext System for Design Information Management," technical report (CR-84-15), Beaverton, Ore.: Tektronix, Inc.

DeWeese, L.C. (1976), "Computer Content Analysis of 'Day-Old' Newspapers: A Feasibility Study," research publication (GMR-2176), Warren, Mich.: General Motors Research Laboratories.

Doyle, J. (1978), "Truth Maintenance Systems for Problem Solving," technical report (419), Cambridge, Mass.: MIT AI Laboratory.

Englebart, D., and English, W. (1968), "A Research Center for Augmentating Human Intelligence," in *Proceedings of the Fall Joint Computer Conference,* vol. 33, Arlington, Va.: AFIPS Press.

Fahlman, S.E. (1979), *NETL: A System for Representing and Using Real World Knowledge,* Cambridge, Mass.: MIT Press.

Feiner, S., Nagy, S., and van Dam, A. (1982), "An Experimental System for Creating and Preserving Interactive Graphical Documents," *ACM Transactions on Graphics, 1* (January), 59–77.

Flores, C.F. (1981) "Management and Communication in the Office of the Future," Ph.D. Thesis. University of California, Berkeley.

Gilfoil, D.M. (1982), "Warming Up to Computers: A Study of Cognitive and Effective Interaction Over Time," *Proceedings of the Human Factors in Computer Systems Conference*, Gaithersburg, Md., 245–250.

Goldberg, A. (1984), *Smalltalk-80: The Interactive Programming Environment*, Reading, Mass.: Addison-Wesley.

Goldstein, I., and Bobrow, D. (1981), "An Experimental Description-based Programming Environment: Four Reports," technical report (CSL-81-3). Palo Alto, Calif.: Xerox Palo Alto Research Center.

Griffiths, T.V., and Petrick, S.R. (1965), "On the Relative Efficiencies of Context-free Grammar Recognizers," *Comm. ACM, 5* (May), 289–300.

Heidorn, G.E. (1978), "Natural Language Dialogue for Managing an On-line Calendar," *Proceedings of the Association for Computing Machinery*, Washington, D.C., 45–52.

Kaplan, R.M., and Bresnan, J.W. (1982), "Lexical-Functional Grammar: A Formal System for Grammatical Representation," in J.W. Bresnan, ed., *The Mental Representation of Grammatical Relations*. Cambridge, Mass.: MIT Press.

Kelley, J.F. (1983), "Natural Language and Computers: Six Empirical Steps for Writing an Easy-to-use Computer Application," Ph.D. thesis, Johns Hopkins University.

Kelley, J.F., and Chapanis, A. (1982), "How Professional Persons Keep their Calendars: Implications for Computerization," *Journal of Occupational Psychology, 55* (December), 241–256.

Kelly, E.F., and Stone, P.J. (1975), *Computer Recognition of English Word Senses*, Amsterdam: North-Holland.

Kincaid, C.M., Dupont, P.B., and Kaye, A.R. (1985), "Electronic Calendars in the Office: An Assessment of User Needs and Current Technology," *ACM Transactions on Office Information Systems, 1* (January), 89–102.

Lenat, D.B., Borning, A., McDonald, D., Taylor, C., and Weyer, S. (1983), "KNOESPHERE: Building Expert Systems with Encyclopedic Knowledge," *International Joint Conference on Artificial Intelligence*, Karlsruhe.

Nelson, T.H. (1981), *Literary Machines*, Swarthmore, Penn.: T.H. Nelson.

Newell, A. (1973), "Production Systems: Models of Control Structures," in W.C. Chase, ed., *Visual Information Processing*, New York: Academic Press.

Orciuch, E., and Frost, J. (1984), "ISA: Intelligent Scheduling Assistant," *IEEE First Conference on Artificial Intelligence Applications*, Denver, Colo.

Phillips, B. (1978), "A Model for Knowledge and its Applications to Discourse Analysis," *American Journal of Computational Linguistics*, microfiche 82.

Phillips, B. (1984), "An Object-Oriented Parser," in B.G. Bara and G. Guida, eds., *Computational Models of Natural Language Processing*, Amsterdam: North-Holland.

Phillips, B., and Hendler, J.A. (1982), "A Message-Passing Control Structure for Text Understanding," *Proceedings of the International Conference on Computational Linguistics*, The Hague: Mouton.

Phillips, B., Messick, S.L., Freiling, M.J., and Alexander, J. (1985), "INKA: The INGLISH Knowledge Acquisition Interface for Electronic Instrument Troubleshooting Systems," technical report (CR-85-04), Beaverton, Ore.: Tektronix, Inc.

Phillips, B., and Nicholl, S. (1986), "INGLISH: A Natural Language Interface," in K. Hopper and I.A. Newman, eds., *Foundation for Human Computer Communication*, Amsterdam: North-Holland.

Quillian, M.R. (1969), "The Teachable Language Comprehender: A Simulation Program and Theory of Language," *Comm. ACM, 8* (August), 459–476.

Reimann, B.C., and Waren, A.D. (1985), "User-oriented Criteria for the Selection of DSS Software," *Comm. ACM, 2* (February), 166–179.

Rivest, S., Shamir, A., and Adelman, L. (1978), "A Method for Obtaining Digital Signatures and Public Key Cryptosystems," *Comm. ACM, 2* (February), 120–126.

Robertson, G., McCracken, D., and Newell, A. (1979), "The ZOG Approach to Man-Machine Communication," technical report (CMU-CS-79-148), Pittsburgh, Penn.: Carnegie-Mellon University.

Schank, R.C., and Abelson, R.P. (1977), *Scripts, Plans, Goals, and Understanding*, Hillsdale, N.J.: Erlabaum.

Simmons, R.F. (1973), "Semantic Networks: Their Computation and Use for Understanding English Sentences," in R.C. Schank and K.M. Colby, eds., *Computer Models of Thought and Language*, San Francisco, Calif.: Freeman.

Stone, P.J., Dunphy, D.C., Smith, M.S., and Ogilvie, D.M. (1966), *The General Inquirer: A Computer Approach to Content Analysis*, Cambridge, Mass.: MIT Press.

Tennant, H.R., Ross, K.M., and Thompson, C.W. (1983), "Usable Natural Language Interfaces through Menu-based Natural Language Understanding," *Proceedings of the Human Factors in Computer Systems Conference*, Boston, Mass.

"The Automated Office in the 1980s," *Dun's Review*, 3 March 1980.

Turoff, M., and Hiltz, S.R. (1980), "Structuring Communications for the Office of the Future," *Office Automation Conference Digest*, Atlanta, Ga.

Turoff, M., and Hiltz, S.R. (1984), "Telecomputing Impacts on the Office," *IEEE Conference on Office Automation*, New Orleans, La.

Walker, D.E., and Hobbs, J.R. (1981), "Natural Language Access to Medical Text," *Proceedings of the Fifth Annual Symposium on Computer Applications in Medical Care*, New York.

Weinreb, D., and Moon, D. (1981), *LISP Machine Manual*, Chatsworth, Calif.: Symbolics Inc.

14

Computer-Based Intelligence Support: An Integrated Expert Systems and Decision Support Systems Approach

Andrew P. Sage
Adolfo Lagomasino

This chapter summarizes research and design needs for intelligence-based support, especially in areas of command and control. It argues strongly for an approach that integrates (especially in the areas of inference analysis) contemporary approaches in artificial intelligence for expert system construction and management science or systems engineering approaches for the design of decision support systems. A discussion of knowledge representation and information processing highlights the need for this. An approach that accommodates both probabilistic and logical support and that is able to cope with several types of imperfect information is described.

The research described here was supported by the U.S. Army Research Institute under Contract MDA 903-82-C-0124.

14.1   INTRODUCTION

Intelligent systems for decision support are computer-implemented procedures that seek to combine expert knowledge about a domain with expert methods of conceptualizing and reasoning about that domain. They integrate this with "formal" methods of reasoning about the domain. The inferential power of such computer programs rests upon a knowledge base that puts together factual information about the domain with the heuristics or informal "rules of thumb" experts use to rapidly find solutions to problems and with the formal reasoning methods that are needed when approaching an unstructured problem about which experiential familiarity is slight.

The goal of an intelligent system for decision support is to encode in a computer program the facts an expert has and the methods of reasoning about them, together with formal methods of reasoning about unstructured situations. In that sense, an intelligent system may be viewed as a descriptive model of an expert reasoning process about a problem domain and a normative system to aid in formal reasoning when this expertise does not exist. Although intelligence support systems have the potential of encoding cognitive biases or prejudice, they may be very attractive to planners and decision makers because they could be set up as on-line decision support systems in situations in which time limitations are an important factor. There are methods, currently under investigation, that enable detection of inconsistent reasoning, and it is hoped that such efforts may be extended to enable detection of at least some of the identified cognitive biases associated with human information processing.

14.2   KNOWLEDGE REPRESENTATION AND PROCESSING IN DECISION SUPPORT SYSTEMS DESIGN

Approaches that will enable effective knowledge representation, and associated inference activities, in large knowledge bases have been the subject of investigation for many researchers. An appropriate representation can be used to describe the four different types of factual knowledge elements that may be captured in a knowledge base: objects, events, performance, and meta-knowledge. It will assist in identification of the values that need to be associated with facts in order to enable judgment and choice. The purpose of a particular knowledge representation is to enable the use of knowledge for: retrieving factual information from the knowledge base that is judged relevant to the task at hand, reasoning about these facts in the search for a resolution of the task requirements, and acquiring more knowledge. Several approaches for the representation of knowledge as they apply to the control and generation of dialogue for human-system interaction are discussed in Sage and Lagomasino (1984).

14.2.1 Knowledge Base Management System (KBMS)

A knowledge-based management system is one of the three fundamental components of an intelligent system for decision support. In almost every instance in which there will exist multiple decision makers, there will exist the need for individual knowledge bases and organizational knowledge bases. Some of the desirable characteristics of a DBMS include the ability to cope with a variety of data structures that allow for probabilistic, incomplete, imprecise, and other forms of imperfect data and the ability to cope with data that are unofficial and personal, as contrasted with official and organizational.

In order to construct a knowledge base, it is first necessary to identify a knowledge representation scheme. A representation scheme is a collection of data structures, operations that may be applied on the data structures, and integrity rules that are used to constrain or otherwise define permissible values of the data. There are at least five models that may be used to represent data. The most elementary of these is the *individual record* model. The *relational model* is a powerful generalization of the record model. A relation is the fundamental data structure in the relational model, and there may be a number of fields in any given relation. The relational model enables mathematical set operations in terms of addition of new records, updating fields within existing records, creating relations that may be contained in records, deleting relations that may be contained in records, joining or combining two or more relations based on their containing common fields, selecting records by virtue of their containing certain specified relations, and projection (e.g., to enable selection of a subset of the fields that exist in a relation).

The hierarchical or tree data model is a relatively efficient representation of data. In a *hierarchical model*, the structure represents the information that is contained in the fields of a relational model. In a hierarchical model, there will be certain records that must exist before other records can exist, since every data structure must have a root record. Because of this structured aspect of the model, it will be necessary to repeat some of the data that need be stored only once for a relational model. The *network model* is a generalization of the hierarchical model in that there are links between records, which enables a given record to participate in several relationships. There are often major problems associated with insertions, deletions, and updating in both the hierarchical and network data models due to the need to maintain a consistent data base. These do not exist in the relational model since the same data are never entered more than once. Also there is additional search complexity since a search can start anywhere in the network structure. However, searches are generally more efficient than they are in the relational model.

Due to the need to accommodate intelligent capabilities in a decision support system, it is desirable to consider a *production rule model* as a fifth data model. This will enable inferences to be made. Thus this is a particularly desirable form of data model when we desire to use many predictive management information system capabilities. The IF-THEN response to "what if" queries is especially natural in this representation. As will be shown, this representation allows for efficient meta-level control, through decision-support-type approaches, of the production rules in an expert system knowledge base. Knowledge representation formats also include frame, script, and schema representations. These representations are much like the cognitive maps that humans construct of the world around them. At this point, there does not seem to exist operational data models based on these representations, and surely this is an area of contemporary research need. Additional discussion of data base management system (DBMS) design approaches can be found in Sprague and Carlson (1982) and Date (1981, 1983). The three-volume *Handbook of Artificial Intelligence* edited by Barr, Cohen, and Feigenbaum (1981, 1982) discusses knowledge representation from an AI perspective.

14.2.2 Model Base Management System (MBMS)

It is necessary to provide inference capability in an intelligent system. This requires some sort of model base management system (MBMS). It is through the use of model base management systems that we are able to provide for sophisticated analysis and interpretation capability in a decision support system. The single most important characteristic of a model base management system is that it should enable the decision maker to explore the decision situation through use of the knowledge base by a model base or algorithmic procedures and management protocols. This can occur through the use of modeling statements, in some procedural or nonprocedural language; through the use of the model subroutines, such as mathematical programming packages, that are called by a management function; and through the use of data abstraction models. This approach facilitates updating and use of the model for explanatory and explication purposes.

The use of multiple models can potentially accommodate the desire of the typical decision maker for flexibility. Thus a mixed scanning approach might be incorporated in which a conjunctive or disjunctive scanning mechanism is used to allow for an individual scan to eliminate grossly unacceptable alternatives. After this is achieved, further evaluation of alternatives might be accomplished by a compensatory tradeoff evaluation or one based on a dominance search procedure (Sage and White 1984).

To provide flexibility, the MBMS should provide, upon system user request, a variety of prestructured models that have been found useful in the past, such as linear programming and multiattribute decision analysis model, and procedures to use these models. It should also allow for the development of user-built models and heuristics that are developed from established models, which will either become permanent parts of the MBMS or will be considered as ad hoc models. It should also be possible to perform sensitivity tests of model outputs and to run models with a range of data to obtain the response to a variety of "what if" questions.

14.2.3   Dialogue Generation and Management System (DGMS)

The dialogue generation and management system portion of a decision support system is designed to satisfy knowledge representation and to satisfy control and interface requirements of the intelligent system for decision support. It is the DGMS that is responsible for presentation of the outputs of the system to the decision maker and for determining, acquiring, and transmitting their inputs to the KBMS and the MBMS based on its knowledge about the decision maker's goals regarding the specific decision situation. Thus the DGMS is responsible for producing output representations, for obtaining the decision maker's inputs that result in the operations on the representations, for interfacing to the memory aids, and for explicit provision of the control mechanism that enables effective dialogue between the user and the KBMS and MBMS.

There are a number of possible dialogues. These are inherently linked to the representational forms that are used for the DBMS and MBMS. Menus, spreadsheets, tradeoff graphs, and production rules are some of the formats that may be used as a basis for dialogue system design. Generally, several of these should be used, since the support system user may wish to shift among these formats as the nature of issues and experiential familiarity with the issues changes. The DGMS should be sufficiently flexible so as to allow review and sensitivity analysis of past judgments and to provide partial judgments based upon incomplete information. Of course, the DGMS should be "user friendly" through provision of various HELP facilities, prompting the decision maker, and other abilities that support the knowledge of the support system user.

14.3   MANAGEMENT OF INTELLIGENT SYSTEMS

Limits associated with the cognitive capacity of the human mind, time limitations, and many other competing concerns of the decision maker are constraints that affect adequate formulation, analysis, and interpretation of complex large-scale issues. A design goal for intelligent systems and processes that will assist in various problem-solving tasks is to reduce, to the extent possible, the effects of the aforementioned constraints so as to enable the efficient and effective use of information that will lead to quality judgments in routine and familiar task environments and in unfamiliar task conditions.

An appropriate framework in which knowledge could be organized and utilized efficiently and effectively is desired. This is especially needed as studies have shown that the way in which a task is framed exerts a very strong influence upon the way in which task requirements and task resolution efforts are determined (Kahneman, Slovic, and Tversky 1982; and Sage 1981). This requires that we be able to address the modeling of intelligent systems for decision support from several perspectives. Our interest here is to describe implications that arise in the design of intelligent systems for decision support that incorporates systems management activities. Of particular interest will be those components at the interface between the cognitive process level of systems management and the problem level and those at the knowledge meta-level, which will enable effective modeling of the intelligent system itself.

14.3.1   The Problem Level

At the problem level in the systems management process, there are a number of abilities that an intelligent system for decision support should have. It should assist the decision maker in the *formulation* or framing of the decision situation in the sense of recognizing needs, identifying appropriate objectives by which to measure the successful resolution of an issue, and generating alternative courses of action that will resolve the needs and satisfy objectives. It should also provide support in enhancing the abilities of the decision maker to obtain the possible impacts on needs of the alternative courses of action and to understand systems behavior. This *analysis* capability must be associated with providing the ability to study the response or changes in the existing situation due to potential intervention, so as to enhance the ability of the decision maker to provide an *interpretation* of these impacts in terms of predefined and evolving objective measures. This interpretation capability will lead to evaluation of the alternatives and selection of a preferred option. Associated with these must be the ability to acquire, represent, and utilize information or knowledge and the ability to implement the chosen alternative courses of action. All of this must be accomplished with due consideration given to the particular rationality perspective that is used for decision making.

14.3.2   Cognitive Process Level

Several intelligent systems design complexities arise at the cognitive process level of systems management. These relate to the forms, frames, or perspectives associated with acquiring, integrating, and applying vast amounts of knowledge. These forms range from the systemic framework of formulation, analysis, and interpretation at the problem level, which is characteristic of formal operational or holistic thought, to intuitive affect, which is characteristic of concrete operational and holistic thought. The reasoning perspectives invoked at the cognitive process level of problem resolution depend upon the task requirements, the experiential familiarity of the decision maker with the task, and the rationality perspectives that are used for task resolution (Sage 1981, 1982; and Linstone 1984).

14.4   KNOWLEDGE AGGREGATION NEEDS IN INTELLIGENT SYSTEMS FOR DECISION SUPPORT

Various assumptions about the nature and characteristics of the contingency structural elements of task and environment and the human problem solver's familiarity with these are considered essential in the design of intelligent systems in order to enable effective and efficient organization of knowledge about specific situation domains. Due to these assumptions, not all specific domains of knowledge are suitable for building intelligent systems for decision support. Gevarter (1984) identifies four characteristics that a domain of knowledge must satisfy at the knowledge level in order to allow an intelligent system to be built that is based *only* on expert knowledge:

1. There must be at least one human expert who is acknowledged to perform the task well.

2. The primary sources of the expert's abilities must be special knowledge, judgment, and experience.

3. The expert must be able to articulate that special knowledge, judgment, and experience and also explain the methods used to apply it to a particular task.

4. The task must have a well-bounded domain of application.

There will exist many situations in which these requisite conditions are not satisfied. A decision support system is a generic dual of an expert system and is intended for use in situations in which at least one of the aforementioned four conditions do not apply. It appears that this will often occur. For this reason, there is motivation to seek support system design incorporating features of *both* the expert system, whose design assumes availability of relevant expertise, *and* the decision support system, the design of which assumes that this expert knowledge, and its availability in a well-structured format, cannot be assumed.

The representation of knowledge suggests the existence of some form of prior knowledge that enables the system to perform the function of acquisition and aggregation of the new knowledge in with the existing knowledge so as to enable decision support. This must be such as to enable expansion, contraction, replacement, and residual shifts with respect to knowledge in the knowledge base. Also, notions of knowledge "quality." need to be associated with various knowledge representations and updated as new knowledge is received.

Information-seeking efforts are necessarily concerned with the process by which information that is relevant to a situation is obtained from the environment. A knowledge representation system must be able to provide a description and an explanation of the situation, for example, to enable generation of a set of *beliefs* or *knowledge*, organized into a "representation," about the situation. It should be noted that what may be a belief to one person may be knowledge to another (Abelson 1979), and this relates to perceived information quality.

There must be also a generalization component or inference mechanism that is equipped with some form of basic logic to enable access to the knowledge base for formation of inferences and judgments. A fundamental question arises from this discussion concerning how a priori knowledge and the generalization component influence the operation of the complete intelligent system for decision support.

There are two perspectives that are relevant here concerning how individuals go about the retrieval of information, the use of information for reasoning, and the feedback process that enables acquisition of new knowledge. One perspective is that learning is performed by an elementary-to-complex process in which simple things are learned first followed by more advanced concepts. The other perspective is based on the belief that learning starts with complex statements about the description of a situation. Through decomposition into simpler statements, a system is able to increase its understanding concerning the specific situation domain.

As a means of illustrating the two perspectives of the knowledge acquisition process, it is useful to compare problem-solving activities and natural language understanding in some detail.

Most artificial intelligence systems that are in use today are based on the first perspective with respect to acquisition and aggregation of new knowledge. They use the elementary-to-complex perspective and do not typically verify, validate, or otherwise seek to determine the consistency of the resulting knowledge base. The resulting lack of control with respect to questions of validity of the resulting knowledge base is characteristic of an incomplete intelligent system. If this perspective is used exclusively, then some essential components of an intelligent system have been omitted or the interaction between the support system and the user has been modeled inadequately.

Systems that operate at the other extreme of the knowledge acquisition spectrum, such that learning proceeds in a complex-to-elementary fashion, have been difficult to implement. In reality, both modes of learning are appropriate, and both are used by the human problem solver. Integration of the two approaches is clearly desirable, and this is a major concern of this chapter.

14.5 INFERENTIAL SUPPORT FOR KNOWLEDGE AGGREGATION

Inferential activities based on imprecise, incomplete, inconsistent, or otherwise imperfect knowledge is becoming more important in the design, implementation, and operation of expert systems. *Inference* is concerned with the generation of theories and hypotheses beyond those originally given. In planning and decision-making activities, the information that is usually available initially is limited so as to allow satisfactory performance of judgment and choice. Hence, inference is an essential activity for systems intended to aid in the learning process.

Several approaches for making inferences from available information have been developed. These range from strict probabilistic Bayesian reasoning to less mathematically rigorous approaches. Analysis of systems based on these methods reveals discrepancies on the results obtained due largely to the differences in the underlying assumptions in which they are based. Quinlan (1983) contrasts several of these approaches and classifies their dissimilarities in terms of:

1. The way in which the uncertain information about propositions is represented
2. The assumptions that form the basis for propagating information
3. The control structure used for this propagation
4. The treatment of inconsistent information

Sage and Botta (1983) also present a summary of contemporary research involving inference mechanisms in expert systems, concentrating on the extent to which these mechanisms can be Bayesian.

Most of the existing research concerning inference uses probability theory as the standard for the representation, aggregation, and interpretation of information. However, while such theories have the advantage of modeling the uncertainties present in human discourse, there are at least two potential difficulties. Occasionally, the semantic correspondence of probabilistic expressions to natural language expressions is questionable. Also, there are forms of information imperfections other than "uncertainties," and the probabilistic representation of these other forms, while often possible, is sometimes cumbersome at best.

A large number of studies in cognitive psychology indicate that human judgments of probability values are often inconsistent with the simple axioms of probability. A comprehensive review of these efforts can be found in Sage (1981). Often, these errors are of considerable magnitude — not just small deviations usually expected from intuitive, subjective assessments. Failure to follow the rules of probability are generally attributed to errors of application and errors of comprehension of such rules. An *error of application* exists if there is evidence that people know and accept a rule that they did not apply. If people do not recognize the validity of the rule they violated, it is called an *error of comprehension*. Since both types of errors are described in terms of violations to the rules of probability, we could as well claim that the errors are the result of a misrepresentation of human judgments about uncertainty. An *error of representation* refers to the semantic correspondence between the natural language expression and the symbolic representation and rules of aggregation used for inference. Errors of representation may result in a set of inconsistent hypotheses. So, an inferential inconsistency may indicate an error in representation, but the contrary is not true (i.e., agreement does not necessarily reflect understanding of semantic principles). Consequently, questions arise concerning how to detect and avoid errors of representation and which framework to use in modeling uncertainty, imprecision, and other forms of information imperfection as well.

Inferential activities based on logical interconnection of elements in a hierarchical net or tree are called *hierarchical inference*. Hierarchical inference usually entails a series of inversion, aggregation, and cascading processes to compute the likelihood of an underlying hypothesis and observable evidences based on their logical relations. *Inversion* involves reversing the logical relation among elements in the network in order to calculate more easily the desired relation. In a Bayesian model, the process of inversion is represented by Bayes theorem. When a datum D is perceived to have an impact on the occurrence of an event H, the relation between D and H is given by:

$$P(H|D) = \frac{P(H)}{P(D)} P(D|H)$$

so the perceived effect of the likelihood of H given D is expressed in terms of the perceived effect of the likelihood of D given H. *Aggregation* is the task of assessing the impact of a set of data on a given hypothesis based on the immediate logical relations between the data $(D^1, D^2,...)$ and the hypotheses H. Symbolically, we have $P(H/D^1, D^2,...) = R[P(H/D^1), P(H/D^2) ...]$ where R is the function that aggregates the local relations $P(H/D^i)$, for various i, to form the global relation $P(H/D^1, D^2,...)$. *Cascading* is the combination of a series of immediate relations on a chain of sequential impacts to assess a global relation. For example, if a datum D is perceived to have an effect on an event E, and this in turn effects $H(D{\rightarrow}E{\rightarrow}H)$, then the process of cascading consists of calculating $P(H/D)$ based on the local relations $P(H/E)$ and $P(E/D)$.

The general case of hierarchical inference involves a number of processes of inversion, aggregation, and cascading. A node in the hierarchical inference net represents a finite partition of exclusive and exhaustive possible states. It may be a set of hypotheses, a set of observable or unobservable events, or more generally just data.

The impact of a given state D_i on a state A_j is given by Bayes inversion theorem as:

$$P(A_j|D_i) = \frac{P(A_j)}{P(D_i)} P(D_i|A_j) \qquad (1)$$

Conditioning on the states of the intermediate node B to calculate $P(D_i|A_j)$ and then inverting and cascading the result gives us:

$$P(A_j|D_i) = \frac{P(A_j)}{P(D_i)} \sum_{k=1}^{h} P(D_i|A_jB_k) P(B_k|A_j) \qquad (2)$$

In decomposition for cascading, it is usually assumed that the relation among the states of adjacent nodes is unaffected by the occurrence of states at other nodes. In this case, the likelihood of state D_i, given that B_k occurred, is independent of every state A_j so $P(D_i|A_jB_k)=P(D_i|B_k)$. For the chain of nodes $A \rightarrow C \rightarrow E$, Equation 2 becomes:

$$P(A_j|E_l) = P(A_j) \sum_{k=1}^{c} \frac{P(C_k|E_l) P(C_k|A_j)}{P(C_k)} \qquad (3)$$

Equation 3 is sometimes referred to as the "modified Bayes theorem" (Gettys and Willke 1969) and has been used in a class of procedures called "probabilistic information processing" [Edwards et al. 1968] to help people overcome the suboptimum behavior they show when revising probabilities of interrelated events. Use of this equation requires the assessment of large amounts of data that may be very difficult to assess intuitively in complex hierarchical inference structures. For example, the meaning of the likelihood or probability of a new state given all previous information is difficult to understand when it comprises the conjunction of a large number of states. In addition, the complexity in the processing, storing, and assessment steps increases rapidly with the number of nodes in the network. This has led to the common criticism of using a formal Bayesian framework for inference (Kelly and Barclay 1973). Recent work, especially that by Pearl (1982a, 1982b, 1983) indicates that this criticism may not be fully justified.

An interesting and efficient scheme for the propagation of beliefs or evidence in hierarchically organized inference structures has been recently reported by Pearl (1982a, 1982b). The scheme relies on decomposing an inference task into a series of simpler intuitive inferences linking each stage in the hierarchy to produce a global assessment. The computation of the global assessment is simplified by reformulating the general Bayesian procedure for hierarchically organized inference structures discussed here. Data can be communicated among adjacent nodes and used to update the information at every node throughout the network. The decomposed Bayesian processing, characteristic of this scheme, allows updating to be performed by a series of local updating processes between each node and its neighbors, rather than by a central processing as in the general Bayesian framework. The likelihood of the various states of a given node depend on the entire data observed. Hence, the impact of the entire data on a given node can be decomposed in two disjoint sets of data — data obtained from the network rooted at that node and data from the network above the node. At node A let $D_d(A)$ stand for data obtained from the network rooted at A (i.e., nodes $B^1,...,$ B^L and nodes in the networks rooted on these) and let $D^u(A)$ be data obtained from nodes in the network above A (i.e., B and nodes above it, $A^1,...,A^M$ and nodes rooted on these). This decomposition prescribes how information obtained from above and below some node should be combined. A series of manipulations leads to

$$P(A_i) = ag(A_i) g(A_i) \tag{4}$$

where $g(A_i)=P(D_d(A)|A_i)$ represents the probabilistic support attributed to A_i by the nodes below it; $q(A_i)=P(A_i|D^u(A))$ represents the probabilistic support received by A_i from the nodes above it; and a is a normalization constant defined as $a=P(D_d(A)|D^u(A))^{-1}$. $P(A_i)$ is in fact a conditional probability conditioned on the existing state of knowledge.

Updating the values of g and q at every node in the light of new information allows for the calculation of the probability or likelihood of the state of every node. The calculation of g at a node involves only data obtained from the network rooted at that node. The data obtained from the network rooted at A is equivalent to data obtained from each of the networks rooted at nodes adjacent to A. This says that g can be calculated at a node if the g's of the nodes immediately below it and the conditional probabilities quantifying the relation between these nodes are known.

The data above A, $D^u(A)$, required to calculate $q(A_i)$, can be decomposed into two disjoint sets: $D^u(B)$ and D_d (siblings of A). Following the same reasoning as just used, we obtain a result that enables us to compute $P(A_i)$ and $P(B_j)$ without requiring normalization. These results indicate that information to perform the local processing can be represented at each node by assessed conditional probabilities relating adjacent nodes in the hierarchy and computed values of g and $P(.)$ at each node.

To initialize the inference net for propagation, we need the assessed conditional probabilities at each node. At an observational node, every state is equally likely to occur in the absence of any information, hence $g(.)$ is set to 1 at every observational node. From this, the value of g at every other node can be calculated. From the prior probability at the top node and the computed values of g, the probability of the states of each node can be calculated. Once the net is initialized, the occurrence of a particular state at an observational node will cause g to be updated. This information is then propagated up to update the g's of all other nodes and then down to update the likelihood of the states of each node.

In contrast with strict Bayesian procedures, Pearl's scheme requires only the assessment of a prior probability for the node at the top of the hierarchy, that is, the last stage of the hierarchical inference structure usually representing the hypothesis being studied. The probabilities of all other stages in the structure are uniquely determined by the assessed conditional probabilities at each node, thus reducing somewhat the amount and complexity of prior information required. On the other hand, Pearl's work relies on more strict independence assumptions in order to obtain computationally tractable results and also requires prior knowledge about the distribution of the underlying hypothesis being studied.

One of the major criticisms of this and similar Bayesian approaches is the need to identify point values about the probability of events. Usually, a point value assessment of the probability of an event is an overstatement about our actual knowledge of the likelihood of occurrence of that particular event. In response to the need of representing imprecision of Bayesian probability values, Dempster (1967) utilized the concept of lower and upper probabilities to deal with the subjective imprecision of uncertainty measures. Shafer (1976, 1981) presents a comprehensive exposition of this novel idea as well as extensions to the theory of inference based on the concept of upper and lower probabilities. The basic idea of this concept is that instead of representing the probability of an event A by a point value $P(A)$, it may be bounded by a subinterval of $(0, 1)$. That is, the exact probability $P(A)$ may be unknown but bounded. This kind of representation has solid grounds in the Dempster-Shafer theory of basic probability and for that reason has received considerable attention recently.

Of particular interest in this research is the work of Toulmin, Rieke, and Janik (1979) in that they have constructed an explicit structured model of logical reasoning that is suited for analytical inquiry and computer implementation. The model is sufficiently general that it can be used to represent logical reasoning in a number of application areas.

Starting from the assumption that whenever we make a claim there must be some grounds in which to base our conclusion, Toulmin states that our thoughts are generally directed from the "grounds" to the "claim." The grounds and the claim are statements that express facts and values. As a means of stating observed patterns of stating a claim, there must be a reason that can be identified to connect the grounds and the claim. This connection is called the "warrant," and it is the warrant that gives to the grounds-claim connection its logical validity.

We say that the grounds support the claim on the basis of the existence of a warrant that explains the connection between the grounds and the claim. It is easy to relate the structure of these basic elements with the process of inference, whether statistical, deductive, or inductive. The warrants are the set of rules of inference, and the grounds and claim are the set of well-defined propositions or hypotheses. It will be only the sequence and procedures, that are used to come up with the three basic elements and their structure in a logical fashion, that will determine the type of inference that is used.

Sometimes, in the course of reasoning about an issue, it is not enough that the warrant will be the absolute reason to believe the claim on the basis of the grounds. For that, Toulmin allows for further "backing," which in his representation supports the warrant. It is the backing that provides for the reliability, in terms of truth, associated with the use of the warrant. The relationship here is analogous to the way in which the grounds support the claim. An argument will be valid and will give the claim solid support only if the warrant is relied upon and is relevant to the particular case under examination. The concept of logical validity seems to imply that we can only make a claim when both the warrant and the grounds are certain. However, imprecision and uncertainty in the form of exceptions to the rules or low degree of certainty in both the grounds and the warrant does not prevent us on occasion from making a "hedge" or a vague claim. Very commonly, we must arrive at conclusions on the basis of something less than perfect evidence; and we put those claims forward not with absolute and irrefutable truth but rather with some doubt or degree of speculation.

To allow for these cases, Toulmin adds "modal qualifiers" and "possible rebuttals" to his framework for logical reasoning. Modal qualifiers refer to the strength or weakness with which a claim is made. In essence, every argument has a certain modality. Its place in the structure presented so far must reflect the generality of the warrant in connecting the grounds to the claim. These qualifiers also relate to conditions of validity on the set of facts used as the basis for the grounds. Possible rebuttals, on the other hand, are exceptions to the rules. Although modal qualifiers serve the purpose of weakening or strengthening the validity of a claim, there still may be conditions that invalidate either the grounds or the warrants, and this will result in deactivating the link between the claim and the grounds. These cases are represented by the possible rebuttals.

The resulting structure of logical reasoning provides a very useful framework for the study of human information processing activities. The order in which the six elements of logical reasoning have been presented serves only the purpose of illustrating their function and interdependence in the structure of an argument about a specific issue. It does not represent any normative pattern of argument formation. In fact, due to the dynamic nature of human reasoning, the concept formation and framing that results in a particular structure may occur in different ways. The six-element model of logical reasoning is shown in Figure 14.1.

FIGURE 14.1
THE SIX-ELEMENT MODEL OF LOGICAL REASONING

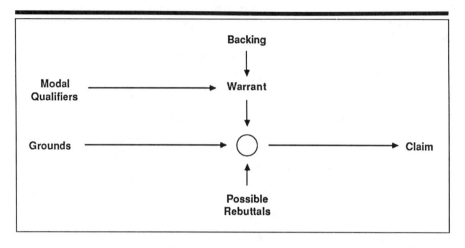

The effects of various forms of inquiry upon issues of representation and detection of judgmental errors in human information processing have been investigated (Lagomasino and Sage 1985a, 1985b, 1986), using this structure of rational argument. The frameworks for Bayesian inference just discussed require probability values as primary inputs. Since most events of interest are unique or little is known about their relative frequencies of occurrence, the assessments of probability values usually require human judgment. Substantial psychological research has shown that people are unable to elicit probability values consistent with the rules of probabilities and that they are suboptimum in revising probability assessment when new information is obtained.

Tversky and Kahneman (1981) have shown that dominance of causal over diagnostic information exists in assessing conditional probabilities. They concluded, in a series of experiments, that if some information has both causal and diagnostic implications, then people apparently assess conditional probabilities primarily in terms of the direct causal effect of the impacts, instead of weighing the causal and diagnostic impacts of the evidence. Thus, if A is perceived to be the cause of B, people will give higher probabilities to $P(B|A)$ than to $P(A|B)$. Burns and Pearl (1981) conducted a study to test the validity of judgments made by these two forms of reasoning. Thus they investigated whether causal or diagnostic judgment is a more natural way of encoding knowledge about every-day experiences. Their results demonstrated that neither one was found to be more accurate than the other. In a similar study, Moskowitz and Sarin (1983) reported that individuals found it easier and showed more confidence in assessing $P(A|B)$ if B is causal to A.

This apparent contradiction of results may be explained by the differences in the contingency task structure within which the experiments were performed. It suggests that the choice of which form of inference to invoke depends more on the level of familiarity of the observer with the task at hand and the cognitive style that determines the way in which the knowledge was originally perceived. Most structuring procedures for decision making rely on the "divide and conquer" approach under the assumption that judgment is improved when a complex, ill-defined problem is decomposed, analyzed, and solved by a set of smaller, well-defined problems. The findings of these studies, aside from having implications on the validity of the "divide and conquer" approach, imply that the form of representation of judgments used should correspond with the meaning of the judgments assessed.

Falk and Bar-Hillel (1979) have recognized the importance of distinguishing between probabilistic and logical support. *Probabilistic support* refers to the increased likelihood of the occurrence of an event A, given that another event B has occurred. That is, A supports B if $P(B|A) > P(B)$. *Logical support* exhibits the relation of implication between two premises, denoted $A{\rightarrow}B$, that fails to hold only if the first is true and the second is false. Logical support is transitive; if $A{\rightarrow}B$ and $B{\rightarrow}C$, then $A{\rightarrow}C$. When $A{\rightarrow}B$ it is also true that $B{\rightarrow}A$. With these definitions, the distinctions between probabilistic and logical support should be apparent. Logical support does not imply conditions similar to those that follow from probabilistic support. $A{\rightarrow}B$ is logically equivalent to $B{\rightarrow}A$, but it says nothing about the truth of $A{\rightarrow}B$ or $B{\rightarrow}A$. Likewise, probabilistic support is not transitive, and logical support must be transitive. A major point in this distinction is when to apply these two methods of representation in inferential activities. We are concerned with this issue because, as previous research has shown, the method used to represent human judgments may strongly influence the validity and consistency of these judgments.

It is especially important to note that we can ascribe uncertainty to the truth of logical support by referring to the probability by which A implies B, $P(A{\rightarrow}B)$. The importance of this will concern us next in the development of a general framework for inference. Much of our research has been concerned with developing a framework of inference suitable for assessing and structuring complex problems that derive from the logic of reasoning of Toulmin and the calculus of probabilities to make inferences on the likelihood of the events or premises that comprise the inference structure. Assessments by the decision maker in the form of logical support relations among the events are used to structure the problem, and assessments in the form of set inclusion inequalities among the events and their relations are combined using the probability calculus to draw inferences.

The framework and process for inference support developed here is applicable to a general class of networks of interrelated propositions. Specifically, it can be applied to finite connected networks in which the number of propositions is finite and every pair of distinct propositions is joined by at least one chain of relations. We have developed a procedure that describes the information-processing elements involved in the structuring and analysis of an issue within this framework. The information-processing functions associated with the use of the framework for inference described here involves four steps:

1. Initial problem framing
2. Hypothesis generation
3. Parameter value assessment
4. Hypothesis evaluation and situation assessment

The intent of the first step is to capture those elements and relations that constitute an issue and to represent them in a form that is suitable for inference. The inference network developed here is not necessarily hierarchical as contrasted with the case of Bayesian inference. We are able to deal with structures that correspond to a very general type of inference network. Nodes in the network represent the propositions of interest in the particular issue. Inferential links between propositions are defined in terms of the set of consistency relational equations, including the set of consistency relations and any other assessed relations between the propositions at each node. The probability value of the propositions at each node is underconstrained, and acquisition of information about the relation between the nodes is the primary means of further constraining the probability values of the propositions at each node.

Given the assessed initial problem frame, the task of hypothesis generation involves the generation of reasonable hypotheses that are based on situational perception and information needed for the task at hand. In most cases this involves the specification of alternative hypotheses at each node. Ideally, the set of hypotheses under consideration at each node should be mutually exclusive and exhaustive. This task also involves the selection of the basic premises and possible rebuttals relevant for each inferential link.

The parameter value identification step provides for the continual assessment of the parameters of the inference model. This includes the assessment of probability values of the propositions at each node as well as the probability values representing the uncertain logical relations at each inferential link. These assessments can be related and represented imprecisely in the form of bounded intervals and/or linear inequalities on the set of parameters. Achieving the task of parameter value assessment with minimal imprecision will depend strongly on the quality of the information available and the person's perception and familiarity with the task at hand.

The hypothesis evaluation and situation assessment step involves probability categorization, over a set of alternative hypotheses, of the probable situations as captured by the information that is provided to the inference model. Given the set of consistency relational equations for each link in the inference network, we can calculate the probability values for the propositions at each node. These probability values will usually be stated in the form of bounded intervals and linear inequalities. If more precise information is required, then further assessments about the relations and propositions in the network must be performed. This suggests the generation of alternative hypotheses and the assessment of more precise parameter values. The information-processing tasks required in the use of the framework for inference based on logical reasoning describes an iterative process suitable for situations in which knowledge about it is ill defined or imperfectly described.

The objective of this portion of our research has been to investigate various approaches for inference based on imprecise knowledge and to advance the state of research in the area of representation of natural language expressions about uncertainty and imprecision. We have investigated a new approach for inference based on logical support relations that differs considerably from Bayesian approaches, which rely on probabilistic support relations. This new approach has the interesting feature of being computationally simple, capable of working in a general class of inference networks, not relying on idealistic independence assumptions, and not having to make a clear distinction between hypothetical and evidential types of information.

14.6   CONCLUSIONS

In the context of devices to aid in human information-processing activities, there exist two design philosophies concerning the proper relationship between the input component and the generalizing or inference mechanism. One advocates the view that these components should be considered as operating separately; with the input component in charge of knowledge acquisition, and representation considered as if it was independent of the generalizing sector that is in charge of aggregation or inference. This approach offers simplicity in system design at the expense of effectiveness. The mode of representation of information will influence the success or failure of the inquirer in arriving at a solution. This deficiency seems to be characteristic of many current information systems. They are passive, and it is up to the user to recognize an information need and then seek out the required information.

The other approach considers that the two sectors are essentially nonseparable and that each supports and enhances the functioning of the other; but this in turn complicates the system design, perhaps by a considerable amount. In this approach, the internal interactions of the input and generalizing sector are capable of generating user-system interaction. There are various ways in which a system can initiate a dialogue with a user. These include identification of:

1. "Gaps" in the knowledge base that prevent the system from making inferences or from adequately summarizing the information in a sector of the knowledge base

2. An inconsistent set of information followed by detection of the inability of the system to resolve it

3. Sufficiently imprecise information that makes it not possible to suggest an appropriate course of action

4. Inability of the system to satisfy the desired goals of the user.

Identification of these potential deficiencies and use of prompts based on them for the purpose of computer-control dialogue are necessary for intelligent system design for decision support. To be fully responsive to the needs of users, research concerning this subject should be integrated with research involving human information processing and associated inference structures.

In this chapter and in the associated research, we have been especially concerned with situations in which there are many perspectives and experiential familiarity with a particular judgmental task. It is argued that this requires attention to combining the skill-based and rule-based features of an expert system with the formal reasoning–based knowledge developed through use of a decision support system. This could be especially fruitful in accomplishing meta-level-model-based management. A structured inference procedure to accomplish this type of control, based on the use of imperfect information as well as probabilistic and logical support, was described.

REFERENCES

Abelson, R.P. (1979), "Differences Between Belief and Knowledge Systems," *Cognitive Science,* 3:355–366.

Barr, A., and Feigenbaum, E.A. (1981, 1982), *The Handbook of Artificial Intelligence,* vols. 1 and 2, Los Altos, Calif.: William Kaufman, Inc.

Burns, M., and Pearl, J. (1981), "Causal and Diagnostic Inferences: A Comparison of Validity," *Organizational Behavior and Human Performance,* 28(3):379–394.

Cohen, P.R., and Feigenbaum, E.A. (1982), *The Handbook of Artificial Intelligence,* vol. 3, Los Altos, Calif.: William Kaufman, Inc.

Date, C.J. (1981), *An Introduction to Database Systems,* Reading, Mass.: Addison-Wesley.

Date, C.J. (1983), *Database: A Primer,* Reading, Mass.: Addison-Wesley.

Dempster, A.P. (1967), "Upper and Lower Probabilities Induced by a Multivalued Mapping," *Annals of Mathematical Statistics,* 38(2):325–339.

Edwards, W., Phillips, L.D., Hays, W.I., and Goodman, B.C. (1968), "Probabilistic Information Processing Systems: Design and Evaluation," *IEEE Transactions on System Science and Cybernetics,* (SMC-4), pp. 248–265.

Falk, R., and Bar-Hillel, M. (1979), "Probabilistic Dependence between Events," Hebrew University of Jerusalem, October.

Gettys, C., and Willke, T.A. (1969), "The Application of Bayes' Theorem When the True Data State is Uncertain," *Organizational Behavior and Human Performance,* 4:125–141.

Gevarter, W.B. (1984), *Artificial Intelligence, Expert Systems, Computer Vision and Natural Language Processing,* Park Ridge, N.J.: Noyes Publications

Ishizuka, M. (1983), "Inference Methods Based on Extended Dempster-Shafer Theory for Problems with Uncertainty/Fuzziness," *New Generation Computing,* 1:159–168.

Kahneman, D., Slovic, P., and Tversky, A. (1982), *Judgments under Uncertainty: Heuristics and Biases*, New York: Cambridge University Press.

Kahneman, D., and Tversky, A. (1982), "Variants of Uncertainty," *Cognition*, 11(2):143–157.

Kelly, C.W., and Barclay, S. (1973), "A General Bayesian Model for Hierarchical Inference," *Organizational Behavior and Human Performance*, 10(3):388–403.

Lagomasino, A., and Sage, A.P. (1985a), "An Interactive Inquiry System," *Large Scale Systems*, 9:231–244.

Lagomasino, A., and Sage, A.P. (1985b), "Representation and Interpretation of Information for Decision Support with Imperfect Knowledge," *Large Scale Systems*, 9:169–191.

Lagomasino, A., and Sage, A.P. (1986), "Imprecise Knowledge Representation in Inferential Activities," in M.M. Gupta, ed., *Approximate Reasoning in Expert Systems*, New York: Elsevier North-Holland.

Linstone, H.A. (1984), *Multiple Perspectives for Decision Making: Bridging the Gap Between Analysis and Action*, New York: Elsevier North-Holland.

Moskowitz, H., and Sarin, R.K. (1983), "Improving the Consistency of Conditional Probability Assessments for Forecasting and Decision Making," *Management Science*, 29(6):735–749.

Pearl, J. (1982a), "Distributed Bayesian Processing for Belief Maintenance in Hierarchical Inference Systems," UCLA Cognitive Systems Lab, (UCLA-ENG-CSL-82-11), January.

Pearl, J. (1982b), "Reverend Bayes on Inference Engines: A Distributed Hierarchical Approach," presented at the AAAI National Conference on Artificial Intelligence, August 18–20, Pittsburgh, Pa.

Pearl, J. (1983), *Heuristics: Partially Informed Strategies for Computer Problem Solving*, Reading, Mass.: Addison-Wesley.

Quinlan, J.R. (1983), "Inferno: A Cautious Approach to Uncertain Inference," *The Computer Journal*, 26(3):255–266.

Sage, A.P. (1981), "Behavioral and Organizational Considerations in the Design of Information Systems and Processes for Planning and Decision Support," *IEEE Transaction on Systems, Man, and Cybernetics*, (SMC-11) September, pp. 640–678.

Sage, A.P., and Botta, R. (1983), "On Human Information Processing and Its Enhancement Using Knowledge-Based Systems," *Large Scale Systems*, 5:208–223.

Sage, A.P., and Lagomasino, A. (1984), "Knowledge Representation and Man Machine Dialogue," in William B. Rouse, ed., *Advances in Man-Machine Systems Research*, Greenwich, Conn.: JAI Press, pp. 223–260.

Sage, A.P., and White, C.C. (1984), "ARIADNE: A Knowledge Based Interactive System for Planning and Decision Support," *IEEE Transactions on Systems, Man and Cybernetics*, 14(1):35–47.

Shafer, G. (1976), *A Mathematical Theory of Evidence*, Princeton, N.J.: Princeton University Press.

Shafer, G. (1981), "Constructive Probability," *Synthese*, 48:1–60.

Sprague, R.H. Jr., and Carlson, E.D. (1982), *Building Effective Decision Support Systems*, Englewood Cliffs, N.J.: Prentice Hall.

Toulmin, S., Rieke, R., and Janik, A. (1979), *An Introduction to Reasoning*, New York: MacMillan.

Tversky, A., and Kahneman, D. (1981), "Causal Schemas in Judgments under Uncertainty," in D. Kahneman, P. Slovic, and A. Tversky, eds., *Judgments under Uncertainty: Heuristics and Biases*, New York: Cambridge University Press.

V

NEXT GENERATION TECHNOLOGY

Jean Piaget, the father of human intellect development theory, explains the evolution of thought as humans mature from childhood through young adulthood in terms of two higher cognitive modes: "concrete" and "formal" thought. The "concrete" thinker relies largely on perceptual experience—what can be seen, heard, felt or otherwise sensed and simple judgment guides for thought and problem solving. The "formal" thinker, on the other hand, is capable of abstract thought, independent intellectual effort, reliance on internal (rather than perceptual) stimuli, and use of advanced analytical powers. The normal child matures from solely a "concrete" thinker and problem solver, to one who is capable of "formal" thought.

The more recent work of several cognitive science researchers has indicated that expertise arises not from mental analytical power, but from perceptual abilities. In the expert, the whole-situation recognition capacity is refined to the point that predictions or decisions, learned through experience (after buying and wearing out 30 three-piece suits), intuitively accompany situation recognition without need for calculation.

The point is that proficient decision makers may not be following rules. If you ask a typist to think about which finger is being used to type each letter, the typist's speed will slow down. If you ask tennis players how they snap their wrists when serving, their strokes become "self-conscious" and unnatural.

The eminent Dutch psychologist and chess master Adrian deGroot argues for the existence of a nonverbalizable mental capacity (distinct from factual knowledge), which he calls "intuitive experience." deGroot asserts that the great chess player internalizes not squares with pieces on them, but rather a very special sense of "fields of force," a cluster of potential actions, a space of and for evolving events. This intuitive experience is only actualized by situations, and it cannot be described by the expert. Experts tend to reason holistically, by analogy with previous similar experiences, rather than by explicit analysis and/or computation. Herbert Dreyfus, the author of *What Computers Can't Do* (Harper & Row 1984), uses this line of reasoning as the basis of a skill-acquisition process description when he states "the significant pattern pervading the skill-acquisition process . . . is the progression from abstract, rational understanding, and decisionmaking in terms of isolated elements and rules relating them, to immediate situation recognition and response based on holistic similarity to prior concrete experiences."

The point is that AI/ES has yet to provide technology that can perform as well as humans in numerous situations. No computer program exists that can play cards one minute, balance its checkbook the next, and then go out and drive a car. The roadblock to developing such a computer program is, in part, that the human mind is still a puzzle, it is still not well understood.

In chapter after chapter up to this point, authors have repeatedly returned to this issue and to their needs to better understand the cognitive processes of their domain subjects in order to improve their ESs or ESSs and in order to better support the user. Computerized chess programs do not play chess the way grand masters play it, and until we understand entirely how the grand master plays chess, no amount of increased ES speed or size will lead it to beat the grand master.

The following information will be included in Part V:

1. Chapter 15 explores a subject that has totally defied AI/ES technology to date—that of common sense reasoning and learning as applied to creative problem solving. In short, the study of "the ability of humans to find new and creative solutions to problems" has led the author to model creative processes to better understand them.

2. Chapter 16 explores one subject under the heading of creativity—that of automated analogy systems. The author provides a deeper probing of this subject and of the inability of current AI/ES technology to perform and exploit analogical reasoning.

3. Finally, Chapter 17 explains progress made on building an analogical reasoning system that is capable of inventiveness and innovative behavior.

The material presented in these chapters explores the frontier of what is known in several AI/ES topics. There are no easy, cheap solutions to advancing the state of the AI/ES technology. The benefits of current ES and ESS applications is only a harbinger of things to come, and ESs and ESSs are only the first generation of AI technology to successfully begin the transition to business applications. Part V attempts to show some of the benefits that might be gained by next-generation AI technology as well as some of the progress already being made toward that goal.

15

Modeling Creativity for Management Support Via Artificial Intelligence Approaches

Chen-Hua Chung

Business management has become increasingly unstructured and more complicated as a result of broad and rapid technological changes. For this reason, there is a greater need for new and creative methods, so that effective managerial problem solving or decision making can be enhanced. Unfortunately, creativity has not been a design consideration in most decision or management support systems. It is not even sufficiently addressed in artificial intelligence (and expert systems) research. In this chapter, we explore various issues associated with modeling creativity for management support via artificial intelligence approaches. Three types of AI programs are examined: (1) creativity acquisition programs (CAP), (2) creativity facilitation programs (CFP), and (3) intelligent and creative programs (ICP)., A single program alone is not sufficient for effective management support. Management support systems should be developed as a network of subsystem interfaces. Creativity and synergistic effects can also be brought about through the process of subsystem interfaces.

15.1 INTRODUCTION

In recent years, the notion of artificial intelligence (AI) has become very popular both inside and outside the field of computer science. The most successful applications of AI research have been in the development of "automatic consulting systems," better known as expert systems (ESs). Although reports on the successful applications in business management have been rare, the enormous potential of ES and AI for management should not be ignored.

The research in the use of computer and information technology to support management, namely, decision support systems (DSSs) or management support systems (MSSs), has been limited to a specific decision or a specific class of decisions (Scott Morton 1983). This development is somewhat similar to that of the existing expert systems that operate in highly specialized domains. Incidentally, most business decisions or managerial problems are rarely well defined. One of the assumptions (or expectations) of the development of the DSS concept was that DSS can support less-structured or unstructured decision-making process such as upper-level or strategic planning (Keen and Scott Morton 1978; and Sprague and Carlson 1982). Also, the MSS concept should emphasize the fact that an organization is an integrated and complicated management system (Chung 1985a). Business management has become increasingly unstructured and more complicated as a result of broad and rapid technological changes. For this reason, there is a greater need for creativity, so that effective managerial problem solving and decision making can be enhanced.

Unfortunately, creativity has not received adequate attention in the research and development of DSSs or MSSs. It is not even sufficiently addressed in most AI studies and applications. This is due partly to the difficulty in the computerization of the creativity concept and partly to some misconception of creativity in AI research.

From the viewpoint of managerial problem solving, creativity is "the ability to break through constraints imposed by habit and tradition so as to find 'new' solutions to problems" (Ackoff and Vergara 1981). The notion of creativity implicitly suggests that it is sometimes desirable or even necessary to break through constraints or rules imposed upon the problem-solving process. This idea certainly would not be readily acceptable to those people who are preoccupied with the procedural or logical reasoning in conventional computer programming or AI techniques. However, as will be further explored later, modeling creativity via the computer or AI approach is technically feasible. It should also be emphasized that the incorporation of creativity into decision or management support systems is not just wishful futuristic thinking. It is a managerial necessity. As the business environment becomes more and more complicated and competitive, an organization needs to seek creativity to gain strategic advantages. Creativity is the means for both survival and growth.

Generally speaking, the use of AI approaches to model creativity for management support can be accomplished at three levels:

1. As a knowledge acquisition system (KAS) — a program used to extract knowledge (creativity in this case) from "experts" (i.e., creative persons)

2. As an automatic consulting system — a program used to facilitate or enhance the creativity of users and/or decision makers

3. As an intelligent computer — a program that is itself creative

With the current state-of-the-art technology of AI, particularly the expert systems technology, the systems of the first two levels can be developed with relative ease. The design of an intelligent and creative system of the third level would require more sophisticated AI technology and is parallel to the AI research in the future. Thus this type of parallel system would be the most challenging and would provide the most rewarding research in the applications of AI to management.

In Section 15.2, the literature of creativity is briefly reviewed. Section 15.3 discusses the first two types of programs from the preceding list — that is, the programs that extract and/or enhance creativity. In Section 15.4 the programs of the third type are explored, and Section 15.5 emphasizes the managerial implications of the study and suggests directions for future research.

15.2   AN OVERVIEW OF CREATIVITY

The literature relevant to creativity has been sporadic. However, Ackoff and Vergara (1981) provide an excellent review of creativity related particularly to problem solving and planning. Table 15.1 summarizes their study of the nature of creativity.

From the viewpoint of AI application, it is rather irrelevant whether creativity arises from conflict or harmony within an individual, as the argument goes between the psychoanalysts and the humanistic psychologists, respectively. Creativity may result from outside pressures as well, or it may come from the removal of constraints, particularly self-imposed ones. What is more important is to explore the creative thinking process, which should eventually be captured and incorporated (i.e., simulated) in the AI programs.

The logic theorist and the general problem solver (GPS) developed by Newell, Shaw, and Simon (1957) and Newell and Simon (1963) were initially designed as problem-solving programs. However, some implications of creative thinking can be drawn from *how* the program "solves" problems. Specifically, creative thinking is simply treated as a special

TABLE 15.1
SUMMARY OF THE NATURE OF CREATIVITY*

Origin-Oriented Approaches	Process-Oriented Approaches
Psychoanalysts	*The Associationists*
Creativity arises from conflicts within an individual. The creative process involves externalizing the internal products of imagination through the interaction of primitive and more mature types of thinking (Freud 1970).	An individual's creativity is a function of his ability to invoke and explore remote associations in selecting a response to a problem (Mednick 1962).
Humanistic Psychologists	*Gestalt Psychologists*
Creativity arises when there is no conflict within an individual. The creative process involves the release of natural creative potential through the removal of inhibitions from the individual and obstructions from his environment (Fromm 1959).	Creative thinking proceeds neither by piecemeal logical operations nor by disconnected associations, but by more determinate restructuring of the whole situation (Wertheimer 1959). Creativity lies in the ability to redirect a line of thought taken in solving a problem (Maier 1970).
Psychometricians	*Information Theorist** *
Each individual's natural creative potential is limited by his genetic endowment and can be measured by standard tests. The creative process involves the interaction of two contrasting types of thinking: "divergent" which converts information into a variety of unconventional alternatives, and "convergent", which aims at unique or conventional outcomes (Guilford 1977).	Human thinking process can be simulated as the process of information processing in computer programs. Creative activity is a special class of problem-solving activity characterized by novelty, unconventionality, persistence, and difficulty in formulation (Newell, Shaw, and Simon 1962).

*Adapted from Ackoff and Vergara (1981).
**Not directly quoted form Ackoff and Vergara (1981).

kind of problem-solving behavior (Newell, Shaw, and Simon 1962). A problem is a "maze" or a set of paths connecting the initial and terminal states. To solve a problem is to select a desirable path from the subset of all possible solutions. Creativity lies in the design or the discovery of heuristics in finding the right path(s). Ideally, a creative program would be able to invoke adaptive changes (i.e., some improvements) in heuristics. This leads to the issue of the learning capability of the program.

The design of heuristics usually involves the use of some criteria and constraints to reduce what otherwise would have been an unlimited search space. Koestler (1973) argued that creative ideas would come from outside the space defined by these criteria and constraints and therefore denied the possibility of the creativity of such a search program.

The disagreement here may be just a matter of how the term *creativity* is defined. Analogous to the distinction between effectiveness and efficiency as defined by Drucker (1954), the discourse can be interpreted in the following way: the search within the delimited space is to get things done right (efficiency), while the search outside that space is an intent to get the right things done (effectiveness). This analogy is valid to the extent that the thinking processes associated with efficiency and effectiveness resemble the search processes inside and outside the delimited space. As pointed out by Bennett (1983), discovering how to be more effective requires "divergent" thinking (as the decision maker is stimulated to expand the set of open decision possibilities), while discovering how to be more efficient requires "convergent" thinking (as the decision maker uses tools to achieve results in reduced time or at reduced cost). It is generally believed that creativity is necessary for achieving both effectiveness and efficiency. In this sense, the distinction suggested by Koestler becomes trivial. This is particularly true in business management for which effectiveness and efficiency are both important. (Certainly, one may argue that effectiveness should always be given higher priority than efficiency). On the other hand, as will be discussed later, creative thinking tends to be divergent rather than convergent.

The definitions of creativity offered by the associationists and the Gestalt psychologists do not directly refer to the use of a (computer) programming approach. However, their ideas (e.g., "remote association" and "restructuring of the (whole) situation") are very helpful in understanding the nature of creativity.

In addition to the concepts summarized in Table 15.1, creative thinking also can be explored from other angles. For example, Bruner (1962) defines creativity as an act that produces "effective surprise." From the perspective of organizational problem solving or decision making, *surprise* means a new way of doing things, while *effective* means the way of doing things that would improve the organization's status quo or would push forward the process of achieving its goal(s). Thus the effectiveness of the surprise should be evaluated in terms of organizational goals. If the surprise is a positive influence on organizational problem solving or goal achieving, then the surprise would be effective. Otherwise, it is only something unexpected and cannot be called "creative." For example, in most program or systems design processes, the designer may run into some "Aha!" experiences (Mostow 1984). However, these surprises may not be effective in terms of the design objectives. Only the "Eureka" experiences are the effective surprises that are most desirable and most precious.

Bruner (1962) also suggests that all the forms of effective surprise result from "combinatorial activity"—that is, a placing of things in new perspective. This view is somewhat similar to what the Gestalt psychologists called "a restructuring of the (whole) situation." To further explore the nature of creativity, we use the modeling concept in Management Science/Operations Research (MS/OR) to illustrate the combinatorial interpretation of the creative process. In general, there are two phases in modeling: the inclusion process and the structuring process (Nugent and Vollman 1972). During the inclusion process, the modeler is to determine what variables are "significant" enough to be included in the model. In structuring the chosen variables, the modeler again must consider what relationships among variables are "significant." There may be numerous combinations of variables (to form relationships) and numerous combinations of relationships (to form higher-level relationships, or the so-called meta-relationships). However, not all of them will be considered significant. The significance judgment implicitly involves the use of a confidence level. That is, the modeler believes that a particular variable or relationship should be included at a 95 percent confidence level. In other words, if the problem or the decision-making situation reoccurs a sufficiently large number of times, the variable(s) or the relationship would appear relevant in 95 percent of the cases, while those variables or relationships consistently beyond the confidence interval would be remote associations. The remote associations are the combinations that are least likely to impact the results of problem solving or decision making, based upon the modeler's subjective judgment. The combinations within the confidence interval are usually the result of the modeler's "rational analysis" of the problem situation and therefore contain few surprises.

Using the confidence interval construct, we can conceive creativity as effective combinations that lie outside the modeler's confidence interval. Unfortunately, these remote associations are usually overlooked in most decision analysis because they are considered the least likely to occur. However, it is important to remember the words of Harlan, Christianson, and Vancil (1962): "It is a waste of time to do a careful analysis of three alternatives and to select the best of the three if a fourth course of action which is far better is completely overlooked. Analysis is no substitute for imagination."

Due to the combinatorial nature of the choice of variables and relationships, the number of alternatives within the confidence interval usually consists of only an extremely small portion of all the possible combinations. Thus a rational analysis can capture only a few of far too many possible alternatives. The so-called rational analysis actually limits our choice to those within the confidence interval. Outside the confidence interval, the potential for creativity is virtually unlimited.

A combination of variables and relationships is one type of description or "knowledge representation" of the problem. Restructuring the whole situation (in the sense of the Gestalt psychologists) is the same as changing the knowledge representation of the problem. As will be further discussed in the later sections, one way to facilitate creativity in an AI program is to initiate changes in problem representation.

There exists no AI program that is itself creative. Although some programs may have surprised the designer or the users, none of them has been designed for the purpose of generating "effective surprises." A more viable approach would be to develop a program that can induce or enhance human creativity. This approach has the same spirit as the current research and development in expert systems. In a sense, the facilitation of human creativity would be treated as a specific problem domain. Through man-machine interactions, the expert system, working as a creativity facilitator, would stimulate or guide the human (creative) thinking process.

In the following sections, we will discuss the programs that facilitate human creativity and some design issues associated with a creative program. A focus on management support will be maintained.

15.3 PROGRAMS THAT FACILITATE HUMAN CREATIVITY

As previously mentioned, there are two types of programs that can be developed to extract or facilitate human creativity. The first type of programs resemble the knowledge acquisition system (KAS) in building an expert system. (For detailed discussions on the architecture of expert systems, see Chapter 1, Figure 1.1 in particular.) The KAS is used to elicit expert knowledge (in this case, creative ideas) from experts or creative persons. The second type of programs are themselves expert systems that can be used to facilitate or enhance the creativity of users. That is, the users can consult with the program for help in generating creative ideas. The distinction made between the two types of programs is only for the convenience of discussion. Eventually, the KAS for creativity probably would not be used as a stand-alone system. At most, it would be only part of the ES for enhancing creativity. In other words, we can assume that with the help of the program (i.e., the ES), any person (i.e., the user) can become creative. Therefore the user no longer would need to rely on other "experts."

15.3.1 Creativity Acquisition Program (CAP)

With the notion of "creativity acquisition," it is implicitly assumed that, (1) creative persons exist and can be identified, (2) creative persons use problem-solving techniques that differ from those used by "ordinary people," and (3) the thinking process of creative persons can be captured via (or translated into) computer programs.

Issues related to the first two assumptions have been vigorously pursued by psychologists or researchers in creativity. The traits approach had been used to identify the personality characteristics of a creative person (McClelland 1962; and Crutchfield 1962). However, it is commonly believed that different individuals would possess different degrees of creativity in different problem areas. Thus a generalized creativity acquisition program (CAP) would be useful in eliciting creativity from different persons for different problem domains.

The purpose of creativity acquisition may be twofold. First, what the program seeks from the creative person(s) is simply some creative ideas in tackling the particular problem. The task of this program then is no more difficult than performing knowledge acquisition for ordinary expert systems. Second, the focus of the acquisition task can be placed upon the "creative thinking process." That is, we expect the program to capture how the person develops creative ideas. This leads to the third assumption — that is, the thinking process of creative persons can be captured and transferred into programs. This is an important yet difficult task. Like a KAS for expert systems, the CAP would require the creative person to explain "how he or she got that idea" or "how he or she got that way." Sometimes it may be too much to ask a person to explain his or her own thinking process. Even the most disciplined mind is never bound by logic (MacLeod 1962). Creative persons may rely heavily on intuitive or illogical thinking. They may not be aware of how they developed the ideas, particularly when the creative ideas were the result of some kind of "sudden enlightenment."

To create a program to capture the creative thinking process would require research in creativity, similar to what many psychologists and researchers have been doing for decades. Since building a "research machine" may not be our intention, it would be reasonable to directly incorporate into the program the research results in the creativity literature. That is, what is really needed is a creativity facilitation program with embedded creativity enhancement techniques reported in the literature. Thus we may be able to do away with the creativity acquisition program. With emphasis placed upon problem solving in specific domains, the creativity acquisition program can be reduced to an ordinary knowledge acquisition routine for expert systems.

15.3.2 Creativity Facilitation Program (CFP)

If the "techniques" used by various creative persons can be captured and generalized, then the generalized results would be instructive to "ordinary" people. In other words, the generalized methodologies can serve as facilitation tools for creativity.

Various procedures for enhancing creativity have been reported in the literature. Ackoff and Vergara (1981) provide an extensive review of some of the most well known and widely used procedures, including: brainstorming (Osborn 1963); dialectical approach (Churchman 1966; Emshoff and Mitroff 1977; and Mason 1968); synectics (Gordon 1961); and so forth. If these procedures are built into the user-machine interface routine (of an ES), then the routine can be called a "creativity facilitation program" (Chung 1985b).

The program can facilitate user's creative thinking in various ways. For example, it can suggest directions or provide checklists for deliberation. It can reason through user's inputs and help the user review his or her own thinking process. Frequently, new ideas are sparked by reviewing old ones. With built-in reasoning capability, the program can be helpful in editing or summarizing the unorganized "chunks" in the user's thinking and eventually producing some concrete ideas. The program also can use words, sentences, or pictures to stimulate the user's associative thinking. Thus it is also desirable to incorporate some graphics routines into the facilitation program. It certainly takes creativity to build a program that facilitates creativity. As van Dam (1984) points out, graphics is well on its way to being the standard form of communication with computers. Some studies have reported the effects of graphical presentation methods on decision making (DeSanctis 1984). Further study will be needed to explore what kinds of graphics techniques can best enhance creativity. Similarly, sound effects can also be considered. This leads to another important issue in the design of a creativity facilitation program. That is, how to create the right atmosphere for generating creative ideas via human-machine interactions. We may have to go beyond merely talking about the "user-friendliness" of these programs.

Some creativity enhancement procedures (e.g., brainstorming) emphasize the effect of group process. In terms of computerized creativity facilitation, both the group members and the group processes can be simulated in the program. The user, as a "member" of the group, becomes creative via the exchanges with the "computerized members" in the program. On the other hand, the implementation of creativity facilitation needs not be limited to one user and one program. In business management, particularly at higher levels of an organization, the problem-solving or decision-making process usually involves the interfaces among more than one functional area or problem domain (Chung 1985a). It is desirable to have one (creativity) facilitation program for each problem domain and to have these programs (and their users) interface with one another. With the architecture and technology of networking, such inter-program exchanges can be accomplished with little difficulty. The interfaces among different problem areas, with or without the use of computer programs, are themselves a creativity facilitation process. By exchanging ideas among different problem domains, people can look at their own problems from different angles. The interfacing process goes beyond the confidence intervals discussed earlier. Creativity can be brought about through the process of interdomain interfaces.

As Scott Morton (1983) pointed out, the research and development in DSSs (or MSSs) have been limited to a specific decision or a specific class of decisions. The facts that an organization is an integrated whole and that most decisions are related to one another have not been adequately addressed. Chung (1983, 1985a, 1985c) defined DSSs (or MSSs) as an integrated network of subsystem interfaces. Specifically, each subsystem of an organization (e.g., a functional area or a level of the organizational hierarchy) may have its own models for decision support. However, to enhance the effectiveness of managerial problem solving, it is necessary to interface the models of various subsystems. The facilitation of creativity and the enhancement of effectiveness can be considered the synergistic results of subsystem interfaces. Thus a multi-CFP environment would be most appropriate for the process of subsystem interfaces.

15.4   INTELLIGENT AND CREATIVE PROGRAMS (ICP)

An intelligent and creative program is able to generate creative ideas itself. This statement may be contrary to the beliefs of most ES (or AI) researchers, since many current developments in building ESs have resulted from attempts to deviate from this statement.

As Hayes-Roth, Waterman, and Lenat (1983) discussed, the early AI research was dominated by a naive belief that a few laws of reasoning coupled with powerful computers would produce expert and superhuman performance. Later, as experience accrued, the severely limited power of general-purpose problem-solving programs ultimately led many researchers to work on narrowly defined application programs (Ernst and Newell 1969; and Newell and Simon 1963, 1972). This is where the development of expert systems concept began.

Feigenbaum (1977) pointed out that the power of an expert system derives from the knowledge it possesses, not from the particular formalisms and inference schemes it employs. With the belief that "knowledge is power," tremendous efforts have been devoted to knowledge acquisition and the building of knowledge bases. Knowledge engineering then becomes an important research topic. Shifting the focus from an inference-based paradigm to a knowledge-based paradigm, most AI researchers believe that the power of an intelligent program to perform its task depends primarily on the quantity and quality of knowledge it has about the task (Buchanan and Feigenbaum 1982). In other words, the power of the intelligent program is limited by the quantity and quality of the knowledge supplied to the program. With this belief, AI researchers may have self-imposed some constraints on the capability of the program. This may also be the reason why creativity has not been an issue actively pursued by AI researchers.

This section explores the issues related to the design of a creative program. Feasibilities and difficulties in modeling creativity into an AI program will be addressed. Some lessons drawn from AM (Lenat 1976) and EURISKO (Lenat 1983a, 1983b) will be examined as will some reflections from the methodologies employed by these programs. AM and EURISKO are programs that were constructed as experiments in "learning by discovery." Although not designed with the purpose of seeking creativity, they are two of the few AI programs that are most relevant to the notion of creativity. We then examine some AI programs that simulate human information processing or cognitive processes. A typical example of such a program would be ACT by Anderson (1983). Finally, we summarize some design strategies for building creative AI programs.

15.4.1   AM and EURISKO

The AM program by Lenat (1976) was initially constructed as an experiment in "learning by discovery." AM discovers concepts and conjectures in elementary mathematics and set theory. Initially, AM is given a substantial knowledge base of 115 simple set-theoretic concepts. The concepts are represented internally as frames, each containing the same fixed set of slots or facets. The slots are used to store data related to concepts (e.g., its definition, examples, interestingness, etc.). Initially, most slots of most concepts are blank. AM uses a collection of 242 heuristic rules for guidance as it tries to fill in those blanks. The rules are organized in a production-system architecture. (For detailed discussions on this architecture, see Chapter 1 of this text). The heuristics are used to fill in slots of some concepts, to verify the contents of a slot for correctness and interestingness, to create new concepts, to add new tasks to the agenda, or to modify the interestingness of a task on the agenda. The search procedure of AM is a type of best-first search, since it always chooses the most interesting task from the agenda. AM has 59 heuristics for assessing the interestingness of concepts and tasks. The interestingness mechanism is the key to the function of the task agenda and the search process of AM. According to Cohen and Feigenbaum (1982), "Without heuristic guidance and the agenda mechanism, AM would be swamped by a combinatorial explosion of new concepts. However, the fact that it creates only 200 new concepts and that half of them are acceptable to a mathematician shows that its search is quite restricted."

In Section 15.2, we used the analogy of a modeling process and the notion of confidence interval to illustrate the concept of creativity. The choice of significant variables and relationships in building a model implies the use of a confidence interval for the chosen parameters. Due to the combinatorial nature of the possible choices, the number of the combinations eventually included in the model consists of only an extremely small portion of all the possible combinations. The variables and relationships not included in the model are those outside the confidence interval. These remote associations are usually the source of creativity. With the theoretically infinite number of possible combinations outside the confidence interval, the potential for creativity is virtually unlimited. The same analogy can be applied to the evaluation of AM.

The 59 heuristics for assessing the interestingness of concepts and tasks are designed based upon rational analysis by the designer of AM. These rules, as the guidelines for AM processing, represent the rules within the designer's confidence interval. Thus the application of these rules will not produce surprises in the sense that as long as the guidelines are followed no erratic behavior will occur. Certainly, it is rather difficult to judge whether the performance of AM has been overly constrained by these interestingness rules. However, these rules may have caused the suspicion that AM is simply "a large LISP program in which various procedures call each other in a partly pre-programmed way," (Ritchie and Hanna 1984). It is certainly necessary to have rules of one kind or another to guide the search or the processing of a program; otherwise, the program might wander around aimlessly or fall into the trap of combinatorial explosion. Nevertheless, overly restrictive guidance may limit the power and the potential for creativity of the program. Similarly, the blind trust in the power of knowledge, as advocated by many AI researchers of the knowledge-based paradigm, may unknowingly confine the power of the program by supplying too much knowledge to the program. The supposedly intelligent program then becomes less intelligent. Feigenbaum (1977) had a point when he said that the power of an expert system derives from the knowledge it possesses, not from the particular formalisms and inference schemes it employs. However, this may be true only for the designing of expert systems, and may not necessarily be plausible for the entire AI research. If the objective of AI research is to develop some intelligent (and creative) program, then it is certainly undesirable to rely on spoon-feeding (i.e., preprogrammed instructions) or to use too many do's and don'ts (i.e., too detailed guidelines and constraints). Albert Einstein once said, "Imagination is more important than knowledge." This statement should be seriously considered by all AI researchers.

We are not in the position to evaluate the AM's 59 heuristics for assessing interestingness. However, if these rules can be somewhat relaxed or refined, the potential for creativity may be enhanced. (Of course, it would be necessary to incorporate some other constraining methods to avoid the danger of aimless search). If too much emphasis is placed upon channeling the program's behavior, the machine intelligence would then be limited by human intelligence.

Lenat (Davis and Lenat 1982) stated, "AM is forced to judge a priori the value of each new concept, to lose interest quickly in concepts which aren't going to develop into anything. Often, such judgments can only be based on hindsight. For similar reasons, AM has difficulty formulating new heuristics that are relevant to the new concepts it creates. Heuristics are often merely compiled hindsight."

EURISKO (Lenat 1983a, 1983b) is an extension of AM with the task to learn new heuristics the same way AM learns new math concepts. The interestingness mechanism is not the focus of change in EURISKO—the AM's descendant. Instead, Lenat has found that a better representation plays a crucial and unique role in theory formation. In AM the heuristics were represented in "two opaque lumps of LISP code" (IF slot and THEN slot). In EURISKO, "a heuristic is—like a math concept always was in AM—a collection of about twenty or thirty slots, each filled with at most a line or two worth of code (often just an atom or a slot list" (Lenat and Brown 1984). This new representation is a functional decomposition of the program along two dimensions: slots and values. This leads to the assertion that theory formation is the mapping between form (i.e., the structures) and content (i.e., the meaning). The role of representation in theory formation is consistent with our earlier assertion that knowledge representation is an important factor in creativity. A new representation is, using the terms of Gestalt psychologists, a restructuring of the (whole) situation. Theory formation, like any creative act, is a restructuring of the forms and the mapping between forms and contents.

The progress from AM to EURISKO can be considered an enhancement of intelligence or creativity (if any) of the program. An important factor contributing to the progress would be the representation of heuristics. From the perspective of creativity, the significance of EURISKO research might be its underlying potential as a "model for cognition." According to Lenat and Brown (1984),

> The paradigm underlying AM and EURISKO may be thought of as the new generation of perceptrons, perceptrons based on collections or societies of evolving, self-organizing, symbolic knowledge structures. In classical perceptrons, all knowledge had to be encoded as topological networks of linked neurons, with weights on the links. The representation scheme being used by EURISKO provides much more powerful linkages, taking the form of heuristics about concepts, including heuristics for how to use and evolve heuristics. Both types of perceptrons rely on the law of large numbers, on a kind of local-global property of achieving adequate performance through the interaction of many small, relatively simple parts.

Creative thinking, as a special kind of human information processing, would be best addressed in the context of some cognitive models.

15.4.2 AI Programs for Cognitive Process

The AI approach to modeling the cognitive process can be traced all the way back to the endeavors of the information theorists such as Newell and Simon. The recent developments in cognitive science represent the increased interest in AI approaches to cognitive processes. Quite a few models of cognition have been developed and are important to the evolution of cognitive science. They include GPS by Newell and Simon (1963), Feigenbaum's EPAM (1963), Quillian's (1968) semantic memory model, the MEMOD model by Norman et al. (1975), HAM by Anderson and Bower (1973), and others. To explore the modeling of creativity, we only discuss here the adaptive control of thought (ACT) model by Anderson

(1976, 1983). All the other models have been comprehensively reviewed by Cohen and Feigenbaum (1982).

ACT is an extension of Anderson's human associative memory (HAM) program (Anderson and Bower 1973). While HAM is a model of human memory, ACT is designed as a general model of cognition. In order to simulate the control of the transition from thought to thought and to simulate its direction, ACT employs a production system architecture that consists of three memories: working, declarative, and production. The working memory of ACT is a short-term memory for active concepts. According to Anderson (1983), "working memory contains the information that the system can currently access, consisting of information retrieved from long-term declarative memory as well as temporary structures deposited by encoding process and the action of production." The production system formalism is used to represent human cognition as a set of condition-action pairs. The condition specifies some data patterns; and if elements matching these patterns are in working memory, then the production can apply. The action specifies what to do in that state. The basic action is to add new elements to working memory. Anderson called the production systems "cognitive S-R (stimulus-response) theories."

At any time, only parts of ACT's memory are active. Activation can spread through the declarative network as nodes activate adjacent nodes. A piece of information will become active to the degree that it is related to current sources of activation. Activation then is a relevancy heuristic for determining the importance of various pieces of information. In other words, the processing of the ACT program is guided by the activation mechanism. Therefore the key to creativity would be in fine tuning the rules constraining the activation mechanism. For example, with the assignment of "strength" of the connection between nodes, the current ACT program has been trying to minimize the occurrences of "remote associations." The capacity limit (i.e., the bottleneck, the constraints) on the processing of activation, not the activation itself, is a deterrent to creativity.

According to Anderson (1983), there are two reasons why activation is treated as a limited resource. First, imposing a limit on activation serves the computational function of forcing a choice among competing patterns. Second, activation may require the expenditure of finite metabolic resources even though its exact neural analog is unclear. The first reason was mainly a practical consideration in programming ACT. However, we believe the capacity limit can be increased as computer power is increased. The second reason for assuming limited capacity for activation would be valid to the extent that ACT attempts to simulate human cognitive process. From the point of view of enhancing the program's creativity, there is no need to assume that the machine (i.e., the program or the system) would have a limited amount of "cardiac output" as the human body does.

Parallelism in human cognition, which has not been incorporated in ACT, is another aspect that should be addressed in a creative program. The potential for creativity can be greatly enhanced with the inclusion of parallelism.

15.4.3 Some Strategies for Creative Programs

In this section, the examples of AM/EURISKO and ACT are used to explore various issues associated with modeling creativity into AI programs. Some strategies for designing a creative program are also summarized. This is only a suggested rather than an exhaustive (not even comprehensive) list.

1. The power of knowledge should not be overemphasized.

2. An oversupply of constraining rules in guiding the processing of the program should be avoided.

3. The formalism of problem (or knowledge) representation should be a design factor in enhancing the program's creativity.

4. A simulation of human cognitive process may be included in the program. However, the program need not be constrained by the limitations that have been applied to the human body.

5. Parallelism should be incorporated.

6. Like the case of creativity facilitation programs, it is desirable to build creative programs based upon the construct of (a network of) subsystem interfaces.

15.5 CONCLUSION

The purpose of this chapter was to explore the issues associated with modeling creativity for management support via AI approaches. In the process, a critical assessment of the research and development in AI and expert systems has been given as well.

We have investigated the nature of creativity and some issues associated with the design of AI programs that either enhance human creativity or possess the capability of being creative itself. We have seen that AI research (and expert systems development, in particular) has been somewhat constrained by the preoccupation with rational analysis and logical linkage. Although a computer program can be executed only in an "absolutely logical" way, this should not imply that in simulating the process of human information processing only the logical thinking process can be translated into the program. According to MacLeod (1962),

> Simon and his colleagues may be pardoned for having concentrated first on the simulation of clean, logical thinking. Thinking in its clearest form is easier to reproduce than is the ordinary muddy thinking in which most of us indulge . . . . When the machine can accurately replicate human stupidity in all its profundity, then we shall have a model that will enable us to test a theory of thinking as thinking actually taken place.

The shift away from the inference-based paradigm to a knowledge-based paradigm was mainly the result of perceiving the "severely limited power" of general-purpose problem-solving strategies (e.g., GPS). The focus of AI research may have been shifted. Nevertheless, the concentration on the "clean, logical thinking" has never been changed. It is true that AI does not require that an intelligent program demonstrate human intelligence. We, however, would suspect that the intelligence and the power of an AI program may have been "severely limited" by excluding the "muddy" (and possibly creative) thinking from the program.

The concentration on rational and logical thinking has not been unique to computer science and AI. For decades, people in MS/OR have been trying to capture the rationality in decision making. As Simon (1980) said, "One of the crowning achievements of the social sciences in the past two or three generations has been to elucidate the concept of rationality, a concept that is central to understanding human behavior."

In Section 15.2, we pointed out that the use of the modeling concept has implicitly incorporated a prerequisite of rationality. (This is also true in the use of simulation, statistical generalization, management science, or any quantitative analysis for decisions.) With the confinement of a confidence interval, most MS/OR/STAT techniques have addressed mainly the "efficiency" rather than the "effectiveness" problems. With the emphasis on rationality, we have been trying to minimize "surprises" and therefore quite possibly have excluded many creative ideas from our decision-making process. We certainly do not deny the value (or even the necessity) of these techniques for decision making. However, with the focus on rationality, have we left any room for creativity?

In the DSS literature, there has been an intentional focus on improving managerial effectiveness rather than managerial efficiency (Keen and Scott Morton 1978; and Moore and Chang 1983). However, creativity has never been a design consideration in the DSS literature. With models as an important element in DSS (Bonczek, Holsapple, and Whinston 1981; and Sprague and Carlson 1982) and with the limited modeling concept discussed previously, we suspect that the potential for improving managerial effectiveness may have been limited by excluding creativity as a DSS design factor.

On the other hand, with the increased attention received by the potential applications of AI and/or expert systems in supporting management (as evidenced by the publication of this text), the importance of incorporating creativity into the programs or systems that support management should not be overlooked. Care should also be taken in transferring the AI/ES technologies to management support systems. For example, the origination of expert systems was to provide automatic consulting systems for "specific problem domains." These domains are usually well defined. Unfortunately, in business management the problems are quite often less structured or unstructured. We may be able to define

FIGURE 15.1
THE ORGANIZATION OF EXPERT SYSTEMS INTERFACES

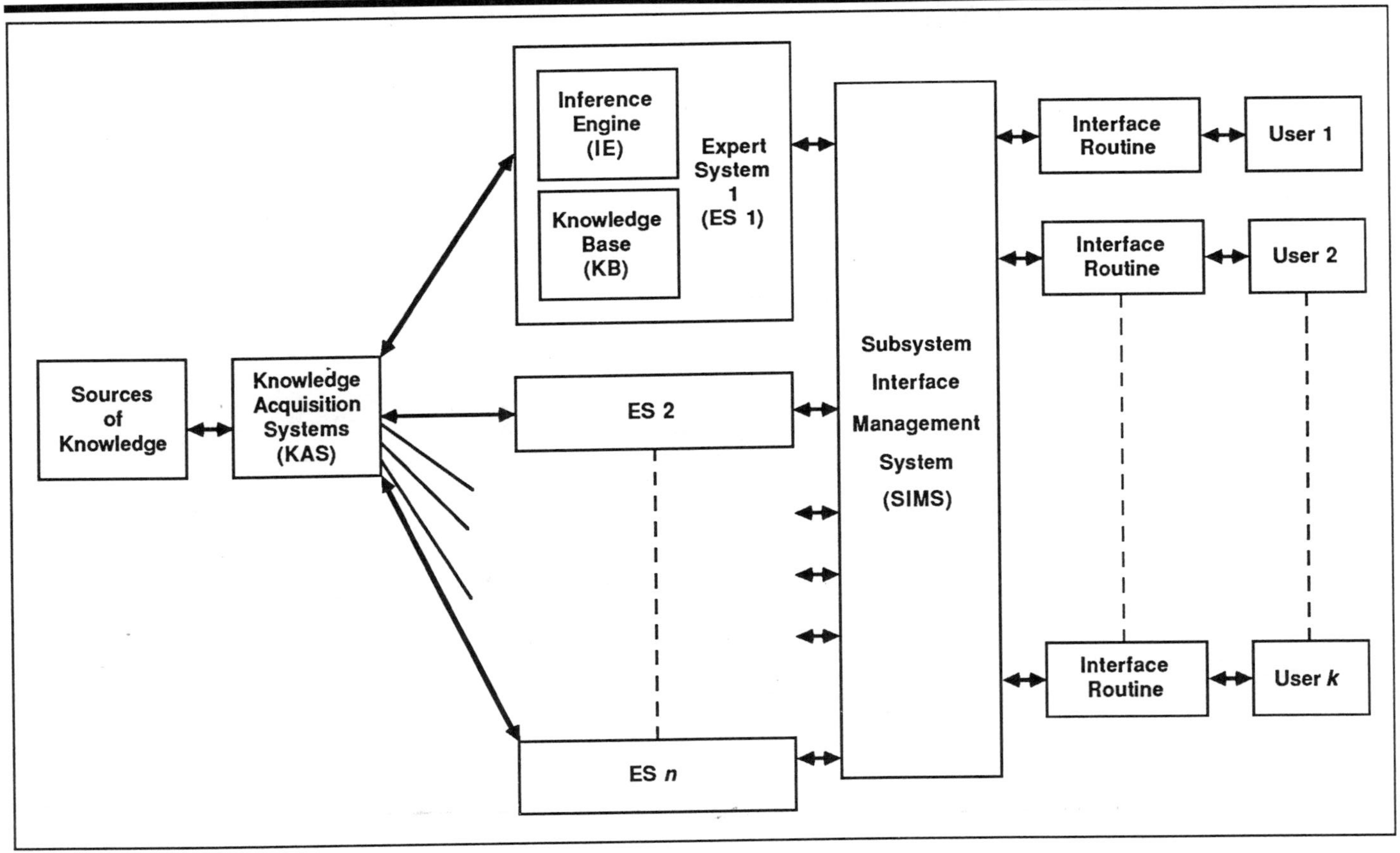

some specific decision problems, such as production planning, financial planning, and so forth. However, we can at best find suboptimal solutions to these problems. A global optimum for the overall organization is usually not guaranteed. Similarly, we may be able to find "experts" for individual problem areas. However, there is rarely an expert in management who can master every problem area. It is more practical to have a collection of experts who specialize in their own problem domains. To accomplish managerial effectiveness, these experts need to be coordinated and to interface with one another. A management support system is a network of subsystem interfaces. This same spirit should be applied to the introduction of expert systems into business management. Instead of a single expert system, a collection of expert systems, one (or more) for each problem domain, is needed. These expert systems then should be coordinated and integrated. Figure 15.1 depicts the organization of a group of expert systems under the environment of subsystem interfaces. These subsystem interfaces may bring about the enhancement of creativity. Thus the concept of subsystem interfaces should also be applied to the modeling of creativity for management support. That is, no matter whether we have a creativity facilitation program or a program that is itself creative, the programs should be built under the architecture of a network of subsystem interfaces so that managerial effectiveness can be enhanced.

REFERENCES

Ackoff, L., and Vergara, E. (1981), "Creativity in Problem Solving and Planning: A Review," *European Journal of Operational Research*, 7 (1): 1–13.

Anderson, J.R. (1976), *Language, Memory, and Thought*, Hillsdale, N.J.: Erlbaum.

Anderson, J.R. (1983), *The Architecture of Cognition*, Cambridge, Mass.: Harvard University Press.

Anderson, J.R., and Bower, G.H. (1973), *Human Associative Memory*, Washington, D.C.: Winston.

Aronofsky, A., ed. (1969), *Progress in Operations Research*, New York: John Wiley and Sons.

Bennett, J.L. (1983), *Building Decision Support Systems*, Reading, Mass.: Addison-Wesley.

Bonczek, R.H., Holsapple, C.W., and Whinston, B. (1981), *Foundations of Decision Support Systems*, New York: Academic Press.

Bruner, J.S. (1962), "The Conditions of Creativity," in H.E. Gruber, G. Terrell, and M. Wertheimer, eds., *Contemporary Approaches to Creative Thinking*, New York: Prentice-Hall.

Buchanan, B.G., and Feigenbaum, E.A. (1978), "DENDRAL and Meta-DENDRAL: Their Applications Dimension," *Artificial Intelligence*, 11 (1): 5–24.

Buchanan, B.G., and Feigenbaum, E.A. (1982), "Foreword," in R. Davis and D.B. Lenat, *Knowledge-Based Systems in Artificial Intelligence*, New York: McGraw-Hill.

Buchanan, B.G., and Shortliffe, E.H. (1983), *Rule-Based Expert Systems: The MYCIN Experiments of the Heuristic Programming Project*, Reading, Mass.: Addison-Wesley.

Chung, C.H. (1983), "The Design of Subsystem Interfaces for Decision Support Systems," paper presented at TIMS/ORSA Joint National Meeting, Chicago.

Chung, C.H. (1985a), "A Network of Management Support Systems," *OMEGA*, 13 (4): 263–276.

Chung, C.H. (1985b), "Towards A Computerized Creativity Facilitation Program," working paper, University of Kentucky.

Chung, C.H. (1985c), "Network of Subsystem Interfaces—A Framework for Research and Development in Management Support Systems," working paper, University of Kentucky.

Churchman, C.W. (1966), "Hegelian Inquiring Systems," internal working paper, no. 49, Space Science Laboratory, University of California at Berkeley.

Cohen, P.R., and Feigenbaum, E.A. (1982), *The Handbook of Artificial Intelligence*, vol. 3, Los Altos, Calif.: William Kaufmann.

Crutchfield, R.S. (1962), "Conformity and Creative Thinking," in H.E. Gruber, G. Terrell, and M. Wertheimer, eds., *Contemporary Approaches to Creative Thinking*, New York: Prentice-Hall.

Davis, R., and Lenat, D.B. (1982), *Knowledge-Based Systems in Artificial Intelligence*, New York: McGraw-Hill.

DeSanctis, G. (1984), "Computer Graphics as Decision Aids: Directions for Research," *Decision Sciences*, 15 (4): 463–487.

Drucker, P.F. (1954), *The Practice of Management*, New York: Harper & Row.

Duda, R.O., Gasching, J.G., and Hart, P.E. (1979), "Model Design in THE PROSPECTOR Consultant System for Mineral Exploration," in D. Michie, ed., *Expert Systems in the Micro-Electronic Age*, Edinburgh, Scotland: Edinburgh University Press.

Emshoff, J., and Mitroff, I.I. (1977), "On Strategic Assumption Making: A Dialectical Approach to Policy Analysis and Evaluation," working paper, Wharton Applied Research Center, University of Pennsylvania.

Ernst, G.W., and Newell, A. (1969), *GPS: A Case Study in Generality and Problem Solving*, New York: Academic Press.

Feigenbaum, E.A. (1963), "The Simulation of Verbal Learning Behavior," in E.A. Feigenbaum, and J.A. Feldman, eds., *Computers and Thought*, New York: McGraw-Hill.

Feigenbaum, E.A. (1977), "The Art of Artificial Intelligence: Themes and Case Studies of Knowledge Engineering," *Proceedings of The Fifth International Joint Conference on Artificial Intelligence*, 1014–1029.

Feigenbaum, E.A., and Feldman, J.A., eds. (1963), *Computers and Thought*, New York: McGraw-Hill.

Freud, S. (1970), "Creative Writers and Day Dreaming," in P.E. Vernon, ed., *Creativity*, Baltimore, Md.: Penguin.

Fromm, E. (1959), "The Creative Attitude," in H. Anderson, ed., *Creativity and Its Cultivation*, New York: Harper.

Gordon, W. (1961), *Synectics*, New York: Harper.

Gruber, H.E., Terrell, G., and Wertheimer, M., eds. (1962), *Contemporary Approaches to Creative Thinking*, New York: Prentice-Hall.

Guilford, J.P. (1977), *Way Beyond the I.Q.*, Buffalo, N.Y.: Creative Education Foundation.

Harlan, N.E., Christenson, D.J., and Vancil, R.F. (1962), *Managerial Economics: Text and Cases*, Homewood, Ill.: Richard D. Irwin.

Hayes-Roth, F., Waterman, D.A., and Lenat, D.B., eds. (1983), *Building Expert Systems*, Reading, Mass.: Addison-Wesley.

Kastner, J.K., and Hong, S.J. (1984), "A Review of Expert Systems," *European Journal of Operational Research*, 18 (3): 285–292.

Keen, P., and Scott Morton, M.S. (1978), *Decision Support Systems: An Organizational Perspective*, Reading, Mass.: Addison-Wesley.

Koestler, A. (1973), *The Act of Creation*, New York: Dell.

Lenat, D.B. (1976), "AM: An Artificial Intelligence Approach to Discovery in Mathematics as Heuristic Search," Ph.D. thesis, Stanford University.

Lenat, D.B. (1982), "The Nature of Heuristics," *Artificial Intelligence*, 19 (2): 189–249.

Lenat, D.B. (1983a), "Theory Formation by Heuristic Search, The Nature of Heuristics II: Background and Examples," *Artificial Intelligence*, 21 (2): 31–59.

Lenat, D.B. (1983b), "EURISKO: A Program that Learns New Heuristics and Domain Concepts, The Nature of Heuristics III: Program Design and Results," *Artificial Intelligence*, 21 (2): 61–98.

Lenat, D.B. (1984a), "Computer Software for Intelligent Systems," *Scientific America*, 251 (3): 204–213.

Lenat, D.B., and Brown, J.S. (1984b), "Why AM and EURISKO Appear to Work," *Artificial Intelligence*, 23 (3): 269–294.

Lindsay, R.K., Buchanan, B.G., Feigenbaum, E.A., and Lederberg, J. (1980), *Applications of Artificial Intelligence for Organic Chemistry: The DENDRAL Project*, New York: McGraw-Hill.

MacLeod, R.B. (1962), "Retrospect and Prospect," in H.E. Gruber, G. Terrell, and M. Wertheimer, eds., *Contemporary Approaches to Creative Thinking*, New York: Prentice-Hall.

Maier, N.R. (1970), *Problem Solving and Creativity*, Belmont, Calif.: Brooks/Cole.

Martin, W.A., and Fateman, R.J. (1971), "The MACSYMA System," in *Proceedings of the Second Symposium on Symbolic and Algebraic Manipulation*, Los Angeles, Calif.

Mason, R.O. (1968), "Dialectics in Decision Making: A Study in the Use of Counter Planning and Structured Debate in Management Information Systems," Ph.D. thesis, University of California at Berkeley.

McClelland, D.C. (1962), "On The Psychodynamics of Creative Physical Scientists," in H.E. Gruber, G. Terrell, and M. Wertheimer, eds., *Contemporary Approaches to Creative Thinking*, New York: Prentice-Hall.

Mednick, A.A. (1962), "The Associative Basis of the Creative Process," *Psychological Review*, 69 (3): 220–232.

Michie, D., ed. (1979), *Expert Systems in the Micro-Electronic Age*, Edinburgh, Scotland: Edinburgh University Press.

Minsky, M.L. ed. (1968), *Semantic Information Processing*, Cambridge, Mass.: MIT Press.

Moore, J.H., and Chang, M.G. (1983), "Meta-Design Considerations in Building DSS," in J.L. Bennett, ed., *Building Decision Support Systems*, Reading, Mass.: Addison-Wesley.

Mostow, J. (1984), "Rutgers Workshop on Knowledge-Based Design," *SIGART Newsletter*, 90 (October): 19–32.

Newell, A. (1969), "Heuristic Programming: Ill-Structured Problems," in A. Aronofsky, ed., *Progress in Operations Research*, vol. 3, New York: John Wiley and Sons, 360–414.

Newell, A., and Simon, H.A. (1963), "GPS: A Program that Simulates Human Thought," in E.A. Feigenbaum and J.A. Feldman, eds., *Computers and Thought*, New York: McGraw-Hill.

Newell, A., and Simon, H.A. (1972), *Human Problem Solving*, New York: Prentice-Hall.

Newell, A., Shaw, J.C., and Simon, H.A. (1962), "The Process of Creative Thinking," in H.E. Gruber, G. Terrell, and M. Wertheimer, eds., *Contemporary Approaches to Creative Thinking*, New York: Prentice-Hall.

Newell, A., Shaw, J.C., and Simon, H.A. (1957), "Empirical Exploration with the Logic Theory Machine: A Case History in Heuristics," *Proceedings of Western Joint Computer Conference*, pp. 218–239. Reprinted in Feigenbaum, E.A., and Feldman, J.A., eds., *Computer and Thought*, New York: McGraw-Hill.

Norman, D., Rumelhart, D.E., and the LNR Research Group (1975), *Explorations in Cognition*, San Francisco: Freeman.

Nugent, C.E., and Vollman, T.E. (1972), "A Framework for The System Design Process," *Decision Science*, 3 (1): 83–109.

Osborn, A.F. (1963), *Applied Imagination*, New York: Scribner's.

Pople, H.E. Jr. (1981), "Heuristic Methods for Imposing Structure On Ill-Structured Problems: The Structuring of Medical Diagnostics," in P. Szolovitz, ed., *Artificial Intelligence in Medicine*, American Association for the Advancement of Science, Boulder Colo.: Westview Press.

Pople, H.E. Jr., Myers, J.D., and Miller, R.A. (1975), "DIALOG: A Model of Diagnostic Logic for Internal Medicine," in *Proceedings of the Fourth International Joint Conference on Artificial Intelligence.*

Quillian, M.R. (1968), "Semantic Memory," in M.L. Minsky, ed., *Semantic Information Processing,* Cambridge, Mass.: MIT Press.

Ritchie, G.D., and Hanna, F.K. (1984), "AM: A Case Study in AI Methodology," *Artificial Intelligence,* 23 (3): 249–268.

Scott Morton, M.S. (1983), "State of The Art of Research in Management Support Systems," paper presented at the Colloquium on Information Systems, Harvard Business School.

Shortliffe, E.H. (1977), *Computer Based Medical Consultation: MYCIN,* New York: Elsevier.

Simon, H.A. (1980), "The Behavioral and Social Sciences," *Science,* 209 (4): 72–78.

Simon, H.A., and Feigenbaum, E.A. (1964), "An Information-Processing Theory of Some Effects of Similarity, Familiarization, and Meaningfulness in Verbal Learning," *Journal of Verbal Learning and Verbal Behavior,* 3 (5): 385–396.

Slagle, J.R. (1961), "A Heuristic Program That Solves Symbolic Integration Problems in Freshman Calculus: Symbolic Automatic Integrator (SAINT)," Ph.D. thesis, MIT.

Sprague, R.H. (1980), "A Framework for the Development of Decision Support Systems," *MIS Quarterly,* 4 (4): 1–26.

Sprague, R.H., and Carlson, E.D. (1982), *Building Effective Decision Support Systems,* Englewood Cliffs, N.J.: Prentice-Hall.

Stefik, M. (1981a), "Planning with Constraints (MOLGEN: Part1)," *Artificial Intelligence,* 16 (2): 111–139.

Stefik, M. (1981b), "Planning and Meta-Planning (MOLGEN: Part2)," *Artificial Intelligence,* 16 (2): 141–169.

Szolovitz, P., ed. (1981), *Artificial Intelligence in Medicine,* American Association for the Advancement of Science, Boulder, Colo.: Westview Press.

van Dam, A. (1984), "Computer Software for Graphics," *Scientific America,* 251 (3): 146–159.

Wertheimer, M. (1959), *Productive Thinking,* New York: Harper.

16

Automated Analogical Problem Solving and Expert Systems

Lance B. Eliot

This chapter introduces the manager to an emerging field of study in artificial intelligence: automated analogical problem solving. Expert systems have been characterized as brittle and lacking in the reuse of prior experiences; the coupling of an expert system with an automated analogical problem solver holds great promise as one solution to these weaknesses. Using the expert system adoption design provided in Chapter 1, this chapter examines a simple illustration of binding an automated analogical component with an expert system. Prior research on analogy as a form of human cognition, and the development of analogy in automation, is traced and provides a useful survey of the field.

16.1 INTRODUCTION

Studies of human problem solving frequently reveal the pervasiveness of analogy usage (Sternberg 1977), yet few studies of human behavior have concentrated on analogy as a particular cognitive strategy. Fewer still are the automated systems that make use of a systematized analogical process as a problem-solving technique. This chapter is a review of current understanding of the analogical thinking process, its implementation as computer-based automation, and its future potential in developing expert systems.

Analogies, whether studied as human or computer based, have important implications for management. Peters and Waterman (1982) have identified the importance of intuition, decision rules, and heuristics in their analysis of managers and organizations. Their findings suggested that the starting point of decision making, at least in sorting through information, was with heuristics such as associations, metaphors, and analogs. Studying analogy as a form of decision making may lead to improved understanding of management behavior and could provide a foundation for new expert systems to conduct certain managerial tasks.

The use of an automated analogical system, coupled with an expert system, will be illustrated by expanding the expert system described in Chapter 1. Chapter 1 provided a simple expert system that could offer advice on selecting problems that are appropriate for expert system adoption. As indicated in the first chapter, the expert system fulfilled three key features required of an expert system, namely: (1) it is able to ask about the particular problem of concern; (2) it can render an opinion regarding the problem and possibly reach a solution to the problem; and (3) it can elaborate on its decision by some explanation mechanism.

Yet, consider the repeated use of the Chapter 1 expert system in its presently designed state. If this system were used to evaluate a series of expert system adoption situations, what would it "know" about the different situations and their specific circumstances? Would the system learn from a previous experience that one rule, such as the success rule "top management supports an expert system approach," could be abrogated by an impending management change in the organization? Or, would the system realize that in the context of an R&D expert system development effort, that perhaps the entire set of rules in optimality is not as critical as the success rule set?

These selected rule questions are not as important as the theme underlying them, that is, the expert system should be able to "learn" as it proceeds to solve problems and reuses the problem-solving process. Obviously, there are several ways in which the expert system can be instructed to evolve from its prior experiences. This chapter considers one important approach—the use of an automated analogical problem-solving component that works with the expert system to solve the overall problem of concern.

Three sections will be used to describe analogy and expert systems development. First, a brief history of analogy as a research topic is supplied. Much of the research on analogy has appeared in literature on cognition and developmental psychology. A separate focus on analogy has been treated in the computer science literature, with only minor reference made to prior studies on humans and analogy performance. Section 16.3 examines recent advances in computer technology, especially in artificial intelligence, that have revealed the value of analogylike techniques in constructing intelligent systems. Section 16.4 merges expert system development with various aspects of studies on analogy. These analogy aspects arise from the two major strands of study on analogy given in Section 16.2 (how do humans use analogies) and Section 16.3 (how have computer systems been programmed to make use of analogies). Finally, Section 16.5 proposes future recommendations for managers, researchers, and expert system developers.

16.2   HISTORY OF ANALOGY STUDIES

Leatherdale (1974) has extensively examined the history of analogy and provided a probing analysis of its role in science. Analogy has historically been an overloaded term. Analogy may be used to signify things related by a relation or may be used to signify a relation itself. Jevons (1958) argued that analogy has been used primarily as a resemblance between the relations of things, not between things themselves. Mill (1949) suggested that it is more common to treat analogy as a wider range of resemblances.

Leatherdale determined that analogy has traditionally been defined as a resemblance between two things, either as (1) a general unanalysed resemblance between two things, or (2) a resemblance in an intermediate experience form. The former, (imported analogy) is the kind reported by a flash of insight that may accompany an analogy discovery, while the latter (manifest analogy) is analogy as normally discussed in logic.

Logic, such as induction, makes use of analogy at a common sense level and has been described as using manifest analogy (Heese 1963). Analogy in logic, starting as a mathematical ratio, has gradually evolved to a much wider meaning (Sternberg 1977). Bacon (1960) traced the development of the scientific method and indicated that manifest analogy may have served as the root for development of science and the scientific method. The most notable initial use of the analogy concept was in the 1400s by Aristotle. Aristotle has often been credited with development of both analogy and metaphor concepts (Lloyd 1966). Generally, analogy is considered a more fundamental concept and simpler than the metaphor (see Miller 1979 for a comprehensive distinction).

Leatherdale argued that manifest analogy has not played a critical role in the history of science. This common sense level of analogy was not sufficient to lead to scientific progress; instead, imported analogy shares greater responsibility. Imported analogy, also known as creative analogy, has been used for scientific discoveries (Hadamard 1949) that frequently require novel perceptions (Nyman 1953). For example, Galileo (1957) recognized and used the analogy of motion of a ship to make discoveries in another subject, that of projectiles.

Imported analogies do not suddenly appear, according to Leatherdale, rather they are amorphous entities that breed and fully form over long periods of time. Discrete areas of thought may be brought together, ranging from areas quite similar to very remote ones. Imported analogy requires multidimensional insight and nonlinear thinking. Even superficial analogies may be of significance (Moles 1957). A simple analogy may cascade into other inferences and reveal a whole new perspective (similar to scientific discovery as identified by Kuhn 1962).

Leatherdale defined an analogical act as the process of noticing, perceiving, or attending to an analogy. First, there must be recognition that an analogy should be formed. Next, reformulation occurs. Reformulation consists of importing an analog from some other area of experience and applying it to a topic analog. A topic analog resides in a knowledge area for which some reordering or explanation is sought. Usually, the imported analog is from a familiar domain that is of relevance to the topic domain.

Oppenheimer (1956) described analogy as the similarity of structure involving two sets of particulars that are different, yet have structured parallels. He argued that these structuring elements are artifacts discovered in the world and not just invented. One example he provided of analogy used in this fashion was the Babylonian predictions of astronomical events. The Babylonians constructed the needed mathematical regularities without an understanding of celestial mechanics, but the regularities did reflect their observations, patterns, and predictions.

Sternberg (1977) has conducted important research and surveyed prior literature on analogical reasoning. Using an information-processing paradigm for studying human behavior (Simon 1976), Sternberg proposed a meta-theoretical framework on research in problem solving and used analogy as a field of study for his framework development. Sternberg's framework examined specific aspects of cognition and analogs by postulating that there are identifiable elementary information processes that operate upon internal representations of objects or symbols (an elementary information process is called a *component*).

Components have properties (e.g., duration, difficulty, probability), functions (e.g., meta-component, performance acquisition, retention, and transfer), and levels of generality (e.g., general, class, specific). Sternberg concentrated on components used during analogical reasoning in problems of the A is to B as C is to D type (e.g., $A:B :: C:D$), where D is omitted as part of the task problem. Analogies of $A:B :: C:D$ form have served an important role in studies of intelligence and IQ (Piaget 1970; and Spearman 1923).

Sternberg emphasized the need for research with practical implications, since the little that is currently known regarding components is based on tasks that may not require true real-world performances. Yet, his studies of analogy, using an $A:B :: C:D$ form, may suffer from a lack of realism. Gick and Holyoak (1980, 1983) argued that Sternberg focused on analogical reasoning, not analogical problem solving. Analogical problem solving involves complex analogies that extend beyond a simple proportion form.

After some initial hypotheses were tested through several experiments, Gick and Holyoak developed a framework for studying analogical problem solving. Their framework makes use of mappings, schemas, and semantic retrieval rules to describe the cognitive processes that appear to occur during an analogy problem-solving process. Work by Gick and Holyoak follows similar studies by researchers examining analogies in geometry (Polya 1957) and geography (Collins et al. 1975) and makes use of current theories of schema-based models (Rumelhart 1975; Schank and Abelson 1977; and Thorndyke 1977).

Gick and Holyoak defined analogical problem solving as consisting of four essential steps: (1) build a mental representation of a base problem and solution and build a target base; (2) notice that some aspect of the target serves as a retrieval cue linking back to the base; (3) map the base and target; and (4) generate an analogous solution, or extended mapping, for the target. These steps may occur in parallel and on several levels of abstraction. In order to describe an analogy, their framework makes use of a special notation combining propositional functions, predicates, relations, and labeled arcs.

According to Gick and Holyoak, skilled analogical problem solving requires identifying both analogous and disanalogous elements that are embedded in the base and target. Mapping relations may be successful (known as *mapped identities* and *structure-preserving differences*) or potentially problematic mapping failures (known as *structure-violating differences* and *indeterminate correspondences*). A complete analogy is an isomorphism without mapping failures, with all of the mappings between identities or between structure preserving differences. An analogy with mapping failures is an incomplete analogy.

Empirical research covered by Gick and Holyoak has examined four topics regarding analogical problem solving: (1) establishment that problem solvers in certain domains can use analogies to generate solutions; (2) establishment of the separation of noticing and application acts; (3) exploration of the factors involved in single-base transfer; and (4) exploration of the factors involved in multiple-base transfer.

Analogies may be misapplied and be both a benefit and a cost to problem solving (Gilovich 1981). Although analogies may direct problem searches into a direction away from a solution, they may also lead the way out of a path that does not lead to a solution (Reed, Ernst, and Banerji 1974). An analogy may also be expository, that is, it may be used as a descriptive mechanism whether an analogy is present or not, as was used by informants in a hospital capital budgeting case analyzed by Meyer (1983, 1984).

Organizational development researchers Woodworth and Nelson (1979) identified an analogy between organizational development and the curing rituals of primitive people. Their analogy was used to stimulate creative thought concerning approaches to organizational theory. Keidel (1984) studied the use of sports analogies by managers as managers explain organizational performance. Use of such analogies provide terminology for explaining the actions of organizations, and, as argued by Keidel, they can significantly shape management behavior in perceiving organizational events and decisions.

One amusing example of analogy use in an organizational setting was that reported by Anderson (1975) in which designers were trying to develop a dripless catsup bottle. After some difficulty in developing such a bottle, the designers considered certain biological features of a horse and formed an analogy leading them to a double inner and outer opening for the bottle problem. Biological analogies, including this bottle design case, have been previously reported by Gordon (1961) and Mawardi (1959).

The history of analogy suggests that the pervasiveness of analogies is apparent, yet cognitive processes that underlie analogies are still not well understood. Prior cognition research focused on analogical reasoning processes concerning $A:B :: C:D$ problems, which appear to be less complex, and perhaps different, from those found in analogical problem solving. Recent attention in analogy research has begun to examine a wider spectrum of behavior used in solving full analogies dealing with real-world situations.

16.3 AUTOMATED ANALOGICAL COMPONENTS AND SYSTEMS

Carbonell (1983) has reviewed previous studies of analogical systems as reported in computer science literature (e.g., Kling 1971; and Winston 1980) and indicated that very few such systems have been constructed or even investigated. He argued that analogy has a central role in human inference and provides a powerful computational mechanism for artificial intelligence applications. Yet most, if not all, traditional artificial intelligence models used for problem solving lack any capability for using prior experiences in solving new problems.

Carbonell proposed that an analogical inference engine could be incorporated into artificial intelligence models. His engine might be used in simplified versions of real-world problem-solving situations. New problem situations that did not have a prior analog would be unable to make use of the analogical inference engine. An engine of this kind could be supported by other standard problem-solving techniques such as those described in Newell and Simon (1972).

A general problem-solving process could link to the engine as needed. Carbonell proposed that the engine consist of two phases: (1) reminding and (2) transforming. *Reminding* serves to recall previous problem/solution pairs and computes similarities to a current problem. A final similarity metric would be calculated that included four analogy aspects: (1) the initial state of the new problem and the initial state of the recalled problem, (2) the final states of each, if available, (3) the path constraints of each, and (4) the applicability score based on preconditions.

Transforming, a term for the second phase of Carbonell's engine, takes a recalled problem/solution sequence and transforms it into a new problem/solution that satisfies the new criteria. Thus the transform problem space will contain an initial state (the solution from the recalled problem) and a goal state (the solution specification for solving the new problem). Transform operators are used in the problem space to map one solution sequence into another sequence in an effort to solve the new problem.

Carbonell identified many transform operators, including processes such as general insertion, general deletion, sub-sequence splicing, subgoal preserving substitution, operator reordering, sequence inversion, and others. A difference metric is calculated and tested throughout the transformation procedure and allows systematic control of transform operator usage. Generally, the greater the store of prior related experiences, the greater power the engine has in contributing to a problem-solving process.

An interesting derivation emerges from Carbonell's inspection of his own proposal. He identified that the engine could be modified to receive both a positive exemplar set (successful analogies) and a negative exemplar set (unsuccessful analogies) and be required to learn by example in order to formulate a generalized plan. The engine and its parent problem-solving system could equally call on one another in a recursive fashion. Simon (1976) has indicated that problem solvers may proceed in a problems-within-problems fashion; in other words, stages unfold in a cyclical manner from what is the problem to what are the alternatives and back to what is the problem.

Carbonell (1981) has described the construction of a system, known as POLITICS, that plans against adversaries using counterplanning strategies in international politics. Planning and the development of counterplans led to his research on automated analogical systems. Developing a parser to examine a sentence and discover metaphors (a related issue to analogical problem solving) was examined by Carbonell (1982) and provided several interesting ideas for codifying knowledge to represent metaphors.

Evans (1968) developed one of the first significant analogy problem-solving systems. His program solved geometric analogies, yet had arguable grounding in relation to human behavior to solving such problems (Dreyfus 1979). Winston (1980) constructed an analogy system to demonstrate that simple situations could be analyzed with a computerized analogy program. Again, his system was based on a questionable interpretation of how humans solve analogies. Yet, it provided important insight into how such a program (one performing in an apparently analogical manner) could be implemented. Key ingredients identified included: extensible relations representation, importance-dominated matching, analogy-driven constraint learning, analogy-driven learning, and classification-exploiting hypothesizing.

Kling (1971) developed a small analogical reasoning system using a computer program called ZORBA. Kling's work was also one of the first significant attempts at programming the analogy process. ZORBA was essentially a heuristic program that took theorem pairs, as stated in a form of predicate calculus, and generated simple analogies between them. Although his system was designed using behavioral paradigms of analogical reasoning, many severe limitations existed both in behavioral explanations that constituted analogical processes and in the computer program itself.

Stelzer (1983) has developed a mathematical form for constructing analogies across subject matters. His axiomatic approach classifies analogous relationships into types and parallels some research on human analogy classifications. Silverman (1985) has performed similar work on analogical problem solving by working forward from behavioral aspects, focusing on experienced practitioners in a systems-engineering domain, to develop a problem behavior graph that could then be used to create a production system. The work by Silverman represents a renewed effort in constructing automated analogical systems using as a basis some understanding, even if incomplete, of the human analogical problem-solving process.

16.4 EXPERT SYSTEMS AND ANALOGICAL PROBLEM SOLVING

Prior work on automated analogical problem solving has focused on automating analogies for isolated tasks and generally has not attempted to couple together expert systems and analogical problem solving. Currently, there are three dominant modes in which such a coupling might take place: (1) the use of analogical problem solving as an expert technique within the domain of concern; (2) the use as a connector to another expert system or at least to other domains of knowledge; and (3) the use as an expository device during man-machine interaction, particularly during the expert knowledge acquisition stage or during the end-user explanatory stage.

Chapter 1 characterized expert systems as brittle, narrow focused, and unable to reason from first principles, analogies, or common sense. Automated analogical problem solving can lead to expert systems that are less brittle and may allow potentially more robust systems in their ability to solve new problems that resemble old ones. Another advantage in developing analogies is that thinking about analogies requires even further elicitation of a problem than just considering the rules and facts of an expert system itself. Providing the necessary structure and data to an automated analogical engine may reveal facets of a problem situation that were previously not considered.

The three modes of automated analogy and expert system coupling are each complicated in their own respective constructions. The first mode, use of automated analogical problem solving as an expert technique, will be examined by expanding on the Chapter 1 expert system design. The other two modes will be described in a generic fashion following the expanded design. It is these last two modes that are linked to the future frontier of expert systems as it affects the use of expert systems in management (as described in Chapter 1). Specifically, the frontier consists of at least three requirements: (1) enhancing the language system to allow more natural input, (2) providing readily convertible written inputs, and (3) interfacing with existing computerized aids.

In the introduction to this chapter, several questions were posed regarding the ability of the expert system to "learn." Of course, human intervention on the part of a knowledge engineer, whose job would be to change the rules themselves, is one way that the system could be modified. But the expert system would merely reflect the learning of the knowledge engineer and not its own form of internal learning. Requiring a knowledge engineer's constant intervention could be both costly and problematic (e.g., the engineer might unintentionally insert erroneous rules if having to continually update the system).

One automated alternative would be to include meta-rules. Meta-rules represent rules about rules in the knowledge base. Thus a well-developed set of meta-rules could help control the use of the knowledge base by the system itself during the problem-solving process. Humans exhibit the use of meta-rules during problem solving. For example, a manager might monitor his or her own progress during an expert system adoption consideration and conclude that relevancy rules were of little concern in the last project and that certain features of the new project also suggest that the relevancy rules probably do not apply in this newer context.

Unfortunately, meta-rules often require additional rules regarding the meta-rules themselves — a kind of meta-rule on meta-rules. This cyclical requirement can continue, requiring more and more rule additions to the knowledge base and further complicating the problem-solving process in a loosely structured manner.

A formalized and structured form of capturing the essence of the needed meta-rules could be accomplished through an automated analogical component. Seven basic steps can be used in adopting the automated analogical component:

1. Determine the vital data elements.

2. Determine the mapping relationships among data elements identified in step 1.

3. Select the analogical inference engine.

4. Provide the new problem.

5. Invoke the analogical inference engine, which then renders analogies.

6. The end-user asks questions concerning resultant analogies.

7. The analogical component updates its analogies knowledge base.

Steps 1 through 3 are static steps that are done once for a specific domain and expert system, while steps 4 through 7 are dynamic steps that reoccur with each usage of the automated analogical component. Analogies are represented here in problem-solution pairs, and the initial two steps establish the structure of these pairs.

Chapter 1 described an expert system to aid in deciding when an expert system adoption would be appropriate. The design already depicts data elements, such as length of time for solving the chosen problem (found in a feasibility rule), and these same entities will be used for the problem portion of problem-solution pairs. Solutions currently are rather simplistic, a yes or no indicating whether the adoption is warranted, but they could be enhanced by adding additional data elements.

Each adoption situation, no matter whether a "success" of yes to adopt or a "failure" of not to adopt, might also include other items in the solution structure. For example, a "yes" adoption could require that after the expert system is adopted actual project data, such as number of rules in the resulting expert system, be included with the problem-solution pair for the particular project. Subsequently, new problems might be able to explore meaningful results from the expert system beyond a "yes" (adopt) or "no" (do not adopt) decision.

Besides establishment of problem-solution pairs, there is the need to elicit mapping relationships among data elements. There are horizontal mapping relationships and vertical mapping relationships. Horizontal relationships reach across problem-solution pairs and serve as the basis for measuring the correspondence between one problem and another problem (and their solutions too). Vertical relationships tie problem-solution pairs together within themselves and represent how data elements within a pair are related to one another.

The Chapter 1 expert system contained a series of feasibility rules. A horizontal relationship could be established between one specific rule and the same specific rule in another pair. For example, a problem that typically takes a few minutes to solve may be considered mapped with great similarity to another problem that also takes a few minutes, and it may be mapped with less similarity to a problem that takes hours to solve. The analogical inference engine would make use of this horizontal mapping relationship as part of a decision as to whether two given problems are analogically related to one another.

Is it critical that two problems be similar in the amount of time required to solve them, in order to be considered analogically related here? First, before answering the question, notice that merely asking this question brings up an issue that probably was not raised when the rule itself was formed by a knowledge engineer. Having to specify the complete structure of the analogies tends to cause elicitation beyond the scope of the original expert system rule construction alone.

In any case, this specific rule dealing with time of the task being considered may not be a critical element to match. Recall that analogies have successful matches (i.e., mapped identities and structure-preserving differences) and potential failure matches (i.e., structure-violating differences and indeterminate correspondences). Here, the time rule may be a successful match even if the times are greatly dissimilar; this would be allowed as long as the relationship established allows a structure-preserving difference to exist between this rule in two different problems.

Difference metrics are used to calculate and compare data elements and their mapping relationships. The metric values serve the same purpose as certainty factors described in Chapter 1. They are convenient and easily manipulated formalisms for "intuitive" judgments that must be used by the automated analogical component. A simple scale of -100 to $+100$ might be used to represent mapping degrees, with thresholds for successes and failures (i.e., less than zero might be structure-violating differences, zero might be indeterminate correspondences, up to $+20$ might be structure-preserving differences, and $+20$ to $+100$ might be used for mapped identities).

The analogical inference engine searches for analogies and uses the problem-solution structure selected in steps 1 and 2 given previously. The analogical inference engine is a general mechanism and relies on the data elements and mapped relationships to reflect the specifics of the domain (in the same way that an expert system has a general inference engine mechanism and reflects the domain through the facts and rules). An analogical inference engine may employ various techniques for finding analogies. Two techniques, forward examination and backward examination, are quite simple and will be illustrated with the expert system adoption domain.

Suppose an expert system adoption decision was being made for a company known as the Thompson Corporation. Further, assume that the corporation had already made the adoption decision 40 separate times, with 8 actual projects being adopted. Thus the analogies to be used consist of 40 problem-solution pairs, each pair containing data elements and mapped relationships created specifically for the expert system adoption domain. Eight pairs contained "yes" adoptions, while 32 contained "no" adoptions (i.e., their solutions indicated "yes" or "no").

Using forward examination, the analogical inference engine would inspect each problem-solution pair and compare each old problem to the new problem under consideration. Forty problem-to-problem inspections would occur, and the resulting comparisons would lead to a final analogy metric indicating the degree of correspondence for each problem to problem. The analogical inference engine would then report on the pairs and rank them according to their correspondences.

Returning to the Thompson Corporation example, suppose the engine discovered 6 problem-solution pairs with high correspondence to the current problem, 14 with low correspondence, and the remaining 20 with virtually no correspondence. Assume that the 6 high correspondences were all "no" adoption decisions. The results would seem to lend evidence to a "no" decision (i.e., experience suggests that similar adoption considerations have all led to a "no" adoption). If the expert system arrived at the "no" conclusion via its direct solving process, then both procedures provide even stronger support for a "no" vote.

Using backward examination, the engine would inspect problem-solution pairs in a manner different from the forward examination. The engine would first be given a proposed solution to the new problem, and then the engine would inspect full pairs (i.e., both solutions with solutions and problems with problems). The engine would select matching solutions first and then proceed to inspect problems. Finally, a ranking and reporting would be provided by the engine.

Thus, using the Thompson Corporation example again, suppose that the "yes" adoption was an answer proposed for a new problem of adoption. The engine would preselect the 8 projects containing the "yes" adoption solution and then proceed to compare only those potentially analogous problem-solution pairs. Rather than inspecting each pair in an exhaustive fashion, the engine starts in essence at the end ("here is what I want to get to") and proceeds to find problems with data elements and mapped relationships that best match the current problem.

Where did the current problem and its potential solution come from? Step 4 in the seven basic steps to automated analogical development indicated the need to provide a given problem. An automated analogical system acting on a stand-alone basis would probably have a natural language front-end processor to allow input of a given problem from a human user. An expert system attached to an automated analogical component would pass the appropriate items to the analogical inference engine, and the expert system would contain rules concerning the use of the analogical component.

The expert system would not have to always make use of the analogical component, just as a human problem solver may decide to "do it by formula" alone. This especially could be true if few analogies were available or if the certainty factor derived by direct method was so high that the expert system assumed little additional evidence was needed from another problem-solving technique.

In these analogical inference engine examples, the case of a "no" vote by one unit, perhaps the expert system by its direct rules, and a "yes" by the other, here the analogical component, would present a conflict in the decision-making process. Human problem solvers must confront the same possibility (a kind of "the formula says one thing, but my experience tells me another" cognition problem). How would these conflicts be resolved in the automation? The answer depends on the kind of binding between the expert system and the analogical component.

Current sophistication of analogical systems and expert systems indicates that for the time being an analogical component will probably serve as an adjunct to the expert system decision-making process. Recall that true analogical problem solving requires the ability to notice that an analogy may be fitting in a given situation, while here the expert system makes use of the component on a rather blind basis (essentially omitting the notice act and proceeding directly to the application act). Eventually, there may be a blending of analogical components directly into expert systems, as opposed to automated analogy serving as a slave problem solver.

Steps 6 and 7 of the automated analogy development complete the decision-making process. First, step 6 indicates that the analogical reporting should be able to explain its "reasoning" process. This would be accomplished by displaying the appropriate data elements and mapped relationships for analogically related pairs. A user may wish to see successful high corresponding pairs as well as the failures, or less corresponding pairs. The explanatory feature could be stand-alone, or it could act through the expert system explanatory capabilities.

Returning once again to the Thompson Corporation, the manager obtaining 6 high corresponding pairs, 14 low ones, and 20 with almost no correspondence might be curious as to why the 20 other adoption consideration situations were so different. Perhaps there is an error on the part of the manager in describing the current situation and minor changes would make it more like previous situations. Or perhaps this new situation, which at first seemed to be just another usual problem, contains aspects that should be monitored carefully due to their uniqueness. The conventional expert system designed in Chapter 1 would have reported a yes or no decision with a certainty factor and could indicate the rules used to lead to that decision, but it would not be able to provide much insight as to how this problem stacks up against prior problems.

Finally, step 7 completes the analogical component by requiring the storage of the new pair, increasing the problem-solution knowledge base. A fully automated analogical component would also update its knowledge regarding problem-solution pairs. Updating would include the incorporation of additional patterns reflecting new relationships between previously stored pairs and the new pairs and would bring about changes in mapped relationships and data elements dynamically.

This expansion of the first chapter expert system was meant to suggest how an automated analogical component might work coupled with an existing expert system. An expert developing an expert system is likely to reflect on previous expert systems projects when considering a new development project. The expert might make use of a general framework directly (as given in Chapter 1), yet the expert might also compare circumstances of the new project with those of old ones. Thus the analogical component adds a new dimension by allowing a greater context sensitivity to problems. The analogical component described is illustrative of current work in the automated analogy field, although many complex issues were not covered due to the simplicity of the illustration.

16.5   OTHER MODES

The previous example focused on automated analogy as an expert technique. Two other modes, automated analogy as a connector to other expert systems or knowledge bases and automated analogy as a man-machine interfacing mechanism, are briefly explored next.

Using analogical problem solving in a man-machine interaction mode could provide a powerful explanation scheme. In discussing a problem and its solution to the user, a sympathetic analysis might be provided (i.e., in terms that the user can understand and perceive in a sensible fashion) in order to help a user "get across" the issue being explained (see Rumelhart and Norman 1981). As well, the analogical feature could be used to store expert judgments provided by users, or perhaps other expert systems, and to build upon its own expert knowledge base.

Various types of expert systems, such as interpretation systems, prediction systems, and others, could make use of an analogical problem-solving feature. Development of an expert system normally requires the investigation of human expert behavior in a particular domain. A knowledge engineer might use analogies to discover and codify expert knowledge. In fact, an initial expert system might be constructed for a selected domain by a knowledge engineer and then allowed to learn by analogy as an expert describes additional problems and solutions.

A superior expert system would be able to make statements about its own knowledge and to decide when analogies serve as a cost or benefit to a decision process. Human behavior has been described as using analogies both successfully and unsuccessfully. Even an automated analogical problem-solving system would be expected to produce both successful and unsuccessful analogies; although it should be prevented from acting on unsuccessful analogies, while not ignoring the possibilities that such analogies may pose in solving later problems.

Several dangers exist for construction and use of automated analogical features. Just as behavioral research suggested that human experts suffer from reasoning biases, so might a similarly performing analogy system. Incorrect inferences may be made, and remain uncovered, in a vast store of analogies. Further, these inferences may reappear in sets of analogies and remain hidden for awhile, providing short-term satisfactory results yet possibly resurfacing in long-term decision making. Backing out of analogies is just one topic area of human analogical problem solving that is still poorly understood.

Unfortunately, the current generation of expert systems provides little evidence in the linkage between analogical problem solving and expert system construction and modification. Additionally, expert systems are often suspect due to a lack of confirmed behavioral foundation for their behavior, that is, is an expert system really performing in the same manner as a true expert? Recent advances in analogical problem-solving research, as identified in previous sections, may lead to a new generation of expert systems.

Silverman (1983) proposed a problem-processing system that would prompt a user for information, search for analogs, and provide appropriate problem results. A prototype expert system, known as INNOVATOR, has been described by Silverman (1985) and is intended to serve as an aid to management during modeling and simulation.

An alternative paradigm for expert system construction proposed by Coombs and Alty (1984) focused on discovery learning. An expert system, in their view, should act as an advisor rather than a director. They argued that human experts are often called upon to support problem solving, not act as problem solvers per se. A knowledge-based system following a guidance mode would have different priorities from a traditional expert system. Their prototype, MINDPAD, suggested how a guidance system would be constructed.

A computer program called TIMM, described by Kornell (1984), automated certain aspects of knowledge acquisition. A critical feature of the program was an inference procedure that modeled human analogical thinking. The system could generate plausible events in the domain and then interact with a user to determine the success of its generations. Future new situations could be codified into the knowledge base as a result of the programs' "learning," and the expert system could be less fragile. Kornell argued that most current expert systems tend to make unpredictable inferences at the edge of their knowledge domains, while an analogical inference engine could allow a more graceful degradation.

16.6 CONCLUSION

This chapter has described analogies in both human and machine formations. Automated analogical problem solving as a component to link with expert systems was reviewed and illustrated by expanding the expert system design given in Chapter 1. Analogical problem solving holds great promise as an automation tool, particularly in its capacity to make expert systems less brittle and more capable to accept inputs, render robust decisions, and explain internal reasoning processes.

Davis (1984), providing an important caution, warns that there is no philosopher's stone that will solve problems across all problem domains, and analogical problem solving is certainly not a philosopher's stone. Instead, analogical thinking is a pervasive form of human thought that should be considered in the development of expert systems. Expert systems can make use of both prior behavioral research and prior computer analogy systems.

There is a common story told concerning a research project that sought to develop an artificial intelligence system to control a robot arm for stacking blocks (Kay 1984). One final, "great" solution was to just build intelligent blocks that would waddle over to the arm. Rather than requiring human experts to think in terms not using analogies, as is the case with most current expert systems, new expert systems might "walk" to their users by explaining and collecting knowledge through analogical thinking.

Automated analogical problem solving represents an important frontier in the development of next-generation technology. Hertz (1984) argued that there is an "AI wall" that appears to be holding back breakthroughs in artificial intelligence — that is, our inability to program the computer to recognize and produce metaphors. This chapter has suggested that the wall is indeed ahead (i.e., metaphors and analogies) and that future research should concentrate to some extent on automated analogical problem solving.

REFERENCES

Anderson, J.R. (1975), *Language, Memory, and Thought*, Hillsdale, N.J.: Erlbaum.
Bacon, F. (1960), *The New Organon* (F.H. Anderson, ed.), New York: McGraw-Hill.
Carbonell, J.G. (1981), "Counterplanning: A Strategy Based Model of Adversary Planning in Real-World Situations," *Artificial Intelligence*, 16 (2): 295–329.

Carbonell, J.G. (1982), "Metaphor: An Inescapable Phenomenon in Natural Language Comprehension," in W.G. Lehnert and M.H. Ringle, eds., *Strategies for Natural Language Processing*, Hillsdale, N.J.: Erlbaum.

Carbonell, J.G. (1983), "Learning by Analogy: Formulating and Generalizing Plans from Past Experience," in R.S. Michalski, J.G. Carbonell, and T.M. Mitchell, eds., *Machine Learning: An Artificial Intelligence Approach*, Palo Alto, Calif.: Tioga.

Collins, A., Warnock, E.H., Aiello, N., and Miller, M.L. (1975), "Reasoning from Incomplete Knowledge," in D.G. Bobrow and A. Collins, eds., *Representation and Understanding: Studies in Cognitive Science*, New York: Academic Press.

Coombs, M., and Alty, J. (1984), "Expert Systems: An Alternative Paradigm," *International Journal of Man-Machine Studies*, 20 (3): 21–43.

Davis, R. (1984), "Amplifying Expertise with Expert Systems," in P.H. Winston and K.A. Prendergast, eds., *The AI Business: The Commercial Uses of Artificial Intelligence*, Cambridge, Mass.: MIT Press.

Dreyfus, H.L. (1979), *What Computers Can't Do*, New York: Harper and Row.

Evans, T.G. (1968), "A Program for the Solution of Geometric Analogy Intelligence Test Questions," in M. Minsky, ed., *Semantic Information Processing*, Cambridge, Mass.: MIT Press.

Galileo, G. (1957), *Discoveries and Opinions of Galileo* (S. Drake, ed. and trans.), New York: McGraw-Hill.

Gick, M.L., and Holyoak, K.J. (1980), "Analogical Problem Solving," *Cognitive Psychology*, 12 (1): 306–355.

Gick, M.L., and Holyoak, K.J. (1983), "Schema Induction and Analogical Transfer," *Cognitive Psychology*, 15 (6): 1–15.

Gilovich, T. (1981), "Seeing the Past in the Present: The Effect of Associations to Familiar Events on Judgments and Decisions," *Journal of Personality and Social Psychology*, 40 (1): 797–808.

Gordon, W.J. (1961), *Synectics*, New York: Harper and Row.

Hadamard, J. (1949), *An Essay on the Psychology of Invention in the Mathematical Field*, Princeton, N.J.: Princeton University Press.

Hayes-Roth, F., Waterman, D.A., and Lenat, D.B., eds. (1983), *Building Expert Systems*, Reading, Mass.: Addison-Wesley.

Heese, M.B. (1963), *Models and Analogies in Science*, London: Cambridge University Press.

Hertz, D.B. (1984), "Myths, Models, and Metaphors: The AI Wall," *Applied Artificial Intelligence Reporter*, 2, (October): 2.

Jevons, W.S. (1958), *The Principles of Science*, New York: McGraw-Hill.

Kay, A. (1984), "Inventing the Future," in P.H. Winston and K.A. Prendergast, eds., *The AI Business: The Commercial Uses of Artificial Intelligence*, Cambridge, Mass.: MIT Press.

Keidel, R.W. (1984), "Baseball, Football, and Basketball: Models for Business," *Organizational Dynamics*, 12, (Winter): 5–18.

Kling, R.E. (1971), "A Paradigm for Reasoning by Analogy," *Artificial Intelligence*, 2 (2): 147–178.

Kornell, J. (1984), "Embedded Knowledge Acquisition to Simplify Expert Systems Development," *Applied Artificial Intelligence Reporter*, 2 (August/September): 28–30.

Kuhn, T.S. (1962), *The Structure of Scientific Revolutions*, Chicago: University of Chicago Press.

Leatherdale, W.H. (1974), *The Role of Analogy, Model, and Metaphor in Science*, Amsterdam: North-Holland.

Lloyd, G.E.R. (1966), *Polarity and Analogy: Two Types of Argumentation in Early Greek Thought*, London: Cambridge University Press.

Mawardi, B.H. (1959), "Industrial Invention: A Study in Group Problem Solving," unpublished Ph.D. dissertation, Harvard University.

Meyer, A.D. (1983), "Determinants of High-Tech Medical Innovation," unpublished manuscript, University of Wisconsin-Milwaukee.

Meyer, A.D. (1984), "Mingling Decision Making Metaphors," *Academy of Management Review*, 9 (1): 6–17.

Mill, J.S. (1949), *A System of Logic Ratiocinative and Inductive Being a Connected View of the Principles of Evidence and the Methods of Scientific Investigation*, London: Cambridge University Press.

Miller, G.A. (1979), "Images and Models, Similes and Metaphors," in A. Ortony, ed., *Metaphor and Thought*, London: Cambridge University Press.

Moles, A.A. (1957), *La Creation Scientifique*, Geneva: Geneva Press.

Newell, A., and Simon, H.A. (1972), *Human Problem Solving*, Englewood Cliffs, N.J.: Prentice-Hall.

Nyman, A. (1953), "Induction et Intuition," *Theoria*, 19 (4): 22–41.

Oppenheimer, R. (1956), "Analogy in Science," *American Psychologist*, 11 (6): 127–135.

Peters, T., and Waterman, R. (1982), *In Search of Excellence*, New York: Harper and Row.

Piaget, J. (1970), *Genetic Epistemology* (F. Duckworth, trans.), New York: Columbia University Press.

Polya, G. (1957), *How to Solve It*, Princeton, N.J.: Princeton University Press.

Reed, S.K., Ernst, G.W., and Banerji, B. (1974), "The Role of Analogy in Transfer Between Similar Problem States," *Cognitive Psychology*, 6 (3): 436–450.

Rumelhart, D.E. (1975), "Notes on a Schema for Stories," in D.G. Bobrow and A. Collins, eds., *Representation and Understanding: Studies in Cognitive Science*, New York: Academic Press.

Rumelhart, D.E., and Abrahamson, A.A. (1973), "A Model for Analogical Reasoning," *Cognitive Psychology*, 5 (4): 1–28.

Rumelhart, D.E., and Norman, D.A. (1981), "Analogical Processes in Learning," in J.R. Anderson, ed., *Cognitive Skills and Their Acquisition*, Hillsdale, N.J.: Erlbaum.

Schank, R., and Abelson, R.P. (1977), *Scripts, Plans, Goals, and Understanding: An Inquiry into Human Knowledge Structures*, Hillsdale, N.J.: Erlbaum.

Silverman, B.G. (1983), "Analogy in Systems Management: A Theoretical Inquiry," *IEEE Transactions on Systems, Man, and Cybernetics* (SMC-13) 6 (November/December): 1049–1075.

Silverman, B.G. (1985), "Expert Intuition and Ill-Structured Problem Solving," *IEEE Transactions on Engineering Management* (EM-32), 1 (February): 29–33.

Simon, H.A. (1960), *The New Science of Management Decision*, New York: Harper and Row.

Simon, H.A. (1976), "Identifying Basic Abilities Underlying Intelligent Performance of Complex Tasks," in L. Resnick, ed., *The Nature of Intelligence*, Hillsdale, N.J.: Erlbaum.

Spearman, C. (1923), *The Nature of "Intelligence" and the Principles of Cognition*, London: Macmillan.

Stelzer, J. (1983), "Analogy and Axiomatics," *International Journal of Man-Machine Studies*, 18 (1): 161–173.

Sternberg, R.J. (1977), *Intelligence, Information Processing, and Analogical Reasoning: The Componential Analysis of Human Abilities*, Hillsdale, N.J.: Erlbaum.

Thorndyke, P.W. (1977), "Cognitive Structures in Comprehension and Memory of Narrative Discourse," *Cognitive Psychology*, 9 (5): 77–110.

Winston, P.H. (1980), "Learning and Reasoning by Analogy," *Communications of the ACM*, 23 (12): 689–703.

Woodworth, W., and Nelson, R. (1979), "Witch Doctors, Messianics, Sorcerers, and OD Consultants: Parallels and Paradigms," *Organizational Dynamics*, 7 (Autumn): 17–33.

17

Expert Systems Issues in "Innovator": Representations and Heuristics

Barry G. Silverman
Vassilis S. Moustakis

An expert system–based assistant called INNOVATOR is being developed to provide computerized support for institutionalized innovation. Based on the belief that a computer will someday invent, but at present can only support inventor/engineers, INNOVATOR is the focal point of a four-pronged research program aimed at: (1) developing a more scientific understanding of the cognitive behavior of innovators, (2) translating the cognitive results into computerizable form, (3) evolving a generic version of INNOVATOR, and (4) applying the generic version to actual institutions. These four sets of activities and results to date for NASA and U.S. military applications of INNOVATOR are described in this chapter.

17.1 INTRODUCTION

The process of innovation (and development) is often defined to encompass the spectrum of activities associated with creating a discovery, an invention, an innovation, a development, or a technology (or system). Much has been written about how each of these types of creations are brought into being—that is, about the innovation process. While there are many differences between these types of creations, most investigators, regardless of their perspective (e.g., economic, sociological, psychological, etc.) point to the use of analogy as playing a critical role in the innovator's "tool-kit" (Gilfillan 1935; Hadamard 1945; Polya 1954, 1957; Usher 1954; Gordan 1961; Rossman 1964; Hesse 1966; Koestler 1960; Sahal 1981; and Silverman 1984a).[1]

Despite the importance placed by innovation process theoreticians and practitioners on analogy in the act of insight and despite the vast amount written on it, analogy is still a poorly understood subject. For example, Usher (1954) claims "only a more complete psychological analysis can furnish a full awareness of the complexity of the act of insight and the range of problems to which it gives a solution" (p. 83). Psychologists are similarly convinced of the importance of analogy, particularly in the measurement of human intelligence. Again, however, despite a large amount of psychological literature on the analogy topic, and "despite its everyday pervasiveness and theoretical importance, analogical reasoning is still only poorly understood" (Sternberg 1977, p. 354).

In today's world of institutionalized innovation in which firms depend for their very existence on the innovation process, it is inexcusable that so vital a tool as analogy is so poorly understood. Without a proper understanding of how analogies are formed, what role they play in the innovation process, what biases their users tend to commonly make, what knowledge is most critical to effective formation of the analogies, and what intermediate steps are essential to formation of "good" analogies, there can be little hope of supporting innovators or of improving the process of innovation in the firm. Understanding the analogical paradigm is also vital to an appreciation of how organizations can most effectively manage the transition to new technological eras.

This chapter describes the INNOVATOR research program and expert systems-based framework that address the "analogy gap" in or-

---

[1]An *analogy* is defined in this article as a common and mundane human technique for indicating one or more respects in which two entities are similar. Analogical problem solving, whether in the fields of science, invention, innovation, engineering, or everyday problem solving, may be viewed as a comparison between two "things" or situations that can be classified into three aspects: (1) an analysis of the problem to be solved (the *target*) into an abstract description; (2) an analysis of a past situation (the *base*) into some abstract description, this time consisting of a problem-solution pair; and (3) a relevant mapping between the two descriptions that permits the definition of the target problem to somehow be advanced and also helps solve the target problem (i.e., analogies to be preserved, disanalogies to be discarded, and partial analogies to be adjusted).

ganized innovation (see Figure 17.1). The foundation of this program is a continuing series of studies of the cognitive behavior of inventors/engineers, aimed at evolving a "more complete psychological analysis" of the act of creation (see Section 17.2). Although far from complete, the cognitive investigations have given rise to a skeleton of a prescriptive model of innovation (Section 17.3) that is of sufficient detail to provide a focus and framework for development of a generic knowledge-based support system. This generic framework or shell is, in turn, the focus of investigations into the most appropriate combination of (1) knowledge representation forms, (2) problem processor structures, and (3) computer-to-human-language interfaces. Section 17.4 describes this research, its results, and how two early applications of INNOVATOR — one already implemented for NASA and one being implemented (and already in pilot or prototype form) for the U.S. military — provide validity assessment and evaluation feedback to the long-term research goal. As a by-product, the NASA application of INNOVATOR is also explained in Section 17.4.

17.2 RESULTS OF COGNITIVE RESEARCH ON ANALOGICAL REASONING

This section attempts to describe the authors' attempts to derive a cognitive model of the inventor/innovator and to derive a model of the process of analogical reasoning along with a set of relevant dimensions over which the "goodness" of an analogy could be evaluated. The background investigations and the cognitive model resulting from this research are summarized in this section. This section also serves to explain the particular problem domain that the knowledge-based systems presented in Section 17.4 were designed to support.

17.2.1 Research Methods: A Hybrid Knowledge Elicitation Paradigm

Three well-known paradigms and a fourth paradigm have been combined into a "hybrid paradigm" for knowledge elicitation from expert innovators. The well-known paradigms are (1) traditional knowledge engineering, which essentially leaves the elicitation issue up to common sense or "brute force," (2) the rule-induction or example-oriented paradigm of Michie (1974) in which the experts are confronted with cases for which solutions are known, small alterations in the cases are discussed, and new rules (solutions) are thus induced by the discussion, and (3) protocol analysis (see Waterman and Newell 1971), which begins with tape recording the thought process, spoken out loud, of the subject during problem solving. This verbal protocol tends to be fairly "chaotic," and the

FIGURE 17.1
THE INNOVATOR RESEARCH PROGRAM OVERVIEW

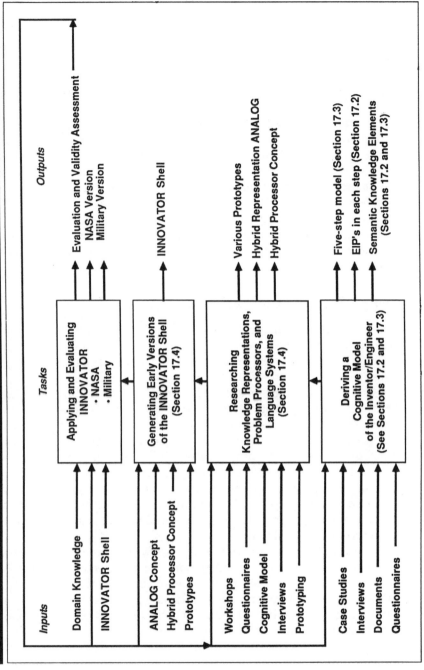

task of protocol analysis is to translate this raw material into more accessible representations. Ideally, the final output of a protocol analysis is a description of the subject(s) as an information-processing system in a form that can be directly implemented as a computer-based expert system.

A fourth paradigm involves assembling a mathematical model of the situation from available documentation and what is known from the three other paradigms. This "hybrid" approach utilizes the prescriptive (somewhat "naive") knowledge embodied in the model as a guide to what further problem-solving aspects bear further knowledge elicitation by one of the other paradigms. In simplistic settings (e.g., games, puzzles, straightforward problems or when a "captive" audience of experts exists), one of the three known paradigms may prove optimal. In complex settings (e.g., innovation), the hybrid paradigm becomes a necessity. This is due to (1) the lack of experts from which to elicit a knowledge base (they are too busy), (2) the multiyear time span over which problem solving occurs, and (3) the fact that teams of experts and not gurus contain the knowledge base.

17.2.2   Types of Knowledge Elicited

Investigations on analogical reasoning applied the hybrid paradigm to the spacecraft planning and design process for ground support systems at NASA Goddard Space Flight Center (GSFC) in Maryland, where specific investigations into professional analogy were conducted by the authors. In particular, the authors focused upon the engineering managers and their contractors (hereafter, collectively referred to as *system innovators*) within the Mission Operations and Data Systems Directorate – a group that designs and operates highly innovative facilities (ground systems) that control near-earth, unmanned satellites once they are placed in orbit. As each new satellite enters the systems-engineering cycle, NASA must plan out, design, develop, test, integrate, and operate ground systems in six distinct areas including command, control, attitude, orbit, data capture, and telemetry processing. The specific satellites are unimportant to the purposes of this chapter.

Space permits only a brief sampling of the types of knowledge states and elementary information processors (EIPs) collected from the NASA elicitation studies. By way of overview of the general protocol, a system innovator wishing to obtain a cost estimate (or design) for a future spacecraft (S/C) ground facility #1 looks for an analogy to the cost (design) of an existing and somehow similar (S/C) ground facility #2. Analogy between facilities 1 and 2 is based on a number of interrelated cues such as functional requirements, hardware architecture, and complexity of software. The system innovator then identifies and eliminates disanalogies, adding new elements as needed to complete the project plan, cost estimate, or design effort. A simple illustration of this use of analogy is shown in Figure 17.2, which represents a small segment of the second-level functional requirement document of a base system or analog. A cost for facility 2 is derived by placing dots next to each functional requirement of facility 1 (no dots if a requirement is not germane, one dot for a direct correspondence, multiple dots for increased complexity in facility 2). A complexity multiplier is derived as the ratio of the number of dots to total functional requirements of facility 1. The multiplier is then used on the facility 1 cost estimate to derive the cost estimate of facility 2. While seemingly trivial, the heuristics just described can only effectively be utilized by domain experts who recognize the interrelationships of requirements, system resources, and weights ("dots").

FIGURE 17.2
THE FUNCTIONAL ANALOGY APPROACH: AN EXAMPLE FOR TWO SPACE CRAFT (S/C) CONTROL CENTER FACILITIES

Functional Requirements

- • 000. **Telemetry and Command**
- • 001. **Network Control Center**
- •• 002. **Science Support Center**
-    003. **Data Capture Facility**
- • 004. **Operations Support Computing Facility**
- • 005. **Mission Planning Terminal**
-    006. **MSFC Simulator**
-    007. **ST Associate Contractors**

-    100. **Telemetry Combinations**
- • 101. **Real-Time Engineering Telemetry**
- • 102. **Data Synchronization & Quality Monitoring**
- • 103. **Data Decommutation**

Rules: • means common function
        item 002 indicates multiple interfaces
        Complexity Factor = common functions/total function = 68/104

Algorithm: Cost = Complexity Factor x $(Cost_{PORTS} + Cost_{PASS} + Cost_{TAV})$
           x Inflation

Source: Sobieski (1982).

A more complicated example involves an eight-year, multiperson effort to plan out and design software for an operations control center (OCC), in this case for space telescope (ST). An OCC typically includes anywhere from three to two dozen computers, each containing large software programs designed to fulfill different functions. This specific instance dealt with the set of computers identified as the applications processor (AP). Further, the STOCC's application processor is extremely large—about 580,000 executable lines of code—and it encompasses two distinct programs.[2] The first is the on-line system (OLS) software, which encompasses 160,000 executable lines of code (estimated) and handles the real-time command, control, and data stream monitoring functions. The second program is the off-line system (OFLS) software, which encompasses the remaining 420,000 lines of executable code and handles the less critical, non-real-time functions.

In protocol analysis the problem-solving behavior of the subject

---

[2]The AP also encompasses a simulator that is not included in these estimates.

FIGURE 17.3
ANALOGY FORMULATION SECTION OF ONE OF THE PROBLEM BEHAVIOR GRAPHS OF THE PROTOCOL ANALYSES

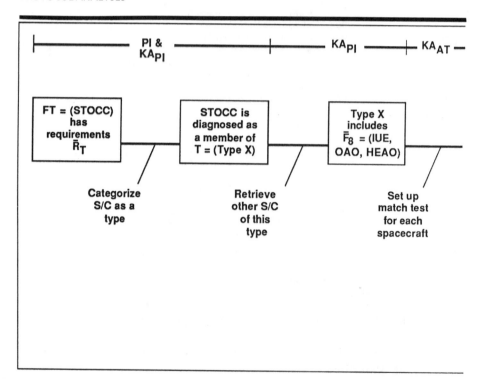

matter expert is described via a "tool" called the problem behavior graph (PBG). PBG describes the entire set of problem-solving states in which each state is a body of knowledge that may be transformed to a succeeding state via elementary information process (EIP) operators. They are elementary in the sense that they are not further broken down into greater detail by the process under consideration. Of course, the level of analysis that is defined as "elementary" will depend upon the type of behavior under consideration and the aspects of behavior that are of interest. A PBG thus consists of a "flowchart" with knowledge states as the nodes and EIPs as the links. The assumption is that behavior in a human information-processing system is the result of sequences of these states and EIPs that can in turn be organized on and replicated by the computer.

The PBG for the entire STOCC is exceedingly large and space permits only one illustrative section of the STOCC-OLS-AP to be displayed in Figure 17.3.[3] The portion of the PBG of Figure 17.3 shows ten knowl-

---

[3]A more complete documentation of this PBG exists in Silverman (1985a).

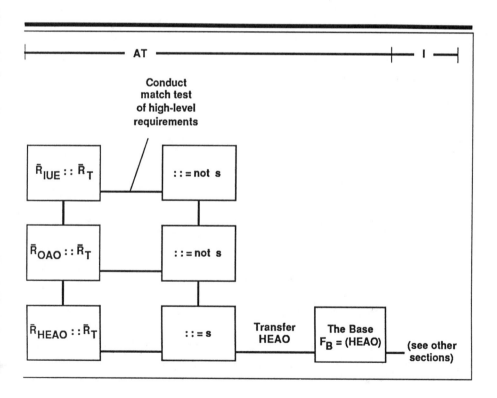

edge states (boxes or nodes) and nine EIPs (links). These states and EIPs encompass the initial attempt by the designer(s) to locate a useful analog or base, F_B, for the target problem, F_T, which is the STOCC-OLS-AP. The PBG reveals two notable features in the search for a base. First, the analogy is performed in terms of similar attributes or requirements, R_T and R_B, for the target and base, respectively (the subscripts *IUE*, *OAO*, and *HEAO* in Figure 17.3 are specific base spacecraft names). R_T and R_B are each fairly large semantic nets that may be thought of as sets of many hierarchically interlinked lists. Second, the search space is minimized via a heuristic known as "typing" the target spacecraft. This may be thought of as similar to the diagnostic classification a medical doctor applies when trying to infer a disease from a set of symptoms. For the case shown, once the STOCC was "typed," only three analogs needed to be searched.

It is interesting from a normative viewpoint to attempt to classify these states and EIPs into broadly defined "steps" that comprise the analogical reasoning process. States and EIPs represent the "bottom" level of cognitive behavior. Paradigms such as analogical reasoning represent the top level that drives the cognitive operations and processes. Between the two levels lies a controlling methodology or set of steps. A mapping out of these steps is done across the top of Figure 17.3. These are the same steps that appear in other segments of the PBG, and their abbreviations are explained in the next section.

17.3   A MODEL OF THE ANALOGICAL REASONING PROCESS

The weaknesses and limitations of analogical reasoning process models cited in Section 17.1 stem in large part from a lack of evidence as just described. The results of the protocol analysis and other investigations do not eliminate this problem. However, they provide insight into the states and EIPs as well as into five distinct but iterative and highly parallel steps (Silverman 1985a, 1985b). The problem-solving steps implied by this behavioral model of analogical reasoning are displayed as the five boxes in the middle of Figure 17.4. These steps are used concurrently and opportunistically as the need arises to tap the analog bases, to define the target problem, and to isolate the target solution. Each step is discussed more fully in what follows. But first several terms need to be defined.

First, it is assumed that the inventor often wishes to create a target *entity* that is too complex to think about as a single item. Instead he or she utilizes a top-down refinement or progressive-deepening strategy to reduce search space and effort. That is, the inventor works out the analogical search at the highest level possible (in true Sussmanian fashion, Sussman 1975). This constrains the search at the next lowest level to a

Target Problem and Solution Space ("BLACKBOARD")

Problem Identification (PI)
- CRITIC
- Entropy Measure
- Stopping Rule

Knowledge Acquisition (KA)
- LIBRARIAN
- Heuristic Search
- Back Chaining

Analog Transfer (AT)
- IDEA MAN
- Similarity Metric
- Means-Ends

Knowledge Transformation (KT)
- CRAFTSMAN
- Forward Chainer
- M-Operator Heuristic
- Plan Debugger

Intro Into Use (I)
- WRITER
- Formatting Rules

Analogical Knowledge System (Bases)

small region. At that level, the solution from the previous level is refined and the search region for the next lower level is scoped. In this chapter, seven such levels will be addressed. First, the entity is decomposed into several target *system classes,* and any given class may be decomposed into several target *system types.* It is usually at the type level that analogous systems (bases) are first encountered: several base systems may exist for each type of each class. Finally, each target or base system is decomposable to subsystem, component, and module levels. The inventor will generally decompose a target entity to whatever tier of this several-level view of an entity (entity as root node, module at bottom) is needed to "recognize" an analogous solution that can be reused and/or transformed into a building block in the solution to the target entity. To this end, each tier of the hierarchy is treated as a *list* of *objects.* Each object in turn is associated with a relatively simple description that includes only a list of *attributes* and possibly their *values.* A given object may have more than one attribute list, but only one attribute list is relevant to a given view of the object.

In order to solve this model, the authors evolved an Analogical Reasoning Integration and Extension Language (ARIEL) that acts as a "blackboard expert system" consisting of a series of functional experts responding to an agenda formulator and a goal setter. ARIEL is thus the language within which INNOVATOR is written. The blackboard is a powerful metaphor in which each of several functional experts (1) take a turn considering the problem established by the goal setter, (2) proceed through to consider how the goal may be achieved, and (3) return answers to the "blackboard." Experts interact opportunistically and according to the "least commitment" principle by: (1) examining the goal and any other items found on the blackboard from its own functional perspective, (2) identifying conflicts, and (3) placing their own concerns, conflicts, and suggested solutions on the blackboard. The agenda formulator places conflicted items on a list of items to be addressed, and the goal setter retasks the various experts once again until all conflicts are recursively eliminated and the feasible set as well as optimal (recommended) solution(s) are delineated.

In the case of ARIEL, the blackboard is the "work space" in which the base problem-solution pairs are offered as candidates and in which transformations made and still needed are recorded. The goal setter and agenda formulator are called the CHAIRMAN and they include respectively (1) the executive that contains meta-knowledge of the analogical process in which the functional experts are laboring and (2) the recursive generator that tracks and causes individual experts to be (re)tasked as per the goal setter's commands. The individual, functional experts are the five "steps" of the analogical process that interact and recurse to achieve the end result. To more clearly explain these five specialists, the reader must understand some of the ARIEL vocabulary:

$B = [b]$:   Set of *base* systems on which analogies will be based.

$T = [t]$:   Set of *target* systems whose resource and functional require-ments are to be estimated via analogical reasoning.

L: A list of objects or attribuites that can be denoted with a subscript B or T for base or target, respectively.

$O = [o]$:   Set or list of objects, elements of which can be subscripted with a B or T for base or target object list, respectively.

$A = [a]$:   Set or list of attributes associated with a given object, which can also be subscripted with a B or T. Between members of O and A sets there exists a many-to-many associative re-lationship. That is, one object can be associated with more than one attribute, while one attribute can be possessed by more than one object.

$M = [M]$:   Set of transform operators via which knowledge about an object from the base system is transformed to knowledge re-lated to the *target.*

$P = (O|a)$:   Probability that an object is associated with a given attri-bute list given a (sub)set of attributes. Subscripts B and T are possible and hold the same meaning as above.

$S(O_i, O_j) = [s]$: $i \neq j$. The similarity metric between two objects belonging in the same or in different lists.

17.3.1   Problem Identification (PI): CRITIC

Problem identification is concerned with the perception of a situation as problematical or unstable and the mutual agreement of all parties in-volved as to a statement of what must be acted upon. The output of this step is an (almost) agreed upon description of the *target* problem, condi-tional on a subjective probability estimate. The problem identification expert acts as "CRITIC," concerning itself with diagnostic critique of in-puts (from human users, from the KA expert, and from the AT expert). Using monotonic reasoning and progressive deepening, the CRITIC re-views symptoms (requirements) and "disease" inputs and decides when a "good" analysis has been achieved.

   The CRITIC, as in the case of each of the five specialists, contains LISP methods that examine the contents of the blackboard and determine an approach that will result in a contribution toward building an overall solution to the problem. The main function of the CRITIC is to aid in the process of problem identification, problem formulation, and require-ments definition. To this end, the CRITIC monitors the contents of R_T and determines what methods are to be employed in order to expand or refine the target problem definition. These methods usually entail the selection of an appropriate problem definition aid being presented to the user (via the WRITER). For example, if it is determined that the problem is being examined at the highest taxonomic level and the domain is not very complex, then the CRITIC would select a simple problem definition aid such as a menu, a block diagram, or a matrix. For more complex domains with deeper and more detailed levels of granularity, a computer visual engineering approach with iconic scene depiction windows might be selected, as described in Murray et al. (1985).

The CRITIC is also charged with the overall responsibility of monitoring the target solution generation process as a whole. These tasks range from seeking additional information from the user or LIBRARIAN to invoking a "stopping rule" when either an optimal solution has been achieved or when successive iterations would produce little or no change in the entropy of the target solution.

17.3.2   Knowledge Acquisition (KA): LIBRARIAN

The purpose of this step is to locate and retrieve candidate base systems from the analogical knowledge system. The knowledge acquisition (KA) expert acts as a "LIBRARIAN," concerning itself with heuristic search and backward chaining recall of candidate analogs from associative memory to support progressive-deepening messages from the other experts (via the blackboard).

The first purpose of the LIBRARIAN is to ensure that F_B contains all possible building blocks within a certain threshold that could be used in constructing a target solution to the problem. In order to accomplish this, the LIBRARIAN keeps a close watch on the status of F_T. Whenever this space is modified or updated, the LIBRARIAN conducts a knowledge base search in an attempt to identify any new analogs that are not currently under consideration. This search essentially involves taking each attribute contained in F_T, searching for each new occurrence of that attribute in the knowledge base, and returning to the blackboard all previously unconsidered bases exhibiting that particular attribute.

The second major task of the LIBRARIAN is to ensure that the knowledge base is properly updated with new information generated either by the user or by the ARIEL system itself. Currently, the LIBRARIAN is configured only to assimilate the final results of F_T as a new base (analog) to be considered for subsequent problem-solving sessions. In later versions of ARIEL it is planned to also incorporate intermediate results, including erroneous paths, and so forth, in order to increase the overall intelligence of the system and to make maximum use of lessons learned during each problem-solving session.

The LIBRARIAN is unique in that it is the only specialist that has access to the ARIEL knowledge base. For this reason, the LIBRARIAN must also respond to user requests for specific reference information, as directed by the CHAIRMAN.

17.3.3   Analog Transfer (AT): IDEA MAN

Within this step, the candidate analogs now stored in L_B for a given O_T are evaluated for similarities in an attempt to select the best analog.[4] The analog transfer (AT) expert thus acts as an "IDEA MAN" specializing in a means-ends analysis mode of testing candidate analogs to see if they satisfy the set of symptoms (goals) provided by the problem definition. If such symptom sets are insufficient to conduct the test, the AT expert sends appropriate messages to the blackboard.

The primary responsibility of the IDEA MAN is to examine the $F_B(O_B A_B)$ space and to evaluate each candidate analog based on the value of the similarity metric for that particular analog and the corresponding attributes contained in F_T. Weighing factors to be used in calculating the similarity rating are provided by the user at the request of the IDEA MAN via the WRITER. The candidate analogs are ranked starting with the analog having the highest similarity rating, along with the value of the rating. This output represents a prioritized and valued space of potential solutions for use by the CRAFTSMAN in generating a composite target solution.

17.3.4   Knowledge Transformation (KT): CRAFTSMAN

This step manipulates base objects and attributes so as to minimize disanalogies and to retain and strengthen analogous features. It then uses the results of its manipulations to fill in missing elements or adjust existing elements within the relevant target object and attribute lists.[5] The knowledge transformation expert acts as a "CRAFTSMAN" via a progressive-deepening, monotonic, forward-reasoning process. The expert requests more analog details and lists via the blackboard and ultimately recommends "treatment plans" (requirement multipliers or resource configurations) for the "disease" (requirements).

The CRAFTSMAN has as its goal a means-ends analysis that leads to the construction of an optimal solution to the target problem, using to the greatest extent possible the existing analogs contained in the knowledge base and provided by the user. At this point in the process, all relevant analogs that have been identified have been evaluated and ranked. In constructing the target solution, the CRAFTSMAN starts with the highest-ranked analog and checks for a similarity value of 1.0, in which case that analog becomes the final solution and the stopping rule is invoked by the CRITIC. If the similarity rating is less than 1.0, the CRAFTSMAN

---

[4]This is the portion of the five-step model that is most commonly treated when AI researchers create AI programs to solve analogy problems (see Evans 1968).

[5]An expert system for this step must be of a scope and complexity comparable to other planning expert systems (see Sacerdoti 1979 or Wilensky 1983).

takes the analog with the next highest rating and constructs a temporary target solution by combining it with the highest-ranked analog. At this point, a new similarity rating is calculated and compared with the rating of the highest-ranked analog. If the new rating is lower, the second highest candidate is dropped from consideration and the third highest candidate is considered in a similar fashion. If the new rating is higher, the temporary target solution becomes the new basis for comparison and the process continues.

An algorithm is inadequate to express the multitude, content, and type of transformation operations. By way of example, suppose base 1 is noticed and transferred as a possible solution state to the target system. However, suppose the goal state is left unsatisfied and part of the base must be "TRUNCATED." A second analog (base 2) is noticed, transferred, and "CONCATENATED." The process is now "STOP," since the merger and transformation of these two analogs is felt to "SATISFY" the criteria of the goal state. TRUNCATE, CONCATENATE, STOP, and SATISFY are example EIPs or M-operators of the KT step. As another set of example knowledge transformation EIPs, it is popular with engineers to apply linear multipliers to requirement list objects as was illustrated in Figure 17.2.

17.3.5   Introduction into Use (I): WRITER

This step encompasses activities related to organizational implementation of the "optimal" solution derived during the previous step, that is, of specifying the completed entity composed of L_T^M. The Intro into Use expert acts as a "WRITER," preparing formats and stylizing the "report," asking via the blackboard for additional information as deemed necessary.

17.3.6   Solution of the Blackboard Model

The derivation of EIPs, states, steps, and a methodological description for analogical reasoning have more than intellectual interest. Although the authors have yet to finish their work under the heading of descriptive and scientific analyses of innovators' protocols, it would be naive to suggest that the normative model just described cannot provide prescriptive guidance to efforts aimed at evolving knowledge-based expert systems for both a generic and application-oriented version.

The construction of a blackboard expert system of the scope and complexity of the one just described is the authors' current research goal. A number of the research issues that comprise this goal will be explored later in this chapter. The reader will recognize various portions of the blackboard expert system in this discussion and will hopefully commiserate with the authors on the critical importance of flushing out the many details and design specifications before rushing into implementation.

17.4.   APPLICATION, EVALUATION, AND VALIDATION

This section explains: (1) the constructs currently used in INNOVATOR to solve the model, that is, emulate an actual inventor/engineer, (2) the application of those constructs to the NASA problem domain, and (3) the validity of the constructs as evaluated by NASA users for their application. These three items are presented in terms of the types and formats of knowledge to be included (Section 17.4.1) and the processing heuristics needing to be applied to the knowledge (Section 17.4.2).

Before presenting this information it is worth pointing out the manner in which evaluation data were obtained. The authors were permitted to run three workshops at NASA and one workshop in the military. During the workshops, innovators were presented with background material on the analogy approach and INNOVATOR system prototypes. These workshops served as a vehicle for examining a number of research questions regarding generic analogical reasoning support system elements. User attitudes/requirements with respect to supporting analogical reasoning were collected via both structured questionnaires and thinking-out-loud reactions following hands-on experimentation with INNOVATOR prototypes. See Silverman (1984a, 1984b) for a discussion of the military version.

INNOVATOR user experimentation was performed using small size samples. However, all subjects represented *actual* and experienced inventors/innovators. From these workshops, INNOVATOR emerged as an analogical support system, the purpose of which is to automate the well-structured, repetitive, menial, and knowledge acquisition/processing-intensive aspects of the analogical problem-solving approach, while leaving human judgment to the more difficult creative steps.[6]

17.4.1   INNOVATOR's Knowledge System

From the entire set of representational systems that could be adopted within INNOVATOR (e.g., predicate calculus, production rules, hierarchical descriptions, semantic nets, frames, and scripts), experts expressed a strong preference for a hybrid knowledge representation system. This hybrid system is called the "ANALOG." Selected user responses are summarized in Table 17.1. These responses indicate a strong level of agree-

---

[6]The reliance of workshop participants on analogy is documented in Silverman (1983, 1984a, 1985c).

TABLE 17-1
A CASE FOR HYBRID KNOWLEDGE REPRESENTATION IN AN ANALOG

	Evidence ($N = 29$)*			
Statement	Disagree	Minor Agreement	Agree	Strongly Agree
When I use analogy:				
1. I rely on the information of whole system pictures	0%	0%	20%	80%
2. I rely on simple decision rules for analogy/disanalogy identification	0%	20%	40%	40%
3. I want to be able to facilitate problem reidentification through use of a variety of techniques (graphs, tables, rules, data bases, etc.)	0%	10%	10%	80%

*Twenty-one from NASA; eight from the military.

ment with respect to being able to use a variety of techniques, to form whole system picture descriptions, and to rely on simple decision rules for analogy/disanalogy identification.

The structure of an ANALOG accounts for the integration of diverse yet interrelated knowledge elements and areas of cognition into an integrated net incorporating interrelated inheritance lattices of requirement and resource objects. A representation of the ANALOG structure is given in Figure 17.5. In this figure the ANALOG knowledge system incorporates an inheritance lattice of frames, a set of rules, semantic nets, other data structures, and problem-processing methods. The knowledge system for the NASA application of INNOVATOR was loaded with 52 such ANALOGS by the authors before being turned over for operation maintenance and completion by NASA employees. The knowledge elements are discussed in the following sections, while the methods are postponed until Section 17.4.2.

Object Lattice of Resources and Requirements   Knowledge related to functional, performance, and operational aspects of base and potential target systems in INNOVATOR are described via system resources and requirements. In the context of an ANALOG, system requirements and hardware/software/staff resource data are organized in semantic nets (see Figure 17.5a). A system requirement may correspond to one of these categories: functional (*what* the system is supposed to do), performance (*how* quickly, *how* many, *how* often), or operational (what impact is the system supposed to have on its environment). Any system requirement consists of subsystem requirements. For example, the subsystem functional requirements of a typical OCC are: (1) real-time commanding, (2) telemetry processing, (3) display processing, (4) stored command management, (5) on-board computer management, (6) mission operations planning, and (7) data base management. Component requirements describe functional processes within each subsystem. Some component functional requirements are also shown in Figure 17.5a.

A semantic net of system resources (hardware and software) is also presented in Figure 17.5a. Hardware is described via major components such as CPU, main memory, or disk memory. On the other hand, software is represented via program module statistics and software complexity factors (see Figure 17.5b). Modules incorporate the individual software programs that are measured in terms of a variety of critical attributes, such as but not limited to executable lines of code, percentage of high-level versus machine language code, and complexity factors that are useful for comparing the level of difficulty of two separate programs composed of equivalent lines of code.

Analog Rule Sets   Rule-based structures have received wide application in expert system implementations, such as MYCIN (Shortliffe 1974), R1 (McDermott 1980), PROSPECTOR (Duda et al. 1978), and the military version of INNOVATOR (Silverman 1984b), to name a few. In theory, there are numerous applications for a rule structure within a given ANALOG. For instance:

Progressive Deepening Strategy (Diagnosis): This relates to the implementation of a heuristic search space aid that helps to identify "classes" and/or class "types" to which an entity belongs. An earlier prototype of INNOVATOR at NASA utilized such a rule-based strategy. It was composed of 30 to 40 rules per entity "class" that could pinpoint the "type" of entity being considered. One such rule for the command management system (CMS) "class" that determines the type as a "type 1" is as follows:

> IF: For CMS considerations, spacecraft (s/c) has fixed memory allocations
> For CMS considerations, spacecraft (s/c) requires explicit commands
> For CMS considerations, spacecraft (s/c) requires input editing
> THEN: For CMS considerations, spacecraft (s/c) is type 1 (ae)

Knowledge Representation: Rule sets also may be implemented to express conditional relationships between the various elements of a semantic net of systems requirements on the one hand and resource frames (nets of frames) and relational tuples on the other hand. That is, once a base is pinpointed, the entire ANALOG can be viewed as a multitude of rules. For example, the generic rule structure of Figure 17.5a would be:

> IF: Given elements of the requirements sublattice F_B are true
> THEN: Given elements of the resource sublattice R_B hold, with resource active values being conditional on a degree of certainty CL.

The implementation of INNOVATOR for the military establishes just such condition-conclusion pairs (Silverman 1984b). For NASA, rule

FIGURE 17.5(a)
PORTION OF THE INHERITANCE LATTICE OF OBJECTS IN AN ANALOG

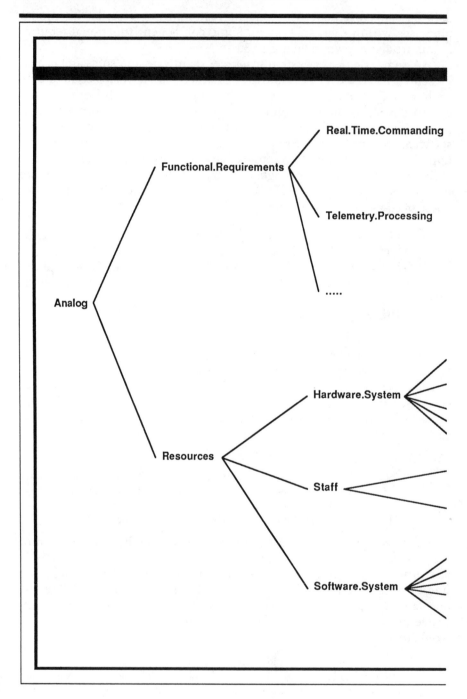

420

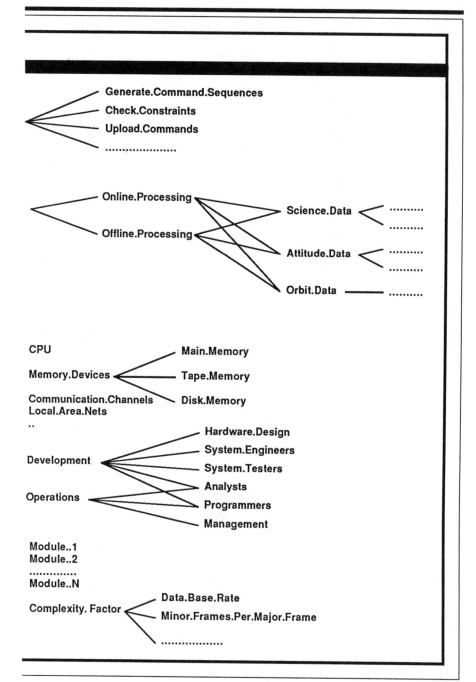

Generate.Command.Sequences
Check.Constraints
Upload.Commands
....

Online.Processing
Offline.Processing

Science.Data
Attitude.Data
Orbit.Data

CPU
Memory.Devices
Communication.Channels
Local.Area.Nets
..

Main.Memory
Tape.Memory
Disk.Memory

Development

Operations

Hardware.Design
System.Engineers
System.Testers
Analysts
Programmers
Management

Module..1
Module..2
....
Module..N

Complexity. Factor

Data.Base.Rate
Minor.Frames.Per.Major.Frame
....

FIGURE 17.5(b)
STRUCTURE OF A TYPICAL OBJECT

```
(Software System

    System:  String
    Parent:  Resource
    Class:   Atom
    Type:    String
    Complexity Factor Variables (CFVs):

            Format & Data Rate:   n-tuple
            Data Base Summary:    n-tuple

    Software Module Variables (SMVs)

            Module 1:   Size, % High Level, Version #, CL
            Module 2:   Size, % High Level, Version #, CL
              .
              .
              .
            Module N:   • • •

    Methods:   Show. Architecture, Display. CFVs, Compute.
               Total.CFV, Set.Guages.SMV, Rule.Set.  Methods ...)
```

sets can only be derived at a macroscopic level since traceability information relating individual requirements to specific resources was not maintained. A macro-level rule set is intriguing, however, and somewhat consistent with cognitive understanding processes such as Simon's chunking (Larkin et al. 1980) and possibly even with the Gestalt instant recognition paradigm (once the problem is known the answer immediately follows); however, it was not adopted here.

Analog Transfer: At this level a rule set may be implemented towards transferring knowledge that relates to a *base* system to a *target* problem situation. Once the semantic net of a target system is pinpointed (refer to the similarity matching paradigm discussed in Section 17.2.2), resource requirement active values are transferred from the base to the target. During this transfer process, active values may also be adjusted (see formulas in Section 17.2.2). A representation of the operation of such a rule set is:

IF: $S(F_B, F_T)$ optimal
THEN: $R_T = M * R_B$

Other Analog Data Structures In addition to atoms, strings, lists, frames, and rules the ANALOG includes bitmaps, relational tuples, and text files. As two examples, in the NASA application ANALOG bitmaps are implemented to convey information related to (1) hardware architecture of a ground facility and (2) a "key" to an instance of an ANALOG — this is a bitmap that provides a layout of knowledge components within each ANALOG.

Relational tuples are implemented in an ANALOG to describe relations between various resource values and dimensions that require large-scale and frequent numerical scaling and/or adjustment by EIPs (see Section 17.4.2). The structure of a few of the tuples for one NASA ANALOG (presented in Figure 17.6) show how a detailed record of staff resource active values by year are portrayed.[7] Staff skill (members of the resource attribute set) categories include programmers, hardware staff, system testers, analysts, management, operators, and others. Each tuple of resource active values is assigned a confidence level (CL) estimate and is adjustable by inflation index tuples and requirement weight multipliers. CL is a subjective evaluator of active value uncertainty, and it expresses the stochastic nature of knowledge with respect to all base systems, where $0 \leqslant CL \leqslant 1$, and an active value tuple with $CL = 1$ is considered 100 percent accurate. A second example of a tuple is set of multiplier operators (M-operators) that can be applied by the user when applying operators (in the KT step) to functional requirement lists (see Figure 17.6b).

Text files are implemented to accommodate textual pieces within an ANALOG. These include HELP facilities, citations, and free comments. Illustrative text files are shown in Figure 17.6a as explanation of the confidence level and in Figure 17.6b as explanation of the M-operators. Free comment text files are used mostly to provide explanation, help, and/or references regarding the sources of resource active values as well as to present other relevant comments.

Evaluations of the ANALOG   Strong user preference was expressed during workshops and interviews with respect to both structure and contents of the ANALOG knowledge organization of INNOVATOR — a few illustrative NASA reactions are summarized in Table 17.2. Two statements related to the structure of an ANALOG from the point of view of analogical reasoning are included in Table 17.2a. The second part of this table summarizes INNOVATOR user agreement on resource requirements of an ANALOG at an aggregated level that have already been implemented in INNOVATOR. However, ANALOG knowledge representation needs to be expanded to include:

1. performance and operational system requirements — current versions of INNOVATOR at NASA and at the military are limited to functional requirements.

2. causal (deterministic and/or stochastic) associations between the requirements and resource at the subsystem and component levels.

---

[7]Actual data are sensitive and are not presented here.

FIGURE 17.6
EXAMPLES OF OTHER DATA STRUCTURES IN INNOVATOR. (a) STAFF RESOURCE ATTRIBUTES AND VALUES FOR A GIVEN OBJECT: TUPLES AND TEXT FILES: (b) REQUIREMENT ATTRIBUTES AND VALUES FOR A GIVEN OBJECT: TUPLE AND TEXT FILE.

(II) S/C RESOURCE USAGE

LAUNCH DATE: 19XX Committed Period I 19XX

(A) STAFF	L-4	L-3	L-2	L-1	L	L+1	L+2	Total (MV)	Conf. Level (a)

(1) Devel. Staff (MY) (b)
    Programmers
    Hardware
    Syst. Test.
    Support
Total Devel. Staff
(2) Oper. Staff (MY) (c)   (Enter values)
    Analysts
    Operators
    Programmers
    Management
    Support
Total Operat. Staff
(3) Total Staff
(4) R & PM Staff (MY)

Notes:
(a) Confidence level (CL) is a subjective evaluator of data uncertainty where O<CL<1. CL=1 indicates 100% accuracy.
(b)
(c)
.. ..

a

(III) FUNCTIONAL REQUIREMENTS (a)

(A) Subsystem Level   Weight

  1.0 Subsystem #1 (Real Time Commanding)   1
  2.0 Subsystem #2   1
  3.0 :   1
       :

(B) Component Level
      Description

1.0 Subsystem #1   Weight

  1.1 Component #1 (e.g. Generate Command Sequences)   1
  1.2 Component #2   1
       :   1
       :

Analogy Instructions

For analogy purposes a "weight" is ascribed to each requirement as an indicator of its intensity. When all weights are set equal to one (1) it represents the base (analogous) S/C. The user may alter these weights by typing over the current entry to reflect modifications/ disanalogies from the base S/C of the new S/C. This can be done in three different ways:

(a) Altering the weights at the Subsystem level.

(b) Altering the weights at the Component level.

(c) Any combination of both (a) and (b).

b

TABLE 17.2
SYSTEM REQUIREMENTS AND RESOURCE KNOWLEDGE IN ANALOG:
A CASE FOR SEMANTIC NETS **(a)** STRUCTURE* **(b)** CONTENTS.**

When I use analogy I want to be able to:	Disagree	Minor Agreement	Agree	Strongly Agree
1. Record/Keep track of system requirements in a readily accessible fashion (in a WBS† sense).	0%	10%	20%	70%
2. Record/Keep track of resource consumption profiles (in a WBS† sense).	0%	10%	0%	90%

Functional and Resource Requirements	Yes	No
Resource Breakdown is desirable for:		
1. Development staff	100%	0
2. Operations staff	100%	0
3. Hardware	100%	0
4. Hardware configuration chart	100%	0
Functional Requirements operators should include:		
1. Linear multiplier generation ability	100%	0
2. Linear multiplier for hardware	100%	0
3. "Technological forecasting" for hardware	100%	0

*N = 21, NASA only.
**N = 7.
†Work Breakdown Structure.

17.4.2   INNOVATOR's Problem Processor

Analogical problem processing has already been described in Section 17.2 in terms of the five-step prescriptive model. This section provides validity assessment of those steps in terms of NASA users reactions. Innovators at NASA are concerned with designing and planning new ground systems in each of six areas: command, control, attitude, orbit, data capture, and data processing. These users unanimously agreed that support elements embodied in INNOVATOR could potentially support them in all subprocesses of analogical reasoning (see Table 17.3a).

Due to contract constraints, the NASA application of the INNOVATOR model of Section 17.3 was degenerated to the following subset of analogical reasoning steps:

1. *Knowledge System:* INNOVATOR provides 40 spacecraft and facility analogs, each of which encompasses the structural elements discussed in the preceding section.

2. *Knowledge Acquisition:* INNOVATOR provides a diagnostic classification or typology framework as a heuristic for search space simplification.

TABLE 17.3
ANALOGICAL PROBLEM PROCESSING ASPECTS OF INNOVATOR

	Yes	No
(a) As an aid in the process of analogical reasoning I would use INNOVATOR in (N = 7):		
— Problem Identification	100%	
— Knowledge Aquisition	100%	
— Analog Transfer	100%	
— Knowledge Transformation	100%	
— Introduction into Use	100%	

(b) Questions related to List of Base "Types" (N = 7)

1. Is four to five spacecraft per type classification enough?   100%
2. Should a *general* type classification be included in each type group (as possible)?   100%
3. Rate the importance of having a matrix of typology definitions/ membership in INNOVATOR (1 = most important, 5 = unimportant):   Mean = 1.40

(c) I would like to have:

	Level of Agreement (N = 10)			
Statement	Disagree	Minor Agreement	Agree	Strongly Agree
A clearly defined procedure or "Handbook" to support performance/training in analogy studies			30%	70%
A data base of relevant analogy information to accompany this "handbook" for performance/ training support			20%	80%
Experts who spend time training nonexperts	10%	20%		

3. *Analog Transfer:* INNOVATOR provides equations for forming subjective probability estimates on members of the $P(O|a_T, a_B)$ and $S(O_T, O_B)$ set.

4. *Knowledge Transformation:* Facilities built in INNOVATOR support the process of transforming knowledge related to base systems to produce target system designs and resource requirements and cost estimates.

5. *Intro Into Use:* A set of multiple representation gauges is provided, which enables the monitoring of results and of current active values. These may be printed as may tabular versions of the same information.

In the NASA version of INNOVATOR the problem identification step is left entirely up to the user as is the decision concerning which of the available transformation heuristics to apply (and at what level and degree). As a result, the NASA version of INNOVATOR should be thought of as an expert's support system rather than being capable of replacing the expert.[8] Discussion turns now to a selection of several of the more interesting features of this aid.

Search Space Heuristics (KA and AT)   In the knowledge acquisition step, innovators begin by diagnosing which one of several "classes" and "types" a target entity falls into. This is the ANALOG base search space reduction technique alluded to earlier. The NASA innovator attempting to plan and design a target satellite's six ground systems (command, control, attitude, orbit, data capture, and data processing) works in precisely the same fashion. He or she begins with a base object sorting. Once a new satellite has been "typed" or classified there are only a few possible bases that need to be explored in any depth as offering analogous plan and design information.

For the NASA application three entity levels thus correspond to the typology sorting process: (1) the satellite is classed in terms of its systems, (2) then each system is associated with a type—I through IV or V, and (3) the actual bases corresponding to that type are retrieved, studied, transferred, transformed, and so forth.

INNOVATOR had to be able to support this "object classification" or typology technique, and during the INNOVATOR experiments two prototype typology search and classification aids were developed for and evaluated by users—rule-based and frame-based.

According to the rule paradigm, system membership conditions in a class type are represented via sets of IF-THEN rules as discussed earlier. An inference engine was thus created for the LIBRARIAN and set to monotonically backchain.

A sample of the dialogue with the backward chaining prototype for the CMS typing session is shown in Figure 17.7.[9] The question-answer dialogue is lengthy and the explanation facility precise. Users at NASA were given this prototype and after experimenting with it concluded it would be useful as a training aid for bringing new employees "up to speed" on typing. As an expert aid, they found the dialogue too slow and felt the explanation/justification facility to be unnecessary ($N = 10$, 100% agreement), since they worked with this material regularly.

To implement a heuristic structure for the ground spacecraft system at NASA, the frame-slot paradigm was thus adopted (a rule-based version is, however, being utilized in the military application of INNOVATOR). A typology frame is defined in each of the six system areas (command, control, attitude, orbit, data capture, and data processing). Each such

---

[8]The NASA version was originally called the "system cost analogy technique."

[9]The author, with the help of J. Liebowitz, created a backward-chaining inference engine for INNOVATOR during this exercise and have since added a forward-chaining option.

FIGURE 17.7
BACKWARD CHAINING THROUGH THE AND-OR GRAPH OF TYPOLOGY RULES FOR A GIVEN
CLASS: ILLUSTRATIVE SESSION FOR CMS

RUN
hello.
I will use my 36 rules to try to establish one of the following 4 hypotheses:
    For CMS considerations, spacecraft (s/c) is type 1 (ae)
    For CMS considerations, spacecraft (s/c) is type 2 (seasat)
    For CMS considerations, spacecraft (s/c) is type 3 (smm)
    For CMS considerations, spacecraft (s/c) is type 4 (st)

please answer my questions with y (yes), n (no), or w (why)

is this true: For CMS considerations, spacecraft (s/c) requires explicit commands?
n
is this true: For CMS considerations, spacecraft (s/c) requires input editing? y
is this true: For CMS considerations, spacecraft (s/c) has loading options/
constraints? w
i am trying to use rule r7
i already know that;
For CMS considerations, spacecraft (s/c) requires input editing
if:
For CMS considerations, spacecraft (s/c) has loading options/constraints
For CMS considerations, spacecraft (s/c) requires s/c activity time line
then:
For CMS considerations, spacecraft (s/c) is type 1 (ae)

is this true: For CMS considerations, spacecraft (s/c) has loading options/
constraints? y
is this true: For CMS considerations, spaceccraft (s/c) requires s/c activity time
line? y
rule r7 deduces For CMS considerations, spacecraft (s/c) is type 1 (ae)
I conclude that For CMS considerations, spacecraft (s/c) is type 1 (ae).

frame includes about four to five type slots to which spacecraft or facility names are associated (see Figure 17.8). A *similarity predicate* (two-argument) is assigned to each typology slot (it can be inserted in the blank column following each S/C name of Figure 17.8). These similarity predicates or coefficients are active values and have identical semantic meaning with [active] *weight values* assigned to functional requirements, i.e., the members of the $[F_B]$ set. Of course, for any two spacecraft or facility-type systems, say S/C #1 and S/C #2, in general:

1. $S(S/C\#1, S/C\#2) \neq S(S/C \#2, S/C \#1)$: This is the asymmetricity property.

2. $S(S/C \#1, S/C\#2)$: May assume any nonnegative value to express *imperfect* similarity between the two systems.

FIGURE 17.8
TYPOLOGY MATRIX: THE FRAME-BASED ANALOG SEARCH HEURISTIC

Type	Command	Control	Attitude	Capture	Processing	Distribution
I	GEOS-C AE-C AE-D AE-E GENERAL	ISEE-C DE-B ERBS GENERAL	SMM	AE NIMBUS-G GENERAL	AE DE GENERAL	SMM
II	SEASAT SMM SIM IUE SIM DE A/B OSO-H GENERAL	SMM AE-C LANDSAT-C ST GENERAL	ERBS	DE ISEE ERBS UARS GENERAL	ISEE SMM ERBS SL (SOPS) GENERAL	ISEE DE-A GENERAL
III	SMM HEAO-C HEAO-A GENERAL	IUE	DE	GRO ST GENERAL	UARS	ST UARS GENERAL
IV	OAO-B OAO-C HEAO-B IUE GENERAL	SPIF		LANDSAT-D TYPE V SL (SIPS)		

3. $S(S/C \#1, S/C \#1) = 1$: Tautological relationship. This is the reason all similarity predicate values at the outset in Figure 17.8 are equal to one by default. In other words, an object type is *perfectly* similar to itself.

A free text explanation feature of ANALOG is also used to provide instructions on setting the active values and to provide object type definitions for novices.

The "general" S/C name of each type slot in the typology frame encompasses the range of system attributes and active values that describe all other object members of that slot (type). This general S/C can be selected by a user interested in obtaining all outputs in terms of the full range (uncertainty bandwidth) of historical results for ANALOGS of that type.

Ideally, a generalized typology knowledge system should be hybrid utilizing both rule and frame constructs. A rule-based system may be used to represent summary typology information, while the attribute value setting of the type and ANALOG is best represented via the frame-slot construct. However, users unanimously selected the frame-slot construct to represent all typology knowledge, and that is what is used in the version of INNOVATOR that was ultimately institutionalized by NASA[10] (see the discussion in Section 17.5).

M-Operator Heuristics (AT and KT) Support provided by IN-NOVATOR (I) in the related steps of analogical reasoning is based on the theoretical framework of analog transfer (AT), knowledge transformation, (KT) and intro into use (I) as discussed in Sections 17.2.2 and 17.3. AT and KT methods send messages to and alter values, while I methods permit the user to monitor results via various gauge and active value graph representations. The goal of this message sending and monitoring activity on the part of the users is to explore answers to questions such as "What would happen to a target requirement set, design, or plan if the base requirement set, design, or plan is transformed via a given M-operator?" Illustrative operational aspects of the problem-processing system for these step "experts" of INNOVATOR include the following items.

1. *Entering similarity factors:* The similarity factor is one of the EIPs NASA innovators most commonly used (Sobieski 1982; Silverman 1983, 1985a) and also represents one of the simple decision rules cited in Table 17.1. INNOVATOR helps the user to derive an analogy/disanalogy

---

[10]In hindsight, the authors feel this was a dominated alternative since many of the current users belong in the "newcomer" category. Nevertheless, given the frame-orientation and contract requirements, the NASA version (as typified by Figures 17.5, 17.6, 17.8, and 17.9 and equations discussed through Section 17.4) was implemented on an IBM personal computer (XT model) using the LOTUS language/system (see Silverman, Moustakis, and Liebowitz 1983; and Moustakis 1984).

similarity factor, the values of which range in the closed interval from zero to one. Implementation is done according to the normalized asymmetric similarity formula (2) of Figure 17.3, in which all functions are simplified to counting and scaling rules. Asymmetry exists because, in general, $S(B,T) \neq S(T,B)$, where T stands for target, B for base, and $S(...)$ is the IDEA MAN's similarity matching model. Similarity is expressed via common functional requirement elements, while an increased level of significance for a certain requirement is acknowledged by editing of active values. The process was already illustrated in Figure 17.3. The only change provided by INNOVATOR is to permit the user to order these weights into an electronic "sheet of paper" and in true progressive-deepening fashion, to permit weights to be entered either at the type level (in the blank columns of Figure 17.7) or at the subsystem and/or component levels (refer to Figure 17.5b).

2. *Resource Forecast:* Elementary information-processing elements embodied in INNOVATOR support the derivation of the target system's resource needs estimates. Resource needs estimates for a target system are derived via a linear transformation of a given base system's resource estimates (active values), which are then automatically adjusted for inflation to the target year(s). For example, from the staff sublattice, staff resource needs are computed via the symbols and formulae indicated below:

(a) *Symbols*

1. Instances of objects of a base system

$R_{Bi}(i) =$ Staff resource estimate of a base system and for the ith skill category and during the ith life cycle cost year, where $1 si \leq 10$; $L - 7 \leq j \leq L + 2$, and $L =$ year of launch. The $r_i(j)$ objects are organized in relational tuple lists.

$F_{Bk} =$ R_{th} functional requirement member of a semantic net $1 \leq k \leq 150$.

$MW_{Bk} =$ "Weight" value of the kth functional requirement. As a default $W_k = 1$ for all k.

$MINF_t =$ Official NASA inflation index for year t organized in a relational tuple.

$A_{Bi} =$ Annual wage rate of the ith staff skill category in *1982* dollars. (Wage is a member of the attribute list of a staff object).

$t =$ Calendar year, $1984 \leq t \leq 1995$.

2. Instances of objects of the target

$B_{Ti}(j) =$ Same as $R_{Bi}(1)$ but estimated via analogical reasoning.

$F_{Tk} =$ k^{th} functional requirement member of a semantic net. Elements of the semantic net of functional requirements of the target are identified by exploring the functional requirement nets of base systems and by querying S/C users.

$MW_{Tk} =$ Same as MW_{Bk}, but the decision maker expresses his or her view on the difference between the target and a base by changing the values of MW_{Bk}. That is, a value of zero would indicate that no association exists between an F_{Bk} and an F_{Tk}, while a value of, say, 2 will indicate multiple or a more intensive presence of F_{Tk} as compared with F_{Bk}.

$COST_i(t, j)$: Cost estimate, based on analogy, for the ith staff skill category in terms of t year dollars, for the jth life cycle year.

(b) *Formulae*

$S(O_T, O_B)$:   Similarity factor of an object of a target with an object from a base. Implemented via the weight value, of functional requirments:

$$S(O_T, O_B) = \frac{\sum_{\forall k \in K} MW_{Tk}}{\sum_{\forall k \in K} MW_{Bk}}$$

$$R_{Ti}(j) = S(O_T, O_B) * R_{Bi}(j)$$

$$COST_i(t, j) = R_{Ti}(1) * A_{B_i} * (1 + MINF_t)$$

and the totals are computed as follows:

$$COST_i(t) = \sum_{\forall j} COST_i(t, j)$$

$$COST(t) = COST_i(t)$$

Users wishing not to alter individual weight values (active values) of functional requirements may obtain aggregate resource forecasts by adjusting the similarity coefficients assigned to the slots of the typology matrix (see Figure 17.7). Again, resource requirement values of a base system are linearly adjusted according to the new similarity coefficient value, and costs are automatically adjusted for inflation. For example, to derive a cost estimate for a target S/C, say S/C #2, which is thought of as being twice as demanding in terms of the data capture class, the similarity coefficient of the relevant base spacecraft, say S/C #1, is changed to 2 and all resource requirement values of S/C #1 are doubled and, if necessary, adjusted for inflation to the year selected.

3. *Gauges:* Changes in active values during the analog transformation process can be monitored via a predefined set of tabular and/or graphic (line and bar chart) gauges. These gauges aid the user in assessing the "what-if" impact of target system requirements and to form multiple system "views." An illustrative bar chart gauge is shown in Figure 17.9. This figure illustrates several features of a forecast for the software resource objects of some S/C entity. Software forecasting works in much

FIGURE 17.9
ILLUSTRATIVE ACTIVE VALUE GAUGES FOR RESOURCE OBJECTS

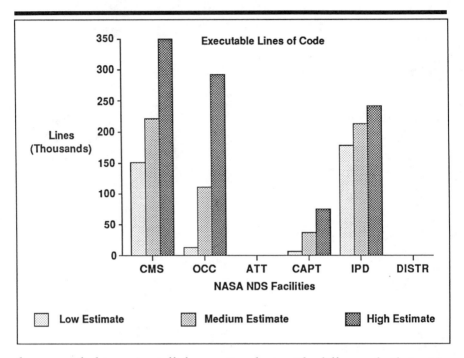

the same fashion as staff forecasting but with different built-in M-operators. In this case, the target entity was decomposed to a single type with each of four classes (command, control, capture, and processing). Figure 17.9 reveals that the user stopped at that level and selected "general" for each type rather than picking a specific ANALOG (hence the range of estimates in each class, rather than single estimate bars). The M-operators applied in obtaining these estimates are simply the weights of the typology frame. Finally, Figure 17.9 is continuously updated as the user explores alternative classes, types, ANALOGS, and M-operators. The same holds true for gauges attached to all other active values.

4. *Evaluation of M-operator Heuristics:* The illustrative EIPs shown here (linear multiplier coefficients, resource forecast, and costing/temporality) and other M-operators provided by INNOVATOR were found to have prevailed in various system sizing/costing studies (see Sobieski 1982; and Silverman 1983). These approaches were also successfully applied by the authors in a spacestation design study (Silverman, Moustakis, and Robless 1985). In addition, these methodologies were unanimously approved during user evaluation workshops and sessions. Indicative user statements validating the utility of INNOVATOR problem-processing elements are summarized in Table 17.4. The first part of this table records the level of user satisfaction/agreement with INNOVATOR ac-

TABLE 17.4
USER EVALUATION OF ANALOG TRANSFORMATION HEURISTICS IN INNOVATOR*

(a) User Requirements

	Level of Agreement (N = 10)			
The following are needed:	Disagree	Minor Agreement	Agree	Strongly Agree
"Experts" who rapidly provide "what-if" or "IF-THEN" answers during analogy-type exercises.			10%	90%
Record/keep track of potentially relevant comparison cases.		10%		90%
Record/keep track of what a decision is intended to accomplish for facilitation of subsequent problem reidentification(s).	10%		10%	80%
Record/keep track of alternatives suggested by the comparison case.			10%	90%

(b) Evaluation of INNOVATOR Support
  1. Rate the importance of support in the following task areas (N = 10): (Rank order: 1 = most important, 4 = least important)

Task	Mean	Coefficient of Variation
• Provide Base System Information	1.1	.27
• Perform (aid) transformation calculations	2.1	.40
• Provide Multiple System Views	2.4	.19

	Yes	No
2. Computation of linear multiplier coefficients: (N = 7)	100%	0%
3. Automated Gauge Availability (via predefined macros): (N = 7)	100%	0%

* User attitudes were captured via different scales.

cording to generic analogical reasoning support requirements. In the second part of Table 17.4, user attitudes versus general INNOVATOR support and user interface elements are recorded.

17.5 CONCLUSION

This chapter documents a series of results of a research effort aimed at the identification of support needs for institutionalized innovation and at the development of a prototype analogical reasoning support system – IN-NOVATOR. The chapter begins by summarizing results of research efforts by which (1) a description of innovators' protocols reveal their reliance on analogy in systems innovation, (2) a protocol analysis pinpoints some of the numerous knowledge elements and elementary information processes (EIPs) innovators utilize, and (3) these elements and EIPs may be organized into a five-step prescriptive model of the innovator's cognition consisting of problem identification, knowledge acquisition, analog transfer, knowledge transformation, and introduction into use. In Section 17.3 each step of this model is elaborated and a generic blackboard expert system is depicted with the five steps being achieved by functional experts called CRITIC, LIBRARIAN, IDEA MAN, CRAFTSMAN, and WRITER, respectively.

The INNOVATOR experiments described in Section 17.4 reveal that this generic structure holds the potential to provide an effective aid to the process of analogical reasoning. Indeed, in January 1984 the first application of INNOVATOR was implemented within the system innovation group at NASA responsible for ground operations supporting near-earth orbiting spacecraft, user training was conducted, and a policy memo was drafted by top management for INNOVATOR's use as part of all new system planning efforts. The NASA application verifies that IN-NOVATOR represents an aid for institutionalized innovation, although this potential needs to be further researched before an entirely generic aid can be completed.

1. *Knowledge System:* Despite the apparent attractiveness of single paradigm worlds (as evidenced by the large number of primarily rule-based expert systems), a hybrid knowledge representation schema appears necessary for INNOVATOR. The knowledge representation form used by INNOVATOR, an ANALOG, incorporates various and diverse representation methodologies such as frames (objects), rule sets, bitmaps, relational tuples, and free-text. Users at both clinical test-bed locations (NASA and the military) where INNOVATOR products were introduced desired the hybrid ANALOG structure.

2. *Problem-Processing System (PPS):* In the same vein, while a trend is toward single- or at most dual-paradigm inference engines (e.g., only backward chaining or backward with forward reasoning), a variety of problem-solving heuristics and techniques are essential for analogical reasoning support. Analogical support elements that rated highest during INNOVATOR experiments on the problem identification and knowledge transformation steps include:

a. An inference engine to classify target entities within a known base system typology. Typology is a taxonomic and heuristic search space reduction technique by which knowledge aspects of past problem situations (bases) are divided into subclasses to facilitate problem identification involving a heuristic search for analogical knowledge.

b. Support for computing a metric for expressing value judgments regarding the degree of similarity between a target system (present problem situation) and alternative base systems (past analogous problem solution pairs). The INNOVATOR prototype at NASA provided support toward the computation of a similarity factor based on the similarity matching model. This support was highly desirable (Table 17.1) and received high evaluation ratings (Tables 17.3 and 17.4). INNOVATOR supports a variety of other knowledge transformation and disanalogy elimination EIPs.

c. Support for "editing" object sublattices, frames, and tuples of base systems was highly praised. Also, research results indicate that an analogical reasoning support system should aid the user in transforming functional requirements and resource active values.

d. Methods to affix graphical gauges by which analogical problem processing results may be monitored continuously.

3. *Language System (LS):* A generic LS for an analogical reasoning support system must be hybrid. Hybridism is extended to include display mechanisms for frames, bitmaps, relations, and gauges as well as to rule-based dialogues and menu commanding. Users at the military welcomed a hybrid LS system structure. However, and to the authors' surprise, early users at NASA rejected rule sets as "too slow" and indicated that rules would be useful only as a training aid for bringing new employees "up to speed." As already mentioned, users regretted this position soon after INNOVATOR was institutionalized at NASA.

Finally, this chapter has identified several analogical reasoning support elements that could be implemented in INNOVATOR (of course, the discussion was limited to a subset of the cognitive steps). However, not all these elements have so far been implemented in INNOVATOR due to contractual constraints. To this end, the current version of INNOVATOR could be expanded to include:

1. Methods to represent associations between elements of the resource and requirements lattices. Put simply, these methods would provide for traces between individual requirements and specific module designs.

2. Methods to model change (e.g., cost growth over the system's life cycle and technological improvement in hardware and software elements).

3. Methods to support the conduct of truth maintenance, whereby all step experts could function probabilistically (e.g., Bayesian analysis, Dempster approach, or certainty factors).

4. Inference engines capable of carrying out each of the heuristic operations of the individual step experts. The research up to this point has verified that primarily simple heuristics are used, and the user evaluations have confirmed the nature of many of these. It is now possible to progress to the next phase of research and to attempt a more complete version of the blackboard expert system of Section 17.3.

As to the most fundamental research question addressed in this chapter, what indeed has been learned about the cognitive processes in innovation? An expert system that can invent seems as far away as ever.

Indeed, more questions have been raised than have been answered. The authors feel, however, that more than just two knowledge-based applications have been successfully attempted. On the one hand, the fact that some degree of structuring and expert system aid was institutionalized is an encouraging sign for the future of research in this topic. That is, research on computerized innovation *can* and *did* produce short-term payoff results to the sponsor. On the other hand, if more questions than answers have been raised (and they have), *then* a fertile research topic has been uncovered. This combination of a fertile long-term research topic producing short-term paybacks to its sponsors is a promising one indeed.

ACKNOWLEDGMENT

Research described in this paper was in part supported by NASA/GSFC (NAS5-27200 and NAS5-26804) and the U.S. DoD (0NR-00014-C-83-0563). The NASA and DoD employees and contractors who so generously participated in and encouraged this research are too numerous to mention here. By the same token, numerous doctoral candidates at George Washington University have contributed to small pieces of IN-NOVATOR for which they hopefully were compensated by the same excitement the authors have received from this project. Finally, the information and/or opinions contained herein are provided by the authors and do not represent official government positions.

REFERENCES

Duda, R.O., et al. (1978), *Development of the PROSPECTOR Consultation System for Mineral Exploration*, SRI Projects 5821 & 6415, Menlo Park, Calif. Oct.

Evans, T.G. (1968), "A Program for the Solution of Geometric-Analogy Intelligence Tests," in M. Minsky, ed., *Semantic Information Processing*, Cambridge, Mass.: MIT Press.

Gilfillan, S.C. (1935), *The Sociology of Invention*, Chicago: Follet.

Gordan, W.J. (1961), *Synetics: The Development of Creative Capacity*, New York: Harper & Row.

Hadamard, J. (1945), *Psychology of Invention in the Mathematical Sciences*, Princeton, N.J.: Dover Publications.

Hesse, M.B. (1966), *Models and Analogies in Science*, Notre Dame, Ind.: University of Notre Dame Press.

Koestler, A. (1960), *The Act of Creation*, London: Macmillan.

Larkin, J., McDermott, J., Simon, D.P., and Simon, H.A. (1980), "Expert and Novice Performance in Solving Physics Problems," *Science*, 208 (20): 1335–1342.

McDermott, J. (1980), *R1: A Rule-Based Configurer of Computer Systems*, (CMU-CS-80-119), Pittsburgh: Carnegie-Mellon University.

Michie, D. (1974), *On Machine Intelligence*, New York: John Wiley & Sons.

Moustakis, V.S. (1984), "System Cost Analogy Technique," dissertation, George Washington University, Institute for Artificial Intelligence. Available from University Microfilms, Ann Arbor, Michigan.

Murray, A., et al. (1986), "A LISP Machine Scenario Generator for the INNOVATOR Expert System," in B.G. Silverman and W. Hutzler, eds., *Artificial Intelligence in Military Applications*, ORSA Monograph, Washington, D.C., pp. 134–169.

Polya, G. (1954), *Induction and Analogy in Mathematics*, Princeton, N.J.: Princeton University.

Polya, G. (1957), *How To Solve It*, Garden City, N.Y.: Doubleday.

Rossman, J. (1964), *Industrial Creativity: The Psychology of the Inventory*, New Hyde Park, N.Y.: University Books.

Sacerdoti, E.D. (1979), *A Structure for Plans and Behavior*, New York: Elsevier.

Sahal, D. (1981), *Patterns of Technological Innovation*, Reading, Mass.: Addison-Wesley.

Shortliffe, E.H. (1974), "MYCIN: A Rule-Based Computer Program for Advising Physicians Regarding Antimicrobial Therapy Selection," Ph.D. dissertation, Stanford University.

Silverman, B.G. (1983), "Analogy in Systems Management: A Theoretical Inquiry," *IEEE Transactions on Systems, Man, and Cybernetics*, (SMC-13), 1049–1075.

Silverman, B.G. (1984a), "The Software Engineering Paradox," *International Test and Evaluation Society Journal*, 5 (1): 1–6.

Silverman, B.G. (1984b), "INNOVATOR: An Expert Systems for Management of Modeling and Simulation," *Proceedings of the International Test and Evaluation Conference*, November, pp. 85–90. Available from ITEA, Lexington Park, Md.

Silverman, B.G. (1985a), "The Use of Analogs In The Innovation Process: A Software Programming Protocol Analysis," *IEEE Transactions*, (SMC-15), pp. 30–44.

Silverman, B.G. (1985b), "Expert Intuition and Ill-Structured Problem Solving," in D. Lee, ed., Management of Technological Innovation, Washington, D.C.: NSF (reprinted in *IEEE Transactions on Engineering Management*, (EM-32), pp. 29–35.

Silverman, B.G. (1985c), "Potential Software Management Cost and Productivity Improvements," *Computer*, IEEE Computer Society, 18 (5): 86–96.

Silverman, B.G. (1985d), "Toward an Integrated Cognitive Model of the Inventor/Engineer," presented at *Conference on Knowledge Engineering and R&D*, Manchester, England and reprinted in *R&D Management*, 15 (2): 342–353.

Silverman, B.G., Moustakis, V.S., and Liebowitz, J. (1983), "Resource Planning By Analogy: The SCAT Support System," *Microcomputers Tools or Toys?*, ACM, Washington, D.C. (chapter's 22nd Annual Technical Symposium).

Silverman, B.G., Moustakis, V.S., and Robless, R. (1985), "Expert Systems and Robotics in the Space Station Era: Design Considerations," *Proceedings of the Expert Systems In Government Conference*, October, pp. 342–353.

Sobieski, S. (1982), "Science and Applications Space Platform Ground System," Greenbelt, NASA/GSFC (photographic copy available from S. Sobieski), 1982.

Sternberg, R.J. (1977), "Component Processes in Analogical Reasoning," *Psychological Review*, 84 (4): 353–378.

Sussman, G.J. (1975), *A Computer Model of Skill Acquisition*, New York: Elsevier.

Tversky, A. (1977), "Features of Similarity," *Psychological Review*, 84 (4): 327–352.

Usher, A.P. (1954), *A History of Mechanical Invention*, Cambridge, Mass.: Harvard University Press.

Waterman, D., and Newell, A. (1971), "Protocol Analysis As A Task in Artificial Intelligence," *Artificial Intelligence*, 2 (March): 261–284.

Wilensky, R. (1983), *Planning and Understanding*, Reading, Mass.: Addison-Wesley.

Epilogue

In concluding this book, it may be noted that artificial intelligence, particularly in the area of expert systems is fast growing and has had several recent successes in business. This is, however, a transition period for managers, many of whom are torn between the hopes and promises on the one hand and their need to pause and gauge the true nature, potential, and impact of this innovation. Unfortunately, the information available to managers is fragmented — highly specific systems for isolated areas of business with little mutual interconnection are being built by knowledge engineers. Most effort is going into the technical; little consideration is being placed on the effect of the innovations on the users or on their value to the organization. It is hoped that this book will help to stimulate a dialogue on these issues and that it has helped the reader to find a realistic use for expert systems in his or her organization.

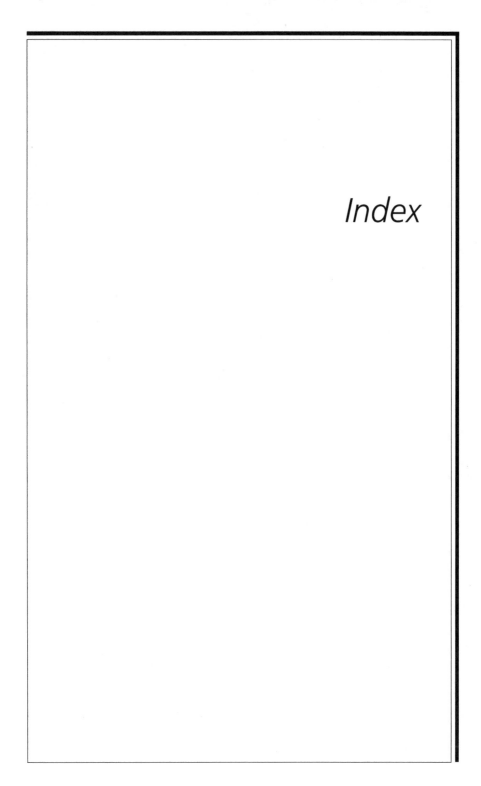

Index